Canada's Century

Canada's Century

Allan S. Evans
Head of History
Emery Collegiate Institute
Toronto, Ontario

I. L. Martinello
Assistant Head of History
Emery Collegiate Institute
Toronto, Ontario

McGraw-Hill Ryerson Limited
Toronto Montreal New York St. Louis San Francisco
Auckland Bogotá Düsseldorf Johannesburg London
Madrid Mexico New Delhi Panama Paris São Paulo
Singapore Sydney Tokyo

CANADA'S CENTURY

ISBN 0-07-082716-8

3 4 5 6 7 8 9 10 THB 7 6 5 4 3 2 1 0 9

Printed and bound in Canada

Canadian Cataloguing in Publication Data

Evans, Allan S., date
   Canada's century

ISBN 0-07-082716-8

1. Canada — History. 2. Canada — Politics and government. I. Martinello, Larry, II. Title.

FC170.E83   971   C78-001070-1
F1026.E83

CONTENTS

PREFACE

Canada's Century is designed for use as a core text by High School students embarking on the discovery of modern Canada. The focus is on Canada since 1945; the ultimate goal is for students to understand the major forces, personalities and issues which are shaping the country's present and will shape its future.

Nonetheless, the authors are aware of the importance of providing a conceptual and historical framework for such a study. Therefore, considerable attention has been given to an examination of the key people and events from Canada's past, particularly since 1900. Indeed, this emphasis has inspired the book's title. The consistent thrust of the presentation is to show how previous political, economic, social and other happenings are interrelated, and have combined to produce the challenging situation of today. This emphasis should be useful in helping the teacher to plan his or her own approach, and in motivating the students to full involvement in the unfolding story.

Canada's Century is made up of six major units. The first two deal with Canadian government and law. These provide students with a working knowledge of the most important and interesting institutions and practices of Canadian political and legal affairs. The third unit is essentially a chronological survey of Canadian history from the turn of the century to the end of World War II. Here the student becomes familiar with the main events, issues and personalities of that period. This provides a solid factual base, plus a conceptual framework from which the students may then move to units 4, 5 and/or 6. These deal respectively with English-French relations, Canadian-American relations and Canadian foreign policy.

Because each unit is self-contained, the book is a flexible learning resource. Most of the units are interchangeable and can be rearranged in almost any order to suit local needs and purposes. Chronology and linear structure are there for teachers who value these qualities.

As experienced teachers and writers, the authors are acutely aware of the need to gear print materials to the actual reading level of the students who will be using them. Every effort has been made to make *Canada's Century* a text that is both enjoyable and comprehensible for High School learners. Where difficult words appear, they are often printed in boldface type, with brief explanations following in parentheses. Vital terms are also set in bold-face type and are summarized, with meanings and examples of use, near the beginning of each chapter. These terms are reviewed at the end of each chapter. Here, in the Things to Think About and Do section, students are also offered a series of questions and exercises, in ascending order of difficulty, to broaden their understanding of the particular chapter.

Canada's Century contains a wealth of visual illustrations: large photos, amusing cartoons, helpful charts and maps, plus special interest inserts of various kinds. These inserts are set off from the narrative by a light coloured "screen". In many cases, they are accompanied by analytical questions, or role-plays, simulations, surveys and exercises designed to help students think, make decisions and clarify values. In addition, there is a variety of documentary material. This has been carefully selected and edited to help people and events come alive in clear focus, but with a view to their readability for High School students.

The attention of teachers and students is drawn to the concluding portion of the book, which deals briefly with the matter of Canada's identity. From the lines of Duke Redbird's poem, *I am a Canadian,* might come the inspiration not only to conclude a study of *Canada's Century,* but perhaps to *begin* it as well.

The Government of Canada

1

INTRODUCTION

How do you react to the prospect of studying government and politics? Many high school students would say that this subject is dull, boring, and tiresome. This attitude may be due to the way government and politics have been studied in the past. Too often the "machinery" of government is what was stressed. This included how a bill is passed, the seating arrangement in the House of Commons, the qualifications of voters, and so on. Of course knowing these things will help you to understand how we are governed. However the true study of government and politics is much more exciting. It includes an analysis of how power is gained and how it is used. Whether we talk about gaining power in a high school student council election or becoming a Member of Parliament in Ottawa, the process is the same.

The humorist Oscar Wilde defined a politician as "an animal who can sit on a fence and yet keep both ears to the ground." Stop for a moment. What does that definition mean? Do you agree with it? Why or why not? Government has also been described as an art, "the art of making men live together in peace and with reasonable happiness." Do you agree that governing is an art? Can you give reasons why this is so? When you study government, you are also studying people. For all of these reasons the study of government and politics should be far from boring. In fact it can be interesting and exciting.

Today, more than ever before, it is vital for Canadians to understand their country and how it is governed. We are faced with serious problems. These include threats of Quebec separating from Canada, an energy crisis and problems with inflation and unemployment. These are issues which we will have to face as citizens. They are also issues which only the government can finally deal with.

Unit Preview/Review Questions

As you study this unit, keep these questions in mind. You may want to return to them when you have finished the unit.
1. Why is government necessary?
2. Why do we have a federal system of government?
3. How do politicians gain and use power?
4. What pressures are brought to bear on our elected politicians?
5. Who exercises power in this country?

2

THE GOVERNMENT OF CANADA

Three centuries ago, the Englishman Thomas Hobbes used these words to describe what life would be like without government:

> During that time when men live without a common power (a government) to keep them all in awe, they are in that condition which is called war, and such a war is of every man against every man . . . In such a condition there is no place for industry . . . no culture of the earth . . . no navigation . . . no knowledge of the face of the earth; no account of time, no arts, no letters, no societies; and which is worst of all, continual fear and danger of violent death, and the life of man solitary, poor, nasty, brutish and short.

1. What problems does Hobbes say a society will have if there is no "common power" (or government) to keep people in line?
2. How will the presence of a government prevent these problems?

Since that time many writers have used this theme in their books. You may have read the book *Lord of the Flies* by William Golding. Perhaps you have seen the film of the book. It tells the **fictional** (made up) story of school boys who survive a plane wreck on a coral island. The boys struggle to survive by getting used to one another and to their surroundings. Television and the movies have also used this theme. There are endless stories of plane-crash or shipwreck survivors on deserted islands who must organize a mini-society. What do all of these stories have in common? In all cases, one of the very first actions of the survivors is to pick leaders. In other words they form a government. Despite the fact that young people on the whole are not "turned on" by the study of government and politics, it is one of the necessities of life. There is no human society known which does not have some way of choosing leaders or forming a government.

Before reading on, study the chart of key words and ideas which follows.

KEY WORDS AND IDEAS IN THIS CHAPTER

Term	Meaning	Sample Use
B.N.A. Act	the British North America Act, passed in 1867	The B.N.A. Act defines the powers of the federal and provincial governments.
		Canada today is an example of a constitutional monarchy.
		Literally, democracy means "the people rule." In modern democracies the people rule through their elected representatives.
		Germany under Hitler was an example of a dictatorship.
		In Canada the executive power rests in the hands of the Prime Minister and his Cabinet.
		Canadian federalism is described in the B.N.A. Act. Section 91 of the Act defines the federal powers. Section 92 defines provincial powers.
		In Canada the highest judicial power is held by the Supreme Court.
		In Canada, the legislative power rests in the hands of Parliament.

Thomas Hobbes' description of society without government sounds very frightening. Does he exaggerate the importance of government? Consider the question from a very personal point of view. How does government affect YOU? Select an average day in your life. You go to school, you eat, you work, play and sleep. It does not look like government has any effect on you. Examine your routine a little more closely. If you made a detailed list of your daily activities it might include many of the following: turning on the radio o television, eating meat and vegetables, walking on sidewalks or riding a ca bus or bicycle, mailing a letter, buying clothes and going to school.

Each of these activities is controlled in some way by some level o government. Explain what re More and more, in our con about) our daily activities. Here are some of the things Canada.

— transportation and comn
— health, education, welfar
— big business and labour
— wages and prices
— development of natural
— foreign trade
— agricultural production

These are all recent government can also make

— pay taxes and fines
— require you to sell your
— forbid you from travellin
— force you to leave the c
— suspend your rights
— send you to jail
— send you to war

This trend of government re

Most people agree on disagreement as to what kin can be reduced to two. "government of the few." O forms. The power to govern is called a **dictatorship.** constitutions. They ARE the governments of Hitler in Ge

Another form of one-pe inherits the position of power.

How The Government Affects Your Life

LW	TW	WEEK STARTING	FEBRUARY 18, 1978	ISSUE	1079	WKS

LW	TW	Title	Artist	Label	WKS
1	1	Stayin' Alive	The Bee Gees	Polydor	5
4	2	Short People	Randy Newman	WEA	7
7	3	We Will Rock You/We Are Champions	Queen	WEA	6
2	4	Just The Way You Are	Billy Joel	CBS	8
11	5	(Love Is) Thicker Than Water	Andy Gibb	Polydor	4
9	6	Emotion	Samantha Sang	Quality	4
3	7	Slip Slidin' Away	Paul Simon	CBS	9
5	8	Desiree	Neil Diamond	CBS	7
16	9	(What A) Wonderful World	Art Garfunkel, James Taylor & Paul Simon	CBS	3
6	10	Turn To Stone	Electric Light Orchestra	U.A.	12
17	11	Theme From "Close Encounters Of The Third Kind"	John Williams/Meco	Capitol/Quality	3
8	12	You're In My Heart (The Final Acclaim)	Rod Stewart	WEA	18
10	13	Here You Come Again	Dolly Parton	RCA	10
13	14	Baby Come Back	Player	Polydor	12
26	15	Lay Down Sally	Eric Clapton	Polydor	2
12	16	Blue Bayou	Linda Ronstadt	WEA	13
14	17	Come Sail Away	Styx	A&M	11
29	18	The Circle Is Small	Gordon Lightfoot	WEA	2
15	19	Closer To The Heart	Rush	Polydor	12
24	20	What's Your Name	Lynyrd Skynyrd	MCA	3
19	21	How Can I Leave You Again	John Denver	RCA	5
20	22	How Deep Is Your Love	Bee Gees	Polydor	21
28	23	Rock And Roll Is A Vicious Game	April Wine	London	2
18	24	You Make Lovin' Fun	Fleetwood Mac	WEA	19
—	25	Night Fever	The Bee Gees	Polydor	1
—	26	The Way You Do The Things You Do	Rita Coolidge	A&M	1
—	27	Peg	Steely Dan	GRT	1
21	28	Hey Deanie	Shaun Cassidy	WEA	6
—	29	Runnin' On Empty	Jackson Browne	WEA	1
—	30	Oh Pretty Lady	Trooper	MCA	1

Read carefully the above chart listing the most popular songs in a recent Hit Parade. You may recognize a number of the tunes. Now try to answer the following questions:
— Which of these songs are sung by Canadians?
— Which of these songs were written by Canadians?
— Which of these songs were produced by a Canadian record company?

At this point, you may be saying to yourself "Hey this is fun, but what does the Hit Parade have to do with the study of government and politics?"

This exercise was intended to make one point: much of what we do in our daily lives is influenced in some way by government — yes, even the songs on the Hit Parade. There is a Canadian law regarding the amount of Canadian content which radio and television stations must broadcast. At least 60% of all the music broadcast by a radio station must be written, produced or sung by Canadians. The records you buy are directly related to their popularity on the radio. So the record you choose may be influenced by the Canadian content in broadcasting law. There are many such laws which touch our lives without our ever being aware of them. You can see the influence that our government has in our affairs, be they small matters or large.

Centuries ago the monarch was all-powerful, much like a modern-day dictator. King Louis XIV of France once stated "L'etat — c'est moi!" — "The state — I am the state!"

In time, the role of the monarchy decreased as the power of assemblies elected by the people grew. These elected assemblies, or parliaments, eventually limited the powers of the monarchs by law. Where parliament and the monarch ruled together under law, the government became known as a **constitutional monarchy.** In most such arrangements the role of the monarchy continued to decline. Its duties became mostly symbolic. Great Britain and Canada are examples of such a system today.

In some countries the power to govern rests in the hands of a privileged class. This group may be thought superior because of birth or wealth or intelligence. Such a government by the "best" citizens is called an **aristocracy.**

1.   THE GOVERNMENT OF CANADA

What form of government do we have in Canada? In theory Canada is a monarchy. The **British North America Act,** states:

"The Executive government and Authority of and over Canada is hereby declared to continue and be vested in the Queen."

The B.N.A. Act was passed in Britain in 1867. At that time Canada remained almost a colony of Britain. As Canada matured and gained her independence, the role of the monarchy became very small. In practice then, Canada is a **democracy,** a "government of the many." All citizens have a voice in choosing their leaders. The word democracy comes from two Greek words DEMOS (people) and KRATOS (power), in other words, the people rule.

Obviously in a country the size of Canada, it is impossible for each citizen to rule directly. The people therefore choose representatives. They govern in our place. These members of government meet in a **Parliament.** In this place new laws are discussed. For this reason Canada's system is known as parliamentary government. Canada's Parliament consists of the following: elected representatives who sit in the House of Commons; an appointed Senate; and the Governor-General who represents the Queen.

Together this group is responsible for making and enforcing the laws of the land.

2.   THE LEVELS OF GOVERNMENT IN CANADA

In 1867 when the Fathers of Confederation created a new Canada, they faced the question "What form of government shall we have?" The sheer size of the country dictated the answer. Canada was a huge country with a scattered population. The people of the Maritimes, Quebec, Ontario and the West saw themselves as groups having their own history, culture and economic interests.

The Government of Canada

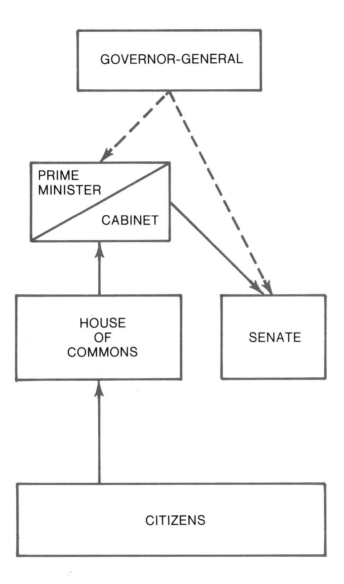

They felt strongly about protecting their unique traditions. Each region was willing to join in political union with the rest of Canada, but not at the expense of their own regional interest.

Even today, these local and regional loyalties remain strong. A person from Halifax will consider himself a Canadian, but also a proud Nova Scotian. A person in Burnaby shares a common bond with all Canadians, but she may also talk of the differences between British Columbians and all other Canadians.

What has allowed these regional differences to continue? It is the unique form of government created in 1867 that we call Canadian **federalism.**

Three levels of government were created in Canada. Each has its own responsibilities. The federal government, through its Parliament in Ottawa, looks after matters that concern all the people in Canada. These include defence and international agreements. The provincial governments, through their own legislatures, look after affairs that concern only the people in their provinces. Hospitals and prisons are two examples of these. Municipal or local governments take care of matters of a purely local nature, such as roads, sewers, etc.

This system lets Canada unite a huge territory. At the same time it should allow people of different regions to follow their own interests, language, religion and way of life.

3.   THE POWERS OF GOVERNMENT IN CANADA

All governments, from the student council at your school to federal government in Ottawa, exercise three basic powers. The first is the power to make laws and regulations. This is called **legislative power.** Once a law is passed, it must be carried out and enforced. That is, people must be made to follow the law. This is known as **executive power.** Finally, the government must have the power to punish those who break the laws. This is called the **judicial power.**

As we have seen, Canada is a democracy. In order to keep our system as democratic as possible we have divided these powers among different groups. In our federal government the legislative power is given to the House of Commons and the Senate. The executive power rests with the Governor-General, the Prime Minister and his Cabinet. The judicial power is in the hands of the Supreme Court and other lower courts throughout the land. This area will be discussed in a later chapter on the law.

THINGS TO THINK ABOUT AND DO

Reviewing Key Words and Ideas

The following terms appeared in this chapter. Try to recall their meaning and how they were used.

aristocracy	dictatorship	legislative power
B.N.A. Act	executive power	monarchy
constitutional	federalism	Parliament
monarchy	judicial power	Supreme Court
democracy		

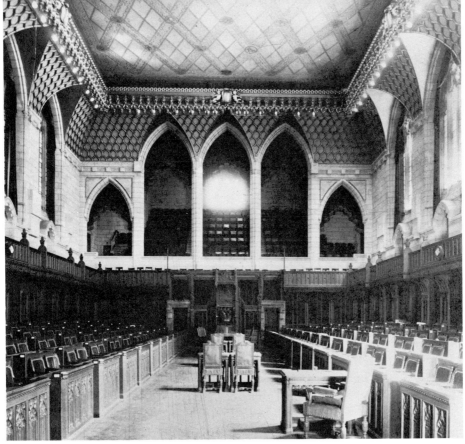

The House of Commons, Ottawa. The speaker's chair is in the centre of the photograph. The members of the government sit in the seats on the speaker's right. The opposition sits on the left. The party leaders sit front row centre, opposite each other.

Remembering the Facts

1. Who is responsible for ensuring that the laws of Canada are enforced?
2. What body of government passes the laws of Canada?
3. The Supreme Court of Canada is the highest executive authority in the land. True or False.
4. Government by the best people in a country is called aristocracy. True or False.

Analyzing Ideas

1. It is usually argued that Hitler's Germany was a dictatorship because it was run by the will of one man. Yet, Hitler was elected by the people with an overwhelming vote. Is a country a democracy if it votes for its government, even though all the powers of government rest in the hands of one man?
2. The Canadian content ruling was designed to boost Canadian performers

on radio and television. Do you think it is fair of the government to force the public to see and hear Canadian performers even though they may not be the very best available?

3. If the government wishes to build a road or an airport, it has the power to expropriate (or buy up) any property it needs. This was the case in Pickering, Ontario when the federal government decided to build a new airport. Dozens of homeowners were forced to sell their homes and farms and move out. Do you feel the government should have such power?

Applying your Knowledge

1. Thomas Hobbes described the situation which might exist if a society had no government. Of course every society today has a government, so his theory may be difficult to prove. Society does come close to a state of "no government" however, in several situations. It might be argued that during rioting and wars no real laws or authority exist. Try to discover what occurred in the rioting in major U.S. cities during the 1960s. Study the behaviour of soldiers during wartime. Is Hobbes right?

2. Try to find out if your favourite radio station is following the rules of Canadian content in broadcasting. Listen to one hour on the radio, and try to figure out what percentage of the programming was "Canadian."

3. It has been said that the number of countries which have democratic governments are in the minority. With the help of your teacher and the encyclopedia, try to make a list of the countries around the world which are democracies. What percentage of the world's nations are run democratically?

3

THE FEDERAL GOVERNMENT

INTRODUCTION

When we speak of the federal government, we are referring to the Parliament in Ottawa. The B.N.A. Act states that "There shall be One Parliament for Canada, consisting of the Queen, an Upper House styled the Senate, and the House of Commons."

The B.N.A. Act also mentions what the powers of this Parliament would be. Section 91 of the Act states:

The British North America Act 1867

Section 91 — Powers of Parliament

91. It shall be lawful for the Queen, by and with the Advice and Consent of the Senate and House of Commons, **to make Laws for the Peace, Order, and good Government of Canada,** in relation to all Matters not coming within the Classes of Subjects by this Act assigned exclusively to the Legislatures of the Provinces; and for greater Certainty, but not so as to restrict the Generality of the foregoing Terms in this Section, it is hereby declared that (notwithstanding anything in this Act) the exclusive Legislative Authority of the Parliament of Canada extends to all Matters coming within the Classes of Subjects next hereinafter enumerated; that is to say, —

1. The Public Debt and Property
Replaced in 1949 by: 1. The amendment from time to time of the Constitution of Canada, except as regards matters coming within the classes of subjects by this Act assigned exclusively to the Legislatures of the provinces, or as regards rights or privileges by this or any other Constitutional Act granted or secured to the Legislature or the Government of a province, or to any class of persons with respect to schools or as regards the use of the English or the French language, or as regards the requirements that there shall be a session of the Parliament of Canada at least once each year, and that no House of Commons shall continue for more than five years from the day of the return of the Writs for choosing the House; provided, however, that a House of Commons may in time of real or apprehended war, invasion or insurrection be continued by the Parliament of Canada if such continuation is not opposed by the votes of more than one-third of the members of such House.

1A. *The Public Debt and Property. (Re-numbered, 1949.)*

2. The Regulation of Trade and Commerce.

2A. *Unemployment Insurance. (Added, 1940.)*

3. The raising of Money by any Mode or System of Taxation.

4. The borrowing of Money on the Public Credit.

5. Postal Service.

6. The Census and Statistics.

7. Militia, Military and Naval Service, and Defence.

8. The fixing of and providing for the Salaries and Allowances of Civil and other Officers of the Government of Canada.

9. Beacons, Buoys, Lighthouses, and Sable Island.

10. Navigation and Shipping.

11. Quarantine and the Establishment and Maintenance of Marine Hospitals.

12. Sea Coast and Inland Fisheries.

13. Ferries between a Province and any British or Foreign Country or between Two Provinces.

14. Currency and Coinage.

15. Banking, Incorporation of Banks, and the Issue of Paper Money.

16. Savings Banks.

17. Weights and Measures.

18. Bills of Exchange and Promissory Notes.

19. Interest.

20. Legal Tender.

21. Bankruptcy and Insolvency.

22. Patents of Invention and Discovery.

23. Copyrights.

24. Indians and Lands reserved for the Indians.

25. Naturalization and Aliens.

26. Marriage and Divorce.

27. The Criminal Law, except the Constitution of Courts of Criminal Jurisdiction, but including the Procedure in Criminal Matters.

28. The Establishment, Maintenance, and Management of Penitentiaries.

29. Such Classes of Subjects as are expressly excepted in the Enumeration of the Classes of Subjects by this Act assigned exclusively to the Legislatures of the Provinces.

And any Matter coming within any of the Classes of Subjects enumerated in this Section shall not be deemed to come within the Class of Matters of a local or private Nature comprised in the Enumeration of the Classes of Subjects by this Act assigned exclusively to the Legislatures of the Provinces.

The Parliament of Canada can make laws about things not listed under Section 91. Many things have happened since 1867. The writers of the constitution could not have foreseen cars, airplanes, televisions, world wars and depressions. Laws have had to be passed dealing with these matters. Parliament has taken its right to do so from the "Peace, Order and Good Government" clause of Section 91.

Before reading on, study the chart of Key Words and Ideas which follows.

1. THE EXECUTIVE BRANCH

In our federal government, the power to carry out and enforce the laws is given to the Prime Minister and his Cabinet. The Governor-General has these powers to a lesser extent.

AS IN THIS CHAPTER

Sample Use

The bureaucracy in Canada's government influences decisions made by our elected officials. This is due to their vast knowledge and experience.

Rather than break cabinet solidarity, a Minister will sometimes resign from the cabinet if he or she disagrees with a decision.

Caucus is the place where ordinary M.P.'s can express their own opinions on the issues of the day. In the House of Commons they are expected to follow the party line.

In Ottawa, offices are set up on a full-time basis by certain groups. They are staffed by individuals whose only job is lobbying M.P.'s.

In Canada the political spectrum extends from the conservative "right" to the socialist "left".

The Canadian Manufacturers' Association and the Canadian Labour Congress are examples of two powerful pressure groups operating in Ottawa.

The throne chair in the
Senate. This chair is used
only by the reigning
Monarch or the Governor-
General. It is a symbol of the
respect given the
Crown in Canada.

The Governor-General

A century ago the Governo
major role in Canada's affairs
His main duty is to make su
the Prime Minister died s
replacement. In this matter h
duty may arise following an
the Governor-General to pi
the advice of the elected M

Another duty of the Gov
Parliament. However this is
custom he cannot refuse to

The Governor-General a
These include opening and closing
state. In sum, the Governor-General is
system of government.

Is the position of the monarchy (through the Governor-General) necessary to Canada?

YES:
— The monarchy is a symbol of our ties with Great Britain.
— The monarchy is a symbol of our British parliamentary heritage.
— The monarchy links Canada with the other thirty-five Commonwealth countries. They too accept the Queen as their head.
— Most people enjoy the pomp and pageantry connected with royalty. It adds colour to the political scene.
— The Queen is above petty politics. She is able to remain neutral. This is an important quality in a symbolic head of state.
— If we abolish the monarchy, we will have to replace it with another position. (Perhaps this would be a President.)

NO:
— The monarchy is only a symbol. It has no real role in our system of government.
— The monarchy is a throwback to the old days when the upper classes ran governments. It goes against the spirit of democracy.
— The monarchy is an issue which divides Canadians. French-Canadians are almost totally against it. English-Canadians are either in favour of it or don't care.
— The role of the monarchy in our government confuses people from other countries. They have a hard time understanding our stress on the *symbolic* nature of the Queen and Governor-General.

Until 1952 the Governors-General of Canada were British. They were chosen from among well known people in British public life. Since then the custom has been to select Canadians for that position. Four distinguished Canadians have held this office.

Vincent Massey (1952-1959)
Georges Vanier (1959-1967)
Roland Michener (1967-1974)
Jules Leger (1974-   )

The Prime Minister:

The most powerful single position in Canada's government is that of Prime Minister. It might surprise you to learn that the position of Prime Minister is not even mentioned in the B.N.A. Act. This is one of the clearest examples of an institution which grew through custom in the British parliamentary system.

The B.N.A. Act merely says that "There shall be a Council to aid and advise

The official residence of the Prime Minister in Ottawa.

the Government of Canada, to be styled the Queen's Privy Council for Canada." The leader of this Privy Council (now the Cabinet) is called Prime Minister.

The duties of the office are not outlined. The role of Prime Minister has changed a lot since 1867. As we have seen, the role of government has greatly increased since Confederation. At the same time, the direct influence of the monarchy has decreased. The result has been a continual growth in the power of the Prime Minister.

Electing a Prime Minister: In the United States, citizens vote directly for their President. We do not vote for a Prime Minister in federal elections. The person who becomes Prime Minister must first be chosen leader by his or her own party. The leader must also be elected to Parliament in his or her own riding. If the leader's party then wins the greatest number of seats in the House of Commons, he or she will become Prime Minister.

Some Recent Party Leaders

Examine closely the background of Liberal and Conservative Party leaders in the charts on pages 19 and 20.
1. From what provinces do the majority of Liberal leaders come? How might this affect their political support in elections?
2. What seems to be the professional and educational background of most party leaders? Do you feel this suitably qualifies them for the position of P.M.?

Liberal Party Leaders in the 20th Century

Name	Age When Elected	Home Province	Selected Leader	Parliamentary Experience	Education	Profession	Religion	Ancestry
Wilfrid Laurier	45	Quebec	1887	1871-74 MLA 1874 MP 1877 Cabinet Minister	Collège-Assumption	Lawyer	Catholic	French
W.L. Mackenzie King	45	Ontario	1919	MP and Cabinet Minister 1908-11 (Department of Labour)	University of Toronto	Civil Servant/ Industrial Relations Advisor	Presbyterian	Scottish
Louis St. Laurent	66	Quebec	1948	Cabinet Minister	Laval University	Lawyer	Catholic	French
Lester Pearson	60	Ontario	1958	Cabinet Minister 1948-1957	Universities of Toronto and Oxford	Civil Servant	United Church	Irish
Pierre Trudeau	48	Quebec	1968	Cabinet Minister 1967-1968	University of Montreal, Harvard, Ecole des sciences politiques, London School of Economics	Lawyer/ Professor	Catholic	French

Conservative Party Leaders 1927-1976

Name	Age When Elected	Home Province	Elected Leader	Parliamentary Experience	Education	Profession	Religion	Ancestry
R.B. Bennett	57	New Brunswick Alberta	1927	Alberta MLA 1909-11 Member of Parliament 1911-17, 1921, 1925-27	Dalhousie University	Lawyer	United Church	English
R. J. Manion	56	Ontario	1938	MP 1917-35, Cabinet Minister 1921, 1926, 1930-35	University of Toronto	Physician	Catholic	Irish
J. Bracken	59	Manitoba	1942	Premier of Manitoba 1922-43	Ontario Agricultural School, Guelph; University of Illinois	Agricultural Scientist	United Church	Scottish/ Irish/ English
G.A. Drew	54	Ontario	1948	Premier of Ontario 1943-48	University of Toronto, Osgoode Hall Law School	Lawyer	Anglican	English
J.G. Diefenbaker	61	Saskatchewan	1956	Member of Parliament 1940-56	University of Saskatchewan	Lawyer	Baptist	German/ Scottish
R.L. Stanfield	53	Nova Scotia	1967	MLA 1949-67 Premier of Nova Scotia 1956-67	Dalhousie University; Harvard Law School	Lawyer	Anglican	English/ Welsh
J. Clark	37	Alberta	1976	Member of Parliament 1972-1976	University of Alberta	Politician	Catholic	Irish/ Scottish

3. Which of the leaders in the charts actually became Prime Minister?
4. Examine the background of each leader. Try to calculate the areas of the country which might support him in an election. Now try to check your predictions with the actual results of the federal elections in which these leaders ran.

Our political system has been affected in many ways by the American experience. One example is the way Canadian political parties choose their leaders. The age of television has turned political conventions into glamour spectacles. As a result, the person with the best "television image" and "charisma" (strong appeal) may be chosen leader. Real issues and answers can be ignored in favour of personalities. In the elections of 1958 and 1968, John Diefenbaker and Pierre Trudeau had dynamic public images. Their opponents, Lester Pearson and Robert Stanfield could not match this appeal. Their lack of "charisma" likely played a part in the election defeat of their party.

When a party is about to elect a new leader, a convention is called. Local party branches from across the country send delegates to this convention. The delegates vote for a new leader from the list of announced candidates. Obviously these delegates will be subject to great pressure from the candidates for their support.

The Prime Minister in Office

The Prime Minister has vast power to exercise. It is his task to make most of the key appointments in government. The Prime Minister chooses Cabinet Ministers, Supreme Court Justices, ambassadors and important civil servants. As leader of the Cabinet, the Prime Minister makes government policy. As leader of the largest party in the House of Commons, he is also responsible for deciding the passage of bills into law. A Prime Minister must call an election at least once every five years. Within this limit however, it is up to him to decide on the date of a federal election.

The Prime Minister also represents Canada in other countries. He and his cabinet must decide foreign policy and negotiate international agreements. Beyond our own borders, the image of Canada and Canadians is often created by the image of our Prime Minister.

In short, the well-being of Canada both at home and abroad rests with the office of the Prime Minister.

The Cabinet

One person could not possibly handle the duties of government. The Prime Minister selects certain members of his party to help him with these tasks. This

Past and Present Party Leaders Left: John Diefenbaker, P.C., former Prime Minister; below: Ed Broadbent, Federal N.D.P., Stephen Lewis, Provincial (Ontario) N.D.P.; bottom; Joe Clark, P.C., leader of the Federal Opposition.

group, together with the Prime Minister, forms the Cabinet. Each cabinet minister is responsible for a certain department, such as Defence, Finance or External Affairs. Each such responsibility is called a **portfolio.** In addition, there are several members of the Cabinet who have no specific duty, but may be used as "troubleshooters" in other departments. These are called Ministers Without Portfolio.

Each minister must answer to Parliament for the affairs of his department. He or she must introduce bills, explain the policies and answer questions for his area of responsibility.

Cabinet ministers also take part in deciding general government policy. These debates take place behind closed doors, and are kept secret. Although there is often great disagreement, once a decision has been reached, each minister must publicly support it. If a member refuses to do so, he or she must resign from the cabinet. This principle is called **cabinet solidarity.**

In selecting members for his cabinet the Prime Minister must choose someone from the House of Commons or the Senate. Normally too he will choose members of his own party. During times of national emergency, such as a war, he may invite members of the opposition to join the cabinet. This happens rarely.

On the surface, it would seem that the Prime Minister's task in selecting the cabinet is quite simple. After all, why not simply choose the best people from

---

George Hees explains why he resigned from the Cabinet in 1963.

Dear Mr. Prime Minister:

As you know, I have been extremely concerned for some time about our defence policy and our relations with the United States.

I have outlined to you, to my colleagues, and to the caucus of the Conservative Party why I consider that our present defence policy does not either fulfill our international commitments or provide for the security of our country. I have also stated clearly that I consider the present attitude of the government cannot but lead to a **deterioration** [worsening] of our relations with the United States.

I had hoped that the views which I expressed would lead to changes in policy which would permit me to remain a member of the government. However, since that time there has been no indication of such change. I feel these matters to be of vital importance to the welfare and security of our country, and therefore I have no alternative but to tender my resignation as a member of your Cabinet.

I do not propose to be a candidate in the forthcoming election.

Yours sincerely,
signed, George Hees

These photographs show some of the duties of the Prime Minister. Above, meeting the Queen, with the Governor-General, Roland Michener. Left, at a press conference. Below, meeting with other politicians.

his party? In fact, the process is not quite so simple. Canada is a large country. Different regions have their own interests. Canada is also a multicultural country. Our population has a variety of languages, religions and ethnic backgrounds. The Prime Minister must take these factors into account.

He must also include the strong people within his own party. This must be balanced by people with administrative skill. As we can see, choosing a cabinet is not an easy task.

In the following chart, what indications are there that religious, language and regional differences have been taken into account by the Prime Minister in his choice of a cabinet?

A Recent Federal Cabinet

	Province of constituency	Religion	Previous occupation
Prime Minister	Sask.	Prot.	lawyer
Minister of Agriculture	Alta.	Prot.	farmer; teacher
Minister of Citizenship and Immigration	Ont.	Prot.	accountant
Minister of Defence Production	Que.	R.C.	lumberman
Minister of Finance and Receiver General	Ont.	Prot.	lawyer
Minister of Fisheries	P.E.I.	Prot.	farmer
Minister of Justice and Attorney General	B.C.	R.C.	lawyer
Minister of Labour	Ont.	Gk. Orth.	businessman
Minister of Mines and Technical Surveys	Que.	R.C.	farmer
Minister of National Defence	B.C.	Prot.	soldier
Minister of National Health and Welfare	Ont.	Prot.	accountant
Minister of National Revenue	N.S.	Prot.	lawyer
Minister of Northern Affairs and National Resources	Sask.	Prot.	teacher
Postmaster General	Que.	Prot.	lawyer; businessman
Minister of Public Works	Ont.	Prot.	lawyer
Secretary of State of Canada	Que.	R.C.	lawyer; businessman
Secretary of State for External Affairs	B.C.	Prot.	lawyer
Solicitor General	Que.	R.C.	lawyer
Minister of Trade and Commerce	Man.	Prot.	lawyer
Minister of Transport	Ont.	Prot.	manufacturer
Minister of Veterans Affairs	N.B.	Prot.	lawyer
Minister without Portfolio	Nfld.	R.C.	lawyer
Associate Minister of National Defence	Que.	R.C.	businessman

A Cabinet Appointment

In recent years more and more women have entered politics and have gained prominent cabinet positions. The Honourable Judy LaMarsh joined the Pearson cabinet in 1963.

As usual, I had to wait to see the Prime Minister.

At lunch, nerves had overcome me, and I remember fretting because I had spilled

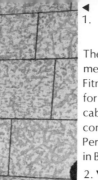

◄
1.

These photographs show some of the duties of a cabinet member. Iona Campagnolo has been Minister of State, Fitness and Amateur Sport. She is member of Parliament for Skeena, British Columbia. 1. entering Room 3405 for a cabinet meeting, 2. meeting with some of her younger constituents, 3. taping the television program "Question Period," 4. recording a radio program for her constituents in B.C., telling the news of the week from Ottawa.

2. ▼

3.
◄

4. ►

soup down the front of my light suit and had nothing with me as a change. What a way to enter the office of the Prime Minister elect!

Pearson asked me to sit down and we chatted for a moment or two about the election, and then he told me that he wanted me to serve in the Cabinet as Minister of National Health and Welfare. I was stunned. What raced through my mind was the size and importance of the portfolio and the amount of important work laid out for it. I wanted to be in the Cabinet, but I had decided by the time I arrived there that I wasn't going to do just any old job — one which calls for no real contribution, but just to be there. I wasn't going to find myself a sop to women voters, and as each day had passed between the election and this interview I got firmer and firmer in my mind about

this. (Whether if such a job had been offered to me I would have had the strength to turn it down is another question, which happily I have never had to answer.) From the night of the election, I had heard that many members had rushed to Ottawa to hang around to be "available" for a call from the Prime Minister and to jog his memory by their presence.... This must be the most difficult time for any Prime Minister, for the less one deserves reward for his contribution to victory, the more vocal he is in claiming it. And if he pressures enough, he often gets it. There is an old Cockney expression that covers the situation, one I often heard derisively repeated at home over the years. "It's the squeaky wheel wot gets the grease." Another is: "It's the coats and pants wot does the work, and the vest wot gets the gravy."

The Honourable Monique Bégin, Minister of Health and Welfare

2.   THE LEGISLATIVE BRANCH

The Members of Parliament

How many of the following questions could you answer:
— Who is your Member of Parliament?
— What is the name of the riding he or she represents?
— How long has he or she represented your riding?
— What specific things has he or she accomplished for your riding?

If we were to look at the electoral map of Canada, the entire country would look like a huge jigsaw puzzle made up of 282 pieces. In fact Canada is divided into 282 electoral districts, called **ridings** or **constituencies.** Each riding sends one representative to the House of Commons. Each representative is called a Member of Parliament.

Conservative M.P. Jim McGrath. He represents St. John's East, Newfoundland. Mr. McGrath has been an M.P. for over 20 years. Some of his recent political appointments have been: Official Opposition Spokesman on Consumer Affairs (1973, 1974); Official Opposition Spokesman on Housing and Urban Affairs (1976); Official Opposition Coordinator of Social Policy and Chairman of Consumer Affairs (1977).

The House of Commons is the highest body in our parliamentary system. It can pass or reject bills, make cabinet ministers account for their actions and even force the government to resign. In practice, Members of Parliament realize that they were partly elected because of the appeal of their party or party leader. They will hesitate to vote against the wishes of their party. As a result, in most cases the vote in the House of Commons will be along party lines. To ensure this **solidarity** (working together as a unit) each party appoints a Party Whip. His or her main job is to make sure Members attend the House of Commons for important votes, and persuade them to support the party's point of view. As you can see when one party wins a clear majority of seats in the House of Commons, it usually gets its own way in running the affairs of state.

Your Member of Parliament seems to be caught in a delicate position. On the one hand he or she was elected by the voters in your riding to represent their wishes and interests in the House of Commons. On the other hand he or she is expected to faithfully support the party's position on important issues in the House. Does the ordinary M.P. have any significant role in the parliamentary system?

The Caucus: The one area where your Member of Parliament is not expected to be a "yes man" is in a **caucus** meeting. The elected members of each party consult regularly, usually once every week, in a private meeting called the caucus. It is a secret session. No minutes are kept. In such meetings, individual M.P.'s are free to state their point of view on issues. The party leaders try to explain their programs to their followers. The M.P.'s can debate policies and try to gather support for their local and regional interests. Obviously many disagreements will come up. But once a decision has been reached in caucus each party member is expected to support the decision in the House of Commons.

The Life of an M.P.: On the surface, being a Member of Parliament does not seem difficult. Members are paid $26 900 annually (as of 1978), with an expense account of $12 000. The sessions of Parliament are usually short (the longest on record was 174 days). M.P.s usually do not have to spend more than six or seven months in Ottawa. They have the privilege of free postal services and are allowed free trips to visit their ridings. They are often asked to free luncheons, and have the chance to rub shoulders with famous people from all over the world. On top of this, some M.P.'s seem to take their jobs casually, and rarely contribute to Commons debates.

On the other hand a Member of Parliament who takes his or her job seriously carries a heavy burden. A Member of Parliament has a number of responsibilities calling for his or her attention. For one thing, an M.P. was elected to represent his or her riding. This means that, on the average, an M.P. looks after the needs of over 83 000 voters. The M.P. has other things to consider. He or she must weigh regional and national interests when making a decision. Of course there is also the pressure to follow party policies.

The Daily Routine of a Member of Parliament: The life of an M.P. may not be all that glamorous. Here is a typical day:

09:00	Arrives at office. Answers mail, makes telephone calls for an hour or two. Handles a great many requests — from young people in the riding who want photographs, to the elderly who are worried about old-age pensions.
11:00	Attends committee meetings. Our M.P. may be a member of one or more Parliamentary committees.
12:00	Lunch
13:00	Returns to office. Speaks to visitors or voters from his riding.
14:00	The House of Commons usually meets in the afternoon and evening. Our M.P. usually attends both question periods.
16:00	Works on speech for the evening question period.
17:30	Dinner
20:00	Evening debate in House of Commons.

The Senate

The House of Commons is the only elected body in our parliamentary system. Yet there is another seemingly powerful body called the Senate. The Senate was created in 1867. There were several reasons for this action. For one thing there was tradition. British Parliament had its House of Lords. This body could put a check on the people's representatives, the House of Commons. At that time it was felt that ordinary voters were not necessarily wise enough to choose a good government. Also, elections for members of the House of Commons came at least once every five years It was likely that many new, inexperienced members would be elected each time. The Senate, whose members were appointed for life, could provide stability to the government.

Another factor to consider was Canada's regional interests. Representation in the House of Commons is based on population. In this way, the provinces with the largest population, Ontario and Quebec, had a great advantage. They could often get their way. The wishes of the smaller provinces would be ignored. Representation in the Senate was organized in this way:

Maritimes	24
Quebec	24
Ontario	24
West	24
Newfoundland (1949)	6
Northwest Territories (1975)	1
Yukon (1975)	1
	104

In this way, each region of Canada was equally represented. Each region could hope to have its own interests defended.

Senators are appointed by the Governor-General on the advice, of course, of the Prime Minister and his Cabinet. To become a Senator one must be at least thirty years old and own property valued at at least $4 000. Today this is not a great deal of wealth. In 1867, $4 000 was worth much more. This was one way of making sure that only the "better" classes would be Senators.

Originally, Senators were appointed for life. They could be removed only if they committed a serious crime, became bankrupt or failed to attend Senate sessions. In 1965, a bill was passed making the retirement age for all future Senators 75. Those already appointed would continue to sit for life. Senators are paid a salary of $26 900 plus an expense allowance of $6 000.

In theory, the Senate has the same duties as the House of Commons. It can pass or reject any bill passed by the House of Commons (except money bills). It may even introduce its own legislation. Senators may be asked to sit on committees to study legislation. Often too, a member of the Cabinet will be selected from the Senate.

In practice however, the Senate is not equal to the House of Commons. The main reason is that the Senate is not an elected body. It is not responsible to the people. The Senate has become a place where Party workers are rewarded for their loyalty and service. The Liberal Party has been in power in Canada for all but 5½ years since 1935. As a result the Senate is largely filled with Liberal supporters. These factors tend to reduce the prestige of the Senate. Its views no longer have a great influence on the government.

Do We Really Need a Senate?

Those who favour keeping the Senate argue that many of the original reasons for its creation still exist. We need a check on government activities, stability, and protection of regional interests. Even many of the defenders however agree that some reform of the Senate may be useful. Some of the most common suggestions are:

1. Since the Senate represents regions, Senate appointments should be made by the provinces. This would also remove the criticism that Senators are rewarded by the party in power for past services.
2. Appointments should include people from all walks of life, not just politicians. This would help give the Senate a broader point of view.
3. Rules regarding compulsory attendance should be passed. Senators, after all, are well-paid. The Senate is sometimes regarded as a "social club" where attendance and debate is minimal.
4. Make the Senate an elected body like the House of Commons. Their views would carry greater authority since they now actually represent the people.

What do you think?

Important Terms

Here are some of the important terms used in the organization of the House of Commons:

SPEAKER: Any debating group needs an **impartial** (fair to both sides) referee. This person makes sure that proper rules and procedures are followed. In the House of Commons, this is the job of the Speaker. He or she must be a Member of the House. The speaker is nominated by the Prime Minister and then chosen by the members of Parliament.

BACKBENCHERS: Backbenchers are Members of Parliament who do not have a specific government responsibility. They do not sit on the Cabinet. They are expected to support their party during debate.

LEADER OF THE
   OPPOSITION: The leader of the second-largest party in the House of Commons is called Leader of the Opposition. All non-government parties are known as "Her Majesty's Loyal Opposition." Their role is to criticize and try to improve government legislation.

PAGES: If you attend a session of Parliament you will notice a number of young people around the Speaker's Throne. They are called pages. It is their duty to run errands for the Members of Parliament; for example, they carry messages.

HANSARD: The daily debates in the House of Commons are recorded in a publication called Hansard. Copies of Hansard are available through the Queen's Printer Ottawa.

Passing a Bill

The main task of Parliament is to create new laws. The responsibility for this falls mainly on the Government. At the opening of a session of Parliament the Governor-General reads the **speech from the throne.** The speech is, in fact, written by the Prime Minister and Cabinet. It outlines the government plans for new laws for the upcoming session. Most bills discussed in Parliament are **government bills;** that is, bills introduced by a Cabinet minister. If a government bill should be defeated in the House of Commons, it is traditional for the government to resign. As you might imagine, great pressure is put on individual M.P.'s to vote along party lines.

It is possible for ordinary M.P.'s to introduce bills of their own. These are called **private member's bills.** These bills may deal with matters of local or national interest. However, the Government usually takes no real position on these bills. Furthermore, very little time is allowed in Parliament for private members' bills. An "early death" is the fate of most such bills.

The procedure for passing any bill in Parliament is the same. A bill introduced in the House of Commons must go through three readings. If it is passed, it will go on to the Senate. Here too it is read three times. If it is passed

Stages in passing a Bill

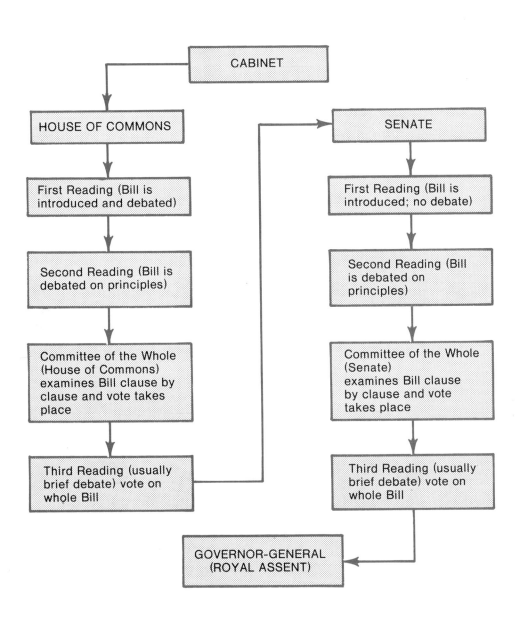

by the Senate, it will go on to the Governor-General. He then signs it and it becomes law. If the bill is rejected by the Senate it will go back to the House of Commons, and begin again.

3.   HOLDING A NATIONAL ELECTION

Voting for our representatives in the House of Commons is the most important political decision most of us will ever make. It has been stated that Canadians are truly "free" only once every four or five years. That is, on the day they vote for a new government. After that, until the next election, they are subject to the decisions of their representatives. This statement may only be a partial truth. Yet it does show how important it is to have informed citizens who choose their representatives wisely. Even so, in each federal election, over a million Canadians do not vote. Often many of these same people complain loudly about how badly their government is run.

Unlike the United States, Canada does not hold its federal elections at preset times. The Prime Minister may dissolve Parliament and call for a national election at any time within five years of the last election.

As soon as an election is called the political parties in each of Canada's 282 ridings swing into action. The major parties will nominate a candidate for each riding. In addition there may be a number of independent candidates (those who have no party attachments). In some ridings, as many as seven or eight candidates might seek election.

The moment the Prime Minister calls an election, the Governor-General officially sets in motion the wheels of the election machinery. The Chief Electoral Officer, a permanent civil servant, begins to prepare the details.

The Usual Steps in a National Election

1. The election is set for a Monday. If the Monday is a holiday then it is held on a Tuesday.
2. Returning officers are appointed to be in charge of elections in each riding in Canada.
3. The returning officers appoint **enumerators** in each riding. Enumerators go from door-to-door to make a list of the eligible voters in the riding.
4. The lists of eligible voters are printed and posted in public places.
5. The candidates are officially nominated and begin campaigning.
6. On election day, the polling stations are open from 08:00 to 19:00.
7. The voter is given a ballot on which to secretly mark their choice.
8. The ballots are counted. Each party sends a representative, called a **scrutineer,** to make sure the ballots are counted fairly. By midnight, the winner is usually known.

Ballot box. *Picture from the sound filmstrip series "Why Do We Have Laws?" courtesy Cinemedia Ltd. Toronto.*

Who is Eligible to Run?

The Canada Elections Act states that any person may be eligible to run for election to the House of Commons who is:
a) a Canadian citizen
b) of the age of eighteen
There are however, a number of people who are not eligible for office. They include:
a) anyone found guilty of corrupt practice during an election;
b) a member of a provincial legislature, sheriffs, or Crown attorneys while they are holding office;
c) anyone holding office or employed by the Government of Canada.

As you can see, a great number of Canadians are free to run for office. However, to be official, their nomination must have two things. It must have the signature of at least ten voters in the candidate's riding. It must also be accompanied by a $200.00 deposit. The candidate will lose this deposit if he or she receives less than half as many votes as the winner. For example, if candidate X wins the riding with 10 000 votes, candidate Y must receive at least 5000 votes or lose his or her deposit.

Who Can Vote?

Long before the actual voting day, an official voters' list is made up by the Returning Officer and the enumerators. The lists are then posted on public places (telephone poles, tree trunks, etc.) The lists include the names and addresses of eligible voters.

The Canada Elections Act also specifies who can vote in Canadian federal elections. The franchise (or vote) is given to Canadians who
a) are eighteen years of age or over
b) are Canadian citizens
c) have been living in Canada for twelve months before the election

Some citizens are denied the right to vote. These include:

a) the Chief Electoral Officer, and the Assistant Chief Electoral Officer
b) the Returning Officer for each riding (except in case of a tie)
c) judges appointed by the federal government
d) people in mental institutions
e) people in prison
f) those found guilty of corrupt acts involving an election

4.   POLITICAL PARTIES

There is a common saying that when three people get together to talk politics they will come up with four different opinions. While this is an exaggeration, it does point out one of the problems of a democracy. If there are so many different opinions among Canadians, how can any common action be taken? Imagine for a moment the situation in the House of Commons if each Member insisted on having things his/her own way. There would be few if any bills passed. Debates in the House would be endless. In practice, we would not have effective government in Canada.

Under these conditions, you can see why political opinions and ideas must be organized under broad categories. This is the role of political parties. Each political party has a **political philosophy,** or point of view. Within this common set of beliefs, there is still room for shades of opinion. Because of political parties, large groups of people can organize and gain control of the government. In this way, they will be able to make laws. Naturally, these should satisfy the majority of people in the country.

Political parties have several other useful roles. They help describe and focus on issues which face Canadians. Political parties try to persuade the majority of people to follow their point of view. To do this, they educate the public in matters of national interest. After an election, the winning party organizes the government and drafts new laws. The losing parties must organize effective opposition. They become "watchdogs" to ensure that the party in power does not become irresponsible.

Obviously, in a democratic system more than one political party is necessary. In fact, in any democratic country there is no limit to the number of political parties. In some countries, as many as a dozen or more political parties run for office. In others, such as the United States, just two parties, the Republican and the Democratic, have any real success. In Canada only the Conservative and Liberal Parties have ever formed a national government. At various times however the New Democratic and Social Credit parties have had strong voices in government decisions.

The main goal of each party is to gain power. To do this it must naturally appeal to the majority opinion in the country. This makes it very difficult for any party with extreme or radical points of view to be elected. Most parties

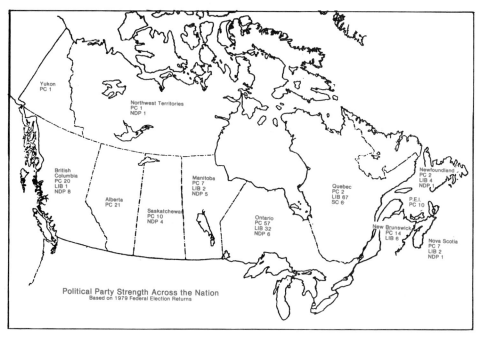

Political Party Strength Across the Nation
Based on 1979 Federal Election Returns

therefore tend to have very moderate opinions and policies. Many people in fact accuse our major parties of having exactly the same philosophy of government. There is in fact a range of political opinion, which allows voters to see the differences between the parties, and so be able to make a decision. This is sometimes called the political spectrum.

The Political Spectrum

Left	Centre	Right
want to change conditions around them as quickly as possible	favour change, but at a cautious pace	believe in keeping tradition and maintaining the present system
believe that key industries, transportation and natural resources should be in the hands of government	believe in some form of government management of the economy	business and industry should be kept in the hands of individuals
believe the government should take care of the needy	tend to be open-minded about approaches and solutions to problems	believe in less government interference in the lives of individuals
are not bound by tradition	respect tradition, but are willing to change if it is the wish of the majority	believe in keeping tradition
the rights of individuals have high priority	believe in law and order, but rights of individuals come first	law and order and discipline have high priority

CANADIAN GENERAL ELECTIONS 1867-1974

Party Standings in the House of Commons

Date of Election			Party Standings							
	Cons.	Libs.	Prog.	UFA.	CCF NDP	S.C.	S.C.R.	Other	Total Seats
Aug.-Sept. 1867	101	80							181
July-Sept. 1872	103	97							200
January 1874	73	133							206
September 1878	137	69							206
June 1882	139	71							210
February 1887	123	92							215
March 1891	123	92							215
June 1896	89	117						7	213
November 1900	78	128						8	214
November 1904	75	139							214
October 1908	85	133						3	221
September 1911	133	86						2	221
December 1917	153	82							235
December 1921	50	117	64					4	235
October 1925	116	101	24					4	245
September 1926	91	116	13	11				14	245
July 1930	137	88	2	10				8	245
October 1935	39	171			7	17		11	245
March 1940	39	178			8	10		10	245
June 1945	67	125			28	13		12	245
June 1949	41	190			13	10		8	262
August 1953	51	170			23	15		6	265
June 1957	112	105			25	19		4	265
March 1958	208	49			8				265
June 1962	116	100			19	30			265
April 1963	95	129			17	24			265
November 1965	97	131			21	5	9	2	265
June 1968	72	155			22		14	1	264
October 1972	108	109			31		15	1	264
July 1974	95	141			16		11	1	264

1. Cons. (Conservatives)
2. Libs. (Liberals)
3. Prog. (Progressives)
4. UFA. (United Farmers of Alberta)
5. CCF/NDP (Co-operative Commonwealth Federation/New Democratic Party)
6. S.C. (Social Credit)
7. S.C.R. (Social Credit *Ralliement*. After the 1968 election, this party became the federal Social Credit Party. The S.C.R. designation is maintained in the above chart to show that all Social Credit Members of Parliament after 1965 have been elected from Quebec. See page 19)
8. Other (Independents — Not allied with any political party.)

5.   THE ROLE OF INTEREST GROUPS

One reason why a Member of Parliament tries to do a good job is the wish to be re-elected. This usually means that representatives will vote according to the wishes of the voters in their riding. However, the government and the individual M.P.'s are often subject to pressures of which many Canadians are not aware. We will look at several of the powerful groups which influence government decisions. There are hundreds of such groups in Canada. They range from labour unions and farming associations to representatives of individual businesses. Any group of people which tries to persuade the government to carry out certain actions is an **interest group.** Their aims may also be for the good of Canada. First and foremost however they seek what is good for the group.

The Mass Media

Over the years one of the strongest groups affecting government decisions has been the mass media. They include newspapers, radio and television. Politicians know that their careers are affected by the amount and the type of coverage which the media gives to them. The media may also come out strongly for or against certain bills. In this way they can influence public opinion. One example of where this is done is the editorial pages of newspapers. In these pages, the personal views of the publishers are stated. As well, certain "letters to the editor" are printed. These can give the impression that a large part of the public is either for or against certain events. The editorial pages of the larger Canadian newspapers can have a great influence on government decisions.

However, the media is not all-powerful. Many people do not bother to read the "news" and "editorials" parts of the newspapers, nor do they listen to the "personal viewpoints" expressed on radio and television. Many other readers and listeners simply come to their own conclusions on the issues. A good example of this occurred during the 1974 federal election. The three major Toronto newspapers, the *Star, Globe and Mail,* and *Sun* all supported the Progressive Conservative Party. Yet on election day, the public gave its support to the Liberal Party.

Pressure Groups

The best known interest groups are those which put organized pressure on the government. They include the Canadian Manufacturers' Association and the Canadian Labour Congress. There are also strong organizations for doctors, teachers, farmers, authors, and many more. The tactic used by these groups to pressure the government is called **lobbying.** Lobbyists are people who try to influence the course of a decision in their favour. Some groups hire professional lobbyists who actually have offices in Ottawa.

6. THE CIVIL SERVICE

Our elected representatives create policies and pass new laws. The less exciting task of putting these policies and laws into practice is left to the group of government employees known as **civil servants.** The members of the civil service are sometimes called **bureaucrats.** They form the largest group of employees in the country. It is estimated that there are over one thousand civil servants for each Member of Parliament. The total number of civil servants at all levels of government in Canada is over 500 000.

Civil servants at the highest level do more than carry out policies. They often directly influence the making of policies. This is largely due to the stability of their position. Cabinet ministers may come and go. They are after all, elected members. They may be defeated at the next election. When a new minister takes over a portfolio, he or she will be starting from the beginning. The new minister will probably rely on the advice and experience of his deputy minister. This civil servant has been on the job for years. In most cases these deputy ministers stay on the job, whether a Conservative or Liberal government takes over. This gives continuity to the ministry. Otherwise it might well end up in chaos.

DEPARTMENT OF FISHERIES

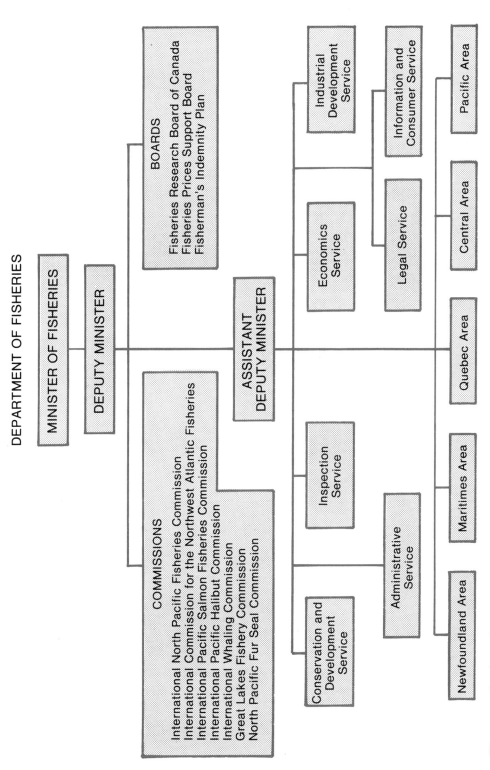

MINISTER OF FISHERIES

DEPUTY MINISTER

BOARDS

Fisheries Research Board of Canada
Fisheries Prices Support Board
Fisherman's Indemnity Plan

COMMISSIONS

International North Pacific Fisheries Commission
International Commission for the Northwest Atlantic Fisheries
International Pacific Salmon Fisheries Commission
International Pacific Halibut Commission
International Whaling Commission
Great Lakes Fishery Commission
North Pacific Fur Seal Commission

ASSISTANT DEPUTY MINISTER

Industrial Development Service

Information and Consumer Service

Economics Service

Legal Service

Inspection Service

Administrative Service

Conservation and Development Service

Pacific Area

Central Area

Quebec Area

Maritimes Area

Newfoundland Area

The organization of one government department

Romeo Leblanc, Minister of
Fisheries and Environment.
Mr. Leblanc is an Acadian
from New Brunswick.

At one time when a new party won an election, it appointed civil servants.
This usually meant great changes. As we have seen, the result could be chaos.
In 1918 the government passed the Civil Service Act. It set up examinations
for government jobs. Most government employees are now chosen on the
basis of these tests. These exams are difficult and candidates must know a
great deal about their chosen field. Today, most candidates must be fluent in
both English and French. If a non-bilingual person is chosen for a bilingual
position, that person must agree to become bilingual. Classes in French or
English and exams are given by the government. Most senior civil servants
probably know more about their field than their superiors, the cabinet
ministers. It has been said that the country might survive an emergency
without an elected government, but not without a civil service.

THINGS TO THINK ABOUT AND DO

Reviewing Key Words and Ideas

The following terms appeared in this chapter. Try to recall their meaning and how they were used.

aristocracy	enumerator	Minister Without Portfolio
backbencher	executive	monarchy
bureaucrats	interest group	the political spectrum
caucus	judicial	Parliament
civil servant	Leader of the Opposition	Party Whip
constituency	legislative	private member's bill
dictatorship	lobbying	speech from the throne

Remembering the Facts

1. The number of elected Members in the House of Commons is
a) 282   b) 284   c) 102
2. What is the voting age in Canadian federal elections?
3. The number of members in the Senate is decided on a regional basis. True or False?
4. Canada's written constitution is known as
a) N.H.L. Act   b) N.B.A. Act   c) B.N.A. Act · d) C.F.L. Act.
5. The retirement age for Senators is 65.   True or False?

Analyzing Ideas

1. What are the characteristics you feel are necessary to a good leader? Make a list of these characteristics and place them in the order of their importance. Why do you think these particular characteristics are important? Which of the following did you include in your list? — intelligence, self-confidence, good looks, courage, honesty, good speaking voice.
2. In a recent debate on capital punishment, the Members of Parliament decided to vote according to their own conscience rather than follow the wishes of their constituents. Do you feel M.P.'s should continue to have this freedom? Why or why not?
3. Our system of representative government has a number of problems. One of these is the problem of unequal representation. Some ridings with a sparse population cover thousands of square kilometres. In such ridings, a Member of Parliament may represent only 10 000 people. In large urban centres, another Member may represent as many as 150 000 people. What are the arguments in

favour and against maintaining such a system? How can this inequality of representation be overcome?

4. The Prime Minister faces a number of pressures when choosing a cabinet. These include regional interests, religious and ethnic factors, party pressures, etc. Should the Prime Minister ignore these factors and simply choose the best person for the job? Explain your answer.

Applying Your Knowledge

1. The mass media (radio, television, newspapers) can be very influential in determining the success or failure of a politician or a political party. Collect the editorial comments from your newspaper for a period of one week. Analyze its stand on political issues. Which political party does it seem to support?

2. Passing legislation in the House of Commons can create problems, especially if there is a **minority government** (a minority government is one in which no party has more than half the seats in the House of Commons). Here is a classroom simulation which can show these problems. Divide the class into groups. Make sure that there is a minority government in power. The opposition should be divided into at least two parties. The government must now attempt to pass a bill (such as raising the drinking age to twenty-one). What compromises and deals must be made in order for the government to succeed?

3. Here is another simulation. Your caucus is about to meet to discuss its stand on the controversial issue of abolishing the annual seal hunt. Assume every member of the class belongs to the same political party. Divide the class in such a way that:

a) Some members represent the Atlantic Provinces fishing community.

b) Some members represent an area in Ontario where the synthetic furs industry has created many jobs.

c) Some members represent the Western provinces, where the International Fund for Animal Welfare has taken out full-page ads condemning the seal hunt. The newspaper editorials have also been against the seal hunt.

d) About one-third of the members of the caucus are neutral.

Set aside a block of time to discuss the issue in caucus. What decision does your caucus make?

4

PROVINCIAL AND MUNICIPAL GOVERNMENTS

1. PROVINCIAL GOVERNMENTS

Introduction

Canada is a federal state. The fathers of Confederation set up federal and provincial governments, and divided certain powers between them. The B.N.A. Act gives the provinces the following power:

Section 92—Exclusive Powers of Provincial Legislatures

92. In each Province the Legislature may exclusively make Laws in relation to Matters coming within the Classes of Subjects next hereinafter enumerated; that is to say,—

1. The Amendment from Time to Time, notwithstanding anything in this Act, of the Constitution of the Province, except as regards the Office of Lieutenant-Governor.

2. Direct Taxation within the Province in order to the Raising of a Revenue for Provincial Purposes.

3. The borrowing of Money on the sole Credit of the Province.

4. The Establishment and Tenure of Provincial Offices and the Appointment and Payment of Provincial Officers.

5. The Management and Sale of the Public Lands belonging to the Province and of the Timber and Wood thereon.

6. The Establishment, Maintenance, and Management of Public and Reformatory Prisons in and for the Province.

7. The Establishment, Maintenance, and Management of Hospitals, Asylums, Charities, and Eleemosynary Institutions (almshouses) in and for the Province, other than Marine Hospitals.

8. Municipal Institutions in the Province.

9. Shop, Saloon, Tavern, Auctioneer, and other Licences in order to the raising of a Revenue for Provincial, Local, or Municipal Purposes.

10. Local Works and Undertakings other than such as are of the following Classes: —

(a) Lines of Steam or other Ships, Railways, Canals, Telegraphs, and other Works and Undertakings connecting the Province with any other or others of the Provinces, or extending beyond the Limits of the Province:

(b) Lines of Steam Ships between the Province and any British or Foreign Country:

(c) Such Works as, although wholly situate within the Province, are before or after their Execution declared by the Parliament of Canada to be for the general Advantage of Canada or for the Advantage of Two or more of the Provinces.

11. The Incorporation of Companies with Provincial Objects.

12. The Solemnization of Marriage in the Province.

13. Property and Civil Rights in the Province.

14. The Administration of Justice in the Province, including the Constitution, Maintenance, and Organization of Provincial Courts, both of Civil and of Criminal Jurisdiction, and including Procedure in Civil Matters in those Courts.

15. The Imposition of Punishment by Fine, Penalty, or Imprisonment for enforcing any Law of the Province made in relation to any Matter coming within any of the Classes of Subjects enumerated in this Section.

16. Generally all Matters of a merely local or private Nature in the Province.

As you can see, the provinces have responsibility for many areas. How are they governed? In effect, the governments of the provinces are a miniature version of the federal government. In the provinces the Lieutenant-Governor replaces the Governor-General. An elected Legislature replaces the House of Commons. Voting procedures and party organizations are much the same. The only real difference is the lack of a Senate in the provincial governments.

Comparison of Federal and Provincial Governments

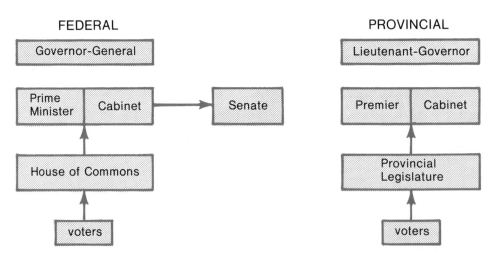

Before reading on, study the chart of key words and ideas on page 47.

Federal-Provincial Relations

You might conclude from Sections 91 and 92 of the B.N.A. Act that the federal and provincial governments have their own areas of responsibility. On the surface there is no cause for dispute. Yet over the years major areas of conflict

KEY WORDS AND IDEAS

Term	Meaning	Sample Use
deficit budgeting	a financial policy whereby the government plans to spend more than it takes in through taxation	Canadian governments practice deficit budgeting. They borrow money to make up for the deficit in their budget. Paying back these loans costs hundreds of millions of dollars yearly.
O.M.B.	Ontario Municipal Board; it was set up to help look after local government	One of the duties of the O.M.B. is to approve the spending by local governments.
regional disparity	some provinces and regions of Canada are more prosperous than others	The federal government tries to lessen regional disparity by aiding "have-not" provinces with grants and subsidies.
shared responsibilities	although federal and provincial governments have their own specific areas of responsibility, on some occasions they divide these responsibilities	Some examples of shared responsibilities are unemployment, old age pensions, immigration, etc.
tariff	a tax placed on imports coming into Canada from other countries	Tariffs are paid by the importer and collected by the federal government.

have come up between the two levels of government. One problem area is taxation. The makers of the B.N.A. Act gave the most important tax sources to the federal government. They did so because it seemed that the federal government would have the greatest expenses. Since 1867, however, a number of provincial responsibilities considered "inexpensive" and "unimportant" have changed. Health and welfare are two examples. Back in 1867, these were not considered important government responsibilities. Since the Great Depression of the 1930s, however, very costly government programmes have been set up in these areas. There was no mention of these areas in the B.N.A. Act. The Supreme Court of Canada decided that the provinces should look after them. Health and welfare came under the "Property and civil rights" clause.

The demand for more schools, better roads, and other provincial services continued to grow. The provinces would soon be struck with the largest expenses. The federal government still had the largest taxing powers. There were two answers. One dealt with money supply. The provinces agreed to give the federal government some of their own taxing powers, such as the inheritance tax. The federal government agreed to share the cost of a number of expensive programmes in return. It also agreed to give grants to the needy provinces.

A second solution was to let the federal and provincial governments share some responsibilities. One example is unemployment insurance. It was a provincial responsibility. In 1940, the provinces agreed to turn control over to the federal government. Other shared responsibilities include:

Some Responsibilities Shared by Federal and Provincial Governments

HEALTH AND WELFARE

Federal — old-age pensions, unemployment insurance, etc.
Provincial — hospitalization; vaccines; tuberculosis tests; sanitoria, etc.

AGRICULTURE

Federal — experimental farms, loans to farms, etc.
Provincial — agricultural colleges, marketing boards, etc.

IMMIGRATION

Federal — quotas on immigrants; checks suitability of immigrants; financial assistance for transportation, education
Provincial — acceptance of proportion of the national quota; selection and direction of immigrants to areas where needed

HIGHWAYS

Federal — financial help to provinces for selected major highways
Provincial — major roads between municipalities

Provincial Premiers Voice Regional Concerns

Despite the intentions of the Fathers of Confederation and the B.N.A. Act, tensions often arise between provincial and federal governments. The differences between the regions of Canada partly account for this. The various provinces complain that the federal government is not sensitive to their needs and desires. Since 1867 the gap between the wealthy provinces and the "have-not" provinces has widened.

On February 10, 1969, a Constitutional Conference was called in Ottawa by Prime Minister Trudeau. The Premiers of the ten provinces attended. They took this opportunity to voice their regional points of view.

Building highways is a shared provincial-municipal responsibility.

Premier Louis Robichaud of New Brunswick spoke for the Maritimes:

Over the years you people from other parts of the Country have heard of this problem of economic **disparity** in our Country which affects us more perhaps than in any other part of Canada.

Over the years we argued that something dramatic should be done to **alleviate** [make lighter] the burden that the residents of the Atlantic area have to support.

Over the years successive governments and people in this Country have been listening to us with very sympathetic ears and over the years a lot of patch work, I should say, has been done.

It is most humiliating for us to appear before this august body and before the Canadian nation and appear like beggars. We are not beggars. We do not want to be beggars. We simply want our fair share of the national wealth...

Our taxes are double what they are in Ontario. In fact the municipal taxes and the provincial taxes are double. That is not all. We, for instance, buy a car in the Atlantic Provinces. Everybody has a car. It is no longer a luxury to have a car. It is a necessity of life. We buy a car which is manufactured in Ontario. We pay $300 to $400 more than the resident of Ontario has to pay for a car, just to buy it; and after that car is purchased then we have to pay much higher taxes than the resident of Ontario has to pay in taxes to operate his car.

Now, in so many areas we are — let us put it bluntly — somewhat discriminated against. Why — because of transportation problems, of course, but I am wondering if something really dramatic should not be done and now. I do not think we can wait any longer.

I do not know what the solution is but let us think for a moment of the abolition of tariffs between the United States and Canada,... along the Atlantic border with the United States.... If that were feasible, do you know what it would mean? It would mean that every resident of the Atlantic Provinces would save approximately $1000 for the purchase of a car — $1000 for the purchase of a car per citizen.

John Robarts, Premier of Ontario, presented Ontario's case:

> I would like to make it very clear that Ontario has always supported the principle of equalization in our Country. I did not realize all the beds in Newfoundland were made in Ontario, nor that all the breakfast food that is eaten there is manufactured in Ontario, but we do realize and understand full well that Ontario's prosperity is based on a whole range of factors. Some of them are just the luck of geography, some of them are the gift of God, and some just the fact that we happen to be part of that great country called Canada.
>
> We recognize this and we are at all times prepared to do our part in ensuring that we have something at least approaching minimum standards across Canada. There must be some meaning to being a Canadian regardless of where you live, regardless of the economic circumstances of the particular area in which you live. This is a very fundamental and a very basic problem.

Alberta Premier Harry Strom stated the West's point of view:

> The economy of the West is based to a very large degree upon the production of certain raw resources... when Westerners examine the Federal Government's priorities in industrial development, the order which they see is the following: the manufacturing industries in Eastern and Central Canada, the raw resource industries of Eastern and Central Canada, then, the raw resources industries of Western Canada and finally, the manufacturing industries of Western Canada.
>
> This order of priorities is not a figment of our imagination.
>
> What Western Canadians legitimately desire, if economic justice is to prevail within Confederation, is that our raw resource industries be given the same priority as the manufacturing industries of Eastern and Central Canada.
>
> We desire this equality of priority to be demonstrated not simply in conference communiqués but in concrete ways....
>
> It is time the Federal Government recognized the harmful effect of the tariff system on the West, and indeed on the economic health of the nation.
>
> For us, the tariff system symbolizes the economic imbalance of Confederation.
>
> We see the logic of protecting infant industries but some of the "infants" are now eighty years of age and we are tired of paying their pensions.
>
> If the Federal Government is prepared to use its influence to secure entrance to foreign markets for Canadian producers, we want it to work as hard on behalf of the raw resource industries of the West....

Premier W.A.C. Bennett spoke for British Columbia:

> In the light of burgeoning provincial responsibilities, particularly in the fields of education, health, and welfare, British Columbia can see no other alternative if Provincial responsibilities are to be met than for the Federal Government to withdraw from the direct tax fields of personal and corporate income taxes and succession duties or estate taxes.
>
> When those changes have been made, it is our view the Constitution should restrict the spending power of the Federal Government to those matters under its jurisdiction....

I want to emphasize that the stresses within the nation at the present time are primarily economic and financial in nature. If we are to achieve that high destiny to which I am sure all of us around this table believe Canada is called, then we must do more to bring about economic opportunity for all citizens in all regions of Canada.

I am not minimizing the importance of such matters as language, culture and constitutional review generally. But I am saying, that if we are to have and develop the kind of Canada we all unquestionably desire, then the scope of our vision must embrace the economic facts of life in Canada, which call for a frank appraisal of what national policy should be adopted to improve the situation. British Columbia believes the solution lies in direct assistance to persons — to people — of low income rather than through large unconditional payments to certain Provincial Governments.

1. What seem to be the main complaints and suggestions of these Premiers?
2. With which position do you most agree? Why?

Paying for government

Have you ever heard the expression that "Nothing in this world is certain but death and taxes"? Benjamin Franklin said this more than 200 years ago. Modern health standards have increased our life span. But taxes seem to go up at an ever-increasing rate. Although taxes often 'hurt', they pay for the government services we are used to receiving. No Canadian would seriously argue that we should do away with police forces, schools, hospitals, postal service and garbage collection. Yet these are but a few of the hundreds of services government provides. A century ago, many of these services did not seem important and were not even provided by government. Today Canadians are demanding more and improved government services. Can we afford them?

The current budget of our federal government is set at over forty BILLION dollars per year. This means that it would take about $2000 for every man, woman and child in Canada to pay off the budget. These figures do not include all the expenses which are borne by provincial and municipal governments. Where do the various governments get the money to pay for the services they provide?

The B.N.A. Act gives the federal government the power to collect the following kinds of taxes:

PERSONAL INCOME TAX — This tax based on a person's annual earnings. This provides the government's largest source of revenue today.

CORPORATION TAX — A tax imposed on the income of a corporation or business.

SALES TAX — This is an indirect tax paid by the merchant on his

FISCAL YEAR 1977-78 ESTIMATES

PROVINCIAL BUDGET DOLLAR

REVENUE   EXPENDITURE

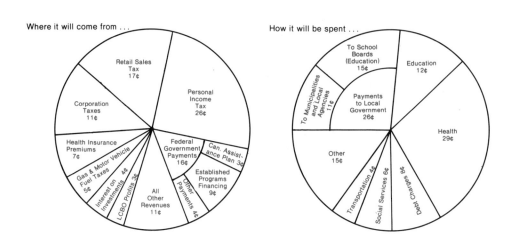

Where it will come from . . .

Retail Sales Tax 17¢

Personal Income Tax 26¢

Corporation Taxes 11¢

Health Insurance Premiums 7¢

Gas & Motor Vehicle Fuel Taxes 5¢

Interest on Investments 4¢

LCBO Profits 3¢

All Other Revenues 11¢

Other Payments 4¢

Federal Government Payments 16¢

Can. Assistance Plan 3¢

Established Programs Financing 9¢

How it will be spent . . .

To School Boards (Education) 15¢

Education 12¢

To Municipalities and Local Agencies 11¢

Payments to Local Government 26¢

Health 29¢

Other 15¢

Transportation 4¢

Social Services 6¢

Debt Charges 9¢

FEDERAL BUDGET DOLLAR

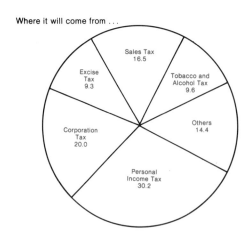

Where it will come from . . .

Sales Tax 16.5

Excise Tax 9.3

Tobacco and Alcohol Tax 9.6

Corporation Tax 20.0

Others 14.4

Personal Income Tax 30.2

How it will be spent . . .

Transfer to Provinces 9.3

Transportation and Communication 7.4

Other 16.4

Economic Development 16.5

Defense 10.0

Public Debt 12.6

Health and Welfare 27.8

total sales for the year. The buyer is usually not aware that he is paying for it. The amount is already included in the purchase price of an item.

EXCISE TAX — Another type of indirect sales tax. Excise taxes are paid by a manufacturer to the government before he sells his product. An example of an excise tax is the tax on liquor.

TARIFF — This is an import tax placed on goods coming in from other countries. The tax is paid by the importer.

Provincial governments also need money to pay for services they give. Their tax sources are not as great as the federal government. The B.N.A. Act allows provinces to raise money through the selling of various kinds of licences (e.g.; automobile, pet, hunting, fishing), corporation income tax, liquor tax, sales tax (e.g.; on gasoline). As well the provinces have the power to collect two other kinds of taxes:

DIRECT SALES TAX — This is different from ordinary sales tax. It is paid directly by the consumer when an item is bought. Most provinces have direct sales taxes ranging from 5% to 11%. Alberta is an example of a province which has no sales tax.

INHERITANCE TAX — When someone dies and leaves property to his/her heirs they must pay a tax on the value of the property.

The third level of government, the municipal, provides some of the most expensive services we use. Municipal governments operate schools, police departments, sanitation departments and public transit. Most of the money for these services comes from PROPERTY TAXES. Property taxes are paid on land and the value of the buildings on the land.

Even with all the taxes available to them, governments at all three levels find it hard to balance their budgets. Like many ordinary Canadians they make a practice of spending more money than they receive. This is called **deficit budgeting.** The government must then borrow money to pay its debts. They borrow from other countries or institutions. Canadian governments at all levels have borrowed a lot in recent years. A large part of our tax money goes to paying back our loans. It has been estimated that the federal government alone spends millions of dollars EACH DAY just to pay back the interest on the money they have borrowed. This issue concerns many economists, especially in times of slow economic growth.

The hidden tax "bite"

We may accept taxes as being inevitable. Yet most of us are not aware of just how much of our income goes back to the government in the form of taxes. A large portion of the price of any item we buy — radio, television, automobile, etc. — is made up of taxes. In the diagram below, we see the impact of various taxes on the price of gasoline. How much would a gallon of gas cost without federal and provincial taxes? As well, taxes will take an additional 75 per cent bite of any future oil price increases.

Pump Price Regular Gasoline

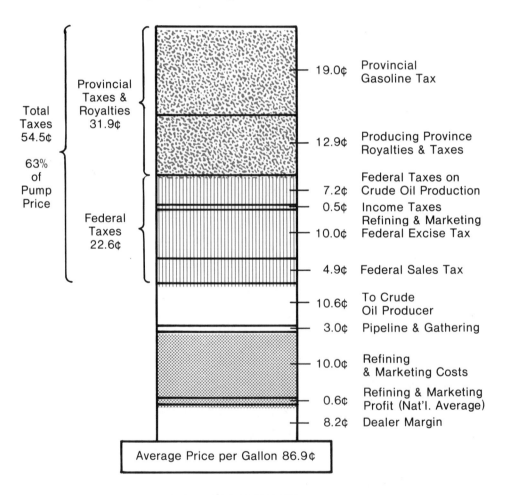

19.0¢	Provincial Gasoline Tax
12.9¢	Producing Province Royalties & Taxes
7.2¢	Federal Taxes on Crude Oil Production
0.5¢	Income Taxes Refining & Marketing
10.0¢	Federal Excise Tax
4.9¢	Federal Sales Tax
10.6¢	To Crude Oil Producer
3.0¢	Pipeline & Gathering
10.0¢	Refining & Marketing Costs
0.6¢	Refining & Marketing Profit (Nat'l. Average)
8.2¢	Dealer Margin

Provincial Taxes & Royalties 31.9¢

Federal Taxes 22.6¢

Total Taxes 54.5¢

63% of Pump Price

Average Price per Gallon 86.9¢

2.   MUNICIPAL GOVERNMENT

Canada is one of the very few countries in the world with three major levels of government. We have already studied the workings of the federal and provincial governments. The third level is the local or municipal government. In many ways, this may be the most important of the three. Municipal governments deal with matters which have direct effect on us. Often, decisions of our federal or provincial governments do not touch us directly. Scarcely a day goes by however when each of us does not make use of the services provided by local governments. Which of the following services have you used in the past week?

— public parks   — schools
— golf courses   — sidewalks
— zoos   — roads
— libraries   — buses or subways
— arenas   — garbage disposal

These and many more are the responsibilities of municipal governments. You can see the importance of these governments. Yet many voters don't act as though they knew this. For federal and provincial elections, the voter turnout is usually close to 70%. Examine the figures for recent municipal elections:

What Per Cent Of Voters Voted In Municipal Elections

City	% of Eligible Voters Who Voted
St. John's, Newfoundland	59%
Halifax, Nova Scotia	47%
Saint John, New Brunswick	40%
Montreal, Quebec	32%
Toronto, Ontario	34%
Winnipeg, Manitoba	54%
Saskatoon, Saskatchewan	35%
Edmonton, Alberta	42%
Vancouver, British Columbia	43%

Unfortunately these figures are typical of municipal elections in cities, towns and country areas right across Canada.

How your local government affects your life

Read the following list of events which might occur in the near future:
— A curfew of 22:00 is placed on anyone under the age of 17.
— The government of Canada agrees to sell nuclear reactors to Rumania.
— Your city firemen go on strike.
— Gasoline prices will rise 10% this year.
— Your house is expropriated to make way for a new road.
— The government agrees to lower transportation costs of Canadian goods travelling across the country.
— There is a bus and subway strike which is likely to last for weeks.

— The city's water purification system malfunctions, and the city may be without water for days.

— The government calls a conference with leading business, labour and political figures to study the economy.

— There has been a rash of burglaries in your neighbourhood, but the police department is understaffed, and can't spare extra men to patrol the area.

List the above "events" in the order of their importance to *you*. After you have completed your list, try to find out which areas are the responsibility of the federal, which of the provincial, and which of the municipal government. The chances are that many of the items at the very top of your list come under the responsibility of the municipal government.

Local government terminology (Ontario)

CITY:	a built-up area with a minimum population of 15 000 people
TOWN:	a built-up area with a minimum population of 2000
VILLAGE:	a built-up area with a minimum population of 500
BOARD OF CONTROL:	in cities of over 100 000 people a Board of Control consisting of a Mayor and a small number of Controllers; Controllers are full-time officials responsible for looking after the city budget and departments
MAYOR:	the head of the municipal council in city government
REEVE:	basically a reeve has the same duties as a mayor; he or she is elected in townships, towns, and villages
ALDERMAN:	an alderman is an elected member of a town council; usually he or she represents a particular area of the town or city

Organization of municipal governments

Section 92, article 8 of the B.N.A. Act, gives the Legislature of each province the right to make laws about municipal institutions. This means that municipal decisions must be approved by the government of the province. It also means that there is a wide variety of municipal governments. The type of government a community has will vary from province to province. It will also depend on the size of the community.

Metro Toronto

In Ontario, the Department of Municipal Affairs set up a special board, the **Ontario Municipal Board** (OMB) to help look after local government. The

City Hall, Toronto

Shared Responsibility

Service	Metro Responsibility	Local Responsibility
Recreation and community services	Regional parks (ravines, waterfront, islands, zoo) Golf courses Regional libraries	Neighbourhood parks and playgrounds Recreation programs Community centres and arenas Neighbourhood libraries
Road construction and maintenance	Expressways Major arterial roads Bridges, grade separations, snow removal and street cleaning are the responsibility of the government in whose jurisdiction the road lies.	Minor arterial roads Neighbourhood access roads Street lighting Sidewalks
Traffic control	Traffic regulation, crosswalks and pavement markings are the responsibility of the government in whose jurisdiction the road lies. Traffic lights are a metropolitan responsibility irrespective of the jurisdiction of the road.	
Water supply	Purification, pumping and trunk distribution system Water is supplied wholesale by the Metropolitan Corpora- tion to the area municipalities who retail it to the consumer	Local distribution system
Water pollution control	Sanitary trunk sewer system and disposal plants Storm drainage is primarily a local responsibility except on metropolitan roads and in a few cases where major storm sewers have been required	Local connecting sewer system
Garbage collection and disposal	Disposal	Collection
Public education	School sites, attendance areas and building programs Operating and capital costs	Operation of school system
Health	Chronic and convalescent hospitals	Public health services
Licensing and inspection	Businesses	Dogs and dog pound Marriage Buildings
Planning and development control	Except for zoning which is a local responsibility, planning and development control are shared by the metropolitan and area municipalities on the same basis as other shared responsibilities.	

Metropolitan Organization

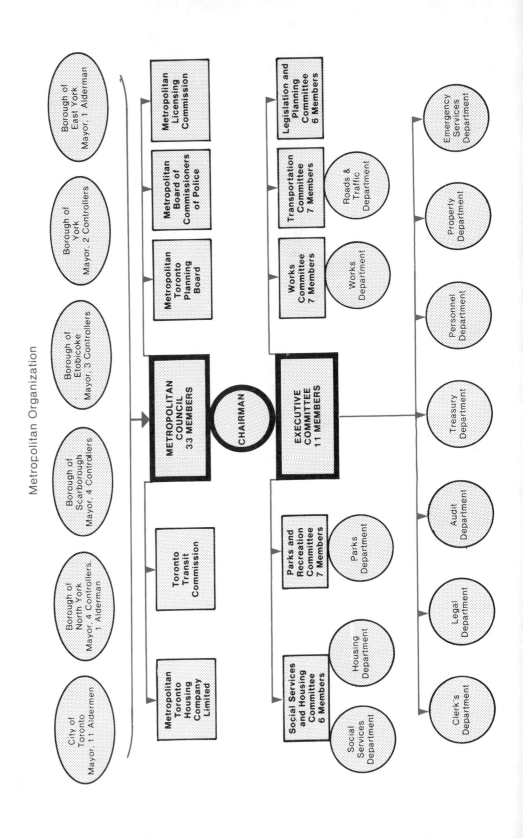

OMB has great powers. One of its duties is to approve spending by each municipality.

The City of Toronto presented special challenge for local government. Originally the area consisted of the city of Toronto and the five boroughs around it — East York, Etobicoke, York, Scarborough and North York. Each borough had, and continues to have, its own mayor and council.

The rapid growth of the area created problems. Transportation, sewage, water supply, road building and taxation were all strained. The Metropolitan system of government was created to ease the problems. The Metropolitan government works in co-operation with the borough governments. It now looks after an area of 1500 km^2 with a population of over 2.3 million.

Halifax

The city of Halifax, Nova Scotia, was the first city founded by the English in Canada. It was built in 1749 as a naval and military base. Over the years, Halifax did not experience the rapid growth of other great Canadian cities such as Montreal, Toronto, Vancouver, Winnipeg and Edmonton.

The founding of Halifax

Today, the most important item in the economy of Halifax is still government. Halifax is Canada's Atlantic headquarters for its naval forces and also its main defence centre. It is also a major industrial, educational, and cultural centre of the Maritimes.

Planning the growth of the city is one of the duties of the municipal government. Although such a task often seems simple on the surface, it takes great management skill. The following example is a good case of the problems in urban planning. The city of Halifax naturally wishes to attract as much industry and building construction as it possibly can. Thus when a number of banks and other businesses unveiled plans for large, high-rise office buildings in the city, it should have been a cause for celebration.

Not so! Halifax is also a leading tourist centre. One of its main attractions is the historical fortress on Citadel Hill, rising 75 m from the harbour. The building of the high-rise offices will block much of the view of the harbour from Citadel Hill. Solution! In 1974 the government passed the Views Bylaw restricting building heights and so protecting the view from Citadel Hill.

Halifax Citadel

Although a small city by some standards, Halifax has a complex government. Halifax is run by a mayor and ten aldermen who make up the city council. They are elected for three-year terms. The city council makes policy for the city. The actual management of the city is left to the City Manager. Through the various committees, the City Manager makes sure that the day-to-day operations of the city run smoothly.

Opposite is a chart showing the organization of the government of Halifax. Suggest *one* area of responsibility of each of the committees listed on the chart.

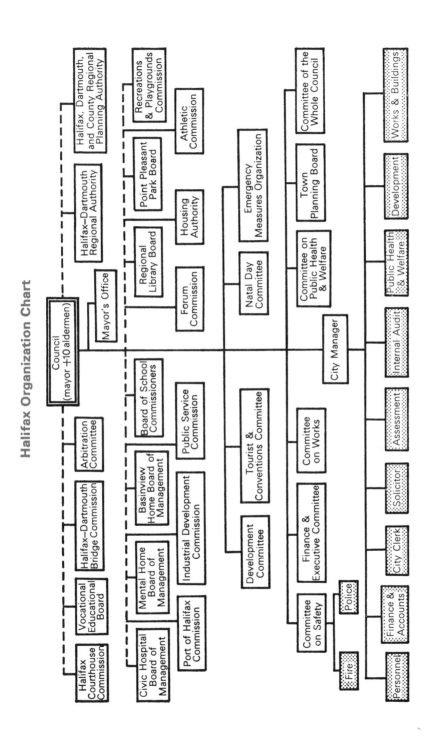

Halifax Organization Chart

Population growth, Halifax, 1749-1976

Year	City	Census metropolitan area (1976 limits)
1749	2 576	
1767	3 022	
1791	4 897	
1802	8 532	
1817	11 156	
1827	14 439	
1838	14 420	
1851	20 749	
1861	25 026	
1871	29 582	
1881	36 100	
1891	38 437	
1901	40 832	
1911	46 619	
1921	58 372	
1931	59 275	
1941	70 488	
1951	85 589	138 427
1956	93 301	170 481
1961	92 511	193 353
1966	86 792	209 901
1971	122 035	222 637
1976	117 882	267 991

Halifax today

Your role in local government

Unfortunately too large a segment of the public is unaware of the role of local government. They do not understand how it works. They seem happy to let others look after the programs and service for which they are paying. How can this be improved? The simplest way is for each citizen to become involved in the political process. Of course we may not all be able to run for office. But we can inform ourselves about what is being done by those in office. How?
— read the newspapers
— attend council meetings
— attend court sessions
— help a candidate in a local election
— talk to your candidate about your concerns
You will probably find that politics is more exciting than you might have imagined.

THINGS TO THINK ABOUT AND DO

Reviewing Key Words and Ideas

The following terms were used in this chapter. Try to recall their meaning and how they were used.

alderman	excise tax	O.M.B.
Board of Control	inheritance tax	reeve
City Manager	Lieutenant-Governor	tariff
deficit budgeting	mayor	

Remembering the Facts

1. The section of the B.N.A. Act which looks after provincial matters is
a) 99   b) 92   c) 91
2. The current budget of our federal government is about
a) $10 billion   b) $20 billion   c) $40 billion   d) $100 billion
3. A tax paid directly by the consumer when purchasing an item is called **indirect sales tax.** True or False.

Analyzing Ideas

1. Governments at all levels annually borrow hundreds of millions of dollars to pay for the services they provide. Should governments continually go into

debt to pay for services? Would Canadians accept a cutback in services in exchange for a balanced budget?

2. Regional disparity is a fact of life in Canada. Do you agree with the principle that the wealthier provinces — Alberta, B.C., and Ontario — should share their wealth with the less fortunate provinces? What actions should the federal government take to equalize the national wealth? How would this affect you personally?

3. Education is a provincial responsibility according to the B.N.A. Act. One of the effects of this is that there is a great variety of educational policies and standards from one end of the country to the other. If you were to move to another province, the subjects and the contents of the courses of study might be much different from what you are now taking. Should there be *one* educational system for all of Canada?

4. Language rights is another area of provincial responsibility. This was intended to help the provinces protect their language and customs. Under this clause, the Province of Quebec passed Bill 101. Among other things, this Bill denies immigrants the right to be educated in English if they wish. Should the federal government use its power to disallow provincial laws in this matter?

5. The voter turnout in Canada for elections at all levels is among the lowest in the world. In Australia there is a $12.00 fine for not voting. There the voter turnout is much higher. Should Canada adopt a similar system to encourage voters to participate in the electoral process?

Applying Your Knowledge

1. Is your municipality considered a village, a town or a city? What is the organization of your local government? Make a chart of the various committees who look after the government of your community.

2. Invite one of the members of your local government to speak to your class. Try to find out what his responsibilities are, what his qualifications for office are, and what problems lie ahead for your community.

3. For the following list of government responsibilities, decide which falls under federal, provincial, or municipal control:

agriculture	education	post office
mining	divorce	civil law
oil	marriage	defence
hospitals	direct taxes	printing money
sewers	prisons	property taxes

II

The Law

1

INTRODUCTION

"Police officer killed by unknown gunman"
"Man holds score of hostages in bank holdup attempt"
"Kidnapping now considered the crime of the '70s"
"Moncton police force demands return of death sentence"
"Mounties accused of illegal bugging"

Headlines such as these greet us almost every day in newspapers across Canada. They leave readers with the impression that crime is on the increase. Statistics would seem to bear out the fact that crime is a growing problem in Canada. Over the past ten years criminal offences have more than doubled. Violent crimes such as murder, rape and robbery are the ones which get the most public attention. Yet by far the largest number of offences committed by Canadians do not involve violence. They may involve the use of drugs, or alcohol. They may be simple automobile offences. Indeed some crimes are committed by people who do not even know they are breaking the law.

On the whole, Canadians know a good deal about the law. They know they must not steal or murder. They know they must not drive beyond the speed limit or drive without a licence. Yet there are hundreds of laws that Canadians either do not know or do not understand. If you break such a law you will still be punished. Our courts say "ignorance of the law is no excuse".

It is important, then, for Canadians to know as much as they can about the law. However, even lawyers do not have knowledge of all the laws at their fingertips. As an ordinary citizen you cannot be expected to know all the laws. You should, however, know how the law operates, and what rights and duties you have under the law. This may be of vital importance to you.

In this unit we will examine criminal and civil law in Canada. You will be asked to actively participate in making decisions about laws through a case study approach. We will also look at your rights as Canadians, the role of the police, our court system and our method of punishing convicted criminals. One chapter will focus on crime committed by young people.

Unit Preview/Review Questions

As you study this unit, keep these questions in mind. You may want to return to them when you have finished the unit.

1. What is a crime?
2. What makes a criminal?
3. What are our rights and protections under the law?
4. What methods are used to deal with lawbreakers?
5. What changes should be made to our legal system?

2

YOU AND THE LAW

If every person on earth were a hermit and had no contact with other people, there would be no need for laws. Fortunately human beings live in social groups. Each person in the group can live a better life. But this means that people must work and co-operate with each other. Unfortunately it seems that some people in society behave in anti-social ways. Some individuals become irritable, some angry, some selfish, some aggressive and some even violent. These hostilities may be turned against other persons or groups in society. Laws are made to protect people from the "bad" actions of others. In effect, the idea of law is to put limits on people's greed, drives and emotions. As individuals, we all have certain freedoms and rights. Sometimes, for the protection of society, the law places limits on these rights. As a famous judge once pointed out, "Your right to swing your fist ends at the point where the other fellow's nose begins."

Imagine for a moment what your world would be like without laws. None of your possessions would be safe — your radio, television, stereo player, bicycle or even your clothes. Someone bigger, stronger or faster could take them from you. Even your person could not be safe from attack. The law of the jungle, "Might makes Right" would take over.

We may not always agree with the laws we live by. In fact, we may not always know what the laws are. However, we are expected to live by these laws. Ignorance is no real excuse and no guarantee against being charged. As we saw in an earlier chapter, in a democracy like Canada our elected representatives make the laws for the good of the majority. If we feel that a certain law is unfair, we have the right to appeal it or work to change it. We do not have the right to break it.

In Canada there are two kinds of laws we live by — **criminal law** and **civil law.** Criminal law protects society against illegal acts. It protects everyone's person and property against other individuals. It also provides punishment for those who break the law.

Following Ms. Wesley's instructions, Rob found her car. His eyes popped! It was a European sports car, the kind he had been dreaming about ever since he first saw it on the cover of Auto Magazine. From the moment he sat behind the wheel he could sense the feeling of power and freedom. Maybe this would be as close as he would ever come to driving such a car again. Who would know if he just went for a little spin around the block first? The car handled like a dream. He pressed a little harder on the accelerator and the car surged forward. But it hit a small, unnoticed pothole and veered to the right. Unable to brake in time or straighten the wheels, Rob saw himself heading for the ditch. The car hit the ditch, rolled over once and became wedged against a telephone pole. It was all over in a flash. Rob, shaken but unhurt, jumped out. As he surveyed the damage, he became frightened. What would he do now? He couldn't go back. He ran.

That evening Rob was arrested by the police and charged with "taking a motor vehicle without consent." Is Rob Randall a criminal?

For an action to be considered a "crime" in Canada it must be subject to the following conditions:

1. It must be forbidden by the Criminal Code of Canada.
2. The accused must have intended to commit the offence.
3. The accused must be able to understand the nature of his action and its consequences.

Does Rob Randall's action qualify as a crime?

In Canada one book deals with criminal law for the whole country. This is the **Criminal Code** of Canada. The Code explains the nature of the offence, sets punishments and tells how criminal proceedings must take place. Alongside the Criminal Code is the body of **precedent.** Precedent refers to decisions made in certain cases by courts in the past. In any new cases of a similar kind, the courts must take the precedents into account.

ERASED CHALK MARKS — YOUTH ACQUITTED

Court follows precedent

TORONTO — The court today acquitted a youth charged with erasing a police chalk mark from the tire of a car parked on the street outside his home.

The youth's lawyer pointed to an Ontario Court of Appeal decision which had ruled that a motorist might erase the police mark from his own car or, if he had the owner's permission, from another car.

The youth admitted that he had erased chalk marks from his own car and also from his neighbour's car parked outside their homes, but his lawyer argued that this act was not against the law because of the appeal court ruling.

Crime Rates

Metropolitan Toronto

Criminal Code Offences Known and Cleared

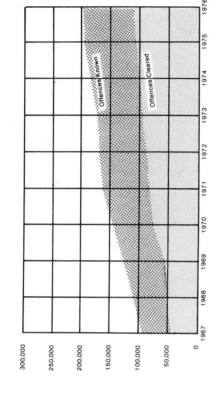

Criminal Code Offences

	1975	1976
Murder	48	50
Attempt Murder	44	30
Manslaughter	5	2
Rape	204	189
Wounding	429	404
Assaults (Not indecent)	7 937	9 342
Robbery	1 945	1 840
Break and Enter	16 549	17 608
Theft Over $200 (Not Motor Vehicle)	9 751	10 531
Motor Vehicle Thefts	7 363	6 356
Total Index Crime	44 275	46 352
Total Non-Index Crime	149 432	148 719
TOTAL	193 707	195 071

Other Offences

	1976
Federal Statutes	6 972
Highway Traffic Act	610 405
Liquor Control Act	24 324
Other Provincial Statutes	2 276
	643 977

Percentage of Offences Cleared by Arrest or Summons

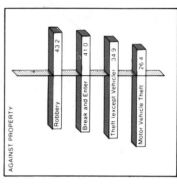

AGAINST THE PERSON

NOT CLEARED   CLEARED

Murder	80.0
Attempt Murder	100.0
Manslaughter	100.0
Rape	77.2
Wounding	71.8
Assault (not indecent)	90.6

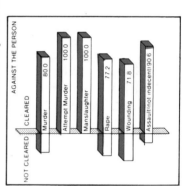

AGAINST PROPERTY

Robbery	43.2
Break and Enter	41.0
Theft (except Vehicle)	34.9
Motor Vehicle Theft	26.4

As we have seen, three conditions must exist for an action to be considered a crime. Often however, it is difficult to determine if an accused person *intended* to commit a crime. It is also hard to prove if he/she understood the nature of his/her actions. If these cannot be proved, no crime has been committed. In fact, it is impossible for certain people to commit a crime. The Criminal Code tells us that:

CHILD UNDER SEVEN.
12. No person shall be convicted of an offence in respect of an act or omission on his part while he was under the age of seven years.
PERSON BETWEEN SEVEN AND FOURTEEN.
13. No person shall be convicted of an offence in respect of an act or omission on his part while he was seven years of age or more, but under the age of fourteen years, unless he was competent to know the nature and consequences of his conduct and to appreciate that it was wrong.
16.(1) No person shall be convicted of an offence in respect of an act or omission on his part while he was insane.
(4) Every one shall, until the contrary is proved, be presumed to be and to have been sane.

Which of the following, if any, are guilty of committing a crime? What might be their defence? What do you think the verdict would be?

A) A thirteen-year-old was babysitting a three-year-old child. She noticed him playing with a book of matches. She took the matches away, and warned him about the dangers of playing with matches. A short while later, she again caught him with the matches in his hands. Angry now, she turned on the stove, and put his hands on the hot burners. The young child suffered second-degree burns. The girl claimed she was trying to teach the child a lesson.
B) A young man who had taken LSD was accused of killing his father-in-law. He stabbed his father-in-law many times with a knife, claiming the man was the devil and was after him.
C) A man had threatened to kill his wife on a number of previous occasions. One night he went out to a tavern. He returned home in a drunken state and actually killed her.

The results:

A) In this case, although the babysitter was aware of what she was doing, the courts decided to dismiss the charges because of her intentions and her age.
B) Insanity was accepted in this case. The jury ruled the young man's mind was so twisted from the effects of the drug that he had no criminal intent.

C) The defence pleaded that since the man was drunk, his mind was not capable of knowing right and wrong. He was in effect, in a state of temporary insanity. This defence was rejected. It was concluded that a person who goes out intending to kill, knowing it is wrong, and does kill, cannot escape punishment by making himself drunk before doing it.

2.   CLASSES OF CRIME

The Criminal Code divides crime into two classes:
1. Offences punished on **summary conviction**
2. **Indictable offences**

Summary Convictions:

Offences punishable on summary conviction are usually not very serious. Most motor vehicle offences come under this class. So do charges of common assault, juvenile delinquency and vagrancy, among others. In such cases, following a **summons** to appear in court, the accused is tried by a magistrate without a jury.

Some Common Offences: Below are some examples of offences punishable by summary conviction.

DRIVING WHILE ABILITY TO DRIVE IS IMPAIRED.

234. Every one who, while his ability to drive a motor vehicle is impaired by alcohol or a drug, drives a motor vehicle or has the care or control of a motor vehicle, whether it is in motion or not, is guilty of an indictable offence or an offence punishable on summary conviction and is liable
(a) for a first offence, to a fine of not more than five hundred dollars and not less than fifty dollars or to imprisonment for three months or to both;
(b) for a second offence, to imprisonment for not more than three months and not less than fourteen days; and
(c) for each subsequent offence, to imprisonment for not more than one year and not less than three months.

Late one evening a drunk driver went off the road and wound up in a field. A police officer found him "sleeping it off" behind the wheel, with the car sitting on its side! The driver was charged with impaired driving, even though the car was off its wheels. The magistrate decided that if a driver is behind the wheel with the intention of driving, he may be charged. The automobile does not actually have to be in motion.

What would be the decision where a drunk is found sleeping in the back seat of his car?

ASSAULT.
244. A person commits an assault when, without the consent of another person or with consent, where it is obtained by fraud,
(a) he applies force intentionally to the person of the other, directly or indirectly, or
(b) he attempts or threatens, by an act or gesture, to apply force to the person of the other, if he has or causes the other to believe upon reasonable grounds that he has present ability to effect his purpose.

A man weighing barely 40 kg started an argument with a man more than twice his size in a neighbourhood bar. The large man realized the smaller man was drunk, and refused to get into a fight. He called the manager, who in turn called the police. As he was being led away, the small man turned to the larger man and threatened to "knock his block off". He was charged with assault.

The magistrate found the man not guilty. He felt that because of his size, and his opponent's size, there was little reason to believe the little man could carry out his threat. If however, a gun or a knife had been used in the threat, he certainly would have been found guilty.

What would be the decision if the larger man had verbally threatened the smaller man?

Indictable offences:

Indictable offences are more serious crimes. They are placed in three different categories, depending on the court in which they are being tried.

CLASS A — This includes the most serious types of crimes, such as murder or treason. These crimes must be tried by a jury in the Supreme Court. In Class A crimes, a **preliminary hearing** is held. The hearing is to determine if there is a reasonable amount of evidence to put the person on trial. If there is not sufficient evidence, the charges are dropped.

CLASS B — These are less serious crimes, such as theft under fifty dollars. These are tried by a magistrate. The trial proceeds in the same way as a summary conviction case.

CLASS C — This includes all other indictable offences, such as burglary, theft and kidnapping. The accused may choose to be tried by a magistrate, a judge alone, or judge and jury. If he/she selects trial by judge or judge and jury, there must also be a preliminary hearing.

Before the trial: Before a trial takes place, the accused is asked to plead "guilty" or "not guilty" to the charges. If the plea is "guilty", there is usually no need for a trial. However, the magistrate will still ask the Crown Attorney, who prosecutes the case, to present his/her evidence. If the magistrate decides the evidence is not sufficient, he/she may change the defendant's plea to "not guilty". A trial will then be held.

If the accused pleads not guilty the case will go through the normal procedure. In Nova Scotia any persons who are to be tried by judge and jury must have the charges against them examined by a **Grand Jury.** The Grand Jury decides if there is enough evidence to put the accused on trial. If it decides the evidence is not sufficient, the accused will be released.

Procedure in Criminal Cases

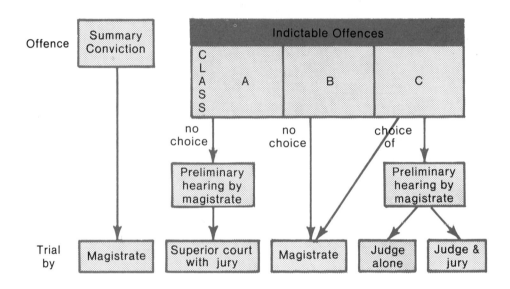

Some Common Offences: Following are some examples of indictable offences:

ACCESSORY AFTER THE FACT — Husband or wife, when not accessory — When wife not accessory.

23.(1) An accessory after the fact to an offence is one who, knowing that a person has been a party to the offence, receives, comforts or assists him for the purpose of enabling him to escape.

(2) No married person whose spouse has been a party to an offence is an accessory after the fact to that offence by receiving, comforting or assisting the spouse for the purpose of enabling the spouse to escape.

(3) No married woman whose husband has been a party to an offence is an accessory after the fact to that offence by receiving, comforting or assisting in his presence and by his authority any other person who has been a party to that offence for the purpose of enabling her husband or that other person to escape.

A group of friends went to a tavern. One of the men had a reputation for causing trouble when he had too much to drink. His friends knew this. Later in the evening the man started a fight with the bartender. He hit the bartender several times before his friends caught him, got him out of the tavern, and drove off in their car. They were all arrested and charged. The man was charged with assault causing bodily harm. His friends were charged with being accessories after the fact. They were found guilty. On what grounds would the judge find them guilty?

ARSON — Fraudulently burning personal property.

389. (1) Every one who wilfully sets fire to

(a) a building or structure, whether completed or not,

(b) a stack of vegetable produce or of mineral or vegetable fuel,

(c) a mine,

(d) a well of combustible substance,

(e) a vessel or aircraft, whether completed or not,

(f) timber or materials placed in a shipyard for building, repairing or fitting out a ship,

(g) military or public stores or munitions of war,

(h) a crop, whether standing or cut down, or

(i) any wood, forest, or natural growth, or any lumber, timber, log, float, boom, dam or slide,

is guilty of an indictable offence and is liable to imprisonment for fourteen years.

A man had an old wooden shed in the back yard of his property. Tearing it down would require too much time and effort. He decided to get rid of it by burning it. A neighbour called the fire department, which promptly answered the call and put out the blaze. The man was charged with arson, found guilty and fined. The man argued that it was his building and he could do what he wanted with it. Why did the judge reject this argument?

MURDER.

212. Culpable homicide is murder

(a) where the person who causes the death of a human being

(i) means to cause his death, or

(ii) means to cause him bodily harm that he knows is likely to cause his death, and is reckless whether death ensues or not;

(b) where a person, meaning to cause death to a human being or meaning to cause him bodily harm that he knows is likely to cause his death, and being reckless whether death ensues or not, by accident or mistake causes death to another human being, not withstanding that he does not mean to cause death or bodily harm to that human being; or

(c) where a person, for an unlawful object, does anything that he knows or ought to know is likely to cause death, and thereby causes death to a human being, notwithstanding that he desires to effect his object without causing death or bodily harm to any human being.

A man had a violent argument with his wife. She ran away from home and went to stay with her mother. The man, angry that his mother-in-law would take sides in the argument, blamed her for the quarrel and decided to take action. He took his rifle, went to his mother-in-law's home and shot at her through the open window. The bullet missed the mother-in-law, but killed a neighbourhood woman who was visiting. The man pleaded that he did not intend to murder the other woman. The court, however, found him guilty of murder. On what basis did it make this decision?

3. CRIMES WITHOUT VICTIMS

Thus far we have studied crimes where the victim is either society in general or individuals within society. We can easily see the need for laws which protect us from assault and injury, and our property from theft or destruction. Indeed, the very definition of crime suggests that someone or something is being harmed by the criminal.

Yet there are thousands of cases in our courts every year where there is no apparent victim. The criminal in these cases appears not to be hurting others, but only him/herself. Some very common examples are involved with drugs, alcohol, suicide, vagrancy and prostitution. Can you think of others? If these actions seem to harm only the offender, why are there laws against them? Let us examine a few of these crimes in more detail.

Drugs: The laws against drugs fall into two categories:
1. trafficking
2. possession
   POSSESSION OF NARCOTIC—Offence.
   3. (1) Except as authorized by this Act or the regulations, no person shall have a narcotic in his possession.
   (2) Every person who violates subsection (1) is guilty of an indictable offence and is liable
   (a) upon summary conviction for a first offence, to a fine of one thousand dollars or to imprisonment for six months or to both fine and imprisonment, and for a subsequent offence, to a fine of two thousand dollars or to imprisonment for one year or to both fine and imprisonment; or
   (b) upon conviction on indictment, to imprisonment for seven years.
   TRAFFICKING—Possession for purpose of trafficking—Offence.
   4. (1) No person shall traffic in a narcotic or any substance represented or held out by him to be a narcotic.
   (2) No person shall have in his possession any narcotic for the purpose of trafficking.
   (3) Every person who violates subsection (1) or (2) is guilty of an indictable offence and is liable to imprisonment for life.

Drugs are also classified as "hard" or "soft". "Hard" drugs are of the addictive type such as heroin and cocaine. "Soft" drugs are non-addictive, such as *marijuana* and *hashish*. Since 1972, some of the soft drugs, such as amphetemines, have been removed from the **Narcotic Control Act.** They were placed under the Food and Drug Act. Penalties under this act are less severe.

A Commission headed by Gerald LeDain investigated the effects of various drugs. It recommended that the penalties for soft drugs be reduced. Some groups in society are actively pushing for the legalization of marijuana. They claim it is no more harmful than cigarette smoking. Their opponents disagree strongly. Many of them say that cigarettes too are harmful and should also be done away with.

In recent years the courts have quietly reduced the penalties against marijuana users. In 1969 one person in four convicted of marijuana use was jailed. Today, few if any users are jailed. Small fines have become the rule.

Hard drugs are a greater problem. These drugs are very expensive. Addicts often spend up to $200 a day to supply their habits. Many become involved in criminal activities such as theft and prostitution to buy drugs. Drug addicts are a major reason for the existence of organized crime in Canada and the United States.

During the time of Prohibition in the 1920s, selling alcoholic beverages was illegal. To get around the law, people made illegal whisky. Organized crime grew quickly on the profits of smuggling whisky. In time, the law was changed to make the sale of alcoholic beverages legal. Will the same thing happen to drugs? What changes in the present law do you think should be made?

Vagrancy: The Criminal Code defines a vagrant as one who "supports himself in whole or part by gaming or crime and has no lawful profession or calling by which to maintain himself". The law may also convict persons of vagrancy if they have a previous record of sex offences and are found loitering in a public place such as a park or schoolground.

Begging in the streets or **"panhandling"** may also be considered vagrancy. Therefore it is against the law.

For a long while "wandering abroad" without a visible means of support qualified a person as a vagrant. A person could not be caught doing just "nothing". Much of the reason for this law stemmed from the hard times of the Depression (see Unit 3, Chapter 2). Thousands of unemployed would roam the streets without a dime in their pockets. Occasionally they would break into homes or stores and steal to support themselves. The vagrancy laws gave police the right to arrest suspicious individuals before another crime could be committed.

Who is the Real Victim? It can be argued that in fact all these crimes do have victims. An alcoholic can make life miserable for his/her family. A drug addict may sustain criminal elements in society. A prostitute may contribute to the lowering of morals in society. A panhandler helps lower society's productivity because he/she depends on others and contributes nothing.

There is another side to the issue. Some argue that in a free society, persons should be free to do as they please, unless it interferes with someone else's rights. They argue that these laws make moral judgements on someone else's conduct. They believe that it is not the business of the law to judge morality. Lastly they point out that drug and alcohol addiction are forms of sickness. Addicts should be treated in hospitals and clinics rather than courts and prisons.

Do you think there is such a thing as a crime without a victim? If so, how should the law treat these offences?

4.   YOUR RIGHTS BEFORE THE LAW

Most Canadians know little about their own rights. The problem is that much of what we "know" is based on American television. There are thousands of laws in existence in Canada. It would be impossible for the average person to be familiar with all of them. You should, however, make an effort to become familiar with your rights before the law. It will help if you are arrested, rightly or wrongly, for breaking the law.

Some Rights We Don't Have

The police do not have to read you your rights.
The police do not have to inform you that you have the right to a lawyer.
Any statement you make to the police if they have not informed you of your rights is still admissable in a court of law.
Evidence, even if gathered illegally by the police, can still be used against you in court.
Under the narcotics laws, police officers can break into any property (except your home) without a specific search warrant.
The R.C.M.P. can be issued with a Queen's Writ of Assistance which entitles them even to break into your home without a warrant.
A police officer does not have to tell you you are under arrest — unless you ask.
A police officer does not have to tell you the charge — unless you ask.

Let us suppose the police suspect you of having committed a theft of over $500 from the store where you work part-time. The following is the sequence of events which might occur.

The Arrest

A police officer comes to your door and asks you to go along with him.

YOU: Why should I?

OFFICER: Just come along.

At this point, the police officer has not made a lawful arrest and you do not have to go along. The officer must tell you you are under arrest, and what the charge is — but remember, only if you ask! If you go along willingly, you cannot claim later that an unlawful arrest was made.

If the officer asks you questions, you may wish to answer. However, anything you say can be used against you in a court of law. It is wise to have a lawyer present. At the same time, you do not have to answer any questions (except your name, age and address). Nor do you have to show the officer your wallet, money or identification. If the arrest is unlawful, the officer cannot hold you for questioning. However do not use force to resist arrest, even if you are innocent of the crime. If the arrest was lawfully made, you could be charged with resisting arrest.

The Role of the Police

Canada's police have one of society's most difficult jobs. On one hand they are supposed to protect society from criminals. On the other hand they are often subjected to abuse from the very people they are trying to help. Besides upholding the law, the police also provide free of charge a number of social services not really within their duty. These might include family counselling, helping lost children, etc. Under a democratic system, the police are really only representatives of the people, trained to enforce the laws.

The police in Canada are not different from other citizens. They do not have special rights or privileges. Like other citizens they are supposed to act within the law. If they break a law, even while on duty, they will be charged.

In Canada there are three kinds of police forces — federal, provincial, and municipal. The federal police force is the Royal Canadian Mounted Police. The R.C.M.P. is known world-wide. They have a reputation for efficiency and of always "getting their man". In Canada, the R.C.M.P. is responsible for enforcing federal laws, such as those dealing with narcotics, smuggling, and shipping. As well, except for Ontario and Quebec which have their own forces, the Mounties act as provincial police forces in the rest of Canada.

The provincial police enforce provincial laws. In rural areas they also enforce the Criminal Code of Canada.

The municipal or city police forces are responsible for enforcing the Criminal Code, provincial laws and city by-laws.

There are in addition other types of police, such as game wardens and customs officers. Some companies also hire their own police forces to protect company property.

The police have a great many hard tasks and responsibilities. As a citizen you also have a duty to help police officers. In fact some of these duties are

These photographs show some of the many aspects of police work. *Pictures (upper right and middle right) from the Sound filmstrip series "Why Do We Have Laws?" and "Police", courtesy of Cinemedia Ltd. Toronto.*

covered by law. The law provides penalties for anyone who obstructs a police officer trying to do his duty.

The law also requires you to help a police officer do his duty if he asks you to do so. This applies to cases where an officer is trying to arrest someone. On the other hand, you cannot be forced to do an illegal act by a policeman.

Police officers in Canada have the right to arrest without a warrant anyone they suspect on reasonable grounds of having committed an *indictable* offence. They may also arrest without warrant anyone they find committing a *summary* offence. Remember, however, that you must be charged with a specific offence. There is no such thing in Canada as "We want you to come down to the station and answer a few questions", or arrest "on suspicion" of something.

The Search Warrant

Since you have been charged with theft, the police officer will want to search your home for evidence. He must have a search warrant issued by the courts. A search warrant is only valid if the details are filled in. Also, it is only good for the day it is issued. A search warrant only permits a police officer to search a place, not a person. However, once inside the place, if the officer has reason to believe a person is hiding anything, he may search that person.

Two R.C.M.P. officers entered the home of a known drug pusher looking for narcotics. It appeared to the officers that the man was putting something in his mouth. One officer quickly grabbed him by the throat to prevent him from swallowing the evidence. The other put his fingers in the man's mouth to search for the drug capsules. The suspect bit the officer's hand. No drugs were found in the man's mouth. One of the charges against the man was assaulting the officer and resisting arrest. The man's lawyer claimed that lawful search did not include the man's mouth. The judge disagreed. He held that since the officers believed the drugs were in the mouth, they had a right to search there.

Writs of Assistance may be used by the R.C.M.P. instead of search warrants. They also entitle R.C.M.P. officers to search your home. The main difference between these two types of warrants is that a Writ of Assistance may be used over and over as long as the officer to whom it was issued remains working for the R.C.M.P. This is one example of the broad powers given in Canada to the R.C.M.P. You should note that any evidence gathered by police officers can be used in court, even if it was the result of an illegal search. The police may also search any vehicle if they believe liquor is being kept there illegally. In the process of a legal search, police officers are authorized to break doors, windows, floors, walls, ceilings and locks if necessary.

```
(Section 429)                                                        FORM 5

                        WARRANT TO SEARCH

            CANADA          ⎞  To the Peace Officers in the said Municipality.
   PROVINCE  OF  ONTARIO    ⎟
      COUNTY OF YORK        ⎟                    WHEREAS it appears on the oath of
     MUNICIPALITY OF        ⎟   ............................................................
   METROPOLITAN TORONTO     ⎠
                               of the Municipality of Metropolitan Toronto
```

that there are reasonable grounds for believing that certain things, to wit: Unregistered firearms
and ammunition for same

which are being sought as evidence in respect to the commission, suspected commission or intended commission
of an offence against the Criminal Code, to wit: Have an unregistered firearm in
his dwelling house
are in the premises   of

at   , hereinafter called the premises.

            THIS IS THEREFORE to authorize and require you, anytime by day or by

            night   to enter the said premises

and to search for the said things and to bring them before me or some other justice.

DATED this 18 day of March   A.D. 1978 , at the Municipality of Metropolitan Toronto.

                                            A Justice of the Peace in and for the
            M.T. 573   Province of Ontario.

At the Station

Now that you have been lawfully arrested, you may be taken to the police
station. Once at the station, you will not get your phone call unless you ask for
one. Even then you may not be allowed to make it. If you did not have a
chance to get a lawyer, you may ask to see the Legal Aid Duty Counsel at
Court the next morning.

   After your arrest, it may be weeks or months before your case actually
comes up in court. Rather than spend this period in jail, you will be allowed
free on **bail.** Bail is a guarantee to the court that you will return for your trial.

Two police officers arrest a suspect. *Picture from the sound filmstrip series "Why Do We Have Laws?" and "Police", courtesy of Cinemedia Ltd. Toronto.*

For simple charges, bail may take the form of a promise to appear "on your own recognizance". For more serious criminal charges, a deposit of money or property will be needed. For a very serious offence such as murder, where the public safety is involved, bail may be denied.

At the police station you may call the Bail Justice of the Peace who will determine your bail. In the United States, bail bondsmen are people who will put up the money for the bail if you cannot afford it. Usually they charge fifteen to twenty percent interest for their services. In Canada bail bondsmen are illegal. You may, however, borrow bail money from friends or relatives.

If you have been set free on bail, but do not appear for your trial, you will lose your bail money. As well, you will be arrested on another charge — absconding bail. This is a serious offence.

If you are charged with an offence but cannot afford a lawyer, the Legal Aid Program will help pay your legal expenses. The Program does not provide the lawyers itself. You are allowed to choose from a list of lawyers in the province. Note that you do not have to be defended by a lawyer. If you wish, you may defend yourself in court, provided that you are competent to carry out your own defence. This is not advisable. As the saying goes, the lawyer who conducts his own defence has a fool for a client. This is even more true for an ordinary citizen.

Fingerprinting a suspect. Fingerprints may be used as evidence in a court of law. *Picture from the sound filmstrip series "Why Do We Have Laws?" and "Police", courtesy of Cinemedia Ltd. Toronto.*

Our Civil Rights

Citizens of the United States and many other countries for a long time had their civil rights guaranteed by their constitution. In Canada, until 1960, these rights had not been set down as specific laws. Of course, as Canadians we exercised a great number of civil liberties. However these rights had always been guaranteed by custom rather than by law. In 1960, the government of John Diefenbaker finally succeeded in passing a Canadian **Bill of Rights.** The provisions are as follows:

Bill of Rights

1. It is hereby recognized and declared that in Canada there have existed and shall continue to exist without discrimination by reason of race, national origin, color, religion or sex, the following human rights and fundamental freedoms, namely,
(a) The right of the individual to life, liberty, security of the person and enjoyment of property, and the right not to be deprived thereof except by due process of law;
(b) The right of the individual to equality before the law and the protection of the law;
(c) Freedom of religion;
(d) Freedom of speech;
(e) Freedom of assembly and association; and
(f) Freedom of the press.
2. Every law of Canada shall, unless it is expressly declared by an Act of the Parliament of Canada that it shall operate notwithstanding the Canadian Bill of Rights, be so construed and applied as not to abrogate, abridge or infringe or to authorize the abrogation, abridgement or infringement of any of the rights or freedoms herein recognized and

declared, and in particular, no law of Canada shall be construed or applied so as to

(a) Authorize or effect the arbitrary detention, imprisonment or exile of any person;

(b) Impose or authorize the imposition of cruel and unusual treatment or punishment;

(c) Deprive a person who has been arrested or detained

(i) of the right to be informed promptly of the reason for his arrest or detention,

(ii) of the right to retain and instruct counsel without delay, or

(iii) of the remedy by way of habeas corpus for the determination of the validity of his detention and for his release if the detention is not lawful;

(d) Authorize a court, tribunal, commission, board or other authority to compel a person to give evidence if he is denied counsel, protection against self crimination or other constitutional safeguards;

(e) Deprive a person of the right to a fair hearing in accordance with the principles of fundamental justice for the determination of his rights and obligations;

(f) Deprive a person charged with a criminal offence of the right to be presumed innocent until proved guilty according to law in a fair and public hearing by an independent and impartial tribunal, or of the right to reasonable bail without just cause; or

(g) Deprive a person of the right to the assistance of an interpreter in any proceedings in which he is involved or in which he is a party or a witness, before a court, commission, board or other tribunal, if he does not understand or speak the language in which such proceedings are conducted.

3. The Minister of Justice shall, in accordance with such regulations as may be prescribed by the Governor in Council, examine every proposed regulation submitted in draft form to the Clerk of the Privy Council pursuant to the Regulations Act and every Bill introduced in or presented to the House of Commons, in order to ascertain whether any of the provisions thereof are inconsistent with the purposes and provisions of this part and he shall report any such inconsistency to the House of Commons at the first convenient opportunity.

4. The provisions of this part shall be known as the Canadian Bill of Rights.

Once arrested, you have the right to a trial without unnecessary delay. With the backlog of cases jamming our courts today, it may take as long as a year before your trial comes up in court. If you cannot afford bail, you will be in jail during that period of time. If your lawyer suspects that the Crown is moving slowly and delaying your trial, he may get your release on a writ of **habeas corpus.** Habeas corpus forces the authorities to justify your arrest. They must show that they are moving as fast as possible to hold a trial. Otherwise you will be released. This is an important safeguard in our legal system. Without it, a person might be kept in jail a lifetime waiting for his trial to come up.

In a Court of Law

Months have passed since your arrest and although you are free on bail, you are impatient to have your name cleared. However the courts have had a busy time and could not schedule your trial early. In any case, your lawyer needed the time to prepare your case. You have been charged with theft. This is an indictable offence, and means you have a choice as to what kind of trial you will have. After consulting your lawyer, you decide to have trial by judge and jury.

Trial by judge and jury is always interesting. The results of a trial often hinge on the character of the jury. Good lawyers will spend much time studying the psychology of a jury. Your lawyer has informed you of the advantages and disadvantages of the jury system. The advantages include:

— the verdict must be unanimous. If even one person in the jury thinks you are innocent, you cannot be convicted.

— juries tend to be from the same social background as you, and might sympathize with your case.

— your lawyer has a right to refuse certain people from getting on the jury. This lessens the chance of bias against you.

— a good lawyer knows what will appeal to juries and how to impress them. On the other hand there may be disadvantages:

— the jury may be prejudiced against you. They may not like your looks, your background, social level, etc.

— if the Crown attorney is better than your lawyer, the jury may be swayed by his/her manner and not the facts.

— juries are not experts on the law. They may reach a wrong decision because of their ignorance of the law.

How Juries are Chosen

Have your parents ever served on a jury? Do you know anyone who has? The chances of serving on a jury are not very high. There are many different kinds of juries (earlier we noted the makeup of the Grand Jury). For criminal cases, normally the jury consists of twelve people. The reason for this number is not totally clear. It has come down from England in the Middle Ages. It is thought to be based on the number of Jesus' apostles.

In order to serve on a jury, you must be eighteen years of age or over, a Canadian citizen and sane. You must own property or be a tenant. Within these requirements everyone is eligible to serve on a jury with the following exceptions:

— those over the age of 70;

— an elected member of government;

A judge addresses the members of a jury. *Picture from the sound filmstrip series "Why Do We Have Laws?" and "Police", courtesy of Cinemedia Ltd. Toronto.*

— judges, magistrates, sheriffs, coroners, jail wardens, court officers or police officers;
— firemen;
— ministers, priests, rabbis and any member of a religious order;
— doctors, dentists, veterinarians, nurses and anyone else connected with the medical profession;
— members of the armed forces;
— airplane pilots and hostesses;
— sailors;
— anyone working for newspapers;
— people working in public transportation;
— people working in communications — e.g. telephone operators
— lawyers and law students;
— tax collectors;
— anyone convicted of an indictable offence.

It may seem after this list that the number eligible for jury duty is not very large. In fact, millions of Canadians are annually eligible for jury duty. How are members of a particular jury chosen from this list?

Your municipal assessor places a "J" beside the name of all eligible jurors. The municipal clerk then chooses a list from these names, in alphabetical order. He chooses twice as many names as are needed for the year, and sends the list to the county sheriff. The sheriff draws by lot the names of people who will sit on the various types of juries. The court clerk then draws names from a box for each individual jury. Even if your name has survived all these tests, you can still be refused by the Crown prosecutor or the defence attorney for various reasons. Amazingly, some people have been selected for jury duty many times.

Once selected, you cannot refuse to serve on a jury without permission of the court. If you refuse you are liable to be fined. Some people try to avoid their obligation. They are afraid that in case of a lengthy trial they may be away from their family and jobs for a long time. Jurors are paid less than $20.00 per day so this may also mean financial loss.

The Trial

At last, a jury has been selected and your trial is ready to begin. Your lawyer has prepared his/her case and has lined up a number of witnesses on your behalf. These people have been ordered to testify by notice of a **subpoena,** sent out by the court.

The trial begins with the Crown attorney addressing the jury. The jury is told that it will be shown beyond all reasonable doubt, that you are guilty of theft, and that the evidence presented will prove it. Your lawyer speaks next and presents his/her opening arguments as to your innocence and the lack of evidence in the Crown's case.

The Crown next parades its list of witnesses. Each witness is sworn to tell "the truth, the whole truth, and nothing but the truth". If a witness should lie on the stand he or she would be charged with **perjury,** a serious offence. After each prosecution witness has testified your lawyer has the opportunity to cross-examine them. On **cross-examination,** only questions relating to the original testimony may be asked. Only eyewitness evidence is admitted. If a witness presents facts which were heard second-hand from someone else, they would not be acceptable. This is called **hearsay evidence.**

During your arrest you repeatedly claimed your innocence. However, if you had confessed your guilt before the trial, or made any statement about the case, it would have been introduced as evidence.

When the Crown attorney rested his case, your lawyer began to present your case. She attempted to show that the evidence presented by the Crown was flimsy and not sufficient to find you guilty. Several witnesses were called to testify to your good character and honesty. On the advice of your lawyer, you did not take the witness stand yourself. On cross-examination, lawyers are allowed to ask leading questions where the answer is already suggested. In the hands of a skilled lawyer, this weapon can be used to confuse the testimony of a nervous witness.

After the Crown attorney finished the cross-examination of your witnesses, both lawyers summed up their cases to the jury. You are perhaps somewhat disappointed that your defence lawyer did not prove someone else guilty of the crime. On television shows this happens every week. Unfortunately in real life this is seldom the case. Cases are lost and won on arguments and weight of

Lawyers often use diagrams to help explain their client's case to the judge or jury. *Picture from the sound filmstrip series "Why Do We Have Laws?" and "Police", courtesy of Cinemedia Ltd. Toronto.*

evidence and the impressions made on the jury. Perhaps, however, members of the jury, like you, are influenced by the exploits of television lawyers, and expect the guilty person to confess. Your lawyer has taken great care to caution them about this attitude in her summary.

During the court proceedings, the judge is under complete control of the trial. He/she may decide what questions, answers, and evidence are suitable and proper. As much as possible a judge must remain fair and impartial in the interpretation of the points of law. At the end of the closing summations, the judge instructs the jury and carefully explains to the jury the laws which apply to this case. They will be instructed on what points they must base their decision. The instruction to the jury is very important. If the judge instructs the jury in the wrong way, or appears to be unfair, retrial may be demanded.

The decision of innocence or guilt is left up to the jury. The verdict must be unanimous — that is, all twelve jurors must agree on the innocence or guilt of the accused. The jury have selected a leader called a **foreman,** who conducts the jury discussion in a closed room. If no unanimous verdict can be reached after a reasonable number of votes and discussions, this is called a **hung jury.** In such cases, the judge may order a retrial with a new jury. If a verdict is reached it is read by the foreman.

You await the decision of the jury as they file back into the courtroom. The foreman reads the verdict — not guilty! The ordeal is over and you are again a free person.

If you had been found guilty, another of the law's important safeguards would have been available, the right of **appeal.** An appeal is a request for a new trial, and must be made within thirty days of conviction. Some of the

reasons appeals may be granted include:
- the judge instructed the jury in the wrong way;
- evidence was admitted into court which should not have been;
- the jury was prejudiced;
- new evidence surfaces after the trial.

If the Crown feels the verdict was unfair, it may also appeal on certain grounds. Cases may be appealed all the way to the Supreme Court. There, a decision is final.

The Court System

The B.N.A Act of 1867 divided the responsibility for Canada's court system between the federal and provincial governments. The federal government is responsible for the Supreme Court of Canada and the Federal Court. The provinces are responsible for all other courts.

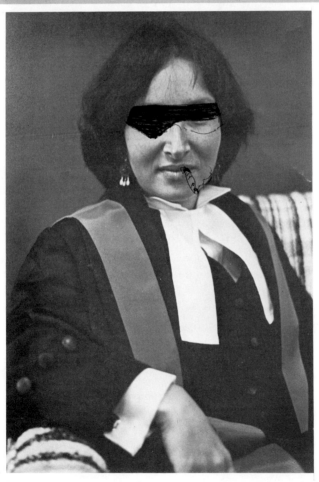

Judge Rosalie Abella, the youngest judge to be appointed in Ontario. Judge Abella presides over Family Courts in the Provincial Court System.

Federal Courts

SUPREME COURT OF CANADA

The court of final appeal in Canada. It also hears cases between the Dominion and the provinces and cases requiring the interpretation of the B.N.A. Act.

FEDERAL COURT
This court hears cases brought against the Crown and cases involving Crown revenues.

Courts of Province of Ontario

SUPREME COURT OF ONTARIO

COURT OF APPEAL	HIGH COURT OF JUSTICE
This court hears appeals from the High Court of Justice and other courts.	This court tries important cases both criminal and civil.

COUNTY COURTS*
These courts try minor criminal cases and civil cases involving only limited amounts (between $500 and $10 000)

SURROGATE COURTS
These deal with estates of deceased persons.

DIVISION COURTS
These hear minor civil cases involving small debts or claims.

MAGISTRATES COURTS**
These hear minor criminal cases and give preliminary hearing to major criminal cases. They also hear certain civil cases.

OTHER PROVINCIAL COURTS
JUVENILE COURTS
FAMILY COURTS
ETC.

This diagram shows the Canadian system of law courts for the Province of Ontario. There are slight variations from this pattern in the provincial court systems of other provinces.

* In Alberta, Saskatchewan, Newfoundland and Northern Ontario, County Courts are known as District Courts.
** In British Columbia, Alberta and Ontario it is called Provincial Court.

If a jury had reached a "guilty" verdict it would have been the judge's duty to sentence you. The Criminal Code may set minimum or maximum penalties. It is up to the judge to decide exactly what the punishment will be. Studies show that in the past judges have been influenced by the following factors:
- the age of the convicted person;
- the person's character and previous record;
- the circumstances surrounding the crime;
- public pressure against certain crimes in the community;
- the judge's own prejudices.

Even a simple trial may be a long and costly affair. Occasionally, justice is not done. However, the system has a number of safeguards which make decisions as fair and impartial as possible in the vast majority of cases. The system is careful to protect the rights of the individual and society. This gives it the appearance of being complicated and slow.

THINGS TO THINK ABOUT AND DO

Reviewing Key Words and Ideas

The following terms appeared in this chapter. Try to recall their meaning and how they are used.

bail	hearsay evidence	search warrant
Bill of Rights	indictable offence	soft drugs
Common law	Narcotic Control Act	subpoena
Criminal Code	panhandling	summary conviction
cross-examination	perjury	summons
Grand Jury	precedent	vagrancy
habeas corpus	preliminary hearing	writ of assistance
hard drugs		

Remembering the facts

1. What is the highest court in Canada?
2. A writ of assistance is similar to
a) a summons   b) a writ of habeas corpus   c) a search warrant   d) a subpoena
3. What is the Criminal Code of Canada?
4. The number of members of a Grand Jury are
a) 12   b) 7-23   c) 100   d) none of these
5. A person who lies in a court of law is guilty of
a) perjury   b) hearsay   c) contempt

6. A person free on bail who fails to show up for the trial loses the bail money. True or false.

Analyzing ideas

1. A young person convicted of smoking marijuana is guilty of a criminal offence. This person will have a criminal record for life. Do you think marijuana possession should be taken off the Criminal Code as an offence? Why or why not?

2. Recently the R.C.M.P. have come under heavy fire from politicians, the media and some segments of the public for a number of illegal activities. Do you think Canada's police officers should be allowed to go beyond the law in order to catch criminals? If so, under what circumstances should this be permitted?

3. Alcoholism has been referred to as an illness, not a crime. Should alcoholics be treated as sick people or as criminals? Should people who commit crimes while under the influence of alcohol or drugs be given more severe penalties?

4. Debate this proposition: If a person is old enough to vote and sign a contract at the age of eighteen, the law should allow him or her to drink at the same age.

Applying your knowledge

1. Explain the difference between an indictable offence and one punishable by summary conviction. Give two examples of each.

2. With your newly found knowledge of court procedure, you are now ready to join Perry Mason as a courtroom lawyer. Set up a fictitious case (it may be murder, or theft, or a traffic violation) and organize a court case around it involving members of your class. Roles in the trial must include the following: judge, Crown attorney, defence attorney, court clerk, accused person, witnesses and jury members.

3. It has been suggested that a person guilty of a criminal offence stands a better chance of being released in a trial by jury rather than a trial by judge alone. What arguments might support this suggestion? What arguments can you offer against it?

4. Fred, the clerk in a large department store, testified in court that he saw Hardnose Harry picking pockets in his store. Harry was sent to prison for his efforts. Several weeks before his scheduled release, Harry was heard to say that the first thing he would do after his release was "to get" Fred.

Is Harry guilty of another crime? Give your reasons for or against.

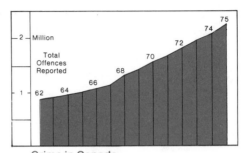

Crime in Canada

This graph shows total offences reported in Canada between 1962 and 1975.

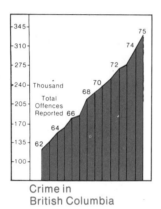

Crime in
British Columbia

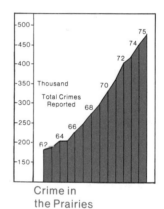

Crime in
the Prairies

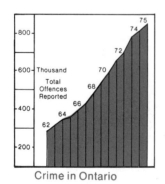

Crime in Ontario

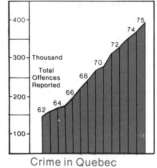

Crime in Quebec

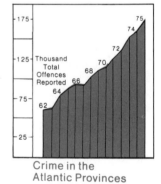

Crime in the
Atlantic Provinces

3

JUVENILE DELINQUENCY

Have you ever
— driven a car without a licence?
— skipped school without an excuse?
— gambled for money?
— damaged public property?
— stolen "little things"?
— drunk alcoholic beverages at a party?

If your answer to any of these questions is "yes," you might by law be considered a **juvenile delinquent.** The **Juvenile Delinquents Act** passed in 1972 defines a juvenile delinquent as "any boy or girl apparently or actually under the age of sixteen" who violates federal, provincial or municipal laws. A juvenile delinquent may also be one "who is guilty of sexual immorality or any other similar form of vice."

Before reading on, study the chart of Key Words and Ideas which follows.

KEY WORDS AND IDEAS IN THIS CHAPTER		
Term	Meaning	Sample Use
juvenile courts	courts which deal only with juvenile offenders	In juvenile courts the media and the public are not admitted to hear the cases.
juvenile delinquent	a young person under the age of sixteen who breaks the law	Juvenile delinquents make up the fastest growing group of lawbreakers in Canada.

Juvenile Delinquents Act	an Act passed in 1972 which specifies the offences and court procedures dealing with juveniles	The Act specifies that a juvenile delinquent may be a person under sixteen who breaks a federal, provincial or municipal law.
probation officer	an officer appointed by the courts to look after juvenile delinquents	Juvenile offenders who are not sentenced to industrial schools may instead have to report to a probation officer.
truancy	a juvenile who fails to attend school or runs away from home	Truancy is a common feature of today's society. A person under the age of sixteen cannot legally leave home.
vandalism	damaging or destroying public or private property	Vandalism is one of the most common types of juvenile offences.

Juvenile Offences
Metropolitan Toronto

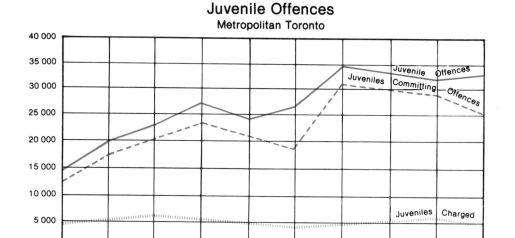

Juvenile delinquency is a major problem in today's society. Crimes committed by juveniles are on the increase. In fact juveniles make up the fastest growing group of law breakers in the country. Many of these crimes are serious — murder, robbery, rape and assault. In the United States, almost a million cases involving juveniles go through the courts every year. One-half of all arrests involve teenagers or young adults. Of those arrested for murder, forty-four percent are under twenty-five and ten percent are under eighteen. Forty-five percent of all arrests for street crimes are of young people under eighteen. In fact the age of fifteen is the peak age for violent crimes.

Of course not all juvenile delinquent acts involve crimes of such serious nature. Many are simply done to get "social acceptance" from other members of the group. Some are just done for kicks." A recent survey in Toronto showed the following results:

Self Reported Delinquent Behaviour

Type of offence	Age 13-14	Age 15-19
	Per cent admitting offence	
Driven a car without a driver's licence	28.6	62.3
Taken little things that did not belong to you	61.0	67.2
Skipped school without a legitimate excuse	13.6	40.8
Driven beyond the speed limit	5.8	51.2
Participated in drag-races along the highway with your friends	6.5	31.1
Engaged in a fist fight with another boy	45.8	56.0
Been feeling "high" from drinking beer, wine, or liquor	11.7	39.0
Gambled for money at cards, dice, or some other game	42.2	66.0
Remained out all night without parents' permission	19.5	25.8
Taken a car without owner's knowledge	5.2	12.5
Placed on school probation or expelled from school	0.7	5.6
Destroyed or damaged public or private property of any kind	44.8	52.0
Taken little things of value (between $2 and $50) which did not belong to you	9.7	16.0

The above are minor offences. Yet several of these offences, committed often, would be juvenile delinquency. Of course many of these incidents go unnoticed or unsolved by the police.

1.   COMMON JUVENILE OFFENCES

There are certain kinds of offences which are most commonly committed by adolescents. These are:

1. **Stealing.** Usually the objects are of small value (under $50). Shoplifting or stealing from lockers in school come under this category.

2. **Vandalism.** Involves the destruction or damage of property for no apparent reason.

3. **Assault.** Verbal threats or abusive language can constitute assault. Often this behaviour leads to fights.

4. **Sexual Deviance.** Intercourse with a female under sixteen years of age.

5. **Truancy** from home or school. Runaways are becoming a common feature of modern society. A person under the age of sixteen cannot legally run away from home. Any adult sheltering a **runaway** is also breaking the law.

Susan and Debbie were waiting in the office of the manager of a large downtown department store. They had been caught by the store detective putting jewellery and cosmetics in their purses. As they were about to leave the store without paying for the goods, he stopped them. Rather than turn them over to the police, he called their parents. When asked why they had tried to shoplift, the girls said they were bored. There was nothing to do, so for kicks they thought it might be fun to try. Besides many of their friends had done it and had never been caught. The manager allowed the girls to go home with their parents. Susan and Debbie were lucky not to be charged in juvenile court.

Ted and Sean got into trouble of a serious kind. Both had been suspended from school for causing a disturbance and getting into fights. They decided to take revenge. One afternoon during a class change they walked back into the school unobserved. They went directly to the boys' washroom and began scratching obscenities on the metal partitions. At the same time with a pocket knife, they began to remove all the ceramic tiles from the walls. As they were about to leave, they were caught by a surprised Vice-Principal who was making his rounds of the halls. The damage was estimated at over $500. Ted and Sean were turned over to the police and had to face charges in juvenile court.

The above cases are examples of two of the most common juvenile offences. In a way they are crimes which affect everyone. Stores pass shoplifting losses on to consumers through higher prices. This means you wind up paying for someone else's "kicks." At the same time, damage to school property is reflected through higher taxes which your parents must pay. Is there anything department stores and schools can do to cut down their losses?

2.   JUVENILE COURTS

Juvenile courts are much less formal than adult courts. Juvenile courts deal only with young people under the age of sixteen charged with offences under the Juvenile Delinquents Act. Juvenile courts do hand out punishment for law-breaking. Their chief aim however is to discourage the young person from committing offences in the future.

The proceedings in a juvenile court are designed to protect the identity and future of the young offender. To this end, members of the public and the press are not allowed in. The only people present are the judge, the court stenographer, the police, the accused and their parents. The court may look into the background of the accused — his home life, school records, etc. The court uses **probation officers** and social agencies such as the Children's Aid Society to help in these matters. If the charge is not serious and the accused has had a reasonably clean record, the judge may place him on probation. We will see in a later chapter what this sentence involves.

Most young people do not have problems living within the rules of society, despite the pressures and frustration of the teen-age years. Yet a minority of Canada's youth insists on breaking the law. They give all young people a bad name in the eyes of some adults. This is reflected in some of our laws, such as **curfews** and other restrictions against young people.

Sociologists and psychologists have tried to find the causes of juvenile delinquency. Many point to a person's social background as a factor. Conditions of poverty, broken homes, and an unhappy family life often lead to delinquent behaviour. There are many other unknown factors which form one's personality. There are many qualities we are born with, others we learn as we are growing. Each of us becomes a unique person with different needs. This is why it is difficult to predict behaviour. In a recent survey, the public was asked what it thought were the factors leading to criminal behaviour.

Would you consider this survey accurate or scientific? Why/why not? Which of the causes below do you think are most responsible for crime?

Why do People Become Criminals?

Cause	Per cent of Total Public
Upbringing	38
Bad environment	30
Mentally ill	16
Wrong companions	14
No education	14
Broken homes	13
Greed, easy money	13
Too much money around	11
Not enough money in home	10
Liquor, dope	10
Laziness	9
For kicks	8
No religion	8
No job	8
No chance by society	7
Born bad	5
Feeling of hopelessness	4
Moral breakdown of society	3
Degeneracy, sex	2
Failure of police	2

THINGS TO THINK ABOUT AND DO

Reviewing Key Words and Ideas

The following terms appeared in this chapter. Try to recall their meaning and how they were used.

assault	Juvenile Delinquents Act	sexual deviance
curfew	probation officer	shoplifting
delinquency	runaways	truancy
juvenile courts		vandalism

Remembering the facts

1. A juvenile delinquent is a law breaker who is under the age of
a) 14   b) 16   c) 18   d) 21
2. A person can legally leave home at the age of 17. True or false?
3. The most common offence committed by juveniles is
a) murder   b) drug abuse   c) stealing   d) skipping school
4. In juvenile court only the juvenile offender and his lawyer are permitted to attend. True or false?

Analyzing ideas

1. The public and the media are not permitted in a juvenile court, and newspapers are not allowed to print the names of juvenile offenders. Do you agree with this practice? Give your reasons.
2. Vandalism is one of the greatest problems in the schools. It is an act in which nothing is gained. Suggest some reasons for the tremendous increase in incidents of vandalism. Try to find out the extent of the damages caused by vandalism in your own school.
3. One suggestion for dealing with juvenile delinquency is to place stricter curfews. Some municipalities are suggesting a 22:00 curfew for those under the age of sixteen. Do you think this is an effective method of fighting juvenile delinquency?

Applying your knowledge

1. A chart earlier in this chapter showed the statistics on delinquent behaviour in the city of Toronto. Without signing your name to the paper, take the test along with other members of your class. Compare the results with those in the survey.

2. Carry out a survey to find out how many members of your class belong to a "gang." Try to find out why they joined such a group, and the range of activities carried out by this group.

3. Check with your local police department to see if they have a Youth Division. Arrange for an officer to speak about the problems of juvenile offenders in your community.

4

PUNISHMENT FOR CRIME

1. Historical Background

Punishment for Crime

Societies have tried to find suitable punishment for breaking the law for a long time. There have been many experiments by various societies for dealing with criminals. In some early societies the punishment for crimes was left up to the family of the injured party. This often led to a system of revenge and feuds. These feuds might last for generations. In some cases the criminal paid the injured party or the victim's family instead.

Certain societies, cut off from European influence, continued until recently to have their own unique forms of punishment. Certain Aborigine groups in Australia punished a murderer in the following way. The accused was placed, without weapons, facing a row of tribesmen about 15-30 m away. First they would hurl insults at the accused. Finally they threw their spears. If the accused was wounded, the procedure would stop immediately. If he/she dodged all the spears one of the victims' relatives would give him/her a ceremonial nick in the thigh with a spear, enough to draw blood. The quarrel was then at an end and everyone went home.

The Comanche Indians of the American Southwest had very few laws. Punishment was carried out by members of the victim's family. In the case of murder, a relative of the dead person might in turn kill the murderer or one of his sons. In the case of horse theft one warrior might punish the offender by killing his horses. Comanches generally admitted their guilt, so fair punishment would not lead to more trouble within the tribe. In disputes where there was doubt, the person with the greatest reputation for bravery was considered in the right.

In traditional Inuit groups, disputes were settled by combat. These included wrestling, head butting and **song duels.** Butting took the form of the two opponents hitting their foreheads against one another until one of the men gave in.

In song duels, the two men took turns singing verses about each other. The verses were intended to insult and ridicule the opponent. This event might go on several hours a day for more than a month. The winner was decided by the applause of the audience who looked on.

As society became more organized, the government took over punishment for crimes. Little thought was given to the motive for criminal behaviour. The main purpose was to punish wrongdoers harshly. In this way governments hoped to discourage other criminals. In the Middle Ages the death penalty was put into effect for almost all crimes. Thus people were put to death for crimes varying from murder to witchcraft to petty crimes such as stealing a loaf of bread. As recently as 1819 in England, the death penalty was in effect for over two hundred different crimes.

There were other forms of punishment involving torture. Branding on the forehead, or cutting off hands were common forms of punishment. As recently as the 1960s in Canada the lash was commonly given to condemned rapists.

The age of the criminal was not a factor in the punishment. In England, there are cases of young children being put to death for petty theft as recently as the 18th century. This leads to the obvious problem. If someone were going to be caught for theft, they may as well commit murder in trying to escape, since the punishment was all the same. The punishment did not fit the crime.

It seems that the seriousness of a crime was considered only in the form of the execution. Persons convicted of a serious offence such as treason might be executed in a very nasty and sadistic way. Forms of execution included: pressing to death; burning at the stake; drawing and quartering; crucifixion; drowning; and being thrown to the lions.

Today only six forms of execution are still officially practised. These are: the guillotine; the garotte (an iron collar is placed around the neck and tightened by a screw until the victim strangles to death); hanging (this method of execution was used for the last time in Canada in 1962; Parliament abolished capital punishment in 1976); the electric chair; gassing (the condemned person is placed in a sealed gas chamber and deadly cyanide gas is released into the chamber); and shooting (a firing squad executes the condemned criminal).

Before reading on, study the chart of Key Words and Ideas which follows.

KEY WORDS AND IDEAS IN THIS CHAPTER

Term	Meaning	Sample Use
capital punishment	a sentence of death imposed by the court for certain criminal offences	In Canada capital punishment was abolished in 1976.
industrial schools	training schools to which juvenile delinquents are sent by the courts in Canada for certain offences	Juvenile offenders are taught normal school courses as well as various trades in industrial schools. They may stay in these schools until they are ready to cope with society.
maximum security prison	a prison which is heavily guarded to insure against the possible escape of prisoners	Those convicted of very serious criminal offences who are considered dangerous to the public are placed in maximum security prisons.
parole	a person sentenced to a prison term may not serve out the entire term in jail. For a portion of his sentence he may be allowed in public if he gives his word that he will behave.	Parole is difficult to get in Canada. Only about one-third of those who apply receive this privilege.
rehabilitation	the idea that a convicted lawbreaker should be re-educated to become a useful law-abiding member of society	One of the chief aims of Canada's prison system is the rehabilitation of criminals.
song duels	a method of settling a dispute used by certain Inuit groups	Instead of going to court, the accuser and accused face each other in a "song duel" in which they insult one another.

2. CAPITAL PUNISHMENT

Capital punishment seems to be on the decline in many countries. However it is a subject which still produces hot debates and arguments. In Canada, the death penalty was abolished by Parliament. However, a survey has shown the majority of Canadians are in favour of keeping it.

Arguments in Favour

Those in favour of the death penalty, the retentionists, argue in the following way:
— Murderers give up their right to live in society.
— The punishment should fit the crime. This principle goes all the way back to ancient times of "an eye for an eye." For the ultimate crime, murder, we should reserve the ultimate penalty, execution.
— If there is no capital punishment, murderers would have nothing to lose by murdering again. They would have nothing to lose in trying to escape by murdering their captors or guards.
— Society needs protection from murderers. We can never be sure that they will change their ways. Capital punishment will prevent a murderer from ever killing again.
— Putting a person in jail for life is not much more humane. Besides, the cost of keeping one person in jail for fifty years is estimated at over half a million dollars.
— Capital punishment has a **deterrent** effect. It would only be used on murders in the first degree — that is, murder which was deliberate and planned. This will cause potential killers to think twice, for fear of losing their own lives. This deterrent effect also builds up in a society over a long period of time. It creates the attitude that murder, because of the method of punishment, is the most serious of crimes.

Arguments against

Those who argue against capital punishment use a combination of the following arguments:
— The death penalty is not a deterrent. Most murders are not planned beforehand. They come about as a result of arguments and fights. Such people do not stop to think about the death penalty.
— According to statistics, those countries who still use the death penalty do not necessarily have a lower murder rate.
— Capital punishment is brutal. No civilized society should resort to such

methods of punishment. It lowers respect for human life.
— There is the chance that a murderer can be **rehabilitated** and turned into a useful citizen.
— Some juries may be less likely to convict a person if the death penalty is in force, because they may be afraid of making a mistake.
— There is always the possibility of executing an innocent person.

Analyze the arguments in favour of and against capital punishment. Which side do you support?

3.   OTHER FORMS OF PUNISHMENT

Canada has abolished the death penalty, but our courts can hand out a great variety of sentences to lawbreakers. A judge may hand out one of the following penalties for criminal offences:

Suspended Sentence: The court will delay punishment in the hope that the convicted person will behave within the law in the future. Generally this is done in cases of minor crimes and with first-time offenders. If the individual does behave, no punishment is given. If they do not behave, they may be returned to court for sentencing.

Probation: This is sometimes attached to a suspended sentence. In this case the individual is under the supervision of a probation officer. The convicted person must report regularly to the probation officer. The officer makes sure that the person is fulfilling the conditions set down by the court.

Fine: The judge may order the payment of a money penalty for certain crimes. This is the case in matters such as traffic offences. If the offender cannot pay the fine, he/she must serve a term in prison instead.

Training Schools: A young person convicted under the Juvenile Delinquents Act may be sent to a training school. The usual age level for these schools ranges from twelve to eighteen. In these schools, young people take the usual school courses. They may also be trained to learn a trade. Sewing, typing, hairdressing, machineshop, electrical work and cooking are some of the courses given. Juvenile offenders may have to stay in such a school until they can show that they are ready to co-operate with society.

Prison: Going to prison is the normal punishment in Canada for serious crimes. Under the Criminal Code, an offender is sent to federal penitentiary for serious crimes (over two years). Those guilty of less serious crimes go to provincial institutions.

A group home for young people in trouble with the law. In several provinces many young offenders are sent to these small home-like settings rather than to training schools.

4. THE PRISON SYSTEM

The prison system is divided into three kinds:

1. Maximum Security — If it is believed the convicted person will make serious attempts to escape and if he/she is dangerous to public safety, they are confined to this kind of prison.

2. Medium Security — If, given the chance, the prisoner would probably try to escape, although he/she is not dangerous to the public, they serve their sentence in this kind of prison.

3. Minimum Security — If the convicted person would not try to escape and is not dangerous, they are sentenced to this kind of prison. In these prisons there are usually no locks, bars, or walls.

Prison Routine

A convicted person entering prison is first taken to a reception centre. Here he/she is given all the items needed in prison, including:

- a set of clothing
- eating utensils
- toilet articles — paper, soap, towels, toothpaste, etc.

The prisoner is then examined by a committee made up of the warden, a prison psychiatrist, a sociologist, a criminologist, a training officer and a minister or priest. Tests and interviews are given. The prison rules are explained.

The daily routine usually varies from prison to prison. A typical day may look like this:

07:00 Wake up, wash and shave in the cells.

Eat breakfast in mess hall.

08:00-11:00 Work or study period. If the prisoner does not report for class, the instructor will inform the guards. The guards will make a search. Guards also handle inmates who refuse to work or cause a disturbance.

11:00-12:30 Lunch.

12:30-17:00 Work or study classes.

17:00-18:00 Evening meal.

18:00-22:00 Free time. Inmates may go to the gym, watch television, play cards, read or write.

22:30 Inmates return to their cells, and the cells are locked.

A typical cell in a detention centre in Ontario. Persons await trial or serve short sentences in these centres.

Privileges

All inmates have the privilege of writing letters to friends on the outside. All mail coming in and going out may be censored. Inmates have to buy their own paper and stamps. Inmates also have visiting privileges. Except for maximum security prisons, inmates are allowed to sit with their visitors in a large reception room. The inmate is thoroughly searched before and after such visits. Visitors are not allowed to hand anything to the inmate.

An inmate who regularly causes trouble and breaks prison rules, may be harshly punished by the warden. The prisoner may be placed in isolation. Here he/she cannot associate with others. Rations may be cut for several days at a time. Physical punishment such as whipping can be given. Today this is seldom done.

A prisoner may also have to serve a longer period in jail. Under a new federal act, all prisoners have the chance to work off one-third of their sentence through good behaviour. This is called *earned remission*. Therefore if the prisoner behaves well, he/she will not serve the full sentence. If the prisoner misbehaves he/she may wind up serving out the entire term.

There are over 7000 prisoners in Canada's federal penitentiaries. Many are not considered dangerous. In some cases they are allowed to go home without guards for a weekend. If they do not return, this is considered an escape. This program has caused concern in the past because of the risks involved. Many in the public and the media have argued that this program should be more tightly controlled. Some say it should be cancelled because of the danger.

Parole is another privilege of the prison system. After serving one-third of his sentence, and inmate of a federal penitentiary unless convicted of a violent crime, may apply to the National Parole Board in Ottawa to grant him a parole. The new federal Parole Act allows each province to set up their own parole boards for inmates of provincial prisons. A person released on parole is literally "on his word." He/she gives his word that he/she will behave within the law in society. During the remaining time on his/her sentence a person must report to a parole officer, much like a person on probation.

Only about one-third of the requests for parole are granted. Interviews are conducted, and reports from the inmate's superiors are considered. No one knows why one person will be granted parole and another one will not. A number of factors are taken into account. Past behaviour, personality, the seriousness of the crime, family contacts and job prospects are some of them. The final decision rests on whether the inmate has changed his/her attitude while in prison.

Are Prisons Useful?

Much of the public would agree that prisons serve a number of useful purposes:

1. They may act as a deterrent. The thought of a lengthy and unpleasant prison sentence may prevent a person from committing a crime.

2. Protection of Society. Those who commit serious crimes present a danger to society. They should be removed until hopefully they can learn to co-operate with others.

3. Rehabilitation. Most people believe that prisons should help the criminal readjust to acceptable behaviour.

4. Punishment. The criminal after all has broken the law and harmed society. He/she should be punished for this action. A crime implies that the person meant to commit it so they must suffer the consequences. This purpose is very close to the revenge theory of "an eye for an eye."

Do prisons rehabilitate? The evidence suggests that they do not. Some prisoners do not need rehabilitation. Their crimes are such that they would probably never commit them again anyway. In these cases prisons are only for punishment. For the others, rehabilitation does not seem to work. Between forty and fifty percent of those released from prison will commit another crime and return. Only twenty percent of prisoners are first-time offenders. The other eighty percent have been in prison before. Certainly this is a high failure rate. One reason for this is that in prison inmates often learn the skills to be better criminals rather than better citizens. Many experts are of the opinion that a new system of rehabilitation is needed. A system which will help the inmate deal with a society he/she may not have seen in years is required. Such a system may still be a long way from reality.

Recently some judges have imposed a different kind of sentence. These force the convicted person to pay back the injured party or to help work in the community rather than going to jail. These sentences are given to offenders who are not considered dangerous or who are not likely to repeat their crime (for example, vandals). Do you approve of this trend?

THINGS TO THINK ABOUT AND DO

Reviewing Key Words and Ideas

The following terms appeared in this chapter. Try to recall their meaning and how they were used.

deterrent	parole	rehabilitation
training schools	probation	suspended sentence

Remembering the Facts

1. There are approximately how many inmates in Canada's federal prisons
a) 25 000   b) 7 000   c) 50 000   d) 100 000
2. The last execution in Canada took place in
a) 1958   b) 1976   c) 1962   d) 1967
3. The percentage of applicants who receive parole in Canada is
a) 33%   b) 10%   c) 50%   d) 80%

Analyzing Ideas

1. The Parliament of Canada abolished capital punishment in 1976. Present an argument in favour of or against the return of the death penalty for murder. Are there *any* offences which you feel should be punishable by death? Conduct a survey of your friends, family and classmates to find out their position.
2. A number of those convicted of criminal offences are placed in minimum security prisons. These people are not considered dangerous to the public. Do you think these people should be given such freedom and trust?
3. Analyze the routine of a typical day in prison. In your opinion is the routine too harsh or too soft on inmates?
4. Debate this resolution: The function of prisons should be to rehabilitate criminals, not punish them!

Applying Your Knowledge

1. It has been suggested that prisons serve to punish lawbreakers and also to rehabilitate them. Are prisons successful in these two purposes?
2. Recently, a number of judges have sentenced criminal offenders to pay back their victims, or work for the community rather than go to jail. For which offences do you think such sentences would be useful?
3. With the help of information provided by the justice department of the federal government, find out the locations of Canada's federal prisons.

5

CIVIL LAW

Thus far we have been dealing with criminal law in Canada. At the start of this unit we mentioned another type of law called **civil law.** Criminal law as we have seen, deals with people whose actions in breaking the law bring harm to other individuals or the community. Civil law, on the other hand, deals with disputes and disagreements between people or groups. These have no direct effect on the community. Such cases include disputes over **contracts,** property or personal relationships. When one party takes another party to court over

A civil case being pleaded in a courtroom. *Picture from the sound filmstrip series "Why Do We Have Laws?" and "Police", courtesy of Cinemedia Ltd. Toronto.*

such matters, it is called a **civil suit.** Unlike criminal cases, society is not involved, and there is no Crown prosecutor trying the case. In civil cases, each side hires its own lawyers to contest the points.

Before reading on, study the chart of Key Words and Ideas which follows.

KEY WORDS AND IDEAS IN THIS CHAPTER

Term	Meaning	Sample Use
caveat emptor	a latin expression which means "let the buyer beware"	Consumers should heed the warning *caveat emptor.* In most cases, the buyer and not the seller is responsible for making sure the merchandise is good.
civil law	the segment of the law which deals with the private rights and agreements between individuals	A dispute over a contract comes under Canada's civil law.
civil suit	court action brought by one person or group against another in matters dealing with civil law	A person may bring a civil suit against another if a contract has not been fulfilled.
contract	an agreement between two parties to purchase something or perform some action; such an agreement is enforceable by law	A contract is legal whether it is verbal, written, or implied.
minor	a person under the age of eighteen	A minor may not legally, sign a contract in Canada.

Let us examine the difference between these two kinds of laws:
Ted the pharmacist had fallen madly in love with Ellen. Unfortunately for Ted, Ellen was already engaged to be married to her boyfriend of many years, Jack. Jack was a regular customer of Ted's drugstore. He picked up all his prescriptions there. In a final attempt to win his true love, Ted decided on a desperate course of action. He added a small dose of a deadly poison to Jack's

next prescription. Unfortunately for Ted his knowledge of poisons was not extensive. The dose he gave Jack was not enough to kill him, although it made him quite ill.

Several days later, the police showed up at Ted's door and arrested him for attempted murder. Why can this be considered a criminal case?

Mary Alice suffered from a persistent allergy for which a prescription medicine was necessary. She had been taking this medicine from the local druggist for several years without suffering any harmful side effects. One afternoon after taking her medicine, Mary Alice became violently ill, and her face broke out in a rash. A doctor was called in and after a period in the hospital Mary Alice recovered. The prescription was analyzed. The results showed that the druggist had mistakenly replaced one element in the prescription for another. This small error had caused the whole problem.

Several days later the unfortunate druggist was notified that Mary Alice was starting a civil suit against him for damages of $25 000.

Why is this not considered a criminal case?

These two situations illustrate the difference between criminal and civil law. Criminal law may seem more exciting to the public than studying civil cases such as contracts. It is a fact that more Canadians get into trouble over contracts than any other branch of the law. There are thousands of laws dealing with civil cases. Obviously we cannot deal with them in detail. However a brief discussion of several examples of the most common problems in civil law will be useful.

A dangerous situation. If the paperboy should step on the skateboard and injure himself, who would be responsible? Why would this be considered a civil and not a criminal case? *Picture from the sound filmstrip series "Why Do We Have Laws?" and "Police", courtesy of Cinemedia Ltd. Toronto.*

1. CONTRACTS

Perhaps the most common legal "jam" most Canadians get into involves contracts. By law, some people cannot be held responsible for signing contracts. These include:

1. minors
2. convicts in penitentiaries
3. Indians on reserves
4. intoxicated people
5. insane people

As a minor, you may not legally sign a contract. Within a very few years however, you may be out on your own. You will face responsibilities of voting, signing contracts, and being sued in court. Young people at this stage are often ripe for being taken advantage of by fast-talking salesmen and merchants. Imagine that you have just begun your first job, and are in the market for an apartment, a car, new furniture, etc. You will probably sign many contracts over the next few months.

A simple contract can take several forms:

1. **Verbal.** A spoken agreement between two parties.
2. **Implied.** Where payment for services is implied. For example, having your car's gas tank filled at a gas station implies you will pay for it.
3. **Written.** The agreement is in the form of a signed document.

Assuming you have the right to sign a contract, and that the contract itself does not break any laws, you are legally responsible for upholding your end of the bargain. The following are several common legal problems you might encounter.

A) Buying a Car

You have just signed a contract to buy a new car. You are anxiously waiting delivery. Several months pass by, and still no car. You desperately need a car to get you to your job. Finally you decide you cannot wait any longer, you would like to buy a car right out of the showroom from another dealer. Can you get out of your contract?

Not really. You should read the fine print in automobile contracts. The agreement you signed would include the following points:

1. There is no time limit set for the delivery of your car. (If you want a time limit, you must agree to such in the contract.)
2. If you fail to take delivery of your car from the dealer within 48 hours of notice, you may lose your cash deposit.
3. The dealer may hold the car for twenty days, then resell it. You will be informed of the time and place of the sale. If he sells it for less than you agreed to pay, the dealer will require you to make up the difference.

B) Buying From Door-to-Door Salespeople

You are a homemaker who has just bought a vacuum cleaner from a door-to-door salesperson. The machine seemed to do a good job in the demonstration. You agreed to pay twelve payments of $20 each, including interest. This would make the total price of the vacuum cleaner $240. This seems a high price. However, the salesperson promised that if you gave a list of your friends' names you might get a better price. You were promised ten dollars back for each friend who also bought a vacuum cleaner.

The next week, you see a similar machine at a store for about $100 less. At the same time, your husband who did not sign the contract is unhappy with the price. Can you return the vacuum cleaner?

Not unless the vacuum cleaner company agrees. A husband does not have to co-sign a contract with his wife. A wife has full legal rights and responsibilities. The **Consumer Protection Act** gives a person the right to change his/her mind on a contract signed in the person's home. However, this must take place within two days of the signing. After this it becomes legal.

C) Books in the Mail

You have just answered an ad which offered free the first book in a series on North American Animal Life. The ad indicated that you were not obligated to purchase any other books. The free book is not all that interesting. However it is free, so you decide to keep it, but you do not ask for any more. Next month, a box with the remaining twelve volumes arrives, along with a bill for the books. Do you have to pay?

The answer is no. In Ontario a person who receives through the mail something he/she did not ask for, may actually keep it. To avoid further problems with the company however, you may wish to send the books back. This can be done in two ways. You may return the box to the Post Office marked "Refused — Return to Sender." They will then be returned at the company's cost. Or you may send a letter to the company and request them to come and pick up the books.

D) Leasing an Apartment

You have been living in an apartment for five months and have seven months left on your lease. Suddenly the building is sold to a new owner. The new owner wants to raise your rent by $20 per month. You refuse to pay. The new owner then wants to evict you and claims he has the right to do so, since you have not signed a lease with him. He refuses to accept your rent money. Can you be evicted?

The answer is no. The new owner was under obligation to find out the existing leases when he bought the property. He must honour any leases signed with the previous owner. He cannot evict you until your lease expires, and he cannot force you to pay a higher rent. If he refuses to accept your rent, you can pay the court. If he wants his money, he can collect it there.

E) Dealing with Repairmen

Your trusty car has finally let you down, and you have had it towed to the nearest repair station. The mechanic who gave the car an inspection gave a quick estimate that the repair bill would be about $100. You then sign a work order. Later that day you pick up your car and become furious when you see the bill — $235! Can you refuse to pay?

You cannot refuse payment. The mechanic's estimate was only a guess. At that point he could not be certain of the damage. When you signed a work bill you gave him the right to make all the necessary repairs. Now you must pay. If you refuse, he may sell your car to recover his money.

In future cases, you should ask for a full written estimate before authorizing repairs to cars or T.V. sets, etc. You can then refuse to agree to the repair if the costs seem high. You can also state a limit as to the amount you will pay. All these things must be done in advance. Once you sign a work order, you are responsible for its terms.

These are but a few examples of the kinds of difficulties many Canadians become involved with. As much as possible the law allows individuals to be responsible for their own actions. The moral in every case is to read over contracts and agreements carefully. The law will not always bail you out. Once again, ignorance is no defence. The old Roman warning **caveat emptor** —"let the buyer beware," is still very much to be heeded.

THINGS TO THINK ABOUT AND DO

Reviewing Key Words and Ideas

The following terms appeared in this chapter. Try to recall their meaning and how they were used.

caveat emptor	Consumer Protection Act	verbal contract
civil law	implied contract	written contract
civil suit	minor	

Remembering the Facts

1. If you sign a contract to purchase goods in your own home, you may cancel the contract if you change your mind within
a) 5 days   b) 1 week   c) 1 month   d) 2 days
2. Which of the following may not legally sign a contract?
a) prisoners in jail   b) minors   c) a wife without her husband's consent   d) Indians on reserves
3. If you tell a plumber to fix your sink, but do not put it in writing, there is no legal contract. True or false?

Analyzing Ideas

1. The old maxim "let the buyer beware" is still very much to be observed today. Do you think the government should pass more laws to protect consumers from making foolish mistakes?
2. Most of the products purchased today come with warranties. It is probable that you have a number of such products in your home. Read the warranties closely. How much responsibility does the manufacturer actually have?

Applying Your Knowledge

1. What is the difference between criminal law and civil law? Which of the following would be considered a criminal matter and which a civil matter?
   a) forging your name on a cheque
   b) mistreating a pet
   c) refusing to pay your telephone bill
   d) driving while under the influence of alcohol
2. Find out a little more about Canada's consumer laws. You may gain reliable information from the following sources: Department of Consumer and Corporate Affairs Canadian Building, 219 Laurier Avenue, Ottawa 4, Ont.
3. If you were the judge, what would be your verdict in the following case?
   Alice entered a contest in which the object was to guess the number of jellybeans in a jar. The prize was a new T.V. set. A week later she was informed that she and another contestant had tied with the closest answer. There would be a quiz to determine the winner. The contest organizer announced that the last person eliminated would be the winner. They drew lots to determine the order of answering. Alice would answer first. Each contestant answered the first four questions correctly. On the fifth question Alice missed. So did her opponent. However, since Alice missed first, the organizer announced that her opponent was the winner. Alice protested that this was unfair to her since both contestants had missed the last question. The organizer claimed his decision was according to the rules. The case went to court.

How would you decide?

III

Canada: 1867-1945 — An Overview

1

CANADA: 1867 - 1914

INTRODUCTION

The period 1867-1914 was a crucial time in Canadian history. In 1867 Canada was a small, politically unimportant country. The nation was still tied to Britain's apronstrings. By 1914 Canada had become a vigorous young nation. It was about to participate in one of the major wars in human history. The period in between was one of great growth and development, both politically and socially.

In 1867 Canada was made up of four provinces — Ontario, Quebec, New Brunswick, and Nova Scotia. By 1914 it contained nine provinces and stretched from sea to sea. Only Newfoundland stayed outside the union. It joined Canada in 1949

These successes were not easily achieved. Canada's giant neighbour to the South, the U.S., was growing quickly. It often threatened to absorb Canada into the United States. The term used to describe this threat was 'expansionism'. Canada was also faced by problems within its borders. These included tying the nation together to form East and West, a Rebellion in the West and arguments between English and French. In this chapter we will examine the major developments in the period between 1867 and 1914. We will try to find answers to the following large questions: What forces were at work to change the political and social scene during these years? What sort of country did these forces produce? Compared to most other countries, Canada is still very young. Yet the difficult decisions made during Canada's 'childhood' helped the nation 'grow up' quickly. They also shaped Canada's future course as a nation.

Before reading on, study the chart of Key Words and Ideas which follows.

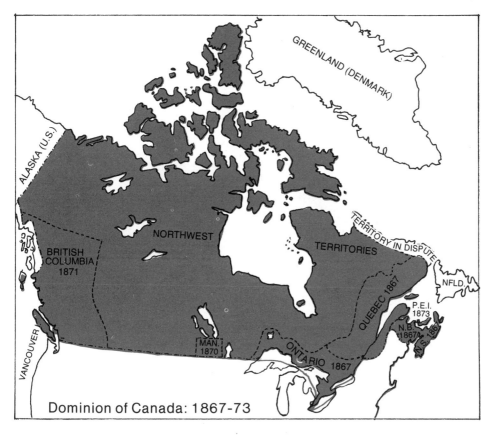

Dominion of Canada: 1867-73

The population, too, was small. Of the 3.3 million Canadians, 80% lived in Ontario and Quebec. This population was also mainly British and French.

	1867	TODAY
French	31%	31%
British-English		
Irish	60.5%	45%
Scottish		
Other	8.5%	24%

What did the future hold for young Canadians in 1867? Many had escaped from poverty overseas, hoping to become wealthy, own land, and "move up" in the world. They believed in the progress and growth of their country. These are probably many of the same values shared by young Canadians today. Yet, for the majority, in 1867 these goals were only wishful dreams. If you had been a young person living in Canada at that time, you would probably have settled for a lifestyle much the same as that of your parents and grandparents before you. Only one Canadian in five lived in towns or cities. For the rest, their way of life seemed destined to remain rural. In the Maritimes shipping and fishing were even then the main features of their economy. In Quebec the lives of most French Canadians were still tied to their habitant farms or lumbering. In Ontario there was a belt of settled communities along the north shore of Lake Ontario from Kingston to Niagara Falls. Outside this belt lay the world of farm, forest, and log cabin.

Rural life in the 1800s must seem slow by today's space-age standards. There were no paved roads, no automobiles and few machines of any type. The steam locomotive connected only the larger towns and cities. Farmers still had to break open and maintain their own roads.

Wood was the main fuel source for homes. Light was provided by coal-oil lamps. The women were expected to cook, spin their own clothes, milk the cows, churn the butter and make the soap for laundry.

Town life seemed a little more lively. You could buy most of life's needs at the general store, even imported cookies and candy. In town you could also expect to find a blacksmith shop, a drugstore, doctor's office, a local newspaper, a bank and several churches. Above all, for entertainment, there were taverns.

Taverns were as plentiful as today's corner milk stores. Every town of modest size had at least three taverns. They were the centres of social and political activity. Each tavern had its own special clients. Liberals would tend to gather at one tavern, Conservatives at a second and neutrals at a third. Here they would discuss the political events of the time. In those days there were no popularity polls and no secret ballot. Studying the tavern population was a simple way of judging the popularity of each party.

The larger cities — Montreal, Toronto, Quebec City, Halifax — could boast of a few paved streets, and gaslighted street lamps. A few of the wealthier houses had running water. Toronto did have horse-drawn streetcars. There was almost no Canadian literature or music. However, plays from London or New York could be seen in large cities. These were attended by the wealthier citizens. The average person, in this age before movies, television, and professional sporting events, had to come up with his/her own leisure activities.

Public education was free. However only a few students went to high school and fewer still attended university. The core subjects of higher education were Greek, Latin, English, History and Mathematics. These prepared the graduate for a career in politics and business. For most of the less fortunate, the future contained dull tedious labour.

A wind of change, however, was sweeping into Canada. It carried new ideas and new hopes. These hopes were based on the promise of the machine age. The **industrial revolution** had already started in Britain and the United States. It was just beginning in Canada. Young people could not dream of instant wealth. Stories of adventurous people, who had started out penniless and almost over night had become millionaires, came north from the United States. The main sources of this new-found wealth were railroads, steel and oil.

Fig. 2 a.—Blouse for Girls of 12 to 15. Front.

Fig. 1 a.—Rubens Hat for a Little Girl.   Fig. 1 b.—High Crowned Hat for a Little Girl.

Fig. 2 b.—Blouse for Girls of 12 to 15. Back.

Fig. 3.—Sash of watered Ribbon and Rep Ribbon.

Fig. 5.—Pelargonium Coiffure.

Fig. 6.—Rose-bud Coiffure.

Fig. 4.—Sash of watered Ribbon and Velvet Ribbon.

Fig. 7.—Bretelles of Swiss Muslin, Insertion and Lace.

Fig. 8.—Visiting Toilette.

Fig. 10.—Fancy Case for Skates.

Fig. 9.—Evening Dress.

FASHIONS AND LADY'S WORK.

Women's fashions in 1873. Make up a page like this one on women's fashions today. Use pictures from magazines and catalogues. What do clothes tell you about how people live during a period in history?

Within a few years, the names of Andrew Carnegie and John D. Rockefeller stood out as examples in these rags-to-riches stories. This same dream took hold in Canada. If Canadians were to achieve these rewards Canada would have to continue to progress and to grow. The obvious direction of growth was westward.

"The Great Trophy of Confederation" was designed to honour Canada's tenth birthday, on July 1, 1877. Each of the seven provinces is symbolized in this drawing. Try to identify each one.

2. ROUNDING OUT THE DOMINION

The motto on the Canadian coat of arms is the Latin phrase **"A mari usque ad mare".** It means "from sea to sea." From the very beginning Canadians realized that if their country was to survive it must be unified from Atlantic to Pacific. Most Canadians placed their hopes for the future on Prime Minister John A. Macdonald. Macdonald was suited to the mood of the times. He too favoured industrial growth and expansion to the West. Almost immediately the new Prime Minister took steps to promote this growth.

Several thousand kilometres to the west was the colony of British Columbia. It seemed eager to join the new Dominion. The main stumbling block was the problem of communication. There were no roads linking British Columbia with the rest of Canada. The obvious answer was the building of a railroad which would link British Columbia to the rest of Canada. However, the giant territory of the Northwest lay in between. It was owned by the Hudson's Bay Company. Canada had to control this huge expanse of land if it was to become a strong nation. During this period settlers in the United States were moving west. They came very close to the Canadian border. The threat of an American takeover of the Northwest forced Macdonald's Conservative government into action. The first step was to negotiate the purchase of the Northwest from the Hudson's Bay Company. In 1869 the deal was completed.

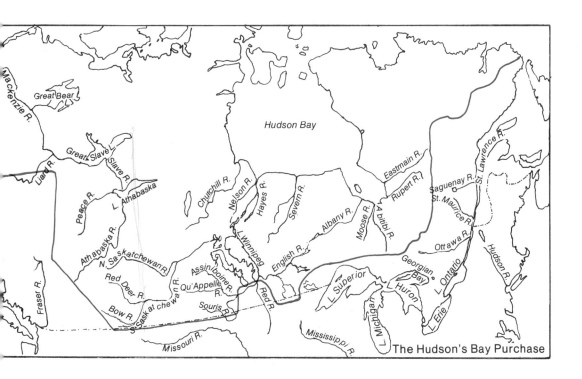

The Hudson's Bay Purchase

THE DEAL

CANADA RECEIVED	HUDSON'S BAY CO. RECEIVED
3.9 million square kilometres = 390 million hectares	— £300 000 ($1.5 million) — 18 000 hectares of land around its trading posts — 1/20 of all the fertile land in the Northwest

Canada's purchase of the Northwest, at the rate of about one penny for every three hectares of land, certainly stands out as one of the greatest real estate bargains of all time.

3.   THE NORTHWEST REBELLION

The purchase of the Northwest also brought the Canadian government its first crisis. The Hudson's Bay Company had given Canada control over not only a vast land, but the people in it as well. This included numerous Indian nations such as the Cree and Blackfoot. It also included about twelve thousand people who lived in the Red River colony.

The majority of the people at Red River were **Métis,** both French and English. The Métis were a proud people. They were part Indian and part European. The Métis considered themselves a separate nation. For many years they had led a wandering life. Their economy was based on the annual buffalo hunt. By 1869 the buffalo herds had almost vanished. Great slaughters in the United States had wiped them out. Many Métis wanted to set down roots as farmers in the Red River area. The sale of the Hudson's Bay lands to Canada caused several concerns. Would the Canadian government guarantee the Métis' land titles? Would it respect the French language and Roman Catholic religion?

When the surveyors sent out by Canada reached the Red River, the Métis naturally became suspicious. On October 11, 1869, a group of Métis put a stop to the work of the surveyors and arrested them. The leader of the Métis was a young man of twenty-five whose name was Louis Riel.

Riel was a born leader. He was well-educated, having studied law and religion in Montreal. Riel had proved to be a good student, but he was proud and hot-tempered. A man who knew Riel described him as follows:

> Riel may have his faults and weaknesses, but he is decidedly an extraordinary man. To begin, his appearance is striking: he has a swarthy complexion with a large head and piercing eyes. He seems quite well educated, and in all gives me the impression of a remarkable man, if unstable.

The Métis decided to keep out the representatives of Macdonald and set up their own Provisional Government. This action angered a number of Canadians living in the settlement, including several Ontario Englishmen. One

Louis Riel

man, Thomas Scott, led a revolt against the Riel government. It failed and Scott and several English-speaking settlers were jailed. Even in jail Scott continued to make trouble. He constantly quarrelled with Riel. At last Riel's patience came to an end and he had Scott executed.

Whether Riel's motives could be defended or not, the execution of Scott proved to be a great mistake. It created a great anti-French, anti-Catholic uproar in Ontario. On the other hand, French Catholic Quebec sympathized with Riel. The seeds of a new and bitter English-French antagonism had been sowed.

Macdonald now had no choice but to send troops to end the "Métis Rebellion". Riel feared for his life and escaped to the United States.

One side effect of the Red River Rebellion was to focus the attention of Canada on the West. The government now took quick action to guarantee the settlers their land and language rights. In 1870 the Red River settlement was admitted into Confederation as part of the Province of Manitoba. Riel became known as the Father of Manitoba. In time he was actually elected as Member of Parliament from that province, but because of a price on his head, he never served.

4.   BUILDING OF THE CANADIAN PACIFIC RAILWAY

Macdonald's fondest dream was to round out the Dominion from East to West. The cornerstone of this "National Dream" was the construction of a great railway to link British Columbia with the rest of Canada. British Columbia had agreed to join Confederation in 1871 only if the railway were started within two years of joining.

John A. Macdonald, Canada's first Prime Minister. He remained in that office from 1867-1891, except for the period 1873-1878.

This seemed an impossible task for the young nation. The costs would be immense. Macdonald himself estimated the cost at $100 million. Later this was proven to be far too low. The railroad itself, if completed, would be the longest ever built. It would have to cross some of the most difficult territory in the world — forests, swamps, prairies and great mountain ranges. It certainly seemed an ambitious project for a country of less than four million people.

Yet great profits might be made in the building of such a railway. Businessmen both in Canada and the United States saw potential. Macdonald's government was soon getting offers from companies on both sides of the border to build his railroad.

Meanwhile Macdonald was busy leading his Conservative Party in the election of 1872. He emerged from the election once again as Canada's Prime Minister. Shortly afterward, the government awarded the contract to build the transcontinental railroad to the Canadian Pacific Railway Company. The Company was headed by Sir Hugh Allan, Canada's wealthiest businessman.

The charter to build the West's "iron road" cost the Canadian government $30 million in cash and over 20 million hectares of some of the best farmland in Canada.

But even as work was beginning on the railroad, a political storm was brewing in Ontario. The Liberal opposition soon produced evidence that Allan and his backers had given large sums of money to the Conservative Party during the 1872 election. In fact over $325 000 had been donated by the Company to ensure Macdonald's re-election. The most damaging evidence

Building the C.P.R. through prairies and mountains.

was a letter from Macdonald to Allan: "I must have another ten thousand; will be the last time of calling; do not fail me; answer today."

The "Pacific Scandal" came crashing down about Macdonald's shoulders. His government was forced to resign. In 1873 the Liberal Party under Alexander Mackenzie governed Canada.

While Alexander Mackenzie was an honest, hardworking and thrifty Prime Minister, he did lack imagination. Mackenzie was also very unlucky. When he became Prime Minister a long period of **economic depression** was beginning. The C.P.R. was the first to be affected by economic conditions. The Liberal government scrapped most of the plans for its construction. Over the next five years only a few short sections of track were laid. British Columbia naturally felt betrayed and threatened to pull out of Confederation.

John A. Macdonald came to the rescue. After the Pacific Scandal of 1873 it seemed his political career had come to an end. But now in 1878 he appeared as the only man who could save the railway, and with it a Canada "from sea to sea". Macdonald's Conservatives swept back into power on the promise of a **"National Policy".**

Macdonald's National Policy consisted of three main projects:
1) completion of the Canadian Pacific Railway
2) raising protective **tariffs** to encourage Canadian industry
3) encouraging immigration to the West

The first order of importance was to finish the railroad. A new Canadian Pacific Railway Company, headed by George Stephen and Donald Smith, was founded. The company agreed to finish the railroad by 1891. In return they received the following generous terms:
— ownership of the railroad;
— $25 000 000 cash;
— 10 million hectares in the rich valley of the Saskatchewan;
— exemption from taxation;
— imports carried duty-free;
— 1100 km of railroad already completed (valued at $30 000 000) to be handed over to the Company.

A young energetic American, Cornelius Van Horne took over construction of the railroad in 1882. In three short years he engineered the railroad from the head of Lake Superior to British Columbia. The last spike was driven at Craigellachie, British Columbia on November 7, 1885, six years before the deadline.

Lord Strathcona drives in the last spike at Craigellachie, B.C.

5. THE REBELLION OF 1885

The same year that saw the triumph of the C.P.R. also witnessed the return of Louis Riel. After the troubles at Red River in 1869, most of the Métis had sold their land cheaply to land agents. They travelled far to the west, to the valley of the South Saskatchewan River.

Here they continued their farming and hunting life. But with the advance of the railroad, their way of life was again in danger. Once again they voiced their complaints to the government. Once more the Macdonald government seemed to ignore the plight of the Métis and their Indian brothers and sisters. Louis Riel agreed to return from the United States and help his people.

At first the Métis drew up a list of simple petitions. They asked for clear title to their lands and justice for the Indians. Macdonald, busy with railroad matters, brushed aside their requests. The angry Métis quickly took up arms in revolt. At Duck Lake the Métis took a detachment of Mounted Police by surprise. After a brief fight, twelve Mounties lay dead; the Saskatchewan Rebellion was on for real. The Métis were soon joined by the Cree Indians under Chiefs Big Bear and Poundmaker.

The newly built railroad quickly proved its worth. It brought troops from the East under the command of General Middleton. After more battles at Frog

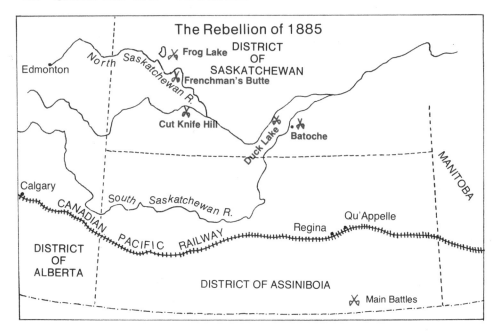

The Rebellion of 1885

Lake, Cut Knife Hill, Battleford and Batoche, the Métis and their Indian allies surrendered. Riel himself was captured.

Later that year at Regina, Riel was put on trial for treason. His lawyers attempted to prove that Riel was insane. The jury, however, believed he was sane, and so responsible for his actions:

> He seemed to us no more insane than any of the lawyers and they were the ablest men in Canada. He was even more interesting than some of them.

They found Riel guilty and on November 16, 1885, he was hanged.

Riel's death caused rioting in Quebec, and a new round of bitter English-French feelings. It would take a long time to heal the wounds.

6.   IMMIGRATION TO THE WEST

The second plank of Macdonald's National Policy was the settlement of the West. Free **homesteads** were offered to draw settlers to the West. The fertile lands of the prairies were divided into townships made up of 36 2.6 km squares. A homestead consisted of one-quarter of a square or 64 ha. Any male over the age of 18 could file for such a homestead. In return he had to promise to live on the land for at least three years, build a home, and break at least 4 ha of soil each year.

In the decade after 1871, the results of this policy were disappointing. In 1871 the population of the west was 73 228. Ten years later the figure was only slightly over 100 000. Instead of a flood, immigration to the west proved to be only a trickle.

The completion of the C.P.R. in 1885 solved the problem of transportation. Before this time, settlers could expect to travel thousands of kilometres on foot and horseback, by cart or by boat, before reaching their destination. Many prospective settlers were naturally frightened of making such a journey. Another spur to immigration was provided by the election of Wilfrid Laurier and the Liberals in 1896. John A. Macdonald died in 1891, still Canada's Prime Minister. After five more years of Conservative rule, the Liberals swept to power in 1896. Wilfrid Laurier was determined to complete Macdonald's National Policy. His energetic Minister of the Interior, Clifford Sifton, took charge of immigration.

In the next few years, Europe and the United States were flooded with pamphlets announcing free land in the Canadian West. These methods were so successful that between 1897 and 1914 over one million Americans emigrated to Canada. Another million came from over thirty different countries in Europe and Asia.

The flood of immigrants finally slowed with the outbreak of World War I in 1914. In the meantime it had filled the West and had produced two new provinces, Saskatchewan and Alberta in 1905. Macdonald's dream of a Canada stretching from Atlantic to Pacific had been realized.

A "soddy" on the prairies. Settlers often had to make do with these homes for years until more permanent homes could be built. It is estimated there were thousands of soddies on the prairies. Examine the picture closely. Can you explain how these homes were built?

Immigration to Canada by Calendar Year, 1867-1915

1867 .... 10 666	1883 .... 133 624	1899 .... 44 543
1868 .... 12 765	1884 .... 103 824	1900 .... 41 681
1869 .... 18 630	1885 .... 79 169	1901 .... 55 747
1870 .... 24 706	1886 .... 69 152	1902 .... 89 102
1871 .... 27 773	1887 .... 84 526	1903 . : 138 660
1872 .... 36 578	1888 .... 88 766	1904 .... 131 252
1873 .... 50 050	1889 .... 91 600	1905 .... 141 465
1874 .... 39 373	1890 .... 75 067	1906 .... 211 653
1875 .... 27 382	1891 .... 82 165	1907 .... 272 409
1876 .... 25 633	1892 .... 30 996	1908 .... 143 326
1877 .... 27 082	1893 .... 29 633	1909 .... 173 694
1878 .... 29 807	1894 .... 20 829	1910 .... 286 839
1879 .... 40 492	1895 .... 18 790	1911 .... 331 288
1880 .... 38 505	1896 .... 16 835	1912 .... 375 756
1881 .... 47 991	1897 .... 21 716	1913 .... 400 870
1882 .... 112 458	1898 .... 31 900	1914 .... 150 484
		1915 .... 36 665

7.   THE LAURIER ERA

The new Prime Minister, Wilfrid Laurier, became the first French-Canadian to hold that office. Stately, elegant and charming, Laurier seemed the perfect person to lead Canada into the twentieth century. His election promised at last to draw together English and French to produce a united Canada. Racial and religious tensions decreased. At the same time, the rest of the world seemed to discover Canada. Laurier came to office at a time when a world-wide depression was coming to an end. Suddenly there were markets all over the world for Canada's raw materials, lumber, wheat and its manufactured products.

A gold strike in the Yukon drew over 40 000 prospectors to the north. It served to further increase the mood of optimism felt all over Canada. There seemed no limit to what the young country would achieve. One English visitor called Canada "the Cinderella of the Western World." Laurier himself declared that the twentieth century would belong to Canada.

The first crack in the dream came in 1899 in a faraway corner of the world. In South Africa, the **Boers,** descendants of the original Dutch farmers in that country, were fighting for their independence from Britain. The Boer's land was rich in diamonds and gold. Britain was determined to gain control of it. Britain asked Canada, as a member of the Empire, to help.

Laurier was placed in a difficult situation. French-Canadians refused to help in what they considered an unjust **imperialistic** war. English-Canadians insisted that Canada should do its duty and aid the mother country. A heated debate followed. Again Canada was divided into two camps, English versus French.

The Yukon Gold Rush: miners crossing the Chilkoot Pass in 1898. The lineup was actually several days long.

After much thought Laurier handed down his decision. Canada would not send an *official* army to South Africa but it would equip *volunteers*. Neither side was satisfied with this compromise solution. French-Canadians felt Laurier had done too much; English-Canadians felt that he had betrayed Britain.

Laurier's popularity received a further blow when his government signed a **Reciprocity Treaty** with the United States in 1911. The treaty reversed one of the cornerstones of Macdonald's National Policy. It removed protective tariffs for Canadian industry. The agreement allowed free trade between the two countries in such products as grain, fish, livestock, fruit and vegetables. Most of the tariff duties were also removed from meat, canned goods and machinery.

The reciprocity agreement had the effect of reducing the price of these goods in Canada. However, many Canadians feared that the competition with U.S. products would also result in loss of jobs. They believed that economic depression would follow. Then they said, Canada would become ripe for takeover by the U.S.

In the election of 1911, Laurier was swept out of office by Robert Borden and the Conservative Party. He would never again sit as Prime Minister of Canada.

It was Borden who would lead Canada into the greatest test of her first half-century, World War I. Over a half million Canadians marched to war in 1914. Of these, 63 000 would never return. Those who survived would find that the old way of life had gone forever.

THINGS TO THINK ABOUT AND DO

Reviewing Key Words and Ideas

The following terms appeared in this chapter. Try to recall their meaning and how they were used.

A mari usque ad mare	homestead	National Policy
Boers	imperialism	reciprocity
Confederation	Métis	tariffs

Remembering the Facts

1. At the time of Confederation the largest portion of Canada's population was made up of
a) French   b) British   c) others
2. The C.P.R. was completed in the year
a) 1873   b) 1885   c) 1891
3. Métis are a population made up of
a) part French, part Indian   b) part English, part Indian   c) both (a) and (b)
4. True or false? At the time of its completion the C.P.R. was the longest railway in the world.

Analyzing Ideas

1. Technological change is proceeding at a much faster rate than in the 19th century. Is it likely that many young people will continue to follow in the footsteps of their parents in choosing a career? If you have given any thought to your future career, how closely is it modeled upon that of your parents?
2. The Riel Rebellions of 1869 and 1885 represent the clash of advancing civilization and a more nomadic form of life. Could the Rebellions have been avoided? What steps would you have taken if you had been Prime Minister of Canada during these times?
3. Debate the following statement:
The building of the C.P.R. was the most important Canadian achievement before 1914.

Applying Your Knowledge

1. Make a list of the most important technological changes introduced in Canada since 1867. How has each of these affected our way of life?

2. A tariff system imposes taxes on products coming into the country. This tends to raise the prices of these products to consumers. Apply your knowledge of tariffs and make a list of the benefits and disadvantages of a tariff system to a country such as Canada.

3. In 1873 Canada suffered a political scandal involving the Prime Minister. Recently the United States has also been the victim of a political scandal. Compare and contrast the results of the scandals on the two countries and the two leaders involved.

At the turn of the century, women participated in almost all sporting activity.

2

A GENERATION UNDER FIRE: 1914-1945

INTRODUCTION

The twentieth century, according to Wilfrid Laurier, was to be "Canada's Century." As the year 1914 unfolded, it certainly seemed like Laurier's statement might come true. Canada was enjoying a great period of prosperity. Her natural resources were at last being developed. Foreign nations were opening their doors to Canadian products.

Canadians could see many reasons for feeling hopeful about their nation. The tensions between French and English had been extreme during the Riel Rebellion (see previous chapter). These tensions now seemed to be coming to an end. Waves of immigrants were opening up the west. The newcomers helped increase Canada's new prosperity. It was an age of exciting new inventions. Both the automobile and the airplane appeared during this period. The future seemed to promise a new, better lifestyle for Canadians.

Then came the tragedy of World War I. It was followed by a period of upheavals. These affected the social, political and economic life of Canadians. Relations between French and English would again be strained. The attitude toward women and their role in society would soon change. Within ten years, the greatest economic depression in history would bring Canada to her knees. In 1939 the second major war within a generation began. Once again war tested Canadians, as they faced the threat of Nazism.

In this chapter we will survey the great political, social and economic changes experienced by Canadians in the period 1914-1945. Canada began the period as a youthful country, still subject to Britain's policies. She emerged as a mature nation.

Before reading on, study the chart of Key Words and Ideas which follows.

KEY WORDS AND IDEAS IN THIS CHAPTER

Term	Meaning	Sample Use
alliance	an agreement between several countries that they will support each other in case of war	Alliances existed in both world wars. In World War I France, England, Russia and Italy were allied against Germany and Austria.
arms race	a situation in which countries compete against one another by building ever larger armies and navies, and supplying them with the most up-to-date equipment	In World War I England and Germany were engaged in an "arms race". Each side sought to gain the upper hand in naval power. It was one of the factors which led to war.
conscription	compulsory enlistment for military service, usually during times of war	The Canadian government introduced conscription during both world wars. The volunteer system had not brought in enough soldiers. Conscription caused political and social problems.
government bonds	notes issued by a government promising to repay borrowed money, usually with interest	Government bonds were issued during both world wars by the Canadian government to help pay for the cost of the wars.
income tax	a tax placed on a person's earnings	Income tax was introduced as a "temporary measure" during World War I. It is still with us today.
inflation	a period in a country's economy during which prices and wages are constantly rising	A mild inflation occurred between 1922-1939 in Canada. It was followed by the Great Depression.
mysticism	the belief that a person can communicate with the spirits of the dead	Prime Minister W.L. Mackenzie King practiced mysticism. Many of his decisions were made after consulting the spirits.

Nazi	a member of the German National Socialist Party whose leader was Adolf Hitler	Nazis believed in the superiority of the German people. The Nazi Party advocated the destruction of so-called "inferior" people, such as the Jews. The party came to power in Germany in 1933.
plebescite	the direct vote of all citizens on an issue of major importance	Mackenzie King issued a plebescite before making a decision on whether to introduce conscription during World War II.
recession	a period of slow economic activity; it is generally a time of high unemployment.	In the years immediately following World War I, Canada's economy suffered a recession. After 1929, the recession grew into a full-blown depression.
socialism	the theory that a community, through its government, should own or control the key industries in the economy, such as communication and transportation	In its Regina Manifesto the C.C.F. Party of 1932 proposed a program based on socialism. Many of its policies are now in effect in Canada.

1. WORLD WAR I

1914

As the year 1914 dawned, Canadians had every reason to feel optimistic. The Canadian economy was at last taking its leap forward. The machine age promised more jobs, easier labour, rapid transportation and adventure. Everywhere business seemed to be growing. The markets of the world were at last opening their doors to Canada's mineral, lumber and wheat exports. Prosperity seemed close at hand.

	1901	1911
Population	5 400 000	7 200 000
Wheat exports	$6 900 000	$45 500 000
Mineral production	$65 800 000	$103 200 000
Manufacturing	$481 000 000	$1 165 900 000
Automobiles	0	22 000

Of course life was still hard for many groups in society. It was still common for those working in factories and construction to labour twelve hours a day or more. Thousands of these workers were killed or injured each year due to unsafe working conditions. Diseases too took thousands of lives. Childhood deaths were quite common. Tuberculosis was the most dreaded disease of adults. Hospitals were not today's modern, well-equipped structures. Rather, they tended to be small, dingy, poorly lit buildings.

Thomas Edison's great invention, the electric lightbulb, was making headway in the cities. Even the large cities, however, seemed primitive by today's standards. In Montreal, horses still had the right-of-way over cars on the streets. In Toronto, the fire department's wagons were still drawn by horse. In most places, Red Flag Laws still prevented cars from going faster than 25 or even 15 km/h.

A leisurely Sunday afternoon stroll in High Park, Toronto, before W.W.I.

By and large Canadians were hopeful about their future. Since Confederation Canada had never been involved in a war. Indeed, at the Canadian National Exhibition in Toronto that year, the theme was "Peace." Few Canadians could suspect that the summer of 1914 would bring their country its greatest crisis since Confederation. For, in Europe, on August 4, 1914, the greatest armies in the history of the world were marching against each other. World War I had begun.

Background to War

It was to be a war unlike any other war in history. In this war, all the resources of the hostile nations would be channelled into the war effort. The raw materials, the factories, the civilian population and the fighting men themselves were all cogs in a great machine. This was to be total war.

The causes of the struggle had been building for decades. In 1871 German armies had defeated the French in the Franco-Prussian War. Since that day each side prepared for the time when the conflict would be renewed. As each side tried to gain the upper hand, they drew other European powers into the web. They did so through a series of alliances. By 1914 Europe was divided into two main camps. On the German side stood the Empire of Austria-Hungary and Italy. This was known as the Triple Alliance. With France were lined up England and Russia — the Triple Entente. (When the war started, Italy joined Britain, France and Russia.)

Each alliance system involved a network of secret treaties. Simply, they promised that if one member of the alliance were attacked, the other two would come to its defence.

The atmosphere of suspicion grew. Each country became involved in an "arms race." Armies and navies were increased, modernized and equipped with the newest weapons. England's proud navy, faced with the threat of a new powerful rival in Germany began an expensive program of rebuilding. Britain's naval budget doubled between 1900 and 1914. She also asked Canada to contribute to this budget. In 1911 this produced a bitter debate in Canada. Should Canada produce her own navy or simply contribute to a larger British navy? Laurier and the Liberals were in favour of a separate Canadian navy. Borden and the Conservatives felt Canada should contribute to the British navy. It was one of the issues which helped to defeat Laurier in 1911. As it turned out, Canada got neither her own navy nor did she aid Britain financially.

It was hoped that since the two alliances were fairly equal in power this would discourage the outbreak of war. However, in a far-off corner of Europe called the Balkans, local wars could not be stopped. Serbia was a small country which had recently been given independence from her former protector,

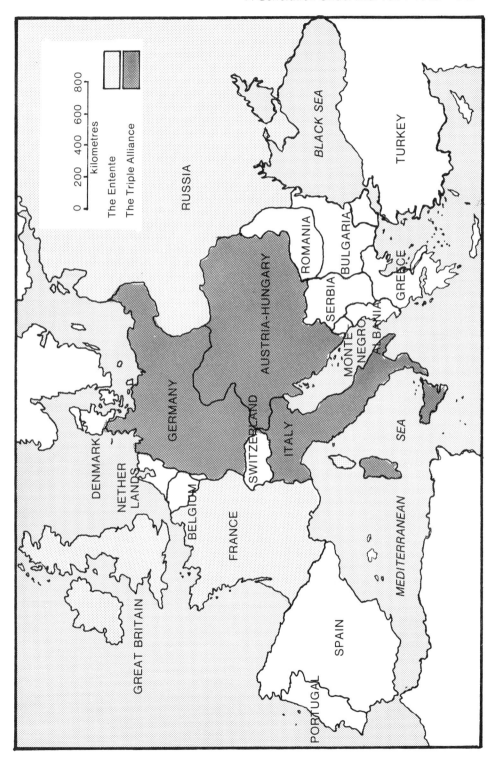

Austria-Hungary. Other groups within the Austro-Hungarian Empire began to demand their freedom as well. They were encouraged in this by Austria-Hungary's enemy, Russia. Because of all these rivalries, the area became known as the "powderkeg" of Europe.

On the fateful day of June 28, 1914, the heir to the Austrian throne, the Archduke Franz Ferdinand, was shot and killed by a young Serbian terrorist at a town called Sarajevo. Austria believed that the Serbian government was behind the assassination. They made a number of harsh demands. Meeting the demands would have meant the surrender of Serbia. Russia came to Serbia's aid. But Austria refused to back down from her demands. The "powderkeg" exploded. War was now inevitable.

When war was declared there were celebrations in all the European capitals. Experts believed the war would be a short one. "Home by Christmas" was the cry of the first volunteers. For most, it would be Christmas, 1918.

The First Blow

Germany came to Austria's aid in this crisis. She had the most powerful army in Europe. However Germany saw herself surrounded. Russia was on one side and France on the other. Across the Channel lay England. Germany felt that her best hope was in landing the first blow.

Russia's army was large, but scattered throughout the huge Empire. It

Canadian soldiers in a trench

would take weeks or months before this army could be ready to fight on Germany's borders. Germany's main concern was the French army. To meet this problem the German generals adopted a plan of attack devised years earlier, the Schlieffen plan.

The Schlieffen Plan was simple but quite effective. It solved the main problem facing Germany in the war: how to defeat the French armies quickly, then return and face the Russian threat.

The shortest path was directly across the German-French border. However this area is very hilly and wooded, making transportation very slow. At the same time, the bulk of the French army naturally waited in this area.

To the north-west, through Belgium, the land was ideal for warfare. It was flat, well-suited for quick transportation, and lightly defended by the French. The Schlieffen Plan was designed to send the bulk of the German army through Belgium. It would then swing west of Paris, and surround the French armies on the border. For the plan to succeed, it depended on speed and timing.

Unfortunately for Germany, the Commander-in-Chief, Von Moltke, made the right wing weaker than the plan called for. At the same time, the German invasion of Belgium quickly brought the British army into action. With the lights of Paris in sight, the German attack slowed down and stopped. The only chance for a short, quick war had vanished. Each side now dug in for a long conflict. From the mountains in the east to the English Channel on the west the two sides faced each other from trenches across a narrow gap called "No Man's Land."

Trench Warfare

The two warring sides prepared for a long conflict. The base of operations became the trench. As the war progressed, trench construction developed into a fine art. For the next four years, soldiers of both armies would eat, sleep and fight in such trenches.

In cold, wet weather, the trenches became slimy, waterlogged mudpits. The water often rose to waist level. The trenches became infested with flies, rats and other disease-carrying parasites. The stench of decaying corpses and garbage often became unbearable. Often soldiers had to endure weeks or even months without washing. In such conditions even small wounds became dangerous and subject to infection and gangrene.

> The familiar trench smell of 1915-1917 still haunts my nostrils; compounded of stagnant mud, latrine buckets, chloride of lime, unburied or half-buried corpses, rotting sandbags, stale human sweat and fumes ...

Clothing usually crawled with lice, the food was monotonous — bread and corned beef. Frosty weather, though uncomfortable, helped by freezing the mud. Even so, the frozen clods thrown up by shells could be as dangerous as shrapnel.

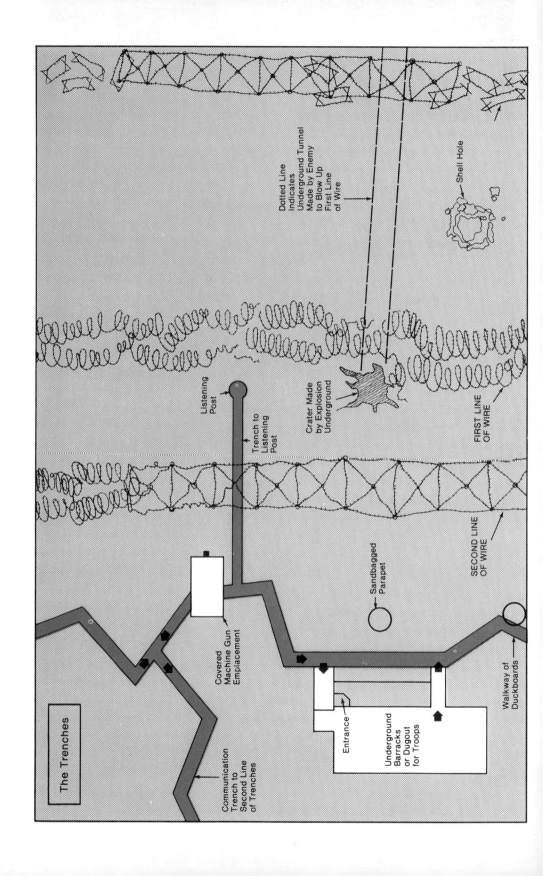

The Trenches

Communication Trench to Second Line of Trenches

Covered Machine Gun Emplacement

Listening Post

Trench to Listening Post

Dotted Line Indicates Underground Tunnel Made by Enemy to Blow Up First Line of Wire

Shell Hole

Crater Made by Explosion Underground

FIRST LINE OF WIRE

Sandbagged Parapet

SECOND LINE OF WIRE

Entrance

Underground Barracks or Dugout for Troops

Walkway of Duckboards

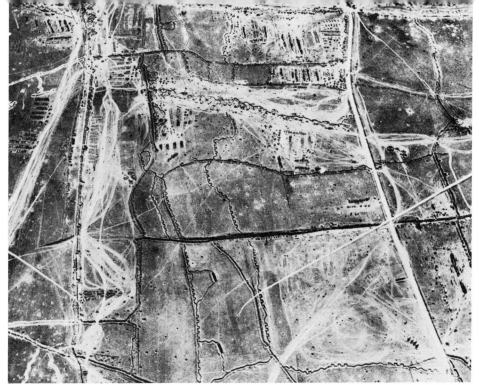

The trench lines at Vimy Ridge in 1917. What details can you observe about trench construction? Can you suggest reasons for this method of construction?

Often the opposing trenches were only 25-100 m apart. The voices and movements of the enemy were clearly heard. Night attacks were common, but at such close range the weapons might consist of clubs or knives. Dawn was the usual time for major attacks and "going over the top." Some soldiers prepared themselves for this ordeal by convincing themselves they would soon be killed. One soldier repeated to himself, "In twenty minutes I'll be dead; in fifteen minutes I'll be dead . . ."

Attackers were cut down by the deadly hail of machine-gun fire, explosive shells and shrapnel. Some would be entagled in barbed wire. Only a few might reach the enemy trenches. If the attack failed, those badly wounded might be left lying for days in "no man's land," dying slowly.

Many soldiers who were subject to these conditions became "shell-shock" victims. Physically they were unharmed, but they suffered nervous breakdowns and were no longer fit for fighting.

The War at Sea

As the war began Britain was still considered the greatest naval power in the world. The German navy, however, had made great strides in the decade before the war. Their ships were large and efficient. Unlike most British ships, they were made entirely of steel. Control of the seas was vital for Britain. Food and armaments arrived by ship. At the same time a strong British navy could *blockade* Germany.

Both sides knew the importance of sea power. They could not risk the destruction of their entire navy in open sea battles. Each side used caution in sending its ships out for action. In fact, there was only one major sea battle in the entire war. The rival fleets met near Jutland on the Danish coast on May 31, 1916. In the battle itself both sides fought fiercely and skillfully. The German navy did more damage than it suffered. However it retreated to port after the battle. Although both sides could claim victory, the German navy never again came out of port.

The Germans answered the British blockade with submarine warfare. This would be the single greatest threat to British shipping. By July, 1915, some two hundred British merchant ships had been sunk by submarines. By 1916 they were sinking 160 ships a month. Germany declared all waters around Britain a war zone. Even neutral ships were in danger. In 1915 the passenger ship *Lusitania* was torpedoed off the coast of Ireland. Over 1200 people died, including 124 Americans. Public opinion was outraged in the United States. It was a factor in bringing the Americans into the war in 1917.

The British blockade of Germany worked well. By 1918 there was a desperate shortage of food in Germany and Austria. Many civilians died of malnutrition as a direct result of lack of vegetables, meat, milk, butter and other essentials.

War in the Air

At the start of the war airplanes were used mostly for **reconnaissance.** The pilots would look for and report signs of troop movement from the other side. Opposing pilots were in fact quite friendly and even waved at each other. This attitude soon stopped. Pilots began to bring up pistols and rifles and shoot at each other. When they mounted machine guns, the first fighters were born.

The German air force had several advantages at first. They had more airplanes than Britain and France combined. They also developed more complex weapons. One danger of firing a machine gun was that you might knock out your own propeller. The German Fokker airplane had a machine gun timed so that the bullets would not hit the propeller blades.

The common strategy in air battles was the "dogfight" in which squadrons of planes would attack each other. The objective in these "dogfights" was to attack the enemy from behind or come at him directly from the sun where he would be blinded. There were no parachutes to save the unfortunate who were hit or had run out of ammunition.

Great aces such as Manfred Von Richthofen of Germany and Billy Bishop of Canada were a special breed of men. On the ground they could be courteous and chivalrous, while in the air ruthlessly efficient. They were also prepared to face death. A French pilot, Charles Nungesser, suffered seventeen wounds which left him with one bad leg, an artificial jaw and gold teeth. He had to be lifted into his plane and flew it with only one leg.

Pilots did not suffer the mud of the trenches. They had good food and clean beds, but they also had the highest death rate of any of the services. The average life span of a flier in 1916 was only three weeks.

The Top Aces

British	French	German
Edward Mannock (73)*	Rene Fonck (75)	Manfred von Richthofen (80)
Billy Bishop (Canadian) (72)	Georges Guynemer (54)	Ernst Udet (62)

*refers to number of hits

Of this list, Bishop, Fonck and Udet survived the war.

Air aces were the "knights of the air" and the first heroes of war. They were instantly recognized everywhere and always received special treatment.

Many Canadians excelled as pilots. By the end of the war almost one-third of the British air force were Canadians. Besides Bishop, other Canadians who gained fame as fliers included Raymond Collishaw, William Barker, and Roy Brown, who, it is generally agreed, shot down Germany's "Red Baron", Manfred von Richthofen.

Billy Bishop in 1917

Canadians At War

When Great Britain declared war on Germany on August 4, 1914, Canada as a member of the Empire, was automatically at war. Above and beyond this duty Canadians, both French and English, rushed to Britain's support.

> Canada is in it to the end. She will not stop until "Rule Britannia" and "The Maple Leaf" sound on the streets of Berlin. One contingent has gone, another is in the course of preparation; and they will all go gladly with the same spirit of patriotic determination. It is Britain's war and it is Canada's war.
>
> *Premier Hearst of Ontario, 1914*

> There are no longer French Canadians and English Canadians. Only one race now exists, united by the closest bonds in a common cause.
>
> *La Patrie, 1914*

Major Jack's painting of Canadian forces in action

At the beginning of the war, Canada's army consisted of only 3000 men. By October over 33 000 volunteers were training near Quebec City. Over the next four years, out of a small population of eight million, Canadians enlisted in the following numbers:

1914 — 59 144
1915 — 158 859
1916 — 176 919
1917 — 63 611

By war's end over 600 000 Canadians had served in the armed forces, of whom 425 000 went overseas.

In spring 1915, the first Canadian troops, the Princess Patricia's Light Infantry Regiment entered the war. Within weeks they suffered the first gas attack of the war at Ypres.

Gas was one of the deadliest weapons introduced in the war. There were two basic types, chlorine and mustard. Chlorine gas killed by suffocation. Mustard gas, which was invisible, was more terrible. This gas caused severe burns on the skin and respiratory tract. It also caused blindness.

Of all the troops at Ypres only the Canadians stood their ground. Ypres was the first of the battles in which Canadians would win great fame as soldiers.

> Suddenly we saw the gas rolling up in a brownish-yellow bank. It was between four and 12 feet high and it wouldn't rise higher unless it was pulled up by the wind.
>
> We saw the French-Africans running away choked with gas, not as a body, but as individuals. We paid no attention to them. We were sorry for them.
>
> I went over to where the line had been broken and where there was confusion. No Canadian troops were running.
>
> The gas was dreadful and suffering was immediate. The only thing we could do was soak our handerchiefs in urine and hold them over our noses.
>
> Thousands were lying around gasping and crying. They were being drowned by the gas. They didn't know how to protect themselves.
>
> But we held our position.

The Battle of the Somme

In 1916, the three Canadian divisions in Europe were organized as the Canadian Corps. They still fought under the British Command, with General Sir Julian Byng at their head.

Soon after they participated in one of the most tragic battles of the war, the Battle of the Somme. Under General Douglas Haig, British and French troops launched an attack near the River Somme. For days British guns pounded the German positions. Haig was certain nothing could survive the shelling, and that advance would be simple. However the Germans had known of the attack for a long time and had dug in. As the British attacked they were met with devastating fire. They fell by the thousands. Some were killed in their own

A tank in No Man's Land. What problems might men and machinery encounter when trying to cross this area? What would be the long-term effects of this war on the soil?

trenches, some in no man's land, some at the enemy wire. Only a few reached the enemy lines, where they were driven back or killed.

The Newfoundland Regiment fighting with the British was destroyed in less than half an hour. Each year on Commemoration Day, July 1, Newfoundland families still mourn their losses from this battle.

By the end of the first day alone, 60 000 British troops had fallen. It was the worst disaster in the history of British warfare. It was only the beginning. Haig refused to give up his plan and continued to pour the troops head-on against the German lines. The slaughter continued without any real gain by either side. When the attack was finally called off five months later, the toll proved frightful. The list of casualties stood at over one million: 420 000 British, 200 000 French and 450 000 Germans. Of the British total 55 000 were Canadians.

Vimy Ridge

Canadians continued to fight well in other major encounters in the war. Their crowning glory came on Easter Monday, 1917 at Vimy Ridge. Vimy Ridge was a point of high ground held by the Germans. It commanded the whole countryside around it. It would be impossible to break through the German line in this area without first capturing the ridge. Countless allied attacks on it

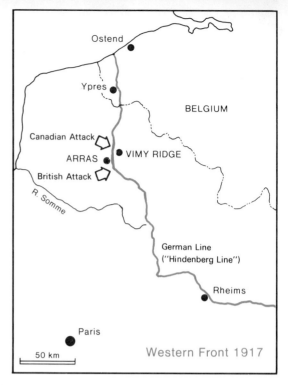

Western Front 1917

had failed. The Germans had fortified the Ridge with trenches, "pillboxes", dugouts, and heavy guns.

The task of taking the ridge was given to the Canadians. With sleet driving at their backs, four Canadian divisions charged Vimy Ridge on April 9:

> It was a cold grey morning but the visibility was good and I could see far over the waste of desolation which was our battlefield. Shells were still falling up front, but the rear areas seemed deserted, save for some batches of prisoners hastening to the cages, and some walking wounded.
>
> But at zero hour all this was changed. The barren earth erupted humanity. From dugouts, shell holes and trenches men sprang into action, fell into artillery formations, and advanced to the ridge — every division of the Corps moved forward together. It was Canada from the Atlantic to the Pacific on parade. I thought then, and I think today, that in those few minutes I witnessed the birth of a nation.
>
> Brigadier General Alex Ross

By noon Canadian soldiers under the command of a Canadian, Major-General Arthur Currie, had taken Vimy Ridge.

1917 proved to be a fateful year and the turning point in the war. A Communist revolution in Russia was successful, and Russia pulled out of the war. This might have been disastrous for the Allies; however in the same year the United States entered the war. The injection of fresh American troops into the conflict proved to be decisive.

In the last stages of the war Canada continued to play a major role in the fighting. In the last "hundred days" Canadian troops were often found to be spearheading assaults on German positions. When the Germans saw the Canadians coming, they prepared for the worst.

Canadian forces attacking Vimy Ridge

The War Ends

At last on November 11, 1918, at 11:00 the Armistice ending the war was signed and the slaughter came to an end.

> I've always thought that the Canadian nation was, in fact, born on the battlefields of Europe. I'm sure that that's true, that the fierce pride developed in the Canadians in their own identity, in their own nationhood, was a very real thing, and it survived over into the peace. Whenever they give the Canadians a chance to show their identity or to be proud of their identity, they are, and they always rise to the occasion.

The cost was high. Sixty-three thousand Canadians had lost their lives. Another 175 000 were wounded. Each country involved in the war suffered great losses. In money terms alone, the war cost the staggering sum of ten million dollars *per hour*. The manpower losses were of course more serious.

The Dead

ALLIES		CENTRAL POWERS	
France	1 600 000	Germany	2 600 000
British Empire	1 100 000	Austria	1 700 000
Russia	3 600 000	Turkey	600 000
Italy	700 000		
U.S.	120 000		
Serbia	1 100 000		
		TOTAL DEAD:	13 220 000

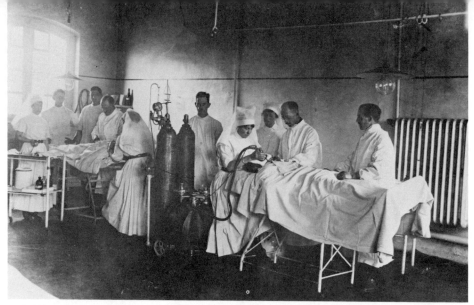

A field hospital behind the lines. Doctors and nurses often worked around the clock on the casualties of war.

An additional 20 million were seriously wounded. The dead and wounded were young men and women in the prime of life. They became known as the "lost generation." Their energies would be badly missed in the future.

Canada on the Home Front

On the home front, Canada's contribution was as important as on the battlefield. Canadian industries immediately switched over to war production. Starting from almost nothing, Canada's factories were producing one-third of the shells fired by the British army in 1917. Factories producing airplane parts and high explosives were built in almost a hundred different Canadian centres. Maritime dockyards built merchant ships. These replaced the ships lost to submarine attacks. Throughout the war Canada supplied most of the food consumed by Great Britain and the British armies.

The huge cost of this effort was estimated at $400 for every person in Canada. It was paid for in two ways. Much of it was raised through the purchase of **government bonds.** This still left Canada facing a huge debt. The government turned to **taxation** to meet the problem. The first tax was the *Business Profits War Tax*. This was a tax placed on profits made by manufacturers on war contracts. A second tax was in the form of a *Sales Tax* on consumer goods. The third and most important step was the *Income War Tax Act* of 1917. This placed, for the first time in Canada, a tax on income. Canadians have been paying income tax ever since.

The issue of compulsory military service **(conscription)** in 1917 (see Unit 4, chapter 3) created a serious political and social crisis. The issue sharply divided English and French in Canada. It left bitter memories long after the war had ended.

The Role of Women

As the men went off to fight overseas, the jobs they had left in the factories were more and more being taken over by women. By 1918 over 30 000 women were employed in key jobs producing supplies for the war effort. The important role played by women in this war effort forced society to change its attitude toward them.

For years women had been demanding political rights. Now as a result of the war, men for the first time were willing to listen. In 1918 Parliament passed a bill which gave women in Canada the right to vote in federal elections.

The Effects of the War on Canada

World War I has been termed Canada's greatest crisis. In four short years on the home front and on the fields of France, Canada matured quickly as a nation. The way of life for most Canadians had changed drastically. Those who had lived and fought overseas had caught glimpses of a different kind of life. They had caught a new feeling of what it meant to be "Canadian." There would be no return to those leisurely days at the turn of the century.

As the Treaty of Versailles was bringing to an end the disastrous war, Canadian soldiers began to return home. Sixty thousand would never again see their country. Many thousands more returned as invalids. Those who did return believed they had fought to make the world "safe for democracy." They

Women building airplanes

hoped that World War I was "the war that would end all wars."

In truth, when the fighting stopped there was less chance of permanent peace and democracy in the world than before the slaughter had begun.

The returning soldiers thought they would receive a hero's welcome. Many would be disappointed. After the first celebrations, it was back to normal. Many soldiers found it difficult after their wartime experiences to adjust to civilian life. Others who had expected to find their old jobs waiting for them were also disappointed. The Canada they had left in 1914 was greatly changed. The war had unleashed new forces in politics, in economics and in society. A new generation would have to cope with these changes in the 1920s.

2.   THE ROARING TWENTIES

The usual image of the 1920s is one of high spirits, fun and good times. Terms usually associated with this period are "the Roaring Twenties," "the Aspirin Age" and "the Era of Wonderful Nonsense." Much of this image comes from movies, novels and music. Is this a true impression of the age? Let us look at the main features of this period.

A family swimming and picnic outing in Prince Edward Island

Political Life

In 1919 Sir Wilfrid Laurier died, and his Conservative rival Sir Robert Borden retired. Arthur Meighen, a brilliant but cold man, was chosen to succeed Borden as Conservative leader. The Liberals chose William Lyon Mackenzie King, a grandson of the man who led the Rebellion of 1837.

At the same time, many people were becoming dissatisfied with the two major parties. Small local parties representing labourers and farmers appeared in different parts of the country. One of these, the National Progressive Party enjoyed great success in the federal elections in 1921. With sixty-five seats they held the balance of power between the Liberals and Conservatives. For the next few years they carried great influence, especially in the west. With the return of prosperity, however, voters returned to the old parties and the Progressive movement broke up.

RESULTS OF ELECTIONS IN 1920s			
	1921	1925	1926
Liberals	117	101	116
Conservatives	50	116	91
Progressives	64	24	13
others	4	4	25

William Lyon Mackenzie King

William Lyon Mackenzie King was a short, stocky, plain-looking man. Before his career ended he would prove to be one of the most important Prime Ministers in Canada's history.

From 1921 to 1930 and 1935 to 1948 Mackenzie King was Canada's Prime Minister. His political style was one of extreme caution. He tended to avoid controversy and put off difficult decisions as long as possible. In this way he hoped to win support from all sides.

King was first elected Prime Minister in 1921. At forty-seven, he was one of Canada's youngest Prime Ministers. By the time of his death in 1950 he was famous around the world as the man who had been Prime Minister longer (22 years) than any other person in the history of English-speaking peoples.

Despite his world fame, Mackenzie King led a very private life. He never married, and although he had many women friends, he seems to have had few romantic interests. King was also a **mystic.** He felt he was being "guided from above" and often attended seances. He believed he received advice from his mother's ghost. It may be unsettling to many Canadians to realize that some of King's important decisions, especially during World War II were made after consulting the "spirits."

Mackenzie King

The Economic Boom

Just before the end of the 1920s experts were announcing that the economy had reached "a permanent plateau of prosperity". The President of the U.S., Herbert Hoover, predicted that "we shall soon with the help of God be in sight of the day when poverty will be banished from this nation". This tide of optimism swept into Canada as well. Was this optimism realistic or were Canadians living in a dream world?

Consider these developments. World War I had created thousands of new jobs and caused industry to expand. Once the war ended, businesses began to convert to peacetime production. Factories which had been building guns, bombs, tanks and airplanes returned to making stoves, sewing machines and automobiles. During the war, while the men were fighting in Europe, many of the factory jobs had been taken by women. Employers soon found that women could handle many factory jobs as well as men. They also found they could appeal to the women's patriotic spirit, and so pay them lower wages.

When the war ended, these conditions continued and many soldiers returned home to find no jobs awaiting them. A minor depression resulted in 1920. As unemployment increased, wages and prices fell sharply. Strikes broke out in many parts of the country.

One such strike took place in Winnipeg and affected workers in almost every trade. It was brought to an end only after a riot had occurred and the Mounties were called into action.

By 1922 the slump was over and consumers were scrambling to buy new products. The result was an upward **spiral** in the economy. Actually upward and downward spirals are quite common in our system of **free enterprise.** Economists tell us that if we were to chart our economy over a long period of time it would not look at all like a straight line. It would look instead like a wave with peaks (economic growth) and valleys (recessions):

This is quite normal. The problem is to prevent a recession from becoming a full-scale depression. We will learn later in this chapter just how such a depression developed.

How does such a spiral begin? If we witness the early 1920s we can see that there was a great demand for consumer goods. To meet this demand there was increased production, and therefore greater sales and more jobs. A byproduct of this is greater profit for the owner and more money in the hands of the workers. With this money, the workers will continue to buy **consumer goods.** Thus a spiral is created:

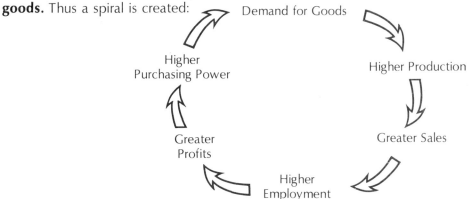

A measure of the economic boom of the 1920s can be seen in the growth of Canadian industry.

	PRE-WAR (1911)	1928
population	7.2 million	9.7 million
wheat exports	$45.5 million	$352.1 million
mineral production	$103.2 million	$285 million
manufacturing	$1 165.9 million	$3 769.8 million
automobiles registered	22 000	1 100 000

Canadian wheat, minerals and pulp and paper reached record sales all over the world. By 1930 Canada stood fifth in the world in the value of her exports.

The Radio and Airplane

The automobile, the radio and the airplane became the great symbols of the 1920s.

The Model "T" assembly line

Radio: The radio brought to Canada the age of instant news and instant entertainment. The first radio station in North America was KDKA in Pittsburgh. Within a short time, however, radio stations had spread all over Canada. One of Canada's great traditions, "Hockey Night in Canada", was first broadcast in 1923. Soon Foster Hewitt's familiar "he shoots, he scores" became part of Canadian culture.

By the end of the decade, there were 79 radio stations piping information and entertainment to 300 000 Canadian homes. The most popular entertainers of the period were singers such as Bing Crosby and Rudy Vallee, and comedians such as Amos 'n' Andy. Jazz, the music of the '20s, was broadcast. Nonsense songs such as "Yes, We Have No Bananas" also became favourites.

The Airplane: The 1920s can also be called The Golden Age of Flight for Canada. It was in the air that young Canadians proved that they were the equals of anyone in the world. Canada had developed great flying heroes both before and during World War I. Names like J.A.D. McCurdy, Billy Bishop and Roy Brown were known around the world for their exploits.

In the 1920s, it was Canada's daring bush pilots who carried on Canada's great flying tradition. Led by the exploits of Wilfred "Wop" May, "Punch" Dickins and "Doc" Oaks, the bush pilots were truly responsible for opening up the Canadian North. By 1929, over 250 bush planes were actively bringing people, food, medical supplies and mail to the distant Arctic outposts under extremely difficult conditions. Without such daring men the treasures of the North would have remained locked in.

More Achievements of the '20s

The decade was also a period of achievements in other fields. In 1919 women were at last granted the right to vote. This overdue action was largely a result

HOUSEHOLD DUTIES

REFRIGERATORS

SAVE FOOD!

CONSERVE ICE!

63-677

45⁰⁰

Made to Fill the Need For a Large-Capacity Refrigerator

63-677 Ice is nature's refrigerant, but if it is to keep food pure and fresh it must have the help of an efficient refrigerator. One that conserves ice as well as protects food from contamination enables you to effect a double saving and gives you the best return for your money. Made to our own specifications and built on the best scientific principles with carefully insulated walls, this large-size Refrigerator is most suitable where large quantities of provisions must be kept fresh. The refrigeration system is of the direct air-cooling type, and the large galvanized iron-lined ice chamber holds about 200 lbs. of ice. Flues are removable. There is ample room for storage in the large provision chamber, which measures 22½ ins. high, 15 ins. deep and 30¾ ins. wide; fitted with two full-depth removable shelves and one half-depth shelf. The cabinet is well made from clear Northern Ash, paneled construction, and is the single-door, front-icing design that does not necessitate high lifting. Finished in Golden color. Hardware is nickel-plated. Selected easy-rolling casters. Refrigerator only, price **45.00**

A refrigerator ad from Eaton's catalogue, 1928. Where would the idea for this refrigerator be obtained? How would this refrigerator work?

of their role in the war effort, and their new role in the work force. Between 1921 and 1930, the number of women employed outside the home rose by forty per cent.

Canadian artists also began to paint the Canadian scene in a new style. Painters Frederick Varley and A.Y. Jackson, along with Arthur Lismer, Lawren Harris, Frank Carmichael, J.E.H. Macdonald and Franz Johnston, made the "Group of Seven" famous throughout the world.

At the same time Canadians were making their mark in the world of science. In 1922 Dr. Frederick Banting conquered the deadly disease of diabetes with his discovery of insulin. This achievement brought Banting a Nobel Prize.

The Stock Market

Another symbol of economic boom is the stock market. Most people are confused by the **stock market.** Have you ever looked at a stock market page? Do you understand the figures, or are you confused like most Canadians?

Actually the principle of the stock market is quite simple. It is a place where shares in private companies are bought and sold. The buying and selling is done by **stockbrokers** who act as agents for private individuals.

Basically, the stock market works in this way: Let us suppose that you, John E. Canuck, had invented a better mousetrap. You set yourself up in business as Canuck Consolidated Mousetrap Ltd. Soon the world is beating a path to your door. Business is booming and you want to expand, but you lack cash. One way to get it is to sell a portion of your company to others. If your company was worth $200 000, you might wish to keep half the company for yourself and sell shares in the other half. The total value of the shares would be worth half the value of your company, or $100 000.

PRICE PER SHARE	TOTAL NUMBER OF SHARES	TOTAL VALUE
$10	10 000	$100 000

So now you have placed these 10 000 shares of Canuck Consolidated Mousetrap for sale in the stock market. A stockbroker will sell them on your behalf (for a fee, of course.) Once the shares are on the market their price may rise or fall. This depends on the *demand* for the shares. If your company is doing well and selling a great number of mousetraps it is likely that many people will want to buy the shares in your company. This demand will push up the price of each share, and result in a profit for the seller. Of course, if sales are poor and the demand is not great, the price may drop. The seller will then lose money.

In the 1920s, stock prices seemed to be constantly rising. Many people saw the prospects of quick wealth, and invested their life savings in the market. Indeed, many fortunes were made in just this way.

3.   THE DIRTY "'30s"

In the summer of 1929 Canadians in all walks of life were looking forward to more happy times, higher wages, good crops and job security. They were prospering. The nation was prospering. Yet within one year this scene had drastically changed. Canada found itself in the grip of a deadly economic depression.

The stock market crash of October 1929 signalled the end of the boom years. It marked the beginning of what would be known in Canada and around the world as "the hungry thirties".

What had happened to cause such a turnabout? Even the experts are not entirely certain to this day. The causes of the depression are very complex. However, we can identify several of them.

The Export Market

Both Canada and the United States are industrialized nations. We rely a great deal on exports to other countries for our wealth. During the 1920s the countries of Europe were buying our products at record levels. As a result, businesses continued to grow and produce more goods.

Unfortunately the export markets soon closed. Europe was still recovering from the effects of the war during the 1920s. It relied on American loans for progress. By 1929 the U.S. had cut off many of these loans. Europe found itself without any buying power.

The effects soon became obvious throughout North America. The economic spiral of the 1920s was now reversed:

Trade dropped to a fraction of what it had been. Factories found themselves with warehouses full of goods they could not sell. Most cut back production or closed for good, and workers found themselves out of a job. The same effects were felt in the lumber and fishing industries.

The Wheat Market:

The worst suffering was felt in the west with the collapse of the wheat market. Even during the boom years of the 1920s the western farmers had not shared in Canada's general prosperity. Despite record wheat sales, competition from foreign producers had kept the price of wheat down.

WHEAT PRICES (ANNUAL AVERAGES)

1925	1929	1930	1931	1932	1933	1936
$1.43	1.03	0.67	0.40	0.38	0.75	1.02

Profits for farmers were still low.

The depression brought tragedy. Competition from the U.S., the Soviet Union, Australia and Argentina continued to be stiff. At the same time Europe no longer had the money to buy our wheat. As a result, wheat prices fell from $1.60 per bushel in 1929 to 38 cents in 1932. The West faced ruin. The results were felt across the country.

The Stock Market

During the 1920s the symbol of prosperity was the stock market. With prices always rising, investing in the stock market seemed a guaranteed path to instant wealth.

Few people were taking into account the risks involved in gambling on stocks. Investors were so sure that stocks would always rise that they even invested money they did not have. They would buy stocks with a **down payment** as low as 20%. They then paid for the rest with a loan from their broker or from the bank. This was called **buying on margin.** These investors hoped to make a quick profit on the market, pay back their loan, and still have a tidy profit left over.

When the stock market began to fall in October 1929, panic set in. The stampede soon started. Everyone wanted to sell their stocks before prices dropped further. This panic selling left stockholders in ruin. It also ruined stockbrokers and banks who had loaned out money for the purchase of stocks.

Stock Prices

	1929		1932	
	HIGH	LOW	HIGH	LOW
American Telephone & Telegraph	310¼	193¼	137⅜	69¾
General Electric	403	168⅛	130⅝	42½
General Motors	91¾	33½	24⅝	7⅝
National Cash Register	148¾	59	18¾	6¼
Remington Rand	57¾	20⅜	7½	1
Sears, Roebuck	181	80	37⅜	9⅞
United States Steel	261¾	150	52⅝	21¼

Chart of Stock Market, 1920-1945

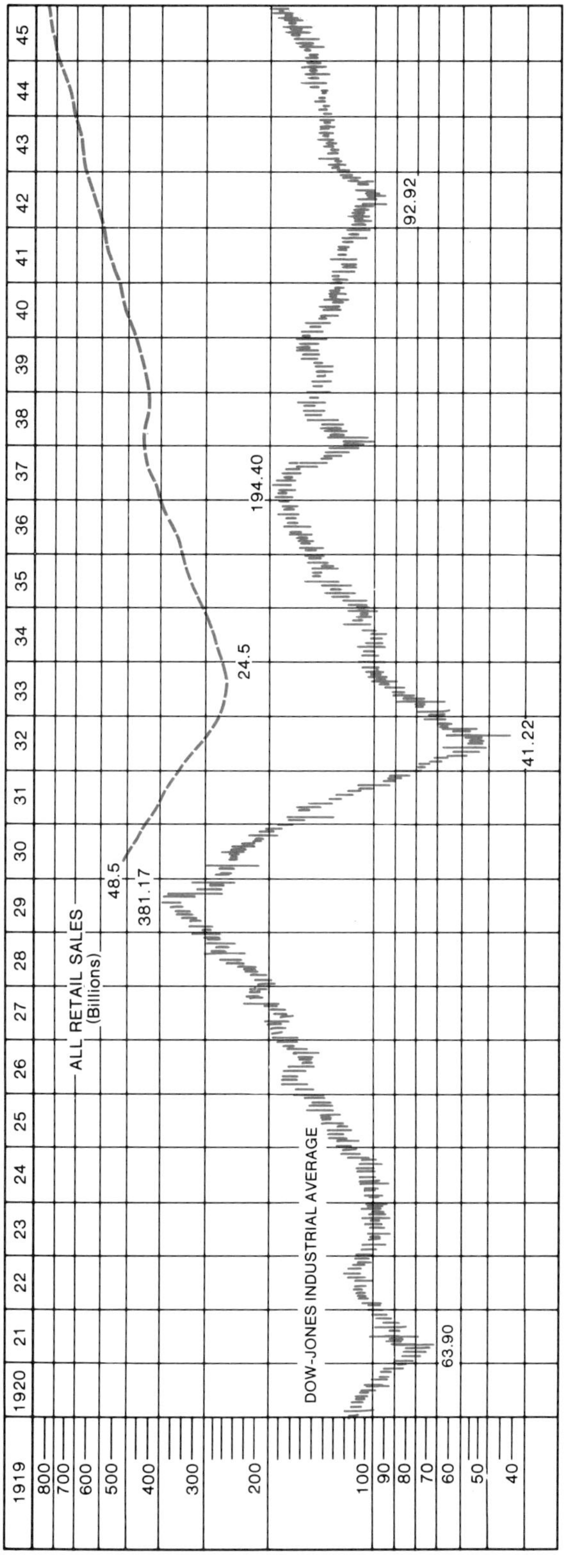

ALL RETAIL SALES
(Billions)

DOW-JONES INDUSTRIAL AVERAGE

48.5

381.17

24.5

194.40

41.22

92.92

63.90

1919 | 1920 | 21 | 22 | 23 | 24 | 25 | 26 | 27 | 28 | 29 | 30 | 31 | 32 | 33 | 34 | 35 | 36 | 37 | 38 | 39 | 40 | 41 | 42 | 43 | 44 | 45

800
700
600
500
400
300
200
100
90
80
70
60
50
40

Effects of the Depression

If the causes of the depression are hard to discover, the effects are very evident. They can best be seen in the following charts:

Per Capita Incomes, 1928-9 to 1933, by Province

	1928-29 average $ per capita	1933 $ per capita	Percentage decrease
Nova Scotia	322	207	36
New Brunswick	292	180	39
Prince Edward Island	278	154	45
Quebec	391	220	44
Ontario	549	310	44
Manitoba	466	240	49
Saskatchewan	478	135	72
Alberta	548	212	61
British Columbia	594	314	47
Canada	471	247	48

Unemployment Statistics (1929-1943)

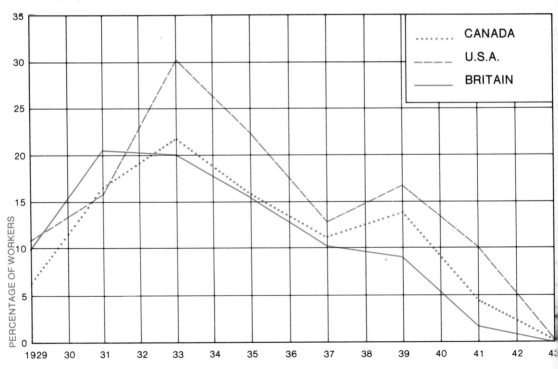

The statistics do not really show the human suffering during this period.

The depression affected everyone — rich, former rich, and poor. Of course, not everyone went broke. There were a lucky few who had timed things just right and sold their stocks or businesses before the crash. As prices shot downward, they were even better off than before the depression.

Most were not so fortunate. There were cases of former millionaires, ruined by the crash, who were forced to live by selling apples or pencils in the street. Others resorted to shining shoes, singing, dancing or begging for enough money to live on.

Many others were worse off still. They could get no jobs at all. At this time in Canada there was no such thing as unemployment insurance or welfare. Those without jobs had to look out for themselves. Thousands of jobless men took up the practice of "riding the rails." These men would jump on freight trains and travel back and forth across Canada looking for work — usually without success.

Many relied on relatives who were better off for charity. Others depended on charitable agencies for handouts of food, clothing and shelter. This was called "living on the pogey." Some became so desperate that they asked to be arrested and sent to jail where they received food and shelter.

In the west, the price of wheat fell so low that farmers burned their grain as fuel. It was cheaper than buying regular fuel. Farmers who could not afford gasoline hitched their cars to horses. These became known as "Bennett buggies." R.B. Bennett was Prime Minister during this period.

To make matters worse, the West suffered through one of its worst periods of drought in history. In 1931 and in the years from 1933 to 1937 droughts crippled the west. Strong prairie winds then stripped the parched topsoil, carried it high in the air and banked it against fences and houses. Many

One of the many farms abandoned on the prairies during the 1930s.

farmhouses were completely covered. Farms were left as sandy deserts. Thousands of farmers simply left the land.

Author James Gray lived through the Depression years and wrote of his experiences in *The Winter Years:*

> We received no cash in relief, and for the first year no clothing whatever was supplied. Relief vouchers covered food, fuel, and rent, and nothing else. But we needed other things — many other things like tobacco and cigarette papers, tooth paste, razor blades, lipstick, face powder, the odd bottle of aspirin, streetcar fare, a movie once a week, a pair of women's stockings once a month, a haircut once a month, and a permanent twice a year. Most people tried to find twenty-five cents a week, every week for a newspaper.
>
> Unexpected needs continually cropped up, like needles and thread, darning wool, a bit of cloth for fancy work, a pattern for remaking a dress, a half-dollar every other month for a cooperative half-keg of beer for a neighbourhood party . . .
>
> . . . morale was built by taking the children to the zoo to feed the bears, by taking a streetcar ride downtown to wander through Eaton's and The Bay, as women did by the hundreds just to get away from their rooms for an hour or two.

Fighting the Depression

When the Depression began, the Liberals under Mackenzie King were still in power. In the election of 1930 they were toppled from power by R.B. Bennett and his Conservatives. Bennett's plan to fight the Depression was to raise **protective tariffs.** He hoped to protect Canadian industry by discouraging foreign imports. He also hoped to use this weapon to force countries to lower their high tariffs. This way he would "blast his way into the markets of the world."

Unfortunately this program failed. Canadian industry continued its tailspin. Finally as the election of 1935 drew near, Bennett unveiled his "New Deal". This plan was modelled on that of President Franklin Roosevelt of the United States. Bennett's "New Deal" proposed to create new laws establishing

- an eight-hour work day
- minimum wages
- an unemployment insurance plan
- elimination of child labour
- control of prices

The voters were suspicious of Bennett and his program. They felt it was just a trick to win the election — after all, he had not solved Canada's economic problems during his first four years in office. In the election of 1935, the voters swept Bennett out of office and brought back Mackenzie King.

A family and their covered wagon on the move in 1933. More than 25% of the population of Canada's Wheat Belt left their homes during the hard times of the 1930s.

New Political Parties

The worsening economy naturally encouraged the growth of new political parties. These parties claimed to have bold new ideas to solve the Depression. Two main parties began during the Depression. These were the Social Credit and the C.C.F.

The Social Credit movement started in Alberta. Its leader was William Aberhart, a school principal and radio preacher. Aberhart claimed that the cause of the Depression was the lack of money circulating in the economy. He proposed to credit every citizen with $25 per month. Of course this idea was very popular in the cash-starved west. The Social Credit took power in Alberta in 1935. They have remained a powerful party in British Columbia and, to a lesser degree in Alberta, ever since.

The C.C.F. (Co-operative Commonwealth Federation) was formed in 1932. Its program was stated in the Regina Manifesto of 1932. It called for

- government ownership of banks, insurance companies, and other financial institutions
- government ownership of transportation, communication and power companies
- fair business practices
- fair wages
- unemployment insurance
- social insurance against sickness or accidents
- socialized medicine

This program was supported by farmers, workers and those who favoured socialism. Under J.S. Woodsworth, the C.C.F. became very popular in the West, particularly Saskatchewan. They have also become a force in national politics. In 1958 the party changed its name to the New Democratic Party.

Key Events Leading To an Independent Canadian Foreign Policy

1918   The Paris Peace Conference. Prime Minister Borden succeeded in having Canada and the other Dominions take part in the Conference on their own, and as members of the British Empire delegation. Each Dominion signed the peace treaty. Parliament approved the treaty separately.

1919   The League of Nations. Canada and the other Dominions joined the League of Nations as independent members.

1923   The Halibut Treaty. For the first time Canada signed an international treaty alone. Until then a British delegate attended negotiations and signed agreements on behalf of Britain. This treaty with the United States dealt with fishing in Canada's coastal waters.

1923   The Imperial Conference. Commonwealth members agreed that each member should have the right to negotiate its own international treaties. Prime Minister Mackenzie King insisted that the Dominions make their own decisions on both domestic and foreign issues.

1925   Locarno Agreements. Germany and France agreed not to use force to settle disagreements between them. Britain agreed to help either country against aggression by the other. The Dominions did not have to accept these terms unless they decided to on their own. None of the Dominions accepted these terms.

1926   The Balfour Declaration. In it the Commonwealth was described as "autonomous (free) communities within the British Empire, equal in status, in no way subordinate to (inferior to) one another in any aspect of their domestic or external affairs, though united by a common allegiance to the crown and freely associated as members of the British Commonwealth of nations."

1931   The Statute of Westminster. The Dominions were given the power to enact extra-territorial legislation. An act of 1865, which said that in any conflict with colonial law British law was supreme, was repealed. It also stated that no British law would extend to the Dominions.

Note: Britain still retained some authority over Canada after 1931. The Judicial Committee of the Privy Council remained a final court of appeal for some Canadian cases. Amendments to the Canadian Constitution (the B.N.A. Act) still require approval of the British parliament. However Britain kept these powers only because Canada could not agree on another way of dealing with these issues.

If you are one of the 75% of Canadians too young to remember 1932:
You could buy large eggs for 29¢ a dozen, a loaf of bread for 5¢, a package of cigarettes for 15¢ and a dozen oranges for 25¢.
If you needed a car, a new Dodge sedan cost $600 and tires for it were $6.00.
A gallon of gas to run your car went for 16¢.
A new dress cost $4.00, while women's shoes were a further $2.00 and a pair of silk stockings sold for 68¢.
A brand new six-room house with garage might go for $3000.00. A dining room suite cost $50.00 and a new washing machine an additional $50.00.
Of course there was the other side of the coin. A job as secretary would bring $20.00 a week. A school teacher could expect to earn $1200.00 a year, a bus driver $1400.00, a waitress $450.00 and a farm labourer $215.00.

After 1935, the economy improved very slowly. The onset of World War II in 1939 brought an end to the Depression. With the need for war materials factories returned to full production. Unemployment dropped. The wheat market recovered. The prosperity cycle once again began to turn. It has continued to this day.

4. WORLD WAR II

Since the end of World War I Canada had gradually won her independence from Britain. By 1939 Canada had full power over her foreign policy decisions. Prime Minister King was determined to use this power in Canada's behalf. He was determined not to rush Canada blindly into another war.

By the late 1930s it seemed as though a second major war within a generation was likely. Adolf Hitler and his **National Socialist (Nazi) Party** were busy rebuilding and rearming Germany. They were also taking territories lost at the end of World War I.

By 1938 Hitler had taken possession of the Rhineland in western Germany. He had also annexed Austria. Now he was threatening Czechoslovakia. British Prime Minister Neville Chamberlain flew to Munich to meet Hitler. He returned to England with a promise from Hitler that the Fuehrer had "no territorial ambitions" in Europe. Chamberlain described the agreement as "peace with honour, peace in our time."

This hope was shattered within months as Hitler annexed Czechoslovakia. The final blow to peace came on September 1, 1939. On that day German airplanes and tanks launched a crushing attack on Poland. England and France as Poland's allies had no choice but to declare war on Germany on September 3.

In 1914 when Britain had declared war, Canada had no choice. In 1939, she was free to make her own decision. There seemed little doubt what that decision would be. Yet, as a symbol of her independence, Canada waited a full week before declaring war on Germany.

> I have never doubted that when the fatal moment came, the free spirit of the Canadian people would assert itself in the preservation and defence of freedom as it did a quarter of a century ago.
>
> William Lyon Mackenzie King, September 1939

Canadians on the Battlefield

At the beginning of the war, Canada's army was ill-equipped to fight a major war. The army listed 4000 officers and men. The Royal Canadian Navy counted 1800 men and the largest force, the Royal Canadian Air Force 4500 men. Yet at the declaration of war, volunteers flocked to enlist. Over 58 000 volunteers were taken in during the first month alone. Many others, including veterans from World War I, were rejected. Indeed out of a population of eleven million, over 1 000 000 Canadians saw military service. This total included 21 624 women who served in the W.A.C. (Women's Army Corps).

Blitzkrieg

In Europe the fall of Poland marked the beginning of a period known as the "Phony War". England and France waited for the expected blow, but nothing happened. All winter the French troops waited behind their strong fortifications, the Maginot Line, but no shots were fired.

On April 9, 1940, the "Phony War" came to an end. Hitler quickly seized Norway and Denmark. On May 10 Winston Churchill became Prime Minister of England, promising his people nothing but "blood, toil, tears and sweat." On the same day, Germany invaded Holland, Belgium and France. The German attack was precise and efficient. It was known as a Blizkreig — or lightning attack. 400 000 Allied troops were quickly surrounded and trapped against the sea at Dunkirk. It seemed the end was in sight. Then the "miracle of Dunkirk" occurred. Between May 27 and June 4 almost 350 000 men were rescued from the beaches. Boats of all sizes and shapes manned by English civilians crossed the channel. This courageous act saved the British army. Even so, the army had lost much of its equipment. France now lay defenceless.

On June 10, Germany's ally Italy declared war on France. On June 22, France surrendered. Britain and her Dominions stood alone against Germany.

The Battle of Britain

Hitler next unleashed the *Luftwaffe,* his air force, against Britain. The Royal Air Force was greatly outnumbered. However, with the help of Canadian pilots, it did hold off the German attacks and inflict great damage. The invention of radar was largely responsible for this success. It warned the R.A.F. of coming

A Canadian sailor recovering after a period of sea duty, proudly displays his tattoo collection. (St. John's, Newfoundland-January, 1943)

attacks. The Germans were unaware of this secret. Churchill showered praise on the R.A.F. pilots by declaring "never in the field of human endeavour have so many owed so much to so few."

Hitler next ordered his bombers to attack the English cities. London, Coventry and Birmingham suffered great losses. However the German air force continued to suffer many losses. By September the massive attacks had come to an end. Only the occasional night bombing of cities continued.

The War Spreads

The war against Germany and Italy spread to North Africa. Here in early 1941 British troops finally proved victorious by defeating Italian troops in Egypt. Germany sent General Irwin Rommel to the rescue. Rommel defeated the British in a number of daring attacks. The Germans regained much lost territory.

War also came to Greece on October 28, 1940. Mussolini launched his attack expecting easy victory. Once again, however, Hitler had to rescue the Italian army. He sent some of his best troops to Greece. On April 27, 1941, the German army occupied Athens.

One of the major turning points in the war now took place. Hitler, feeling that he had nothing more to fear from Britain, turned to the East. His hatred for the Soviet Union was well-known despite the fact he had signed a treaty with that country in 1939. On June 22, 1941, Hitler launched a massive attack on the Soviet Union. He expected an easy victory. He told his generals, "We have only to kick in the door and the whole rotten structure of Communism will come crashing down."

It was Hitler's greatest mistake. Despite stunning victories at the beginning, the German troops soon became bogged down by the Russian winter and heroic resistance from the Russian people. Russia became a huge pit which swallowed some of Germany's finest armies.

At the same time, on the other side of the world, Germany's ally Japan launched a surprise attack on the American fleet at Pearl Harbour. The United States now was committed to war. The invasion of Russia and the attack on Pearl Harbour helped to turn the tide of war against Germany and her allies.

Canadians in Action

In December 1941 the Canadian Army saw its first real action. It took part in the defence of Hong Kong against Japanese attacks. The Canadian position was hopeless. Despite stubborn resistance, Hong Kong fell to the Japanese. Of the 2000 Canadians who took part in the defence, over 500 lost their lives.

Another inactive period for the army followed. In fact Canadian losses to this point were light. There were some casualties in the air battles over Europe. Some sailors lost their lives serving in the North Atlantic. As yet, however, there was no repeat of the heavy losses suffered in the trenches in World War I. All this would change in August 1942.

Canadian soldiers on the beaches at Dieppe

Since the defeat of France (summer 1940) the coastline of Europe had been heavily fortified by the Germans. The Allies were certainly not ready to try an invasion of Europe. However Britain was receiving pressure from her new ally, the Soviet Union. The Soviets wanted a new front opened in the West. They felt that this would reduce the huge German buildup in the Soviet Union. It would then increase chances for a Soviet victory.

The Dieppe raid was planned mainly as a gesture to the Soviet Union. An attack on the French coastline might also provide useful information for a later invasion. The Dieppe fortifications stood on a cliff overlooking a narrow beach below. The cliff was fortified with pill boxes, barbed wire and heavy guns. In the early dawn light of August 19, 1942, 6000 troops, the great majority of them Canadians, attempted to land on the beach. Immediately they came under fire from the waiting Germans. Many never made the beaches. Some penetrated inland, but were driven back. In the end, 900 Canadians lay dead, 500 wounded and another 2000 were captured. It would be the greatest Canadian disaster of the war.

The Home Front

Britain's desperate plight in 1940 made an all-out Canadian war effort vital. The War Measures Act of 1914 was still in effect. This gave the government the power to **censor** the news. It also gave the power to arrest, imprison and deport people. The government could take over any resources thought necessary for the war effort. Parliament was able to pass several acts which strictly controlled Canadian industry. The production of leather, wool, lumber, steel, aluminum and rubber were regulated. Oil, gasoline and food such as meat, sugar, butter, tea and coffee were rationed. They could be obtained by coupons.

As in World War I, Canadian industry rose to the challenge of supplying the Allies' war needs. Shells, rifles, tanks, airplanes, and other army vehicles were turned out in huge volumes. Agricultural production also increased greatly. By 1945 Canada's production had increased to three times its pre-war level. Both the allied war cause and Canadian industry benefitted.

This huge war production again created a large debt. Again the answer was to raise income and corporation taxes. High taxes were also placed on luxury items. The rest of the funds were raised through the sale of Victory Bonds.

The Conscription Crisis

Mackenzie King had campaigned in the election of 1940 on the promise that he would never introduce conscription. In 1917 this issue had bitterly divided Canada. King was determined to avoid such a clash in World War II.

By 1942, however, the Prime Minister was advised by the military that

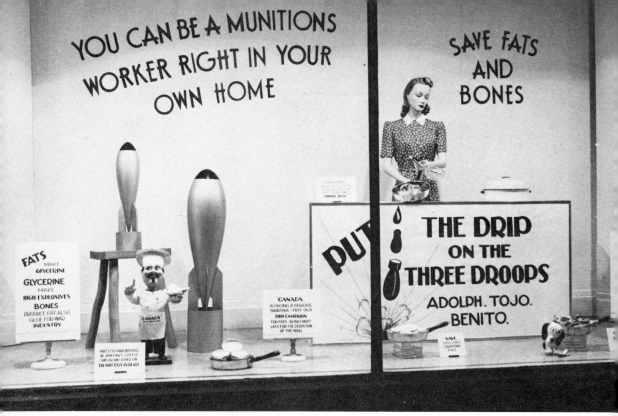

Read these window ads closely. What are they encouraging Canadians to do?

conscription might be necessary. King turned to public opinion. He issued a **plebiscite** which asked:

> Are you in favour of releasing the government from any obligations arising out of any past commitment restricting the methods of raising men for military service?

Across the whole country the vote was 64% in favour, 36% against. However in the Province of Quebec the results were 72% against and only 28% in favour. To soothe French-Canadian feelings, King described his policy as "conscription if necessary but not necessarily conscription". He also said that conscripts would be used for home defense. They would not be sent to fight overseas.

In 1944 a second conscription crisis occurred. By 1944 few men were volunteering for overseas service. Prime Minister King's hand was forced. He decided to send conscripts overseas. In all, 13 000 conscripts served overseas. Feelings in Quebec were very bitter. However, a respected French-Canadian Member of Parliament, Louis St. Laurent, helped to calm the situation. This time, violence was avoided.

The Treatment of Japanese-Canadians

World War II saw many acts of courage and good will on the part of Canadians. It also witnessed one of the most shameful acts in Canadian

Japanese camp, Slocan, B.C.

history. On December 7, 1941, Japan attacked American and British forces at Pearl Harbour (Hawaii) and in the Far East. Canada immediately declared war on Japan along with Britain and the U.S.

In June 1942, Japanese forces landed on the Aleutian Islands near Alaska. At the same time a Japanese submarine was spotted near Vancouver Island. A wave of anti-Japanese hysteria swept British Columbia. About 24 000 Japanese immigrants had settled in that province. Canadian citizens of Japanese origin, many of them Canadian-born, now were considered threats to national security.

The Japanese were removed from British Columbia. Many were placed in **internment camps** inland. Others were sent to various parts of Canada. Their properties were sold publicly for bargain prices, and they were forced to start a new life. The laws against the Japanese were finally lifted in 1947.

The Tide Changes

The year 1943 saw the changing tide of war favour the Allies. In North Africa British troops under Field Marshall Montgomery defeated Rommel's Afrika Korps. By this time American troops under Dwight Eisenhower had also landed in Africa.

In Russia too the Germans met disaster. After months of savage fighting, Russian troops trapped a huge German army of over one-quarter million men. At the end of the battle only 91 000 Germans survived to be taken prisoners. The retreat from the East had begun.

On July 10, 1943, Allied forces began their attack on Europe by landing in Sicily. The drive up the "boot" of Italy involved tough fighting. After long periods of inactivity the Canadian Army got its fill of battle.

At Ortona on the east coast of Italy Canadians fought a bitter month-long battle. In the mud of winter, the Germans put up a hard resistance. They had to be dislodged street by street and house by house. In this battle the French-Canadian unit, the Royal 22nd Regiment (the "Vandoos") greatly distinguished themselves. One correspondent wrote:

> After Ortona Canadians became the acknowledged experts on street fighting. For the rest of the war, officers who had fought there toured Allied military schools lecturing on street fighting. Ortona is a small piece of Canadian history.

For the rest of the war Canadians continued to play prominent roles wherever major battles were fought. They penetrated the last German defenses in Italy. They were also present at the huge Allied assault on Normandy — June 6, 1944, D-Day.

For the Normandy operation, the largest invasion force in the history of the world gathered. It consisted of 300 000 men, 4000 ships and 11 000 aircraft. On the dawn of June 6 this huge army landed on the beaches of Normandy and the invasion of Europe was on.

The Canadian army now under the command of General H.D. Crerar distinguished itself in many battles during the Normandy invasion — at Caen, Falaise and St. Lambert.

Canadian soldiers going through Ortona

By early 1945 the German retreat had begun. British and American troops had crossed into Germany from the west and were racing for Berlin. From the east millions of Soviet troops had cleared Eastern Europe of German occupation. They also drove on Berlin. The Soviet troops reached Berlin first, but by this time Hitler had already committed suicide. Russian and American troops met at the River Elbe, sixty miles west of Berlin. On May 7, 1945, General Dwight Eisenhower accepted the surrender of Germany.

On August 16 on the other side of the world Japan also surrendered, following the destruction of Hiroshima and Nagasaki by atomic bombs. World War II had come to an end.

As in the First War, the cost in manpower was horrendous. Great Britain and the United States suffered nearly half a million dead each. German losses were nearly three million. Canada's losses were nearly 45 000. The most staggering figures were those of the Soviet Union which reported over seven and one-half million dead. The spectre of the terrible new weapon, the atomic bomb remained in the minds of the survivors. The atomic age had dawned.

THINGS TO THINK ABOUT AND DO

Reviewing Key Words and Ideas

The following terms appeared in this chapter. Try to recall their meaning and how they were used.

alliances	income tax	plebescite
arms race	inflation	Red Flag Laws
buying on margin	Luftwaffe	recession
chlorine gas	Maginot Line	socialism
conscription	mysticism	stockbroker
D-Day	Nazi	stock market
government bonds	phony war	

Remembering the Facts

1. Which countries made up the Triple Alliance in 1914?
2. The passenger ship sunk by Germany in 1915 was
a) the Dreadnought   b) the Bismarck   c) the Lusitania   d) the Titanic
3. Women were granted the right to vote in Canada in the year
a) 1912   b) 1918   c) 1929   d) 1967
4. Outline some of the main features of Bennett's "New Deal".
5. What do the initials C.C.F. stand for?

Applying Your Knowledge

Compare the results of the conscription issue in World War I and II. In terms of the military, political and social results, was conscription necessary in each case?

2. Review your knowledge of the stock market. As a class project, every student might bring to school the stock market pages one day, and buy $1000 worth of stocks. Follow the ups and downs of your stocks for one week. At the end of that time determine which student has made the most money on the stock market.

3. There is much discussion today about whether a depression could happen again. Make a list showing which things are similar and which are different today as compared to 1929.

4. Do you agree with Canada's treatment of its Japanese-Canadian citizens during World War II? If not, what should Canada have done?

Analyzing Ideas

1. The construction of trenches and the presence of machine guns in World War I made massive attacks across No Man's Land practically suicidal. Yet, generals on both sides continued to do exactly that. If you had been in command of an army in World War I, what tactics and strategies would you have used to defeat the enemy?

2. William Lyon Mackenzie was Prime Minister longer than any other Commonwealth leader in history. Canadian voters were not aware of his private life and beliefs. Do you think they would have continued to vote for him if they had known about this aspect of his personality?

3. Summarize the key points of Bennett's New Deal in 1935. How many of his proposals have now become law in Canada?

4. In the following chapters you will be reading about Canada in the modern world. You will learn about the problems and decisions Canada faces today in national and international affairs. These areas deal with all aspects of a nation's life — political, social, economic and military. Many of Canada's current problems had their roots in the period we have just studied. Think back and try to make a list of the historical events in the period 1867-1945 which may have influenced the following areas:

— English-French relations
— Canada's foreign policy
— Canadian-American relations
— Canada's status as an independent nation

IV

English-French Relations

1

ONE NATION OR TWO?

INTRODUCTION

On November 15, 1976, the history of Canada changed, possibly forever. That was the date of an important election in the province of Quebec. This election was won by the Parti Québécois (Party of Quebeckers). Most Canadians were surprised at this result. This was because not even the Parti Québécois itself expected to do so well. Just a few months before, Prime Minister Pierre Trudeau had confidently stated in public: "Separatism is dead!"

Canadians also were very concerned about these election results. This was because the Parti Québécois believes in the *separation* of Quebec from the rest of Canada. For this reason, they are called **separatists.** They wish to make Quebec a separate, independent country. It would have its own flag, national anthem and armed forces.

Today, Canada has ten provinces, including Quebec. Try to think what Canada would be like *without* Quebec. Perhaps the best way to start is to imagine a map of the "new" Canada. What would it look like? What problems would be created by Quebec being a separate country and no longer part of Canada? Now think about other things, such as our economy and culture. How would the loss of Quebec affect our physical size? (and do you know by how much?) If Quebec separated, what would Canada lose besides land area? (Make your answer as full and clear as possible.) How would our "image" in the world be affected?

In the 1976 Quebec election, more than half of the voters actually voted *against* separatism. The winning Parti Québécois received only about 41 per cent of the votes. Thus, 50 per cent of the voters rejected separatism. Also, it seems that many of those who voted *for* the Parti Québécois did not want separatism. Rather, they were voting *against* the party in power. This was the Liberal party, which they felt had done a poor job of running the province. The voters wanted a change. They hoped that the Parti Québécois would provide a more honest and effective government.

Still, the election was important for several reasons. First, this was the best showing that the Parti Québécois had ever made. Second, in winning 41 per cent of the votes, they captured 69 of the 110 seats in the Quebec parliament. Therefore, they were now in power as the governing party. Third, the election showed how quickly the Parti Québécois had risen in popularity with the people.

This party had been formed only eight years before, in 1968. This was its third election battle. In each election (1970, 1973 and 1976), it had made large gains in the number of votes that it received. It had become clear that many French-Canadians were becoming very unhappy with Canada. It is very important that English-Canadians should know the reasons for this unhappiness. This is the only way they can hope to understand what is going on in Quebec today. Without such understanding, it might soon be too late to do anything about the problem.

In the next four chapters, we are going to look at the topic of English-French relations in Canada. The first chapter provides a brief review of these relations, from earliest times to Confederation (1867). The second chapter looks at key developments between 1867 and 1960. The third studies changes that took place in Quebec from around 1960 to 1975. The last chapter examines the growth of separatist feeling in Quebec and, to some extent, in other provinces.

Separatism is not unique to Canada

Canada is a *federal* state (review Unit I). This means that the country is divided into several regions. Each region has its own *local* government. As well, there is a *central* government, which handles matters affecting the whole country.

These regions of a federal state usually are called provinces or states. Sometimes, they are distinctive for some reason. They might have special economic interests. Some have unique geographic features. Sometimes they even have dialects, languages or cultures of their own. Such differences can cause a region to feel somewhat apart from the rest of the country. Such feeling can turn into a desire by a region to be completely separate, or independent.

Obviously, this situation exists in Canada. However, it is also found in many other countries. Some Scots want Scotland to be a separate country, not part of the United Kingdom. The Basque people are not completely happy about being part of Spain. Some people in Brittany do not want to be part of France. The accompanying story title appeared recently in a Canadian newspaper. It refers to a separatist problem in Belgium.

Belgian rivals nearer deal on separatism

Belgium is composed of two states. One is Flemish, the other Walloon. This distinction is based on differences of language and culture. To keep the country united, a **compromise** has been worked out. This includes separate government departments for each group in education, economics and culture. There are separate radio and television networks. Even in the armed forces, there are separate Flemish and Walloon units. Only the top command is unified. Its officers usually speak English as a compromise.

In Canada, some people feel that we might have to go as far as Belgium. This might keep Quebec in Confederation. However, it is not certain that most English-Canadians could accept such an arrangement. Also, such a plan might not meet all the needs of French-speaking Quebeckers.

An evening fireworks display illumined the Parliament Buildings in Ottawa on July 1, 1967 — in celebration of Canada's 100th birthday. (Compare with the cartoon on page 192.)

Unit Preview/Review Questions

As you study this unit, keep these questions in mind. You may want to return to them when you have finished the unit.

1. How long have the French been in North America?

2. Why have the French in Canada always been so concerned about the survival of their language and culture?

3. For most of our history, what seems to have been the most common feeling among English-speaking Canadians toward French-Canadians? Why has this been so?

4. Why did Quebec agree to join Confederation in 1867? Have French-Canadians received from Canada everything which they could reasonably expect?

5. What advantages or benefits does Quebec get from being part of Canada?

6. Why has separatist feeling in Quebec grown so rapidly in recent years?

7. What is our federal government (in Ottawa) doing about the challenge of separatism? Can you suggest *other* policies which could or should be tried?

8. René Lévesque and his followers dislike being called "separatists." Instead, some prefer "indépendentistes." Why should they stress the idea of independence (freedom) rather than separation? Which term are *you* inclined to use? Why?

9. There are almost 1 000 000 French-Canadians living outside Quebec (mostly in Ontario, New Brunswick and Manitoba). What would become of them if Quebec separated from Canada? The same could be asked of the 1 000 000 English-Canadians living in Quebec.

FRIDAY, JULY 1, 1977

A political cartoonist's view of Dominion Day celebrations — July 1, 1977. What comment is the cartoon making?

2

HISTORICAL BACKGROUND TO 1867

INTRODUCTION

" ... these French-speaking people ... have, since the British conquest, the bad habit of complaining all the time ... they ignore on what side their bread is buttered and ... bite the hand that feeds them."

"The English Canadian thinks himself instinctively superior to people of French descent."

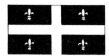

" ... French and English are equal in Canada because each of these linguistic groups has the power to break the country ... neither can force assimilation on the other. But one or the other, or even both, could lose by default, destroying itself from within, and dying of suffocation."

At the present time, the question of English-French relations is the most important issue facing Canada. There appears to be a great deal of bad feeling on both sides. Some English-Canadians regard the French as complainers who are trying to tear the country apart. They resent what they call "the forcing of French down our throats". This is a reference to the Canadian government's effort to promote **bilingualism** (the speaking of both languages) in Canada. Some French-Canadians believe that they are regarded as second class citizens in Canada. They argue that they have never been made to feel equal, or even welcome here. Thus they say that they feel "at home" only in the province of

Quebec. They often accuse English-Canadians of prejudice and discrimination against the French language and culture.

Perhaps we could try to test these rather serious and alarming charges. What is your personal feeling about French-Canadians as a group? What opinions do your family and friends have on this same subject? How typical do you think these views are? Now, to make your efforts more meaningful, try the following quiz. Write the answers in your notebook and be as thoughtful and honest as possible.

Quiz

1. Canada should be considered a   unilingual country
bilingual country
multilingual country

2. Every Canadian should be able to speak   English
French
English and French
English and one other language

3. A member of the House of Commons or the Senate should
be able to speak   English or French
English and French

4. Any person who seeks the office of Prime Minister of Canada should be fluent in both English and French.
Agree   Strongly Agree   Disagree
Strongly Disagree

5. Do you believe that Quebec could survive as an independent nation?
Yes   No   Not Sure

6. Should any attempt at separation by a province be met by force?
Agree   Disagree   Don't Know

7. Can a person who supports the Parti Québécois still be considered a loyal Canadian?
Yes   No   Not Sure

8. The government of Quebec has made French the only *official* language of that province. Do you think this is proper or fair?
Yes   No   Don't Know

9. To get the secondary school graduation diploma, a student should show the ability to talk in French.
Agree   Disagree   Not Sure

10. "This country has two basic traditions, French and English. Both groups must accept this fact. Each group has got to learn to understand and respect the culture of the other."
Agree   Disagree   Not Sure

11. The true separatists in Canada are the English. They seem to deny bilingualism, or at least what it means. By doing this they are, in fact, rejecting Confederation.

Agree　　　　Disagree

12. Three possibilities have always existed for the English-French relationship in Canada. Indicate the one you prefer:

Assimilation of the French

Bicultural partnership

Separation into two independent nations

13. How do you, as an English-speaking Canadian, stand on these issues?

a) desire to learn to speak French

b) accept bilingual street signs

c) hire only people who speak French and English
for the federal civil service

d) acknowledge the right of Quebec to establish
diplomatic relations with other countries

e) agree that a Canadian should be able to
communicate with, and obtain service from, any
branch or department of the federal government,
anywhere in Canada, in English or French, as that
person requires

f) agree that French minorities outside Quebec
should have the same rights and privileges as the
English minority has in Quebec

g) agree that companies operating in Quebec
should use the French language as their primary
language of business there

h) agree that a French-speaking Canadian living in
Ontario or New Brunswick should be able to
communicate with his/her provincial government
and civil service in French

i) agree that French and English should be given
equal status on all stamps, money, cheques, forms
and documents of the Government of Canada

14. How do you react to each of the following statements?

a) "There can hardly be conceived a nationality more **destitute** of (lacking in) all that can **invigorate** (make lively) and **elevate** (uplift) a people, than that which is exhibited by the descendants of the French in Lower Canada (Quebec), owing to their retaining their peculiar language and manners. They are a people with no history, and no literature." Lord Durham, 1839

Agree　　　　Agree strongly　　　　Disagree

Disagree Strongly

b) "As a French-Canadian who speaks only the little bit of English that I learned in school, I cannot feel at home in Canada outside my native province of Quebec. When our family has travelled to other provinces, we have received such comments as 'Speak White' and 'Get back to the reservation'."
Probably happened   Unlikely   Impossible

c) "We must stop making concessions to the French-Canadians; the more you give them, the more they want."
Agree   Agree strongly   Disagree
Disagree strongly

d) "The province of Quebec belongs to all Canadians, not just to the ones who speak French."
Agree   Agree strongly   Disagree
Disagree strongly

e) "With a few exceptions, I think that the English language press has indeed failed to present to its readers a true and adequate picture of contemporary French Canada." Richard Jones, 1972.
Agree   Agree strongly   Disagree
Disagree strongly

f) "The status of the French language in Quebec is a question of social justice . . . . The time has come for us to stop thinking of our future in terms of shaky survival and to recapture the conviction of our true importance: the rightful participation in one of the great linguistic and cultural traditions of this vast world, a world of which we, as Quebeckers, are citizens."
Agree   Agree strongly   Disagree
Disagree strongly

If possible, get other people to complete this same survey. Try to include members of your class at school, perhaps other students as well. (Your family or other relatives, friends, and so on.) It might also be interesting to get the views of strangers on the street, and of people whom you might know in other parts of Canada.

Record the results of the survey. What do most people seem to think about each of these questions? Do the majority agree with *your* personal views? Based on this very limited study, do you think that French-Canadians are correct in thinking that other Canadians dislike them or are prejudiced against their language? If not, how would you explain the fact that many French-Canadians still *believe* this is true? Before reading on, think about these questions.

1. On what experiences with Quebec, or with French-Canadians, did you base your own answers to the survey?
2. How well qualified do you think you really are to make such conclusions?

3. How well qualified were your friends and relatives to make their observations?

4. Is it possible that some of the views of the French about English-speaking Canadians are based on very limited information and experience?

5. How could problems of ignorance and prejudice among English and French Canadians about each other be overcome?

In 1978, Canada had a population of approximately 24 million people. Of these, about 40 per cent were Anglo Saxon. Approximately 27 per cent, or about 6.5 million people, were French-speaking. Thus, while it is true that Canada contains people of many different cultures, the two largest and, in many ways, most important groups are the English and the French. If Canada, as we know it, is to survive, these two groups must live in harmony. At the present time, they are not doing so. Our first task is to try to find out *why*. To accomplish this, we must go back in time to study certain aspects of our past.

Before reading on, study the chart of Key Words and Ideas which follows.

KEY WORDS AND IDEAS IN THIS CHAPTER

Term	Meaning	Sample Use
anglicize	to make someone or something English in nature	The French feared that English-Canadians, backed by Britain, wanted to anglicize them. (Related to assimilation.)
assimilate	to make someone or something similar to (the same as)	The French suspected that England, and English-Canadians, wanted to assimilate them. This would mean that the French language and culture would be absorbed and thus would disappear in Canada.
bilingualism	the use of, or ability to use, two languages	An effort is being made to encourage bilingualism in Canada so that French-Canadians will feel that their language is known and respected in all parts of the country.

mother country	a country which helps to establish, and then controls, a colony or territory	France was the mother country for French-Canadians, just as Britain was for English-Canadians.
nationality	part of a person's identity; refers to the country where a person was born or is a citizen	John A. Macdonald hoped that the English and French would develop the feeling of a common nationality — Canadian.
plebiscite	a public vote, or expression of opinion, on a certain issue	Some French-Canadians wanted a plebiscite held in Quebec to let the people vote on whether they should join Confederation.

1. ENGLISH-FRENCH RELATIONS TO 1791

Different Viewpoints

As you have read, some French-Canadians feel that their place in Canada is not fully recognized by other Canadians. This can be seen, they argue, just by looking at how Canadian history is taught in English Canada. For example, some teachers have begun their courses in Canadian history around the time of the British conquest of New France in 1759. French Canadians are quick to point out, and rightly so, that their ancestors had been settled in Canada for 150 years *before* that event! The following simple sketch suggests the different viewpoints which some French and English Canadians have on the scope of Canada's history.

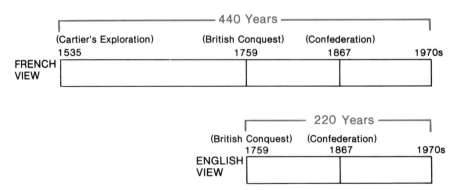

Jacques Cartier at Mount Royal, 1535

Study the time line of the French view of Canada's history. Estimate the percentage of time French Canadians have been part of a united Canada. It comes to about one quarter of the time that French-Canadians have been "present" in North America. Now look at the English view of Canada's history. For English-Canadians, the 110 years or so since Confederation is a much larger portion of *their* history in Canada. How might these different viewpoints affect the attitude of the two peoples toward the idea of belonging to Canada?

Early French Exploration

France played a leading role in the discovery and exploration of North America. Jacques Cartier explored the lower St. Lawrence River in the 1530s. He even tried to establish a permanent settlement along its banks, but failed in this attempt. In the 1600s, daring men such as Samuel de Champlain and Etienne Brûlé explored the upper St. Lawrence River and the Great Lakes. Following in their footsteps came other French adventurers. They pushed the claims of France deeper into the continent. Radisson and Groseilliers went as far west as present day Manitoba; the La Vérendryes reached the foothills of the Rocky Mountains; Marquette and Jolliet probed south from Lake Michigan along the Mississippi River; in 1682, la Salle reached the mouth of the Mississippi at New Orleans. This city keeps both a French name *and* a trace of French culture to this very day. These achievements left France in a powerful position in North America. The empire, which it called New France, controlled some of the most

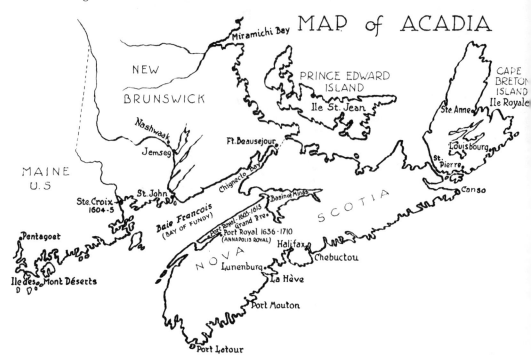

ACADIA

The first attempt by France to set up a colony in Canada took place near the Bay of Fundy in Acadia in 1604. The harsh Canadian winter caused great problems and the following year the colony was abandoned. In time the French returned and small communities of traders, fishermen and farmers were established around the Bay of Fundy. Perhaps the greatest problem for the French was the presence of the English colonies to the south. On three occasions, in 1613, 1629 and 1654 English colonists raided and captured Acadia. On each occasion it was returned to France. In 1713 a treaty between France and England gave most of Acadia to England. In 1755, the French Acadians were caught in yet another conflict between England and France. They were not allowed to remain neutral. Uncertain of Acadian loyalties, the English exiled most of the French to the English colonies, France and England. In time, several thousand made their way back to what is now New Brunswick.

vital waterways on the entire continent. In fact, some historians have pointed out that North America might have become mostly French — with a few changes in history, that is.

New France

The lifeline or major artery of New France was the St. Lawrence River-Great Lakes system. Its heart lay in the 250 km string of settlements between Montreal and Quebec City. Champlain had begun the process of French settlement by founding Quebec in 1608. In the early years, a tiny population struggled to survive in the harsh wilderness. With great effort, the colony slowly began to grow and prosper. By 1755, there were about 60 000 people in New France.

Samuel de Champlain, founder of Quebec

Some English-Canadian historians have suggested in the past that New France was a rather backward and unimportant colony. They hint that the English "did New France a favour" by conquering it in 1759. However, the facts suggest a different story. While it was not rich or powerful, New France deserved respect for its achievements. The fur trade was flourishing. Many towns and villages had been built, and farms cleared, in spite of many obstacles. These included a harsh climate, thick bush and, at times, the hostility of local Indian tribes. France, the **mother country,** was not as helpful as it

A party of voyageurs shooting rapids

might have been. It could have done more to assist New France: by providing money, settlers, supplies and equipment, plus troops for defence when needed.

It is also important to note that New France was developing its own unique culture and style of living. Their ways were freer, more relaxed and less formal than those of France itself. They took time to enjoy life with their families and friends. Families tended to be large, because each person depended so much on the others. They were also very closely knit. Thus, a strong sense of community began to grow. Local arts and crafts developed, all with a French-Canadian flavour or style. Critics have suggested that a "democratic spirit" was lacking in this society. In the modern sense of the word, this is probably true. However, there was no real democracy anywhere in the world at this time. The key thing to remember is that most of the people of New France were very content with their lives. They probably had as much, if not more, personal freedom and peace of mind as the people of France or any other country. Furthermore, they were *proud* of their society and its accomplishments.

The Conquest

Thus, when General James Wolfe captured Quebec for Britain in 1759, the French-Canadians were dealt a crushing blow. They felt embarrassed at being defeated. More importantly, they felt bitter toward France for failing to defend them as strongly as it might have. Also, they felt anxious about their future — what would become of them now that England was in control?

The Battle of the Plains of Abraham, September 13, 1759

British Rule in Canada

The same question faced the British. However, they looked at the problem from a different point of view. It seems that their first reaction was to try to **assimilate** the French. That is, they tried to **anglicize** the French, by absorbing the French culture into that of the English. This would mean bringing large numbers of English-speaking settlers into what is now called Quebec. Few people in England were interested in this idea. The other possibility was to get American settlers to move north from the Thirteen Colonies.

The Royal Proclamation of 1763 was designed to do this. From then on, New France was called Quebec. Its boundaries were changed. Much of the land formerly claimed by New France was taken away. There was a new government for Quebec, headed by a British Governor.

Furthermore, a boundary line was established to control American expansion. This line ran southwest along the Appalachian mountains. Americans were forbidden to settle west of this line. The British hoped that land-hungry Americans would then move north into Quebec. This would create the chance to drown the French language and culture in an ocean of English-speaking settlers. The plan failed miserably. This was because most Americans ignored the restrictions of the Proclamation Act.

Indeed, this was only one of several examples of Americans ignoring British wishes and instructions. After all, the thirteen American colonies were still under the rule of England, just as Quebec was. However, the Americans were stronger and more numerous than the French-Canadians. Thus, they were able to do something about their situation. By the early 1770s, it seemed that an American Revolution was in the making. To Americans, it seemed natural that the French in Quebec would want to join such an uprising. Together, the two peoples could win their freedom from Britain.

Obviously, the same thought occurred to the British government. Therefore, in 1774, they suddenly changed their approach to the French. For the moment at least, they gave up hope of assimilating the French. Instead, they offered many new concessions to them. Among these were:

1. official recognition of the French language
2. permission for the Roman Catholic Church to keep its large holdings of land, and to collect taxes from its members
3. permission for Roman Catholics to hold public office (most French-Canadians were Roman Catholic)
4. full freedom of worship for Roman Catholics
5. permission for French landowners to keep title to (ownership of) their lands
6. keeping of French *civil* law
7. giving back to Quebec of the "Ohio Country" south of the Great Lakes (this land had been taken away by the Proclamation of 1763; it was valuable for the fur trade)

The act which granted these terms was called the *Quebec Act.* Its purpose was to persuade the French not to join an American revolt against Britain. It worked. The French remained loyal to Britain during the American Revolution (1776-1783). They had never had much in common with the Americans. Many French feared that they would be a small minority in an American nation. If so, they would be in even greater danger of being **assimilated** (having their culture absorbed, losing their identity). Also, the French did not expect the Americans to *win* their revolution. Thus, they feared British punishment if they helped the Americans in an unsuccessful revolt.

Results of the American Revolution

In spite of these events, the French had not heard the last of the danger of assimilation. During and after the American Revolution, thousands of Americans poured into Quebec and the Maritime region. These people were called *United Empire Loyalists* because they remained loyal to Britain. They refused to support the revolution. Most of them were English-speaking. They were pro-British in attitude. Their arrival caused great concern among the French. However, Britain was pleased. The Loyalists presented a new hope for the solution of the "French problem."

The French still outnumbered the English by seven to one. However, the Loyalists did not want to live under the terms of the Quebec Act. (Review the act and suggest several reasons for their attitude.) Therefore, Britain immediately made new arrangements. The *Constitutional Act* of 1791 divided Quebec into two units, Upper Canada in the west and Lower Canada in the east. Lower Canada, with its French majority, kept most of the terms of the Quebec Act. Upper Canada was set up as an English-speaking province. It was given British laws and institutions.

2.   UNDER TIGHT BRITISH RULE: 1791-1840

For the next forty years, the two Canadas went their separate ways. The economy and population of Upper Canada grew more quickly. Still, by the 1830s it had fewer people than Lower Canada. In the latter colony, the English remained a minority. Nonetheless, they became increasingly important in the development of trade and local industry. Most French-Canadians remained on the farms, or in the small towns and villages. Their traditional way of life seemed safe, at least for the time being. Perhaps for this reason, they continued to accept British rule. During the War of 1812, their loyalty to Britain was tested just as it had been by the American Revolution. French-Canadian troops fought well in defence of their native land. Their efforts made a major contribution to the defeat of American attacks on Canada.

The Rebellions of 1837

However, trouble began to brew in the 1820s. In both Canadas, the common people began trying to gain more say in their local government. This was resisted by the upper classes in both colonies. Britain also was opposed to making colonial government more democratic. Tension increased rapidly. Finally, in 1837 rebellions occurred in both Canadas. In Lower Canada, the French majority was fighting to gain control of the local government from the English minority. Both rebellions were easily crushed. Even so, Britain sent out Lord Durham to investigate. He was ordered to find the reasons for the rebellions and to recommend solutions to the problem. His famous report, published in 1839, shocked and angered the French.

Louis Joseph Papineau, lawyer, journalist and political reformer. He led the rebellion in Lower Canada in 1837.

The Durham Report

Three hundred years had passed since Jacques Cartier had struggled to build the first French settlement along the St. Lawrence shore. Yet, after a few short weeks in Canada, Lord Durham felt that he knew enough about the situation to describe the French as "a people of no history and no literature." He accused the French of being ignorant, lazy, jealous and hateful toward the English, and of standing in the way of progress in Quebec. He went on to say:

> " . . . I entertain no doubts as to the national character which must be given to Lower Canada; it must be that of the British Empire; . . . that of the great race which must, in the lapse of no long period of time, be predominant [have control] over the whole North American continent . . .
>
> The English have already in their hands the majority of the larger masses of property in the country; they have the decided superiority of intelligence on their side; . . .
>
> If the population of Upper Canada is rightly estimated at 400 000, the English inhabitants of Lower Canada at 150 000, and the French at 450 000, the union of the two Provinces would not only give a clear English majority, but one which would be increased every year by the influence of English emigration; and I have little doubt that the French, when once placed . . . in a minority, would abandon their vain hopes of nationality . . . "

Interpreting the Document

1. What criticism of the French does Durham make in this passage?
2. How would you describe Durham's overall attitude toward the French? On what belief does he base this view?

Lord Durham

3. Why does he feel that the time is "ripe" to aim for the assimilation of the French?

4. What is the main proposal that he makes to Britain to achieve assimilation?

5. What does Durham mean when he refers to the "vain hopes of nationality" of the French?

6. Was Durham right about the French? What evidence can you offer to support your view?

The British government rejected many of Lord Durham's suggestions. However, it did pass the *Act of Union* in 1840. This combined Upper and Lower Canada into one Province of Canada. (By this time, they were known individually as Canada West and Canada East.) The English and French were now thrown together in one government, in which they were expected to co-operate.

3. THE MOVEMENT TOWARDS CANADIAN CONFEDERATION

Lord Durham had predicted that, once united with the English, the French would give up their identity. Britain had passed the Act of Union in the hope that Durham was right. He was wrong. The French did not give up. In fact, they fought even harder to survive. To do so, they worked with the very same political system that had been set up to assimilate them. They used their political power very skillfully. As a result, they were able to defend French interests. Unfortunately, much confusion was produced in the government. No one party or group of people could stay in power long enough to provide stable leadership for the colony. In 1864, George Brown of Canada West described the problem this way: "We have two races, two languages, two systems of religious belief, two systems of everything, so that it has been almost impossible that, without sacrificing their principles, the public men of both provinces could come together in the same government. The difficulties have gone on increasing every year."

Sir E.P. de Taché of Canada East reinforced the point: " . . . From the 21st May, 1862, to the end of June, 1864, there had been no less than five different governments in charge of the business of the country."

As a result of this situation, a committee was formed to consider possible changes that might solve the problem. In May, 1864, it reported: " . . . A strong feeling was found to exist among members of the Committee in favour of changes in the direction of a federative system, applied either to Canada alone or to the whole British North American Provinces."

Thus, both English and French politicians in Canada were looking for a way out of the situation. Some of them thought that the answer might lie in a new and larger political union — one which would include the Maritime provinces.

Delegates to the Quebec Conference

This idea happened to be born at a convenient time. The Maritimes themselves were considering a kind of union of their own. At the Charlottetown Conference of 1864, the Canadas and the Maritimes agreed to consider plans for a Canadian Confederation.

4. DIFFERING VIEWS OF CONFEDERATION

Today, the question facing Canada is: "Will Quebec stay in Confederation?" A follow up might well be: "Why *should* it stay?" Part of the answer to these questions lies in understanding why and how Quebec joined Canada in the first place. There seem to be different views on this matter.

An English View

One point of view suggests that Canada was created mainly for economic reasons. A united country would be able to build roads, canals and railways in an organized way. It could remove all **tariffs** (customs duties) between provinces. These and other measures would encourage industry and make trade easier. As a result, there would be economic prosperity from which all Canadians could benefit. This viewpoint seems to be strongest in Ontario. It tends to suggest that the Maritimes, and especially Quebec, joined Confederation because it was obviously "a good deal." In the process certain things had to be granted to the French. These included a fair voice in government, and recognition of their language, at least in Quebec. Supposedly, there was no intention of creating a bilingual country. The French were not regarded as being one of two equal, founding peoples of the country. It was just that they had to be tolerated. For their part, the French had no "better offer". In fact, they were lucky to have such a chance to join Canada and continue their language. Behind this thinking there seems to lie a feeling that the French were, somehow, inferior. Perhaps there was also the hope that, by placing the French in a minority situation, the English could assimilate them in the long run.

Four opinions on Confederation

Macdonald
"If we wish to be a great people, if we wish to form ... a great nationality commanding the respect of the world, ... if we wish to have one system of government, and to establish a commercial union with unrestricted free trade, this can only be by a (political) union."

Dorion
"I should have desired to make my remarks in French, but considering the large number of honourable members who are not familiar with that language ... ... I strongly fear that it would be a dark day for Canada when she adopted such a scheme as this."

Cartier
" ... Some parties — through the press and other modes — pretended that it was impossible to carry out Federation, on account of the differences of races and religions. Those who took this view of the question were in error. It was just the reverse. It was precisely on account of the variety of races, local interests, etc., that the Federation system ought to be resorted to, and would be found to work well."

Brown
"All right! Confederation through at six o'clock this evening — constitution adopted — ... Is it not wonderful? French Canadianism entirely extinguished!"

1. What advantages are stressed in Macdonald's comments on Confederation? What does he mean by a **nationality?** Do you think that the French-Canadians believed that Canada would consist of only *one* nationality? Would they agree today?
2. How do Cartier's remarks apply to the point made in No. 1 above? Why did Cartier stress the advantages of a *federal* system? How did he think it would help the different "races" and local interests that existed, and still exist, in Canada?
3. What did George Brown seem to think that Confederation would do to the French-Canadians? How does this view compare with those of Cartier and Macdonald? Why might Brown think that Confederation would lead to the assimilation of the French? Has it done so?
4. What note of bitterness or sarcasm can you find in Dorion's comments? Try to discover more about Dorion's reasons for opposing Quebec's entry into Confederation.

A French View

When you really think about it, why would the French join Confederation if they saw things the same way? They certainly didn't *need* the union with Canada — at least not to the same extent that the other provinces needed Quebec in Confederation. It is difficult to imagine Confederation happening if Quebec had not agreed to join. (About as difficult as it is to imagine a Canada today without Quebec!) Perhaps the English minority in Quebec supported Confederation because of the economic benefits which could result. After all, they controlled much of the industry in Quebec by this time. However, the French leaders must have had other reasons for taking their province into the new Canadian union. Some of these were:

1. There would be separate provincial governments in the new system. This way, Quebec could have its *own* government to look after local concerns and protect the "French fact" in Quebec.

2. Provincial governments were given control over such important items as education, property and civil rights.

3. The French language could be legally used in the debates and records of the national government in Ottawa, as well as in the parliament and courts of Quebec.

4. The educational rights of minorities were guaranteed. (Thus, French-Canadians in Ontario, New Brunswick and elsewhere could continue to enjoy whatever separate schools they had when their provinces entered Confederation.)

Georges Étienne Cartier, leading French-Canadian supporter of Confederation

Antoine-Aimé Dorion, outspoken critic of Confederation and bitter political opponent of Georges Étienne Cartier

Conclusion

In spite of all this, the French-Canadians knew that they would be putting themselves in a serious minority position in the new country. The English would outvote them in both houses (Senate and House of Commons) in the new Parliament. Therefore, they must have been willing to *trust* in the good faith of the English majority. Based on the historical record that we have been examining, how good would their reasons be for having such trust? Let us now see whether that trust was kept.

THINGS TO THINK ABOUT AND DO

Reviewing Key Words and Ideas

The following terms appeared in this chapter. Try to recall their meaning and how they were used.

anglicization	conquest	plebiscite
assimilation	federal system	rebellion
bilingualism	mother country	revolution
Confederation	nationality	United Empire Loyalists

Remembering the Facts

1. How did French-Canadians react to the British conquest of New France?
2. How did the British try to assimilate the French in the years immediately after the conquest? Why did these efforts fail?
3. What was the main purpose of the Quebec Act? Was it successful?
4. Why did the British pass the Constitutional Act of 1791?
5. Why was there a rebellion in Lower Canada in 1837?
6. Why were the French angered by the Durham Report?
7. Why did some Quebeckers want their province to join Confederation? Why were other Quebeckers opposed to this?

Analyzing Ideas

1. How might North American history have been different if Quebec had agreed to support the American Revolution?
2. Why were the French-Canadians able to preserve their language and culture in the period 1759-1867? Was it due mainly to their own strengths and efforts, or to the generosity of the English?

3. Does it seem that the French-Canadians were welcomed into Confederation as equal partners? Explain your answer.

Applying Your Knowledge

1. The leader of the 1837 rebellion in Lower Canada was Louis Joseph Papineau. Try to find information about his career, and the reasons behind the rebellion which he led.

2. Set up a role play situation involving either the Quebec Conference, or the debates on Confederation in the Canadian assembly. Assign the appropriate roles. Allow sufficient time for members of the class to research the background and positions of the politicians whom they are representing. Summarize the most important points made in the debate that follows.

3. The class could be divided into two groups, one supporting Confederation and the other opposed. The task of each is to produce a small newspaper, in the style of the 1860s, supporting their point of view. Make full use of headlines, feature stories, editorials, opinion surveys and cartoons. Photographs could be simulated by hand drawings.

A French-Canadian farmhouse near Quebec City

3

FROM CONFEDERATION TO
THE "QUIET REVOLUTION"

Introduction

The years from 1867 to 1960 were very important in the history of Canada. Many of the developments of this period are noted in Unit III, chapters 1 and 2. These years were also important for our topic of English-French relations. In 1867, French-Canadians made up approximately 40 per cent of Canada's population. By 1960, they accounted for only 30 per cent of the population. Generally, the period could be described as one of "ups and downs" in relations between the two peoples. There were quiet times, but these were broken up by events which produced very strong feelings on both sides.

On the whole, the French lost the arguments. This was mainly because they were in the minority. After each setback, they tended to withdraw more and more into a protective shell. Naturally, their outlook became increasingly negative and defensive. This means that their feelings towards Canada became less favourable. They began to take less interest in the affairs of the country. Perhaps they felt that their views were not wanted, or would not be counted for very much. Instead, they concentrated on protecting their language and way of life within Quebec itself. In a sense, they turned that province into a kind of "island fortress." Here they felt comfortable and "at home." They could find shelter from the storms which, from time to time, raged around them.

Before reading on, study the chart of Key Words and Ideas which follows.

KEY WORDS AND IDEAS IN THIS CHAPTER		
Term	Meaning	Sample Use
conscription	compulsory enlistment for military service, usually during times of war	Conscription was used to increase Canada's armed forces in World Wars I and II.

constitutional rights	basic rights specifically guaranteed to people in the constitution of their country	French-Canadians believed that their constitutional rights to French language education, guaranteed in the BNA Act, were taken away in Manitoba and Ontario.
corruption	dishonesty; a willingness to ignore principles in return for a reward such as money	Quebec's troubles in the 1930s were worsened by corruption in its government.
crisis	a *very* serious or dangerous situation	There have been several crises in English-French relations since 1867. These include conscription (twice) and the execution of Louis Riel.
treason	any action which betrays, or helps to destroy, your country	Louis Riel was accused of treason for his leadership of rebellions in the Canadian West. He was convicted and hanged.

Hull, Quebec — the French-speaking mayor goes to jail rather than pay a small fine for a traffic ticket. The reason? — he was served the ticket in English, and the ticket was printed in English.

Ottawa, Ontario — several French-Canadian members of Parliament refuse to stand, for the playing of "God Save The Queen" in the House of Commons.

Toronto, Ontario — A capacity crowd fills Maple Leaf Gardens to watch Team Canada play Sweden in an international hockey match. Hundreds of them *boo* when part of "O Canada" is sung in French.

Calgary, Alberta — a gas station attendant refuses to serve a French-Canadian couple whose car is carrying Quebec license plates.

Unfortunately, each of the above events really happened. None of them took place one hundred years ago, fifty years ago or even twenty years ago. They all occurred later than 1975. Although they took place in different areas and at different times, they are related. They tell us that, after more than one hundred years of union, relations between the English and French in Canada do not seem to have improved. If anything, they are worse. In this chapter, we are going to study some of the developments that have produced this sad and dangerous situation.

1.   THE RIEL AFFAIR

Details of this episode already have been provided in Unit 3, Chapter 1. If necessary, review them before reading further.

The Riel affair created very strong feelings in both French and English Canada. Compare the expressions of opinion quoted below:

This editorial appeared in the Toronto Evening News in 1885:

Ontario is proud of being loyal to England.

Quebec is proud of being loyal to sixteenth century France.

Ontario pays about three-fifths of Canada's taxes, fights all the battles of provincial rights, sends nine-tenths of the soldiers to fight the rebels [Riel's], and gets sat upon by Quebec for her pains. . . .

Hundreds of thousands of dollars are spent in maintaining the French language in an English country. . . .

An anti-French party is springing up in all the Provinces except Quebec. . . .

If we in Canada are to be confronted with a solid French vote, we must have a solid English vote. . . .

If she is to be a traitor in our wars, a thief in our treasury, a conspirator in our Canadian household, she had better go out.

She is no use in Confederation. . . .

As far as we are concerned, and we are concerned, and we are as much concerned for the good of Canada as any one else, Quebec could go out of the Confederation to-morrow and we would not shed a tear except for joy.

If Ontario were a trifle more loyal to herself she would not stand Quebec's monkey business another minute.

Honoré Mercier, a Quebec politician (later to become Premier of that province) gave this speech to a mass rally of 50 000 people in Montreal, also in 1885:

Riel, our brother, is dead, the victim of his devotion to the Métis cause of which he was the leader, the victim of fanaticism and treason: of the fanaticism of Sir John [A. Macdonald] and of some of his friends; of the treason of three of ours [the three French Canadians in the Macdonald cabinet] who, in order to save their portfolios, have sold their brother.]

By killing Riel, Sir John has not only struck our race at the heart but also struck the cause of justice and humanity which, represented in all languages and sanctified by all religious beliefs, demanded mercy for the prisoner of Regina, our poor brother of the North-West.

In the face of this crime, in the presence of these failings, what is our duty? We have three things to do; unite ourselves in order to punish the guilty; break the alliance that our deputies have made with Orangeism and seek, in a more natural and less dangerous alliance, the protection of our national interests.

Louis Riel

Interpreting the Documents

1. Why would English Protestants, particularly in Ontario, be critical of Riel? Why would some of them want him hung? How would the motive of *revenge* enter into their thinking?

2. Which of the charges made in the Toronto editorial were accurate and fair at the time when they were made? Which were not?

3. Would many English-Canadians today agree with any of the feelings expressed in that editorial? If so, which ones? How could they support their views?

4. What does it mean to "identify" with someone? Why would many French-Canadians identify with Riel as their "brother"?

5. Mercier referred in his speech to "Orangeism". What was this?

6. What threat is hinted at in Mercier's final sentence?

7. Two interesting simulations could be developed from the Riel affair.

a) Recreate his trial. Explore the nature of the charges against Riel. Choose witnesses, a jury and key people to act as the prosecuting and defence attorneys. Perhaps your teacher should act as the presiding judge. Afterwards, the whole class could evaluate the trial, and discuss the main points that were made by both sides.

b) Turn the class into the Cabinet of Sir John A. Macdonald. This body had the power to **commute** (reduce) the death sentence on Riel. It chose not to do so. Assign appropriate roles, making sure that each province and each major interest group is represented. Take note of the accusation about the Cabinet made in Mercier's speech, which is quoted above. The Cabinet meeting should be run in a fairly informal way to encourage each person to express an opinion suitable to his or her role. To achieve a high degree of realism, you must keep in mind that the Cabinet is made up of politicians. They are concerned with getting and keeping power, and with practical solutions to real problems.

JUSTICE NOT SATISFIED.

SIR JOHN. "Well madam, Riel is gone; I hope you are satisfied."

JUSTICE.- "No, I am not. You have hanged the **EFFECT** of the Rebellion. I must now punish you as the **CAUSE**."

What is the point made in the above cartoon? Of the Riel affair, Edward Blake (a bitter foe of Macdonald) said: "Had there been no neglect, there would have been no rebellion; if no rebellion, no arrest; if no arrest, no trial; if no trial, no condemnation; no condemnation, no execution. They, therefore, who are responsible for the first are responsible for every link in that fatal chain." Do you agree with Blake?

The final decision, about whether or not Louis Riel should hang, rested with the Prime Minister and Cabinet. Macdonald's government allowed Riel's execution to proceed. This was greeted by cheers in Ontario, but with howls of protest in Quebec. Many French-Canadians felt that this decision had been made for political reasons. They charged that Macdonald valued English votes more than French ones. This made sense, in a way, because the English were the majority. Also, it could be claimed that this was fair and democratic. On *legal* grounds, it was possible to argue either way. However, most French-Canadians felt that a *moral* wrong had been done. Somehow, the bargain of Confederation had been broken.

2. MINORITY RIGHTS IN EDUCATION

When Quebec entered Confederation in 1867 its leaders had insisted that education should be under the control of provincial governments. This was provided for in the British North America Act. Furthermore, that act protected the educational rights of minorities. Section 93 clearly stated:

> (1) Nothing in any such (Provincial) Law shall **prejudicially** *(harmfully) affect any Right or Privilege with respect of* **Denominational** *(belonging to a church or distinct group) Schools which any Class of Persons have by Law in the Province at the Union.*

It went on to say that if any province passed any law harmful to the educational rights of a minority, that minority could appeal to the federal government. This government was given the power to pass whatever measures were necessary to remedy the problem and thus protect the minority. By these terms, the English, Protestant minority in Quebec could enjoy its own separate schools. So could the French, Roman Catholic minorities in Ontario and Manitoba — or so it seemed.

Bad feelings about the Riel episode were still in the air when new trouble broke out in Manitoba. In 1890, that province passed the *Manitoba Schools Act*. This measure cut off the funds to Roman Catholic Schools. Such schools had been guaranteed in 1870, when Manitoba entered Confederation. Most of Manitoba's Catholics were French-speaking. These people felt, quite correctly, that they were being denied their constitutional rights. They appealed to the federal government in Ottawa. However, Prime Minister Macdonald refused to take action. Next, they sought help from the high court in Britain. This body first turned them down, then handed the problem back to the Canadian government. The problem remained unsolved.

In 1896, Wilfrid Laurier was elected Prime Minister. He was a bilingual French-Canadian. Eventually, he managed to win a few small privileges from the government of Manitoba. However, the French in Manitoba did not win back *all* of their educational rights. In fact, in 1916 the Manitoba government passed an *Education Act*. It did away with the concessions won by Laurier. English became the only language of instruction in the schools of the province. A similar situation developed in Ontario. In 1913, the Department of Education announced that French could not be used as a language of instruction past the First Form (Grade 9). There were about 250 000 French-Canadians in the province at this time. They too believed that their proper rights were being denied.

3. CONSCRIPTION IN WORLD WAR I

Canada's part in this war has already been described in Unit 3. By 1917, World War I was in its third year. It was taking a terrible toll in human life. After a visit to the front lines, Prime Minister Borden was convinced that **conscription** was

Wounded Canadian soldiers heading back to England — July 1917

necessary. It was the only way to replace the heavy losses that our troops were suffering. For example, in April and May of 1917, Canadian casualties were 23 939. In the same period, only 11 790 volunteers joined the forces.

Conscription would mean that Canadians would be drafted (forced) into the armed forces. Borden's decision produced a **crisis** in English-French relations. Most English-Canadians agreed with the decision. However, most French-Canadians did not. A long and bitter debate followed. Some of the bad feeling still lingers in the memories of older Canadians who lived through the experience.

Some Of The Arguments Presented By The Two Sides In The Conscription Debate

Pro Conscription (mostly English)
As a colony of Britain, Canada has a moral and legal duty to do everything in its power to help Britain win this war.
If Britain loses this war, Canada will suffer. Much of our foreign trade will be lost. The German navy might blockade the St. Lawrence River, or even the Pacific coast around Vancouver.
In April and May of 1917, our casualties were 23 939 but only 11 790 new volunteers enlisted.
Prime Minister Borden gave Canada's word that we would keep four divisions in the field. Our allies are counting on us.
If we cannot send replacements, our remaining troops will be in even greater danger. Those who died will have died in vain.
By seeing this war through to victory, Canada can be proud. We will win the respect of the world.
You can't back out in the middle of a fight. If we did, in later years we would be looked upon as "quitters" and "chickens" by other countries, and by our own children.
By helping Britain, you help her ally, France. If Canada is ever attacked in the future, we will need the help of these great powers.
French-Canadians have not been volunteering at the same rate as English-Canadians. Conscription will *force* them to do their share.

Robert Borden discussing military affairs with Army officers

Henri Bourassa, publisher of the newspaper *Le Devoir*, was the leader of the anti-conscription forces.

Anti-Conscription (mostly French)

Canada's first obligation is to itself. Britain chose to get into this war, let Britain fight it.

Germany has no quarrel with us. If they *did* try to harm us, the United States would help us. We cannot do anything big enough to decide who wins or loses the war anyway.

The losses are unfortunate, but those who volunteered knew the risks they were taking.

No one realized at the start of this war how long and costly it would become. We have done our share.

Enough blood has already been shed. Bring the other troops home if necessary. Canada does not need fame, and should not take pride in fighting wars.

Let others think what they want. Nothing important for Canada is at stake in this war.

We feel no more obligation to France than to Britain. Neither France nor Britain would shed so much blood for us as we have already shed for them.

French-Canadians are already a minority. They do not wish to throw away their future generations by forcing their sons to fight a British war.

1. As you read these arguments, which side do you take? Switch the order, so that you read the anti-conscription arguments first. Does your opinion change or remain the same? If it changes, why do you think this happens? For a well-founded view, you must do more research.

2. Another reason for French-Canadian opposition to conscription was their complaint that they were being asked to join an "English army". The recruiting officers usually were English. Very few of the recruiting posters were in French. Training, orders and instruction manuals were mainly in English. The sergeants were mainly English. Most promotions went to English-speaking soldiers. Did the French have good reason to complain? Do you think that a two-language army can function reliably in emergencies?

3. A few French-Canadians went so far as to complain that conscription was an English plot to reduce their numbers. It is a fact that the French could replace their losses only through natural reproduction (births). English Canada would recover much more quickly. This was because of immigration *plus* natural

" Daddy, how did you vote in the Big War Election? "

This cartoon shows how the press in English Canada tried to influence voters to support Borden and conscription in 1917. How did this particular cartoon try to achieve this goal?

reproduction. Should French-Canadians still have been expected to enlist the *same* proportion of volunteers as the English?

4. As Prime Minister, what would *you* have done about conscription in 1917?

Conscription was established by the *Military Service Act*. This became law on August 28, 1917. Riots and demonstrations broke out in several Quebec centres. Dozens of people were injured or killed before order was restored.

To justify his stand on conscription, Prime Minister Borden called an election in 1917. He won a sweeping victory. However, of the 65 seats in Quebec, 62 were won by the opposition. Quebec was still solidly against conscription. Once again, they had been outvoted and overpowered by the English majority. A few speeches were made in the parliament of Quebec calling for separation of that province from Canada.

4.   THE PERIOD BETWEEN THE WARS

World War I ended with the defeat of Germany in 1918. As the years passed, the bitter feelings about conscription began to die down. Like other parts of the country, Quebec was somewhat changed by the war. Industries grew larger. More and more people came to live in the towns and cities. Still, for many French-Canadians, the old way of life went on. This was especially true in rural areas. As in all parts of Canada, the younger generation became more interested in education. College graduates tended to follow careers in medicine, law, teaching or the church. This had been a pattern in French Canada for a long time. Some young people moved to the cities. Here, most of them found jobs in factories or business. However, their bosses usually were English. This situation was regarded as normal, and did not seem to cause serious problems at the time.

The same could not be said of the Great Depression. This disaster brought great suffering, from one end of Canada to the other. Thousands of people lost their jobs. Many others had to take cuts in pay. Hundreds of businesses went broke. A new politician, Maurice Duplessis, took advantage of these problems to win power in Quebec. He argued that, since the English ran most of Quebec's economy, they were largely to blame for its troubles. Though not completely true, this idea was quite popular with French voters. Duplessis also promised to "get tough" with Ottawa. He wanted more power and tax money from the federal government. His party, the Union Nationale, did a fairly good job of governing Quebec. Progress was made in the fields of education, transportation and hospital care. But no great victories over Ottawa were won. Moreover, Duplessis often accepted support from powerful English interests. Thus, many aspects of life in Quebec did not change very much.

Maurice Duplessis (centre) surrounded by supporters. What institutions, represented here, gave considerable support to the Duplessis government?

5. WORLD WAR II: CONSCRIPTION AGAIN

As described in Unit 3, the Second World War broke out in 1939. Canada was in it from the beginning. Once again, we fought on the side of Britain and France. Germany was the main enemy. Our Prime Minister was Mackenzie King.

At first, King promised that there would be no conscription. He wanted to keep the country united. However, battle losses became heavy. The promise could not be kept. Conscription was introduced in 1944. At that time, the government eased the blow. It said that conscripted men would be used only for home defence. They would not be sent overseas. However, by the end of the war in 1945, over 13 000 conscripts had been sent overseas.

Despite these facts, conscription was probably not as serious a question as it had been in World War I. This time, the enemy was Adolph Hitler, and most people agreed that he had to be stopped. Also, King clearly tried hard to consult French Canada. He was sensitive about their feelings. He chose a French Canadian, Louis St. Laurent as his main assistant on this issue. St. Laurent won much support with a speech in Parliament in which he said:

"... believing as I do that whenever the majority, after full consultation and mature deliberation, reaches a conclusion of that kind (for conscription), it is proper the minority should accept it and loyally assist in carrying it out. ..."

This cartoon depicts Mackenzie King's skillful handling of the conscription issue during World War II.

Prime Minister Mackenzie King reviews a French-Canadian regiment in Britain during World War II.

6. THE POST-WAR ERA

Between 1945 and 1960, English-French relations were quiet. Life gradually returned to normal after the war. The country was quite prosperous. By today's standards, its problems were fairly minor. Maurice Duplessis remained in power in Quebec until his death in 1959. On the surface, everything appeared to be fine.

Beneath this calm exterior, important changes were taking place in Quebec. The war had created an industrial boom. Thousands of new jobs were created in industry and business. More than ever before, Quebeckers poured off the farms and into the cities. Soon, the old ways were but a memory for most of them.

In the cities, the people were less influenced by the old ties of family and church. Exciting new kinds of futures were open to them. Most of these demanded higher education. Soon, many French Quebeckers began to see things about their province that they did not like. For example, they saw that the English minority ran most of the economy. Worse, they ran it in the English language! French-Canadian workers were not as well paid as the English, yet suffered from higher unemployment. The government was becoming very **corrupt.** Also, it was not nearly as tough with the federal government as it pretended to be. The power of Ottawa over the lives of Quebeckers seemed to be growing. This federal government was almost completely in the hands of English-Canadians. A feeling began to grow among the French in Quebec that some big changes were needed.

As long as he was alive, Maurice Duplessis was able to keep these new forces for change under control. His power over the province was very great. However, his death created the effect of a bursting dam. New energies, new ideas and new hopes for French Canada were released. They came flooding out in all directions. La révolution tranquille (The Quiet Revolution) had begun.

THINGS TO THINK ABOUT AND DO

Reviewing Key Words and Ideas

The following terms appeared in this chapter. Try to recall their meaning and how they were used.

commute (a sentence)	crisis	Quiet Revolution
conscription	Great Depression	revenge
constitutional rights	Orangeism	separate schools
corruption	post-war boom	treason

Remembering the Facts

1. Why did the trial and execution of Louis Riel produce a crisis in English-French relations?
2. Why were French-Canadians bitter about the Manitoba Schools Act?
3. Review the arguments for and against conscription in 1917.
4. How did World War II change life in Quebec?
5. Why was there a "revolution" in Quebec after the death of Maurice Duplessis?

Analyzing Ideas

1. If you are guaranteed certain rights and protection under the law, and then are denied those rights, how would this affect your feeling toward the law? What development, discussed in this chapter, illustrates this point?
2. If a province, or a large group of people, can show that its constitutional rights have been violated, is it entitled to walk out of Confederation? Explain your answer.
3. Do an in-depth study of the strategy used by Mackenzie King to handle the conscription issue in World War II. Why was he so successful in preventing a serious crisis?
4. Try to discover how Maurice Duplessis stayed in power for so long in Quebec.

5. Below is the coat of arms of the province of Quebec:

As you can see, the motto inscribed is: "Je me souviens." How does it translate? What does it imply?

Applying Your Knowledge

1. Imagine that Prime Minister Borden has just announced conscription in 1917. Write a short play depicting the conversation within a family having sons of military age. Part of the class should write action and dialogue for a French-Canadian family, and another for an English-Canadian situation. If there is enough time, act them out in class. How were the families' reactions similar? How did they differ?

2. Investigate the conditions faced by Canadian soldiers in the trenches in World War I. Write a letter home as if you were a French-Canadian serving in the army. What would be your main feelings and complaints?

3. You have probably heard the term "generation gap." Briefly describe what it means. Try to imagine the effect on a rural French-Canadian family of the children moving to the city. Set the scene in the 1950s. How would the ways of the parents appear to the children? What about the other way around? Which generation would be likely to support the 'status quo' (the way things are and have been)? Why?

4

The "Quiet Revolution" and Beyond

INTRODUCTION

As we have seen, English-French relations had followed a fairly steady pattern from the time of the conquest in 1759 to the death of Maurice Duplessis in 1959. Most of the time, each group went its own separate way. These periods of calm were sometimes broken by serious and even violent conflict. Then, feelings would again cool down. Many English-Canadians regarded Canada as a one-language country. English was the official language of government and business. Both of these fields were dominated by English-speaking people. There would be no trouble as long as the French accepted that "this is how it is."

However, by 1960, the mood of Quebec was changing. The French majority there was no longer ready to accept things as they were. In the words of one French-Canadian: "We have survived enough. The time has come to give this survival a positive sense, to fix a goal for it, and to justify it." In short, changes had to be made. The French of Quebec would no longer accept English control of their economy. They would no longer accept the second class position of their language — either in Quebec or in the rest of Canada.

Before reading on, study the chart of Key Words and Ideas which follows.

KEY WORDS AND IDEAS IN THIS CHAPTER

Term	Meaning	Sample Use
backlash	a movement or feeling against a present trend	There is a backlash in English Canada against efforts to please French Canada.

consultation	seeking advice	Quebec has long wanted more consultation between the federal government and the provinces before making important decisions.
controversy	argument, or difference of opinion	There has been a controversy over whether air-traffic controllers in Quebec should be able to work in French as well as English.
independence	being on your own, your own boss, without needing to rely or *depend* on others	Some French-Canadians would like independence for Quebec. It would then no longer be a province of Canada.
revenue	government income, in the form of money	Quebec (and other provinces) would like a larger *share* of Ottawa's revenue.
subsidy	financial aid	Quebec (and other provinces) would like increased subsidies from the federal government.
terrorist	a person who uses violence to try to gain a political goal	Terrorists believing in Quebec's independence carried out bombings, kidnappings and other violent acts in Quebec in the 1960s.

1.   WHY THE QUIET REVOLUTION HAPPENED

The following conditions existed in Canada in the early 1960s. They explain many of the reasons for Quebec's unrest.

● Quebec's rate of unemployment was one of the highest in Canada.

● Many French-Canadian workers were earning less than non-French workers for doing the same job in Quebec.

● The English minority in Quebec had many more rights and privileges than French minorities had in other provinces.

● Many French-Canadians had to speak English to keep their jobs in Quebec.

● Ottawa, Canada's capital, was almost an all-English city.
● Most of the top jobs in the federal civil service were held by English-Canadians.
● There were only a handful (5 or 6) of French-Canadian Cabinet ministers. None of them had a really important department to run.
● The Prime Minister of Canada could speak hardly any French. He seemed to be unaware of the new feelings of Quebeckers.
● The birth rate among French-Canadians was falling rapidly. The great majority of new immigrants to Quebec were sending their children to English schools.
● French-speaking Quebeckers did not seem to have their share of top jobs even in Quebec.
Here are some statistics to illustrate a few of the points made above:

Occupation and Ethnic Origin — Quebec, 1961
(Percentages)

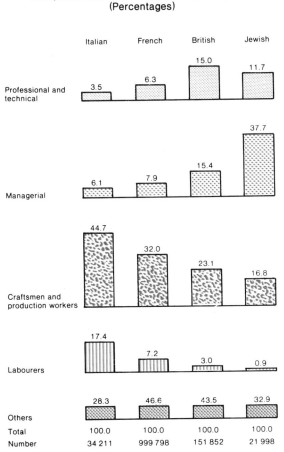

Source: [Report of the Royal Commission on Bilingualism and Biculturalism, Volume 3A, 1969]

Quebec Labour Income

Average Labour Income — Male Workers — Selected Ethnic Groups — 1961

	Income	Index
All ethnic groups (average)	$3469	100.0
British	4940	142.4
Scandinavian	4939	142.4
Jewish	4851	139.8
German	4254	122.6
Polish	3984	114.8
Asian	3734	107.6
French	3185	91.8
Italian	2938	84.6
Indian	2112	60.8

2. THE REVOLUTION BEGINS QUIETLY

As we have seen, the Quiet Revolution did not begin overnight. The forces of change had been at work for many years in Quebec. The death of Maurice Duplessis in 1959 released them in full force. This was made clear in the Quebec election of 1960. The Union Nationale party was defeated. It had been in power for 18 of the previous 23 years. The Liberal party, led by Jean Lesage, now took over. His government began to work on these goals:
1. to clean up the corruption in Quebec's government
2. to improve public services, such as hospitals and transportation
3. to increase wages and pensions
4. to develop natural resources
5. to reform education
6. to develop new industries, under French control where possible

This was a very ambitious and costly programme. To make sure he had public support, Lesage called another election in 1962. The Liberal party slogan was: "Maîtres Chez Nous" (masters in our own house). The Lesage government was re-elected by the voters. Encouraged, it pressed on with its programmes.

Educational reform was a vital part of the Quiet Revolution. Studies showed that many of the buildings themselves were inadequate. Teacher training, plus equipment, was somewhat old-fashioned. Supplies were scarce. Perhaps most important, the **curriculum** (what was studied) was out of date. More attention had to be paid to science, mathematics and business courses. This would provide young French-Canadians with the training needed to qualify for important jobs in industry. In a modern economy, it was not enough for French-Canadians to be doctors, lawyers and teachers. If they were to have influence, they would also have to become engineers, architects, technicians,

These photos depict both the older rural aspects of Quebec and the newer urbanized Quebec.

computer experts, managers and so on. Realizing this, the Lesage government poured millions of dollars into Quebec's educational system.

Even this was not enough. If the Quiet Revolution was to succeed, other things had to happen. The rest of Canada would have to recognize the equality of the French language. The nearly 1 000 000 French-Canadians outside of Quebec would have to be treated with respect and equality. The federal government in Ottawa would have to contain more French-Canadians in important positions. It also would have to grant more powers to Quebec, plus funds to make use of those powers.

3.   THE REVOLUTION BECOMES LESS QUIET

When the Lesage government began to press for these goals, the rest of Canada woke up. The revolution was growing loud. Things had been peaceful for fifteen years. English Canadians had been lulled. They were not in the habit of reading newspapers from Quebec. They did not see the tension building. Therefore, they were rather unprepared for what began to happen. The new demands of Quebec came as a shock to most of them.

Ottawa felt most of the pressure. Premier Lesage accused the federal government of interfering in provincial affairs, particularly education. He asked for the right to pull Quebec out of several programs, such as pensions and medical plans. Quebec preferred to handle these alone. He also wanted Quebec to have more control over its own economic development. This was important for many reasons. It would become easier for French-Canadians to play a greater part in the Quebec economy. This in turn would help the French preserve their language and culture in the province.

Premier Lesage was not yet through — he wanted more. To pay for Quebec's greater powers, he needed more money. Therefore, he asked Ottawa for a larger share of the **revenue** (money) brought in by income tax. In addition, he wanted Ottawa to pay bigger **subsidies** (grants of money) to Quebec.

Finally, Mr. Lesage demanded more **consultation** between Ottawa and the provinces. By this, he meant that the federal government should pay more attention to provincial feelings. It should tell provincial governments about its plans. It should ask their advice and even gain their support more often. It should not simply act on its own in matters that would affect provincial interests.

Naturally, such demands "raised a lot of eyebrows." Still, many other provincial leaders tended to agree with Quebec on these questions. Some of them felt that Ottawa *was* becoming too powerful. More co-operation *was* needed. More money, of course, was always welcome. Still, to many English-Canadians, Quebec was going too far, too fast. Demands like this could

Four of the Leaders of the Quiet Revolution in Quebec

Jean Lesage

Daniel Johnson

Jean-Jacques Bertrand

Robert Bourassa

French President Charles de Gaulle tours Quebec in 1967.

weaken the central government. They could even threaten the unity of the country. Just what was Quebec after? Where would its demands end?

In 1966, opponents of the Quiet Revolution saw a ray of hope. Quebec held another election, but this time the Lesage government was defeated. Many Quebeckers had become alarmed at the huge spending of their government. The changes were too great and too many even for them. The Union Nationale returned to power. They were led by Daniel Johnson. Now, perhaps, things would "return to normal". Such thoughts did not last long. Premier Johnson did not intend to give up the main goals of the Quiet Revolution. He kept the pressure on Ottawa for the same things that Lesage had wanted.

Mr. Johnson also revealed a new plan to help win these goals. This involved closer ties with France. English Canada had kept fairly close ties with *its* mother country. Why shouldn't Quebec renew old bonds with France? The latter might be helpful as a trade partner. It also could supply investment funds to build Quebec's economy. Perhaps it would give "moral support" to the Quiet Revolution. Some English-Canadians panicked. They feared that Quebec might be seeking France's help in becoming partly or fully **independent.**

This fear reached a peak in 1967 when French President Charles de Gaulle visited Quebec. From the balcony of Montreal's City Hall he shouted: "Vive le Québec Libre!" ("Long Live Free Quebec!") English Canada went wild. Letters poured into editors demanding that de Gaulle apologize, be sent home, or worse. He was asked to leave by the Canadian Prime Minister, Lester Pearson. Many French-Canadians were excited by de Gaulle's sympathy for them. But few of them wanted to separate from Canada. They were shocked by the violence of English-Canadian reactions.

Violence of another sort had also begun in Quebec. As early as 1963, a handful of radicals swung into action. They broke into stores and army warehouses to steal guns and ammunition. They painted separatist slogans in prominent places. They planted bombs in public buildings. Such actions were condemned by the vast majority of French-Canadians. Still, they were well publicized in the English press. It was time for Ottawa to act.

Montreal, 17 May, 1963. Bomb disposal expert Sgt. Walter Léja is seriously injured by the explosion of a terrorist bomb placed in a mailbox.

4.   OTTAWA RESPONDS

At first, the federal government was not sure what to do. By 1963, its plans were somewhat clearer. Quebec and the other provinces *were* consulted more, just as Premier Lesage had asked. The provinces were granted more powers, and more money to carry them out. As a result, Quebec set up its own system of pensions, student loans, youth allowances and other programmes. Partly to please Quebec, a new Canadian flag was adopted in 1965. The Maple Leaf emblem replaced the old "Red Ensign." The latter had been too closely identified with our colonial ties to Britain. Therefore, it had been disliked by many French-Canadians. They felt that Canada, as an independent country, should have a distinctive flag of its own.

In another important move, Ottawa set up a special commission in July, 1963. This was called the *Royal Commission on Bilingualism and Biculturalism.* It had two jobs: first, to examine the condition of the French language and culture in Canada; second, to suggest ways to improve this condition. The federal government made another vital point: in future, the English and French would be regarded as equal, founding peoples of Canada. In future, their relations would have to develop in a spirit of partnership. The last traces of the old "master and slave" attitude would have to go.

These were brave words and noble thoughts. However, these hopes could only come true if all Canadians *wanted* it to happen. A few commentators said that it had to happen, or that Canada would be finished within twenty years. Few people took them seriously.

5.   THE "BI AND BI" COMMISSION

In 1965, the Royal Commission on Bilingualism and Biculturalism made an early report. It described English-French relations as poor. It threw challenges to both sides:

TO THE ENGLISH	TO THE FRENCH
1. Stop acting as though Canada is a one-language country, run by and for the English.	1. Stop harping on past injustices.
2. End your prejudice and discrimination against the French.	2. Don't blame the English for all your troubles.
3. Accept the French language and culture as part of Canada's culture and way of life.	3. Claim your full rights under the law and use them more effectively.
	4. Start showing more feeling toward Canada, not just Quebec.

In the next few years, the "Bi and Bi" Commission made several important recommendations. Here are some of them:

A. Declare Canada officially bilingual (done).

B. Make English and French the official languages of the Parliament of Canada and the federal courts (done).

C. In communities where the English or French minority is large enough, provide government services in both languages (partly done).

D. Give students in all provinces a chance to study both languages (done where provinces agreed).

E. Employ more French-Canadians in the government (done).

F. In Quebec, make French the main language of work in government and business (being done).

G. Ontario and New Brunswick should declare themselves officially bilingual provinces (done in New Brunswick).

H. All provinces should provide services in French or English to their minorities (partly done).

I. The region of Ottawa-Hull should be declared the national capital area and made officially bilingual (done).

Reacting to the "Bi and Bi" Report

1. Do you agree with most of these ideals? Which ones? Why?

2. Do you strongly disagree with any of these ideas? If so, why?

3. Turn back to the quiz in Chapter 2 of this unit. Try to remember the answers you gave if you tried it earlier. Have any of your ideas changed? Have any of your opinions become stronger? If so, why?

4. Do you think the "Bi and Bi" Commission wanted all Canadians to become bilingual? Explain your answer.

5. Do you personally believe that all Canadians should become bilingual? Would this be possible?

6. Look up the most recent Canadian census. Make up a chart showing the four or five largest ethnic groups in each province. Which province other than Quebec has the most French-Canadians? Germans? Italians? Ukrainians? Chinese? Greeks?

7. Some people suggest that if French is going to have official recognition, so should the language of other large ethnic groups. These would include German, Italian and Ukrainian. How do you feel about this idea?

6. TRUDEAU: A NEW VOICE IN OTTAWA

An exciting new personality came into politics in the mid-1960s. He was young, intelligent and fluently bilingual. His name was Pierre Trudeau. For years, as a professor and writer, he had been a critic of government. In 1965, he joined the Liberal Party and was elected to Parliament. By 1968, he was Prime Minister of Canada.

The newly elected Prime Minister, Pierre Elliott Trudeau, conducts a working lunch with Jean Marchand (left) and Gerard Pelletier (right). These men were brought into the Trudeau Cabinet to help bring a "new deal" to French Canadians.

To English-Canadians he seemed the perfect person to heal the country's wounds and restore unity. They especially liked his view that Quebec should remain in Canada. Mr. Trudeau was strongly opposed to separatism. He called it a backward step. He said it would be harmful to Canada, but even more costly to Quebec. He also denied that large changes were needed in the Canadian Constitution (the B.N.A. Act). In his opinion, Quebec had all the basic powers needed to protect and advance the French language and culture.

Most French-Canadians were happy about the election of Mr. Trudeau as Prime Minister. They too rejected separatism. However, many of them disagreed with his statements about the constitution. There was a growing feeling, especially in Quebec, that some basic changes were needed.

Instead, Mr. Trudeau concentrated on the growth of bilingualism. He brought many prominent French-Canadians into the government. They were given key positions in the Cabinet and the civil service. Large sums of money were spent to provide language instruction to civil servants who could speak only one language. By 1976, this spending had reached almost $150 million per year. This policy was criticized by some Canadians, for two reasons. First, it obviously was expensive. Secondly, they argued that it was not working. This latter criticism is more important. The amount spent to promote bilingualism in the civil service was only one third of one per cent of the total 1976 budget. Surely this would not be too high a price to pay, if the program worked. Unfortunately, it appeared to be failing.

7.   DIFFICULTIES WITH BILINGUALISM

The Trudeau government learned that the saying is true: It really is difficult to "teach an old dog new tricks." Most unilingual adults are poor students when it comes to learning a second language. Perhaps there was another way? The federal government began to think that it would be better to concentrate on the younger generation. In other words, provide teachers and funds to expand language programmes in elementary and secondary schools across Canada. However, this plan had problems too. One of these was that education was a provincial responsibility. Provinces had always guarded this right very jealously, Quebec most of all. Time was another factor. Could the country wait

In 1976 pressure grew to let French-speaking pilots and air traffic controllers communicate over the air in French. Many English Canadians protested. Investigate this issue. How was it resolved?

until a new generation of bilingual Canadians grew up?

Other problems with bilingualism were emerging as well. A **backlash** was developing in English Canada. People were complaining of the "favouritism" being shown to Quebec. For evidence, they pointed to the numbers of French-Canadians being appointed to key government jobs. They claimed that Quebec was receiving more money from Ottawa than it was paying in through taxes. Montreal was the site for Expo 1967 and the 1976 Summer Olympic Games. (Actually, these events were due largely to the efforts of Montreal itself. Both projects were very expensive, and left Montreal with serious financial problems.)

Perhaps most importantly, English-Canadians felt that French was being "rammed down their throats." An Ontario father kept his child home from classes after "O Canada" was sung in French over the school's public address system. A Toronto radio station broadcast a short comment entitled: "HEY, QUEBEC: GO SUCK A LEMON!" Phone calls and letters poured into the station. They did not condemn the prejudice and intolerance shown in the program. Rather, the vast majority of them said: "Right on!" Equally strong letters began

This photo indicates the popularity of Pierre Trudeau with French-Canadian voters in the late 1960s.

appearing in English-language newspapers. A few excerpts appear below:

"For generations, Quebec has been Canada's baby, spoon-fed, diapered and powdered at the expense of the rest of the Canadian taxpayers."

"Giving in to continual French demands in ... English-speaking provinces, while we observe what is happening in Quebec, is folly to the ultimate degree."

"Given your choice of a bilingual Ontario or Quebec separation, I vote for the break-up of Canada. Mais oui!"

Ironically, bilingualism was also opposed by many French-Canadians. As one observer said: "We are not asking to speak French in Vancouver. We are asking to live in French in Quebec." Another added: "We don't want to feel at home in Winnipeg, or be served in French in your post-office. You write 'luggage' on your airport doors. We'll write 'bagage' and serve you in French in our post-office."

There were English-Canadian supporters of bilingualism. However, they seemed to be in the minority. Also, their position was made more difficult by some rather drastic developments within Quebec.

Could a French-Canadian feel at home in your community?

Most Canadians want our country to stay together. They do not want Quebec, or any other province, to leave Confederation. Some people claim that French-Canadians would identify more with Canada, if they could feel "at home" outside Quebec.

Examine your own community. *How comfortable would you feel in it if you spoke only French?* To answer this question well, consider these points:

1. Could you do your shopping in French?
2. Could you deal with the government, police or other services in French?
3. Could you speak French at work?
4. Could you or your brothers and sisters go to a French school?
5. Does your community have a French-language newspaper? Radio station? T.V. channel? Theatre? Library?
6. What else would be required for you to feel "at home" in the community?

Obviously, it would be impossible for all or even most communities in Canada to be home for both English-and French-speaking people. Fortunately, it also is unnecessary. Still, perhaps bilingualism should be further advanced than it is. How large do you feel a community should be before it could be asked to support bilingual facilities? How large should a cultural minority be before it could expect bilingual services? Apply these standards to your own community. How is it doing?

8. THE QUIET REVOLUTION GETS NOISY IN QUEBEC

In 1970, the Union Nationale government lost power in Quebec. The Liberal party, led by Robert Bourassa, took over. Besides being a fellow Liberal, Mr. Bourassa shared Prime Minister Trudeau's belief that Quebec should stay in Confederation. The signs seemed encouraging.

Then, in October of 1970, a series of shocking events occurred (see chapter 5 in this unit for more details). A radical separatist group kidnapped James Cross, a British Trade official. A few days later they kidnapped the Quebec Minister of Labour, Pierre Laporte. Eventually, Mr. Cross was freed, but Mr. Laporte was killed. The crisis was finally overcome, but not before some extreme statements were made on both sides. Most French-Canadians were repelled by these criminal acts. However, some of them sympathized with the emotions and frustrations of the terrorists. Some English-Canadians could not understand this combination of feelings.

Bilingualism, and English-French relations generally, suffered a more serious blow in 1974. Mr. Bourassa's government passed the controversial "Bill 22." This act made French the "only official language" of Quebec. Here are some of its terms:

● Business firms would be pressed to operate in French. Those which did not would not receive any government contracts.

● Immigrant children wishing to attend English schools would have to take tests in that language. If they could not pass, permission would be denied. They would then have to attend French schools.

● Present English schools could not expand unless granted government approval.

● Official documents, business contracts, product labels, menus and billboards must be printed in French. Special permission would be required to print them also in English.

● Employers must be able to communicate with their employees in French.

Bill 22 did not ban English from the parliament or courts of Quebec. It *did* require that English be taught in French schools.

This act offended many English-Canadians. It created hardships for the 20 per cent of the Quebec population that is non-French. Obviously, it did a great deal of damage to the bilingualism program of the federal government.

9. NOVEMBER, 1976 — SEPARATIST VICTORY!

For weeks in advance, the polls kept saying it would happen. Few people could believe them — until it *did* happen! On November 15, 1976 the Bourassa government was overwhelmingly defeated by the separatist Parti Québécois.

The newly elected Premier of Quebec, separatist René Lévesque, speaks to supporters just after the announcement of his victory of November 15, 1976.

Details of this development are provided in the next chapter. It is enough to say here that the entire country was stunned. Even the Parti Québécois itself was somewhat surprised at its great success.

English-French relations, it seemed, had come to a cross-roads. Or, had they come to the end of the road?

THINGS TO THINK ABOUT AND DO

Reviewing Key Words and Ideas

The following terms appeared in this chapter. Try to recall their meaning and how they were used.

air traffic controller	controversy	Red Ensign
anglophone	curriculum	revenue
Bi and Bi Commission	francophone	subsidies
Bill 22	independence	terrorist
consultation	Quiet Revolution	

Remembering the Facts

1. Summarize the *causes* and *goals* of the Quiet Revolution.
2. What were the reasons for the defeat of the Lesage government in the Quebec election of 1966?
3. Why did the visit of Charles de Gaulle to Quebec in 1967 create a storm of controversy in Canada?
4. What were the main recommendations of the Bi and Bi Commission? To what extent were they carried out?

Analyzing Ideas

1. Why did the federal government's efforts to promote bilingualism run into difficulties?
2. What was the main purpose of Quebec's Bill 22?
3. Should it be possible for a unilingual French-Canadian to get an important government job in Ottawa? Why or why not? Find out whether it *is* in fact possible.
4. In the 1970s, three political figures played key roles in the development of English-French relations. They were: Pierre Trudeau, Robert Bourassa and René Lévesque. A good class project would be to divide up into research teams to develop an information file on these three men. Try to find out about their backgrounds, attitudes and activities. This information will help you to understand the next chapter.

Applying Your Knowledge

1. Imagine that you were a federal civil servant in Ottawa. You speak only in English, and have just been told that, in your job, bilingualism is now required. The ability to speak French also would improve your chances of future promotion. Failure to learn French will cause you to be moved to another, perhaps less important job. What thoughts would run through your mind as you drove home from work that evening? What will you decide to do? What factors will influence your decision? Is it fair for the government to put you in this position? Explain your answer.
2. Consider the possibility of making contact with some French-Canadian students from Quebec. This could be done by individuals or as a class project. Students in the class who study French could be in charge of writing the necessary letters. Others could think of the questions to ask, and the information, photographs or other materials to be exchanged. Such activities should be attempted only with the advice of your teacher and the permission of your school principal.

3. As we have seen, some French-Canadians complain that they do not have enough representation in the federal Cabinet. This is a key body because it advises the Prime Minister. Its members also set government policy for the entire country. As well, they provide leadership for the various departments of government. Do some research to see how the membership and ethnic makeup of the Cabinet have changed over the years. The Canada Yearbook would be very helpful. Ask your teacher and librarian for other suggestions regarding sources. Try to discover the names of the members of Cabinet under the following Prime Ministers:

a) Mackenzie King (in the years immediately after World War II)
b) Louis St. Laurent (around 1955)
c) John Diefenbaker (around 1960)
d) Lester Pearson (around 1965)
e) Pierre Trudeau (around 1969)
f) Pierre Trudeau (around September, 1977)
g) today!

What has happened to the overall percentage of French-Canadians in the Cabinet? How could you account for this? What has happened to the number of *key* Cabinet positions held by French-Canadians? Do the same reasons apply? Does the political party or ethnic background of the Prime Minister seem to be a factor? Can French-Canadians fairly argue today that they are under-represented in the Cabinet? Why or why not?

5

QUEBEC SEPARATISM

INTRODUCTION

> "I feel alive again! We're free at last! We showed those English! Now we can walk with our heads up!"

November 15, 1976. In Montreal and Quebec City, the night air was full of such shouts and cheers in French. There was dancing in the streets. Large groups of people, most of them young, laughed, cried, cheered and sang. One of their favourite chants, which they repeated over and over was: "Québec aux Québécois"! ("Quebec to the Quebeckers!"). These enthusiastic crowds were supporters of separatism. They were celebrating the spectacular election victory of the separatist Parti Québécois.

The Paul Sauvé arena in downtown Montreal was literally packed to the rafters with Parti Québécois workers and supporters. They were waiting for the arrival of their leader, René Lévesque. Suddenly he appeared, moving through the happy crowd, surrounded by aides and bodyguards. He climbed up onto the platform and raised his arms. The crowd cheered wildly and non-stop for almost five minutes. Finally, they quieted enough for him to speak. A rather small, frail man, he appeared very tired. But the strength of a great victory energized him. Overcome with emotion, his eyes partly filling with tears, the new Premier of Quebec began to speak. The words were calm and gentle.

He urged his supporters to keep a friendly, reasonable attitude to Canada. As he spoke, the CBC television cameras in the studio moved close up to the commentators. Most of them tried to play down what was happening. But their facial expressions did not match their words. One of them, Premier Richard Hatfield of New Brunswick, looked stricken. His province has the highest percentage of French-Canadians outside Quebec. New Brunswick guarantees equal rights to French and English, including equality of educational opportunity. Premier Hatfield was very frank. He admitted to being surprised, disappointed and worried by the election results. It was clear that a new chapter in English-French relations was about to be written.

Some Reactions to the Parti Québécois Election Victory

The following reactions were published by a leading Canadian newspaper immediately following the Quebec election of November 1976:

A 20-year-old French-Canadian college student
This person admitted to being strongly in favour of independence for Quebec. He was very happy with the election result. He denied that the P.Q. victory was simply the result of voter unhappiness with the previous government. He claimed that the French in Quebec were in danger of losing their culture and identity. It would be a "waste of time, energy and money" for Quebec to continue in Confederation. An independent Quebec should keep close ties with Canada for economic reasons. However, when asked to comment on English Canada's reaction to separatism, he said: "I royally could not care less what the English think."

A 54-year-old member of Montreal's Jewish community
He was surprised and frightened by the election result. He felt that the P.Q. victory did not mean increased support for separatism. Rather, he saw it as a protest against the previous Bourassa government. He admitted that the Parti Québécois had many talented members. He believed that they were democratic and sensible. Therefore they would not act hastily or foolishly. His attitude must be one of "wait and see."

A 43-year-old French-Canadian housewife
She said she had voted for the Union Nationale. Her brother-in-law was the U.N. candidate in her riding (he lost). After the election results came in, she went out with several friends to celebrate the separatist victory. She said that, if she had to vote again, she would vote for the Parti Québécois. She said that she was not sure why, and that she really did not know a great deal about politics. However, it felt good to see a government pushing for freedom and equality for French-Canadians.

A 37-year-old French-Canadian draftsman
This man worked in Ottawa for the federal government. He was very disappointed with the election result. He claimed that most of his friends and co-workers felt the same way. He said that mature people must see the advantages of remaining part of Canada. He believed that the election results had been swayed by young French voters. They had been "brainwashed" in school by separatist teachers. They had no understanding of the "economic realities of jobs and families." He thought that the youth would change once they were out of school and part of the working world.

Before reading on, study the chart of Key Words and Ideas which follows.

KEY WORDS AND IDEAS IN THIS CHAPTER

Term	Meaning	Sample use
customs union	a trade agreement between two or more countries; they agree to eliminate tariffs or duties in their trade with each other	If Quebec separated, it would want to continue trade with Canada through a customs union.
federalist	in Canada, a person who wants all provinces to remain united within one country	Most Canadians are federalists. They are opposed to Quebec separatism.
indépendentist(e)	a French term, meaning a person who wants independence or freedom for his/her country	Quebeckers who favour separatism refer to themselves as indépendentists, rather than separatists.
regionalism	a tendency of people to identify with, and be loyal to, their region rather than to their country as a whole	Separatism is an extreme form of regionalism.
secession	the act by which a province or state withdraws from a federal union	The separatist government of René Lévesque wants Quebec's secession from Canada.
separatist	a person who wants his/her province to secede from Canada	The separatist movement grew steadily in Quebec through the late 1960s and early 1970s. In 1976, the separatists won power in the Quebec provincial election.

1.   SEPARATISM — IS IT LEGAL?

Separatist feelings are not new to Canada. They have been expressed, from time to time, since Confederation. Also, they are not found only in Quebec. They have been heard in the Maritimes and in the West, particularly in British Columbia and Alberta.

MON., MAR. 14, 1977.

What is the point being made in this cartoon?

The main reason for this is because Canada is divided into regions. Each of these areas tends to have its own identity. This means that it feels somewhat different from the rest of the country.

1. Try to identify the regions of Canada. Make a list of them.

2. What factors have produced this **regionalism?** Explain why they have had this effect. (A full answer should include ideas about geography, history, ethnic groups, culture and economics.)

3. From what region of Canada do *you* come? How strong is your own personal sense of regional identity? Why is this? Do you think that you are typical of your region? Why or why not?

4. Why might it be a good thing for Canadians to have these regional loyalties and identities? On the other hand, what problems might these create?

Pierre Trudeau

"Je suis Fédéralist"

"French Canadians could no more **constitute** (make up) a perfect society than could the five million Sikhs of *the Punjab* (a region of India). We are not well enough educated, not rich enough, nor, above all, numerous enough, to man and finance a government possessing all the necessary means for both war and peace."

René Lévesque

"Je suis Séparatist"

"French Canada is a true nation. It has all the elements essential to national life; it possesses unity as well as human and material resources, including equipment and personnel, which are as good or better than those of a large number of the people of the world."

The issue of Quebec separatism is focused in these two politicians.Both men are from Quebec. Both are fluently bilingual and highly intelligent. Both are dynamic leaders. Each has a great deal of political power. Here the similarities end.

Pierre Trudeau's background is French and Scottish. His father was a very wealthy businessman. The young Pierre went to private schools. He spent much of his youth studying and travelling the world. For several years he was a professor and teacher of law. He also edited and wrote for *Cité Libre*. This publication often criticized the government of Quebec Premier Maurice Duplessis. He also wrote books on Canadian government and politics. In 1968 Trudeau became Prime Minister of Canada. Mr. Trudeau remains strongly opposed to Quebec separation.

René Lévesque was not born into a wealthy family. Perhaps this is why his ties with average people seem closer, and more emotional than Trudeau's. He was a war correspondent in World War II. Later he became a well-known CBC television commentator. He entered Quebec politics in 1960. Lévesque was soon made a member of the Lesage Cabinet. Gradually, he came to the belief that Quebec could not fulfil itself within Canada. When he could not persuade the Liberal party to share his views, he left. In 1968, he helped to form a new separatist group, the Parti Québécois. He was made its first leader that year. In the same year Mr. Trudeau became Prime Minister of Canada.

Could a Province Secede From Confederation?

From time to time this question has come up. Could a province pull out of the Canadian union? There are different opinions on that question. However, most legal experts agree that such an action would be illegal. This claim rests mainly on one simple fact: there is no mention of such action in the British North America Act. The B.N.A. Act is our constitution. It lays down the rules by which our system of government must operate. If the constitution does not mention withdrawal of provinces from the union, then such action cannot be taken. Arguments which support this view are based on what happened in 1867. When the provincial leaders discussed Confederation, they had in mind a union which would last forever. They were not planning a brief or temporary arrangement.

Still, there are points to be made for the other side. They agree that the B.N.A. Act does not mention **secession** (withdrawal by one or more provinces). Therefore, it does not forbid such an action. Also, Canada claims to be a democratic country. It tries to serve the best interest of the Canadian people. What if some of those people, living in one or more provinces, are unhappy? What if they feel that they could do better by forming their own country? Why should they not be allowed to do so? Why should Canada force a province to stay in the union against its will?

Today, there are some people in certain provinces who are in favour of getting out of Confederation. This feeling is strongest in Quebec. It also has some support in British Columbia and Alberta. Some Quebeckers have pointed out that Quebec joined Confederation without taking a vote among the people. They are quite correct. Such a vote would be called a **plebiscite** or **referendum.** No such vote, (one strictly on the question of joining Canada) was held in Quebec, or in any other province for that matter. The decision was made by politicians, elected earlier by the people. Therefore, some Quebec separatists argue that Quebec could leave Confederation the same way it came in. That is, it could leave by a decision of the Quebec government, not by a direct vote of the people.

Another question that comes up is this: If a province wants to leave Confederation, should the decision be made by *its* voters alone, or by all Canadian voters? What is your opinion on this issue? How could you defend your view?

Finally, we come to what is perhaps the most difficult point of the problem: WHAT IF THE PEOPLE OF A PROVINCE WANT TO SECEDE, BUT THE REST OF CANADA IS OPPOSED TO THE IDEA? COULD THE COURTS SOLVE THE PROBLEM? HOW IMPORTANT WOULD **LEGALITY** (the legal right to do something) BE, ESPECIALLY TO THE PROVINCE THAT WANTS TO LEAVE? SHOULD CANADA USE *FORCE* TO KEEP A PROVINCE IN CONFEDERATION?

A few years ago, these questions would have been considered wild and foolish. Today, unfortunately, this is no longer true. The danger of one or more provinces seceding from Canada is *very real*. These questions matter, to all of us. Think about them carefully.

2.   THE RISE OF THE PARTI QUÉBÉCOIS

The rise to power of the Parti Québecois in Quebec was truly amazing. No political party in Canada's history has ever risen so far, so quickly. Separatist ideas go back a long way in the history of Quebec. Still, until recently, very few people held these ideas. As we have seen some Quebec leaders were opposed to Quebec joining Confederation in 1867. At the time of the Riel affair, and the first conscription crisis, a few voices muttered about Quebec leaving Canada. In the 1930s and 1940s, Lionel Groulx spoke and wrote about separation.

However, the thought of separation never really took root in Quebec until the 1960s. It was prompted by the "Quiet Revolution." As we have seen, the main goal of this development was not to take Quebec out of Confederation. Yet, there was a threat beneath the surface. If Quebec's goals were not achieved, separation might occur. Some English-Canadians were openly hostile towards the "Quiet Revolution." In the previous chapter we read many of their statements on bilingualism and other issues. Such remarks encouraged separatist feeling. As one French Quebecker said: "We want the French language and culture to flourish freely in Quebec. If this is too much to ask, then we might as well forget about Canada."

A separatist demonstration in Montreal, 1967

This chart shows the gradual rise in public support for separatism in Quebec.

Results of Selected Polls on Separatism Since 1962

	IN FAVOUR	OPPOSED	UNDECIDED
1962	8%	73%	19%
1965	7%	79%	14%
1968	10%	72%	18%
1970	14%	76%	10%
1973	17%	64%	19%

A number of small separatist parties were born in Quebec in the early 1960s. They were led by such people as Marcel Chaput, Pierre Bourgault and Gilles Grégoire. None were very successful. Altogether they received only 9 per cent of the votes in the 1966 election. However, the movement was strengthened in 1968. In that year, most of the separatist organizations agreed to combine and form one party. Its name: the Parti Québécois. Its leader: the dynamic and popular René Lévesque. Even at this stage, few Quebeckers took the separatists very seriously. Lévesque's predictions about rapid success made many of them laugh. Look at those predictions. How accurate was Lévesque?

Lévesque's Predictions

Prediction	Year of Quebec Election	Results of Quebec Election (other parties not shown)		
		Party	% of Vote	Number of Seats
In 1968, René Lévesque said: 1. In our first election we will win at least 20 per cent of the votes.	1970	Liberals Parti Québécois	45 23	72 7
2. In our second election we will win about 25 per cent of the votes, and we will form the official opposition (i.e. — win the second largest number of seats)	1973	Liberals Parti Québécois	55 31	102 6 (enough to become the official opposition)
3. In our third election, we will form the government of Quebec.	1976	Parti Québécois Liberals	41 33	69 28

The separatists *did* become the government of Quebec in 1976. Still, it is important to remember that they won only 41 per cent of the votes. In other words, 59 per cent of Quebeckers voted against the Parti Québécois. Lévesque had a big advantage in the election. Quebec voters were disgusted with the Liberal government of Robert Bourassa. The Liberals had promised to cure unemployment in Quebec. However, unemployment grew quickly between 1973 and 1976. Taxes and the provincial debt also increased. Scandals rocked the government. They even damaged the personal reputation of Mr. Bourassa. In the 1976 election, the Parti Québécois did not stress separatism. Instead, it asked for support because it could provide good government. A Parti Québécois government would be honest and work better than that of Mr. Bourassa. These reasons were probably as important to Lévesque's victory as his support of separatism. They may have been even more important.

TUES., MAR. 1, 1977.

This cartoon refers to the election strategy of René Lévesque in the 1976 Quebec election. What is the point it makes?

The following opinion polls provide some interesting information. The questions which appear below were asked of Quebeckers a few days before the election of November 15, 1976.

Q: ■ "Personally, do you favour or not Quebec becoming an ■ independent country which would no longer be part of Canada?"

IN FAVOUR	OPPOSED	UNDECIDED
18%	58%	24%

Q: ■ "In general, how satisfied are you with the present ■ provincial government in Quebec:

very satisfied	3%
rather satisfied	23%
not too satisfied	42%
not at all satisfied	25%
Undecided	7%

A poll taken a few days after the 1976 election showed that public support in Quebec for independence had dropped to 11 per cent. However, by February of 1977, yet another poll suggested it had risen to 22 per cent. Sixty-five per cent opposed independence and 15 per cent were undecided.

The question on Quebec separation for today's Gallup Poll was:
"There has been quite a bit of talk recently about the possibility of the province of Quebec separating from the rest of Canada and becoming an independent country. Would you yourself be in favour of separation or opposed to it?"

	In Favour	Opposed	Qualified	Undecided
National..........	14%	73%	1%	11%
Quebec...........	22	63	1	14
Rest of Canada....	11	77	2	10

By May of 1977, support for separatism in Quebec itself had once again fallen below 15 per cent.

1. What do these polls suggest to you about the nature of separatist feeling in Quebec?
2. Try to find an up-to-date opinion poll concerning this issue. How do its figures compare with those of 1977?
3. In your opinion, what factors will decide whether pro-separatist feeling grows or declines in Quebec?

3. CAUSES OF QUEBEC SEPARATISM

The main reasons for the growth of separatist feeling in Quebec can be found in the statements quoted below:

A. "...The fact is, we are considered as second-class citizens, constantly held in contempt by our English counterparts. ... After having all of this thrown at me day after day, you tell me how I can be anything else but a separatist. How can I refuse this last chance to be myself? How can I refuse to be a part, as a full citizen, of a culture, of a country? .... We are only human, and we can take just so much."

B. "We believe that a country, like Quebec, which is three times as large as France, five times as large as Italy, thirteen times as large as Cuba, that such a country which stands among the first producers in the world of hydro-electric power, wood, pulp and paper, iron ore, minerals of all kinds, that this country which is linked to the ocean by one of the main seaways of the world, can live by itself and prosper."

C. "I think of Quebec first because this province is the only one in which I feel completely at home, the only one which allows me to live freely in French twenty-four hours a day."

1. What reasons for separation are stated or implied in A? In B? In C? How do you react to each of these arguments?

This young girl sits in front of a doorway in a Montreal slum. Such poverty has made some Quebeckers desperate for a radical change in government.

2. Do you agree with the suggestion in B that an independent Quebec could survive on its own?

3. Most French-Canadians have a deep emotional attachment to Quebec. Why is this?

4. Even French-Canadian **federalists** (supporters of Confederation) have a strong feeling for Quebec. Prime Minister Trudeau and some members of his cabinet have stated that, if Quebec separated, they would continue to live there. Should they have said this in public? Were they being disloyal to Canada? Explain your answers.

5. What additional reasons could you find for the growth of separatist feeling in Quebec?

Who Are The Separatists?

A survey published by the *Toronto Star* in 1977 identified some characteristics common to most separatists.

		% of Respondents		
	Total	**Extreme separatists**	**Extreme federalists**	**Middle-grounders**
SEX				
Male	50	54	48	49
Female	50	46	52	51
AGE				
18-30	34	56	16	39
Average	39	33	45	37
MARITAL STATUS				
Single	21	29	9	30
Married	66	56	78	58
EDUCATION				
High school or less	61	49	69	59
Technical/ or community college.	22	40	12	18
University/graduate school	17	11	19	23
UNION HOUSEHOLD	41	58	30	39
EMPLOYER				
Self-employed	10	9	14	7
A company	57	47	67	55
Government (municipal, provincial, federal)	31	41	19	37
OWN PROPERTY	49	38	60	45

ETHNIC BACKGROUND

French	73	<u>88</u>	<u>60</u>	77
English	27	12	40	23

SPEAK ENGLISH WITH LITTLE OR NO DIFFICULTY (% of French)

	60	<u>72</u>	<u>46</u>	61

PLACE OF RESIDENCE

Urban	86	<u>93</u>	84	85

VOTING BEHAVIOR PROVINCIAL ELECTION — NOVEMBER 1976

Parti Québécois	60	<u>98</u>	27	64
Liberal	26	2	<u>48</u>	22
Union Nationale	11	—	20	10
Creditiste	2	—	2	4
Parti Nationale Populaire	1	—	3	—

The underscored numbers show where there are significant differences between those in one of the three groups and the population as a whole.

Portraits of Two Separatists

In 1977, *Richard Cyr* was a 26-year-old heavy machinery operator in Montreal. He was a high school graduate. He also had studied at a vocational college. He was married and had one child. He earned about $14 000 per year. He owned no property, but hoped to have his own home one day. He was a union member.

He said that he spoke no English. He did not want French-Canadian children exposed to bilingualism, or even to English media. He was confident that an independent Quebec could survive. Separation might lead to a civil war. Most of the fighting would be with the English in Quebec who "are our number one problem." He said he was not religious. He did not care if the rest of Canada adopted bilingualism. He stated that he would not change his mind unless something shocking happened — "like I dropped dead!"

Madeleine Longpré is from east-end Montreal. In 1977, she was in her mid-fifties and married to a construction worker. Her husband earned about $8 000 per year. She said that Quebeckers have waited too long. They would not change their minds about separating. She claimed that there was growing anti-English feeling in Quebec. She blamed the English hold on the best jobs for this. She had no hope for Canada becoming bilingual because the English were too "hard-headed." Anyway, it would take too long. The French were "fed up with waiting." She felt that Quebec was rich, but lost out by staying in Confederation. She was prepared to suffer a 10 per cent cut in her family's income for the sake of Quebec's independence.

A Dissenting Voice

Alain Marcoux was a 25-year-old worker in Trois Rivières. He was strongly against separatism. He was worried about job opportunities. He had seen many friends lose their jobs in the slow Quebec economy. He did not speak English but wished that he could. He felt that speaking English would increase his chance for a better job. He did not feel that French culture (or identity) was threatened. It was too deeply rooted in Quebec. He felt that many young French-Canadians were too romantic about independence. They did not realize its dangerous results. He believed that the English and French could live together if both sides would try harder.

4.   QUEBEC SEPARATISM: THE RADICAL FRINGE

Most of those Quebeckers who support separatism are opposed to violence. They believe that Quebec should leave Canada peacefully and democratically. The Parti Québécois is a legal party in Canada.

However, since the early 1960s, separatism also has drawn a few **radicals** (extremists) to its cause. One such radical group was known as the *Front de Libération Québécois* (Quebec Liberation Front) or F.L.Q. for short. Its members believed that Quebec could become independent only by using violence. This group was responsible for most of the terrorist acts in Quebec in the 1960s. These acts included robberies and bombings. In a few cases, people were killed or badly injured.

F.L.Q. activity reached a peak in October, 1970. Some of its members kidnapped James Cross, a British trade official, from his Montreal home. A few days later, the F.L.Q. also seized Quebec's Labour Minister, Pierre Laporte, while he was playing with some children on his street. Through these actions, the F.L.Q. hoped to bring attention to their cause. They wanted publicity from the media. Perhaps they also hoped that the government, and English Canadians, would react harshly. This might create sympathy for the F.L.Q. among French-Canadians. The F.L.Q. might then be seen as heroes.

Their aims were only partly fulfilled. They did receive publicity. But almost all of it was bad. The Trudeau government brought in a drastic measure known as the War Measures Act. In effect, this Act suspended everyone's civil rights. This let police arrest and jail people without charging them. Tension was very high for many days. Most Canadians were shocked when the police found the body of Pierre Laporte. It was stuffed in the trunk of a car in a Montreal parking lot. He had been strangled, apparently with the chain of his crucifix.

A newsboy holds up a newspaper with a banner headline announcing the use of the War Measures Act, October 16, 1970.

Mr. Cross was later released, shaken but unharmed. In exchange, the government had to agree to let his abductors escape to Cuba. They were exiled from Canada for life. A total of twenty-three people were convicted and jailed for terrorist acts. These included Jacques Rose and Bernard Lortie. They were sentenced to eight years and life in prison, respectively, for their part in the Laporte kidnapping.

Pierre Laporte

FLQ kidnapper, Marc Carbonneau, who was
exiled from Canada in 1970

Most experts felt that these actions destroyed the F.L.Q. and damaged the separatist cause in Quebec. They might have been right on the first count. It appears they were quite wrong on the second. Perhaps this is partly because of the public reaction to the War Measures Act. Most of the media attacked the government's use of this act. They described it as unnecessary. It was, they said, harmful to human rights in Canada. Civil liberties groups agreed. No doubt, the heavy handed actions of the government had some public support. However, in Quebec, the use of the War Measures Act probably created some sympathy for the separatist cause.

5.   WHAT IF QUEBEC SEPARATED?

To repeat, the separation of Quebec from Canada is not a certainty. Still, it *could* happen. Therefore, it is important to think about its possible effects on the rest of the country. Here are some:

- Canada would lose its largest province (about 14 per cent of its total area).
- Canada could lose about 25 per cent of its population. (Up to 1 000 000 English Quebeckers might leave, but almost as many French-Canadians from outside Quebec might return.)
- Canada would lose about 25 per cent of its **gross national product** (total value of goods and services produced).
- Canada would lose about 15 per cent of its fresh water, 14 per cent of its mineral production and large quantities of hydro-electric power.

- The value of the Canadian dollar would probably fall.
- Atlantic Canada would be physically cut off from the rest of Canada.
- The defence of Canada might be in danger.
- Some experts believe that the rest of Canada might begin to fall apart. Certain other provinces might want to separate.

These comments from letters to a Toronto newspaper suggest other concerns:

- "In my opinion, the existence of Quebec and French Canadians in Canada is one of the few differences between our country and the United States." (WHAT DOES THIS IMPLY ABOUT QUEBEC'S CONTRIBUTION TO CANADA'S IDENTITY? DO YOU AGREE?)
- "... it (Quebec's separation) would be the end of Canada and we would be part of the United States of America in a short time. (DO YOU AGREE WITH THIS OPINION? HOW IS IT LINKED TO THE ONE ABOVE?)

"If Quebec should leave confederation how serious do you think this would be for the future of the rest of Canada — very serious, fairly serious or not very serious?"

(The table also gives results for a similar poll in 1966 but in that study "very" and "fairly" serious categories were combined.)

	Very serious	Fairly serious	Not very serious	No opinion
NATIONAL—Today	46%	27%	22%	5%
—1966	—48—		28	24
Quebec —Today	40	31	22	7
—1966	—51—		20	29
Rest of Canada				
—Today	48	26	22	4
—1966	—47—		31	22
By region today:				
Atlantic	63	14	18	5
Quebec	40	31	22	7
Ontario	51	28	20	2
Prairies	35	29	27	9
British Columbia	48	23	28	2

This Gallup Poll was taken in February, 1977. What had happened to the public mood on the question since 1966? In what region of the country is there the most concern? The least concern? How do you account for these facts?

What would be the boundaries of an independent Quebec?
The changing boundaries of Quebec through history suggest that the province should have to give up land if it separates from Canada, (see maps on page 265.)

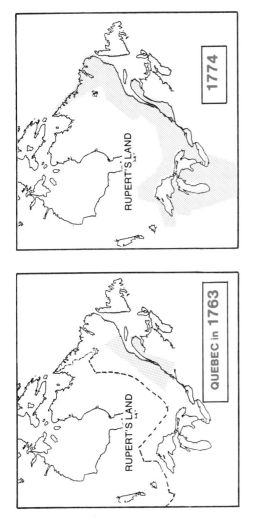

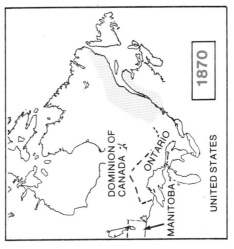

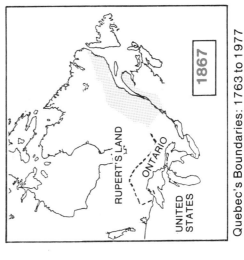

Quebec's Boundaries: 1763 to 1977

The Parti Québécois says that an independent Quebec would lay claim to Labrador, Ellesmere Island, Baffin Island, plus several islands in Hudson Bay and the Arctic Ocean.

Bill 101: Quebec's Language Charter

In the previous chapter, there was mention of Bill 22. This was a measure of the Bourassa government. Its aim was to strengthen the position of the French language in Quebec. The Parti Québécois criticized it when it was introduced. When that party came to power in 1976, it was determined to scrap Bill 22. This was done in the summer of 1977 with the passage of Bill 101.

Opponents of Bill 22 demonstrate in favour of English schools in Montreal. Many such opponents were immigrants to Canada. Why would many of these same people be even *more* upset by Bill 101?

Bill 101 was designed to make French the only official language in Quebec. It was much clearer than Bill 22. It also was easier to enforce in the courts. Here are some important things which the bill did:
- gives every Quebecker the right to work in French
- gives every Quebecker the right to receive education in French
- gives every Quebecker the right to be informed and served by the provincial government in French
- gives every Quebecker the right to speak in French in any public assembly

- gives every Quebecker the right to require that the government, public services, professional corporations, employees' associations and various other enterprises communicate with him in French
- most government documents would henceforth be issued only in French (although people might communicate with the state, and receive a reply, in another language)
- requires all businesses with 50 or more employees to earn "francization certificates" by 1983 (this would mean that their operations were conducted basically in French)
- says that any employee may require his employer to put written communication in French
- states that no employer may dismiss or demote a salaried worker solely on the grounds that he does not speak English well
- requires that public notices, from both government and industry, must be only in French
- strictly limits the right of Quebec schoolchildren to be educated in English

The Quebec government was bitterly attacked by English-Canadians for this act. Premier Lévesque defended Bill 101 on the grounds that the British North America Act gave each province the right to pass laws regarding language. He said that continuing immigration into Quebec was starting to threaten the position of the French majority. Very few of these immigrants were French-speaking. Many of them came from such countries as Italy, Portugal and Greece. Most were sending their children to English schools. Also, the birth rate among French-Canadians had declined. These two facts posed a serious problem. Bill 22 had said that immigrant children who wished to attend English schools had to pass a language test. This test was proving unworkable. Bill 101 tried to limit English education to the children of parents who truly belonged to the English community. It made the following provisions:

- All children who were *legally* in the English school system when Bill 101 became law could remain there. Also, their younger brothers and sisters could attend English schools.
- Children whose mother or father was educated in English primary schools could attend such schools in Quebec.
- Children who were originally from other Canadian provinces could attend English schools in Quebec, *but only if the governments of those provinces would guarantee French education to their French-speaking minorities.*

When Bill 101 was passed, only one province guaranteed the right of education in French. This was New Brunswick. Ontario and certain other provinces rejected Quebec's offer of **reciprocal** (mutual) guarantees in education rights. In 1976, New Brunswick had about 106 000 students in English schools and 54 000 in French schools. Ontario had about 750 000 people of French descent. Of these, about half used French in the home.

In late 1977, some of Quebec's Inuit population protested against Bill 101. They demanded the right to English-language education for their children. They indicated that if Quebec separated from Canada, they (the Inuit) would secede from Quebec. At the time, René Lévesque's government rejected their demand. Here, an Inuit leader confronts a member of the Quebec Provincial Police.

Ontario had promised "adequate" provision of French education, where the number of students made it practical. In 1977, there were 24 publicly supported secondary schools, and 304 elementary schools, offering education in French. Western provinces had lower percentages of French-Canadians. Therefore they had fewer French schools. Manitoba had in effect removed French educational rights in the 1880s. Some of these rights were restored in the early 1970s. There were few French schools in Saskatchewan, Alberta and British Columbia. However, these provinces were working to improve this situation.

1. After the passage of Bill 101, some people suggested that the other nine provinces should do away with French educational rights, and stop all support of bilingualism. What do you think of this idea? Why?

2. The government of Quebec argued that the English minority in Quebec *still* had more rights and protection than the French minority in the other nine provinces. Would you agree?

3. Does a provincial government have the right to tell any of its people the language in which their children will be educated? Explain your answer.

6. HOW WOULD QUEBEC SEPARATION TAKE PLACE?

The Parti Québécois has always said that it would take Quebec out of Canada only if a *majority* of Quebec voters approved. This means that a plebiscite or referendum would be held on the question. Some people feel that *all* Canadians should have a chance to vote on this question, not just Quebeckers. Prime Minister Trudeau made another interesting suggestion: the Parti Québécois should give the same chance to minorities in Quebec. For example, let the Indians, Inuit and English vote to separate from Quebec. (In 1977, a few English Quebeckers formed a group to do that very thing.)

Some Canadians have called for the use of *force* to keep Quebec in Confederation. There are several arguments against this. The bloodshed might be terrible. The other costs would be enormous. Would the effort really be worthwhile if a province wanted out so badly? Also, Canada might not be strong enough to do the job. Our armed forces are fairly small and weak. Probably, there are fewer than 10 000 combat-ready troops in the entire country. Many of them are French-Canadians! (The armed forces contains one almost entirely French-Canadian regiment. This is the "Vandoos", the Royal 22nd Regiment. It is a tough, well-respected fighting force.)

The Parti Québécois believes that a peaceful separation is possible. They would hope to keep an independent Quebec on friendly terms with Canada. They have suggested close military and economic ties. These would include a **customs union** (agreement to remove tariffs or duties on goods) and possibly a common money system. However, Quebec would have its own national flag, anthem and government.

Canadians from outside Quebec do not agree that such a friendly parting could happen. Feelings of bitterness might be too strong. Also, the negotiations would be terribly complicated. One expert has said: "Trying to disentangle Quebec from the rest of Canada economically would be like trying to make eggs from an omelet." What would be the very least that Canada would demand from Quebec?

In a 1976 editorial, the Toronto Star suggested:

- a guaranteed land corridor between Ontario and the Maritimes; this would include railroad and highway links
- a guaranteed right to use the St. Lawrence River and Seaway
- fair compensation for federal **assets** (the value of buildings, equipment and other items paid for by all Canadians) in Quebec
- the transfer from Quebec of nationally-owned companies (such as Air Canada and the C.N.R.)

WOULD YOU ADD ANYTHING TO THIS LIST?

The media have an important role to play in public issues, including Quebec separatism. Press coverage could greatly influence opinion on both sides. What comment is this cartoon making about the press?

7.   COULD AN INDEPENDENT QUEBEC SURVIVE?

Canadians differ widely in their views on this question. Their opinions seem to reflect their wishes. Those who favour independence tend to believe Quebec could survive on its own. Many of those opposed say that it could not.

WHAT DO *YOU* THINK? MAKE A LIST OF THE THINGS WHICH A COUNTRY NEEDS TO SURVIVE. THEN DISCOVER WHETHER QUEBEC HAS THEM.

Obviously, the Parti Québécois feels confident that Quebec *could* survive as an independent country. René Lévesque points out that almost one hundred new nations have been created since 1945. Quebec would have more people, more resources and better technology than most of those countries. Lévesque claims that Quebec has a clearly defined territory, a common language and culture, plus its own history. Montreal is one of the world's great cities. Also, it is the second largest French-speaking city in the world. Above all, separatists argue that Quebeckers *want* to live together in an independent country with its own special identity. So far, the opinion polls do not support this claim.

An independent Quebec would need strong trading ties. At present, Quebec sells more than half of its manufactured goods to the rest of Canada. Quebec could not afford to lose this market. On the other hand, Canada counts on selling about one quarter of its goods in Quebec. Perhaps the two countries would be forced to be reasonable with each other.

An independent Quebec would also need investment funds to develop its industry. The United States is an important source of such funds. It is difficult to tell whether Americans would be willing to invest in the economy of a separate Quebec.

What is the future of English-French-speaking relations?

Emmett Hall

Mr. Hall is a former justice of the Supreme Court. He lived his first twelve years in Quebec, but now lives and works in Saskatchewan. He believes that separatism is "a pack of nonsense" and that Confederation is not in serious danger. In the end, Quebec will not vote to leave Canada. This issue is distracting government attention from important Western concerns. Confederation was created to benefit mainly Ontario and Quebec. It still does so.

Despite Western discontent, Mr. Hall says that no one there takes seriously the idea of Western separatism. He is in favour of bilingualism across the country. He believes that second language training must begin with very young children. He feels that successful bilingualism would help to improve English-French relations.

Laura Sabia

Ms. Sabia is the former head of Ontario's Council on the Status of Women. Her background is Italian. She was raised in Montreal and speaks English, French and Italian. She believes that Quebec will separate from Canada. There is no way to satisfy Quebec's demands without weakening Canada too much. Also, there is no way to *force* Quebec to stay. She has known separatists since she was a girl. They regard Confederation as a great burden to Quebec. She believes that the best approach is to accept the fact that Quebec will go. We should sit down with them and negotiate the best possible terms for both sides. The rest of Canada will be able to survive. However, the Quebec market will still be important for Canada's economy. Therefore we should try to stay on good terms.

Jean Ostiguy

In 1977, Mr. Ostiguy was the president of a stockbroking firm in Montreal. He was an officer in the Canadian Armed Forces during World War II and was wounded in Italy. He saw the 1976 election result as a good thing for Canada. It woke us up to the seriousness of the problem in Quebec. He said: "We have let this happen . . . we certainly have one of the best pieces of real estate in the world, with everything going for us. We've become fat and lazy and spoiled, and maybe this is going to shake us into doing something constructive."

Mr. Ostiguy believes that Canada should take over full control of its constitution from Britain. Then, major changes should be made to meet the reasonable needs of Quebec. The new constitution should be presented to all of Canada through a referendum. The French must be realistic. They must accept the fact that English is the leading language of business in the world today.

Eventually, says Mr. Ostiguy, Quebec will decide to stay in Canada. French-Canadians are too cautious and conservative to go for separation. He believes that independence is partly a romantic goal. It has appeal for French-Canadian youth. However, their interests will change. Also, as they grow older they will become more interested in economic security. Canada offers a better chance of this than does a "free" Quebec.

Gordon Robertson

Mr. Robertson has been a secretary to the Trudeau Cabinet on the matter of federal-provincial relations. He believes that English-Canadians must come to understand Quebec. This can only be done by looking at our history through French-Canadian eyes. He argues that French-Canadians are bitter because we have not respected them. They are proud people. They are very aware of the role played by French explorers and by the voyageurs in our early history. French Canada existed for 150 years before the British Conquest. French-Canadians have not shown loyalty to any country other than Canada for over 200 years. Still, their rights have been violated or ignored. They have not been accepted as valuable or equal members of Confederation. Despite this, Quebec has continued to protect the rights of the English minority there.

Says Mr. Robertson: "From this great difference in attitude between Quebec and the other provinces grew a sense, by French-Canadians, of being wronged — of being humiliated, insulted and trampled upon wherever the English-speaking were in the majority." The English have also controlled the Quebec economy. These two facts have produced support for Quebec separatism.

"We are paying the price today for a hundred years of failure to do what a strong majority could so easily do — to treat with generosity and respect a

Quebeckers willing to suffer setbacks to achieve aims

Separation--if it comes--can and should be peaceful

'Levesque's got us over a barrel'

Majority believe separation would entail higher taxes

Ottawa claiming bilingual victory in public service

Quebec states its case

Language bill: Quebec road signs in French only

More Quebeckers oppose separation

ronto trial in French used for Quebecker

Tell Quebec we care,

Canadian civil war result if Quebec splits, teacher says

uebec language bill a step backwards

Jobs, not language, issue in Quebec,

91 head offices quit Quebec

Unity desire outside Quebec not making large impact

weaker and less numerous community that shares our country." In a 1977 speech, Mr. Robertson called on English-Canada to show greater **tolerance** (understanding and generosity of spirit). He suggested that the terms of Confederation must be changed to suit both English and French-Canadian aims.

8. WILL QUEBEC SEPARATE?

This question will only be answered if and when the time comes. Prime Minister Trudeau is confident that a majority of Quebeckers will say "no." They will see that they are better off to remain in Canada. He seems willing to make some changes in the political system if they strongly wish it. However, he says he will not sacrifice the unity of the rest of Canada. The separatists believe that Quebeckers will agree with their stand. Therefore, it seems that the answer rests with all Canadians. It will depend on our words and actions over the next few years.

THINGS TO THINK ABOUT AND DO

Reviewing Key Words and Ideas

The following terms appeared in this chapter. Try to recall their meaning and how they were used.

assets	federalist	referendum
Bill 101	F.L.Q.	secession
customs union	indépendentist	separatist
exile	radical	

Remembering the Facts

1. In what way is separatism the result of regionalism?
2. Why did the Parti Québécois win the 1976 election in Quebec?
3. Review the arguments for and against the idea that a province can legally secede from the Canadian union.
4. Why has the separatist movement developed in Quebec?
5. How did the "October Crisis" of 1970 affect the separatist movement? Why?
6. How would Canada be affected if Quebec became independent?
7. What problems would Quebec face if it decided to separate from Canada?

Analyzing Ideas

1. It has been suggested that all Canadians be asked to take an oath of loyalty to Canada. Those who refuse should be **deported** (forced to leave Canada). Would this be wise? Would it be legal? Would it be possible?

2. Try to discover why the Parti Québécois is *legal* in Canada. Should it be?

3. One political change which might please French-Canadians would be to abolish the monarchy in Canada. Why would it please them? What other groups in Canada might agree? Should it be done?

4. In the early 1960s a French-Canadian said: "What actually threatens Canada is not change and questioning, but a stubborn refusal to accept change and difference. . . ." What do you think he meant? To what was he referring? Do you agree with him. Why or why not?

5. In September, 1977, René Lévesque admitted that many people in the Parti Québécois wanted Quebec, after independence, to take a neutral position in foreign policy. However, he said he expected that Quebec probably would end up joining the North American Air Defence system with Canada and the U.S. He even admitted the possibility of Quebec joining the North Atlantic Treaty Organization. Why might an independent Quebec want to join these two alliance systems?

6. Canadians who oppose Quebec's leaving Confederation tend to call those who do want to leave *separatists*. However, Quebeckers who favour separatism prefer to call themselves *indépendentistes*. Why would this be? (What differences are suggested in the two terms?)

7. For several years, unemployment has been higher in Quebec than in most other provinces. Some experts say that this should show Quebec that, if it separated, things would get even worse. Others argue the opposite. They say that high unemployment will cause more Quebeckers to support separatism. They would feel that they had "nothing to lose." Which argument makes more sense to you? Why?

Applying Your Knowledge

1. Draw a political map of Canada, or North America, as you think it will appear in 1990. *Boundaries* are the most important point of this exercise. Will there still be a Canada? If so, of what provinces or regions would it consist?

2. Regions of Canada other than Quebec have reasons to be unhappy with their conditions. Try to find out which regions are most unhappy and why. In your opinion, do any of them have good enough reasons for pulling out of Canada? Explain your answer.

3. Conduct an opinion poll in your school or neighbourhood on this question: "How serious would Quebec's separation be for the rest of Canada — very, fairly, or not very serious?" Compare your results with the poll in Chapter 1 of this Unit.

4. Here is a possible class exercise: clip newspaper stories on English-French relations for a two- or three-week period. Cut the headlines off the articles. However, use a numbering or lettering system so that the headlines can later be reunited with the proper articles. Put the articles away. Next, put all the headlines together and use them to try to identify:

a) the current *issues* or *concerns* in English-French relations

b) present *trends* in those relations

c) the attitude or approach of the press to those issues

Then, each student should choose one headline. Using knowledge of the subject, plus the ideas developed so far in the exercise, try to recreate the original article. Finally, have the actual article identified; see how close the "author" came to the original.

5. How would an independent Quebec affect Canada's military security? You may want to return to this question after you have studied Chapter 4, Unit VI, which examines the military and political aspects of Canadian-American relations.

V

Canadian-American Relations

1

INTRODUCTION

News Release:

OTTAWA — JULY 1, 1990

At noon today, the Maple Leaf flag was lowered for the last time from the flagpole on Parliament Hill. Officially, from 13:01, the former English-speaking provinces became part of the United States. It had been just twenty-five years since the Maple Leaf was first unfurled as Canada's own emblem.

Many famous Canadians and Americans had gathered for today's brief ceremony. They were joined by thousands of ordinary citizens. The former Prime Minister of Canada made a short but emotional speech. He talked about what Canada had achieved since its birth in 1867. He described the great strength and other qualities of the Canadian people. Finally, he spoke of his own mixed feelings about the new union with the United States. He said that he was sorry to see the end of Canada. But he thought that all Canadians were excited about joining the greatest nation on earth. He ended his speech with a hope. This was that the new union would add to the strength, happiness and wealth of all Americans — old and *new*.

Then the band began to play. It was made up of United States Marines and former members of the Canadian Armed Forces. 'O Canada' echoed across the Ottawa River for the last time. It could probably be heard on the other side by citizens of the Republic of Quebec. The band played slowly and with great feeling. It was a dramatic moment. Some people were crying. A member of the Royal Canadian Mounted Police lowered the Maple Leaf flag while the band played. The flag was carefully folded. It was handed to an American soldier. The flag will be placed in a Washington museum.

Next, the American flag was slowly hauled up the pole. The band played a stirring version of the 'Stars and Stripes'. At first, some of the crowd did not sing. But by the end, most people were singing loudly. Then the President of the United States spoke to the crowd. He praised the former country of Canada. He welcomed the people and resources of Canada into membership in the United States. He said this was a natural union. It was to be expected. He ended by asking everyone to sing 'America the Beautiful'.

How do you feel about this imaginary scene? Does it bother you? Would you *like* to see it happen? *Could* it really happen? Some people will consider it far-fetched, pure fantasy. But there are some Canadians who believe that Canada's survival *is* in danger. There is the possibility that Quebec might break away from the Canadian union. This might lead other provinces to do the same thing. One or more of these might then ask to join the United States. After all, Canada already is very dependent on the Americans. Why *bother* to keep trying to pretend we are different from them?

Perhaps these are wild ideas. But we must look at all the possibilities. The next few years will probably decide the future of Canada. Most important to that future are our relations with the United States.

This unit will examine those relations, both past and present. It will also look at what might lie ahead.

What Gallup Polls show about Canadian — American Relations

Over the years, several Gallup polls have been taken on the question: WOULD YOU SAY THAT RELATIONS BETWEEN CANADA AND THE UNITED STATES, ON THE WHOLE, ARE EXCELLENT, GOOD, JUST FAIR OR POOR? The following *percentages* show a trend in Canadian opinion on this question.

RATING	1955	1960	1964	1974	TODAY?
Excellent	19	15	11	7	
Good	56	54	57	44	
Just Fair	17	24	26	37	
Poor	2	3	1	6	
Don't Know	5	4	5	6	

NOTE: Figures might not add up to 100 per cent due to rounding.

(a) What seems to be the trend in Canadian thinking about our relations with the United States? What reasons can you suggest for this trend?

(b) Take your own opinion poll. For best results, you should try to question about one hundred people. Ask the same question of everyone. Record their answers carefully. Try to get a broad sample. That is, ask people of different ages, sexes, occupations, ethnic groups and so on. Have at least ten friends or classmates conduct a similar poll. Then, average your findings.

(c) See how your figures compare with earlier years such as 1974 and 1964. Is the trend that you noted in question No. 1 continuing?

(d) Try to find a recent Gallup Poll done on the same question. How do its figures compare with yours?

Unit Preview/Review Questions

As you study this unit, keep these questions in mind. You may want to return to them when you have finished the unit.

1. What ties do we now have with the United States? How strong are they?
2. How and why have these ties developed?
3. How important is the United States to us? How important is Canada to the U.S.? Why?
4. Are relations between our two countries becoming better or worse? Why?
5. Is Canada too dependent on the United States? If so, in what ways? What could be done about the situation?

2

HISTORICAL BACKGROUND

INTRODUCTION

A Canadian Prime Minister has compared living next door to the United States to sleeping with an elephant. He said: "No matter how friendly or even-tempered is the beast, one is affected by every twitch and grunt."

The comparison was, in many ways, a good one. The United States is truly a giant — the world's richest and most powerful country. Physically, Canada is about the same size. However, the United States has ten times our population, about twelve times our economic production and *many* more times our military strength.

The United States is far more important to Canada than any other country. They are our closest neighbour. Moreover, they are our major trading partner. They are our main source of foreign money for investment. The Americans are also our chief military ally. Therefore, Canadian-American relations are very important to both countries, but especially to Canada.

Canadians often have mixed feelings about the United States. Indeed, it has been said that we have a "love-hate" relationship with Americans.

1. What do you think is meant by a "love-hate" relationship? Do you have such mixed feelings about anyone or anything? If so, what and why?

2. Do you have any *positive* feelings about the United States or its people? Such feelings might involve friendship, love, respect, admiration, gratitude, pride and so on. If you do have such feelings, describe them as fully as possible. Then, try to say why you feel this way.

3. Do you have any *negative* feelings about Americans or their country? These could include anger, dislike, hatred, fear, jealousy and so on. Again, if so, describe and then analyze your feelings.

4. If it is helpful, discuss your thoughts on No. 2 and No. 3 above with your family and friends. Then, compare your findings with those of classmates. Make lists of both the positive and negative feelings, and the reasons for both.

5. Try to **interpret** (analyze) your findings. Then **evaluate** (judge) them. For example, are most of them based on the present, or on past developments? (In other words, how important does *history* seem to be as a factor in Canadian feelings about their neighbour?) Also, are most of your findings based on the first-hand experience of people? If not, what *are* they based on — media reports? rumour? prejudice? (In other words, how well founded are the feelings you have listed?)

There are many reasons why Canadians might have positive feelings about the United States. In part, we owe our security, and our high standard of living, to the U.S. Some of us have friends or relatives in that country. Many of us have travelled there. We share a common language. Many of our political and religious beliefs are similar. Most Americans are friendly, generous hosts and polite visitors. It seems that we even have a common sense of humour — we laugh at the same jokes. This seems a minor point, but perhaps it is quite significant. Think about it!

Unfortunately, Canadians also have reasons for some negative feelings about the United States. In the past, the U.S. has been a threat. Americans have invaded us twice. They have seemed ready to do so on several other occasions. A good portion of Canadian history has involved our *reacting* to the American presence. Perhaps this is still true today. Presently, Americans own huge chunks of our country and its economy. Their culture threatens to overpower us. American television, films, music and magazines play a large part in our lives. Many Canadians feel that Americans do not know enough about us. We would like more respect from them. Indeed, it seems that often they take us for granted. The United States is not an enemy country. Yet, it still threatens our independence in many ways.

To deal with the following items, it would be helpful to talk with several Americans. If this is impossible, try to have friends or classmates join you in pretending to be Americans for a while. This should be done seriously, with care.

1. What do you think Americans should know about Canada? Why? How much of this do they appear to know? Why is this? Could the situation be improved?

2. An American president, Richard Nixon, once made a public statement which showed he did not know of Canada's economic importance to the U.S. At that time, we were their main source of imported oil. Then, as now, we were a leading trade partner. How could the president have made such an error? How does this relate to your ideas in No. 2 above?

3. Would Americans likely be more informed, and concerned, about Quebec separatism or a Communist uprising in a small African nation? Which development would be more vital to their interests?

4. What criticisms might Americans make of Canada? How valid would these be? (Explain your answers, and be aware that you are *biased!*)

For many reasons, there has been a recent growth of **anti-Americanism** in Canada. There also is evidence that some Americans are becoming more critical of us. Today, relations still are basically quite good. However, if certain trends continue, trouble might lie ahead. It is very important for Canadians (and Americans) to know about the present state of relations. They also should know the reasons for this situation. These matters will be dealt with in this unit. In the first chapter, we will look at the history of Canadian-American relations, from earliest times to around 1970.

Before reading on, study the chart of Key Words and Ideas which follows.

KEY WORDS AND IDEAS IN THIS CHAPTER

Term	Meaning	Sample Use
annexation	the act whereby one country takes over another	Some Canadians fear annexation by the United States.
anti-Americanism	a feeling of being against the United States or things American	There has been anti-Americanism in Canada both in early and recent times.
blockade	the act of cutting off the foreign trade of another country	During the American Civil War, the North tried to ruin the economy of the South by blockade.
competition	the act of trying to defeat, or be better than, someone else	Since 1945, the United States and the Soviet Union have been in competition with each other.
investment	money, effort or something of value that a person puts into a project	Large sums of money (capital) are needed to get a business started or to help it grow. In Canada, much of this money is foreign. How might this foreign investment threaten our independence?
loyalty	the act or feeling of being faithful to someone or something	United Empire Loyalists were Americans who showed loyalty to Britain during the American Revolution. Many of them came to Canada.
Manifest Destiny	an American belief that the United States would one day take over all of North America	The belief in Manifest Destiny helped to start the War of 1812. It also created anti-Americanism, and fears of annexation, in Canada.

negotiations	bargaining	Canada and Britain held serious negotiations with the United States in 1871, before the Treaty of Washington was signed.
reciprocity	an action between two (or more) parties that is the same on both sides	Canada tried to gain reciprocity in trade with the United States. This involved the lowering, or removal, of tariffs by both countries.
technology	a technical method of doing or making something	The United States has developed the most advanced technology in the world. Much of this is available to Canada. It tends to make our life easier and richer.

How Important are we to Americans?

In February of 1977, Prime Minister Trudeau visited Washington, D.C., the American capital. He was on a very important mission. The Parti Québécois had just been elected in Quebec (see Unit 4, Chapter 5). This event had surprised and worried many Americans. Some business executives wondered if their investments were safe. Military experts were concerned about American security. Was it now in danger? A broken up Canada would not be a reliable ally.

Mr. Trudeau wanted to tell Americans that Canada would *not* fall apart. He delivered this message in an excellent speech to **Congress** (the American Parliament). This speech also was meant for the Canadian audience back home. It was intended to help Canadians to believe in their country.

Trudeau's visit and speech made front page headlines in Canada. This did not happen in the United States. For example, the *New York Times* carried the story on page ten. Americans were more interested in the new budget announced by their government. On American television, the Trudeau visit came up half way through the news programmes. Even then, the first item discussed was the style of clothes worn by the women at the official welcoming dinner!

1. Imagine that a state threatened to leave the American union. Would the President of the United States come to Canada to tell us not to worry? Explain your answer.

Prime Minister Trudeau addressed President Carter and other Americans gathered to greet him upon his arrival in Washington, D.C. — February, 1977.

2. It has been suggested that Mr. Trudeau went to Washington to get American help *against* Quebec separatism. How could the U.S. help? Why might it want to do so?

3. Why might some Canadians feel embarrassed by this Trudeau visit to Washington? Would you share this feeling? Why or why not?

4. Does it surprise you that Americans did not take the Trudeau visit more seriously? Should they have done so? Explain your answer.

1.   THE BEGINNINGS

Both Canada and the United States were "discovered" by European explorers. These explorers sailed for Spain, Holland, England and France. The first three nations set up colonies in what would later become the United States. France started settlements farther to the north. These were mainly in the St. Lawrence Valley and in the present provinces of Nova Scotia and New Brunswick (see Unit IV, chapter 2). They called their colony New France.

By 1750, there were thirteen American colonies along the Atlantic coast. They were controlled by Britain. Their relations with New France were poor. There were several reasons for the strain. The two peoples had different languages and culture. They often competed in business and trading. Religious differences also caused stress. New France was settled mainly by Roman Catholics. Most of the American colonists were Protestant. Britain and France were enemies in Europe. These bad feelings spilled over into their North American colonies.

2. CANADA CONQUERED: AMERICA FREE

The British conquered New France in 1759. But this did not improve relations between the Americans and French-Canadians. One example stands out. Quebec refused to join the Americans in their rebellion against British rule. (Review the Quebec Act for one cause of this action. See Unit IV, Chapter 2.) Many Quebeckers expected the American Revolution to fail. But the long conflict between Quebeckers and Americans was also a reason for their action.

During the Revolution, the Americans tried to invade Canada. Naturally, this increased bad feelings. Along the way, American soldiers sometimes stole food or animals. If they did pay, it usually was with paper money. This was useless in Canada. Some Americans also damaged Roman Catholic churches along their way. Such actions made French-Canadians very angry. When the American force attacked Quebec City, it was defeated.

The American attack on Quebec, 31 December, 1775 (as portrayed by C.W. Jeffreys). Although carried out under cover of darkness and in a raging snowstorm, the attack failed. Over 100 Americans were killed and 430 were captured.

One result of the American Revolution was the arrival of many **United Empire Loyalists** in Canada. These were Americans who had remained loyal to Britain. About 30 000 of them came to Nova Scotia, where they swamped the existing population of 17 000. Perhaps another 10 000 Loyalists settled in present day Quebec and Ontario.

The arrival of the Loyalists affected Canada in many ways. They brought many skills which strengthened our economy. Their numbers increased our military strength. Moreover, they had strong anti-American feelings. This attitude was important in helping to defend Canada against the United States during the War of 1812.

3.   RELATIONS DURING THE NINETEENTH CENTURY

The War of 1812

This war helped to create a sense of unity among Canadians. Our people began to feel that they all belonged to one country. An American victory could have led to a takeover of Canada. Both English and French joined the British in defending our soil.

The War of 1812 was to be the last official warfare between Canada and the United States. Neither country lost land as a result of the war. The Americans and British agreed to limit warships on the Great Lakes. This helped to ease tension and lessen the chances of future conflict. Furthermore, a Canada-U.S. border was decided upon. Both countries accepted the 49th parallel (the present boundary) as the border from the Great Lakes to the Rocky Mountains.

Aging veterans of the War of 1812, photographed at a reunion

Highlights in Canada-U.S. Relations

Time	Political-Military	Economic
1777	First American constitution allows for admittance of Canada into American union	
1783	*Treaty of Paris*—Britain cedes much former Canadian territory to United States	
1812-1814	War of 1812—Canada resists American takeover attempt	
1825		Completion of Erie Canal (1825) enriched New York, at the expense of the St. Lawrence trade and merchants
1837	Canadian rebels given shelter in the United States	
1842	*Webster-Ashburton Agreement*—Britain grants most American boundary claims re Maine and the West	
1844	Slogan of "54° 40' or fight" highlights American presidential election	
1846	*Oregon Treaty*—Britain cedes valuable portions of Columbia River Valley to United States	
1854		Canada signs reciprocity treaty with the United States
1866		U.S. cancels reciprocity
1867	Confederation of Canada	
1871	*Treaty of Washington*—settles British and Canadian disputes with U.S. re boundaries, Canadian fisheries and Civil War incidents	
1874		U.S. rejects Canadian efforts to renew reciprocity
1879		Macdonald introduces "National Policy" to strengthen economic ties across Canada and retaliate against American trade barriers.
1903	Alaska Boundary Dispute	
1908	Formation of the International Boundary Commission	

Time	Political-Military	Economic
1911	Establishment of the International Joint Commission. Also, Laurier defeated, partly over his attempts to revive reciprocity with the U.S.	
1935		Canada and the U.S. reduce tariffs on certain of each other's goods
1938	President Roosevelt assures Canada of American military protection	
1940	*Ogdensburg Agreement*—establishes Permanent Joint Board on Defence	
1941		*Hyde Park Agreement*—establishes wartime economic co-operation
1947		Canada and the U.S. participate in G.A.T.T. (General Agreement on Tariffs and Trade)
1949	Canada and the U.S. join NATO	Establishment of a joint Canada-U.S. committee on trade and economic affairs
1953		
1954		Final agreement on joint project of St. Lawrence Seaway
1956	Canada and the U.S. join in opposition to Anglo-French attack on Egypt	
1958	*NORAD Agreement*—establishes integrated air defence for North America	
1962	*Cuban Missile Crisis*—friction over Canada's delay in putting armed forces on alert	
1963	Prime Minister John Diefenbaker charges American interference in Canadian election on defence question	
1964		Columbia River Treaty signed
1965	P.M. Pearson angers President Johnson with surprise speech calling for pause in American bombing of Vietnam	Canada-U.S. Auto Trade Pact signed
1968		Publication of the Watkins Report on the Canadian economy
1969	Nationalistic speech in U.S. by Canadian Energy Minister J.J. Greene surprises American officials	
1971		U.S. Government alarms Ottawa with 10 per cent surcharge on Canadian goods

Time	Political-Military	Economic
1972		Publication of the Gray Report on foreign ownership in Canada
1973		Passage of the Foreign Investment Review Act by the Canadian Parliament Also, oil crisis causes Canada to increase oil prices and reduce oil exports — U.S. angered
1976	Canada and U.S. both announce extension of their territorial limits to 320 km offshore. This claim includes fishing rights plus mineral rights under the sea.	
1977	Prime Minister Trudeau visits Washington to reassure Americans that Canada will remain united.	René Lévesque, Premier of Quebec, goes to New York to urge Americans to continue investing in his province The Canadian government announces plans to *soften* its role in the approving of foreign takeovers of Canadian businesses Canada and the U.S. agree to terms on the building of a 10-billion dollar Arctic gas pipeline

Border Disputes

The boundary line remained unsettled in several areas. This caused some tension in Canadian-American relations. New Brunswick and the state of Maine argued over their border. The boundary west of the Rockies caused some problems. The countries also disagreed over the dividing line through certain waterways. One example of this was the boundary in the waterways around the southern end of Vancouver Island (page 295). You may wonder why borders through waterways are important. They decide who controls fishing, navigation and shipping. The Alaska Boundary Dispute (page 295) is well known. All of these disputes were settled peacefully. You will have to judge whether Canada gained or lost from the settlements.

Value of Trade between British North America and The United States
(in millions of dollars)

Year	Value		Year	Value
1853	18.9		1861	44.4
1854	32.8		1862	39.0
1855	42.8		1863	45.1
1856	50.3		1864	56.1
1857	46.2		1865	62.0
1858	39.3		1866	73.3
1859	47.3		1867	46.0
1860	46.2		1868	50.3

1. Why did trade increase rapidly between Canada and the United States beginning around 1854?
2. What was the *peak* year for Canada-U.S. trade between 1853-1867? Why was there a serious decline in 1867?
3. Between 1853 and 1866, what was the *percentage* increase in the value of Canada's trade with the United States?
4. Try to discover the annual dollar value of Canada's trade with the United States today. (Chapter 3 of this unit gives you the figures for the mid-1970s. More up-to-date information could be obtained from *The Canada Yearbook* or by writing to Statistics Canada in Ottawa.)

The Rebellions of 1837

Do you remember the story of the Rebellions of 1837? If not, review them in a Canadian History text. The British stopped these rebellions. They wanted to find and punish the leaders. These included Louis Joseph Papineau and William Lyon Mackenzie. Both men fled to the United States. The British then accused the Americans of sheltering criminals. Some Canadians crossed the border to destroy rebel hideouts on American soil. Official notes of protest were exchanged. In time, the bad feelings cooled down.

Trade

In the 1850s, Canada tried to improve trade relations with the United States. We wanted a **reciprocity** agreement. This would lower, or remove, the customs duties on goods moving between the two countries. In 1854 such an agreement was made. It was to last ten years. After this, it could be cancelled or renewed. Refer to the chart on page 289. Did Canada benefit from the reciprocity agreement?

Unfortunately, the United States cancelled this agreement in 1866. Canadian Prime Ministers, such as John Macdonald and Wilfrid Laurier, tried to renew reciprocity. They had little success.

U.S. Civil War

New tensions arose during the American Civil War (1861-1865). To help win the war, the northern states tried to **blockade** the South. This would stop all southern trade. The South's economy would be badly hurt. However, Britain also was hurt by this blockade. Southern cotton was vital to the huge British textile industry. Therefore, Britain continued to trade with the South. It also sold ships to the South. Most of these were later armed. They were used in battle against northern vessels. The best known of these raiders was the *Alabama*. It sank several Northern ships, causing the loss of millions of dollars.

During the American Civil War, soldiers of the Confederacy (the Southern states) raided the Northern town of St. Albans, Vermont. They launched their raid from Canada. This photo shows captured Confederate soldiers accused of the raid outside a Montreal jail. The raid created tension between the U.S. and Canada.

Naturally, such developments made Northerners angry with Britain. Perhaps they would strike at Canada to get back at the British.

Other developments increased Canadian-American tension. Some Southern soldiers came into Canada secretly. From here they raided Northern states. In return, some **Fenians** (Irish-Americans) made a series of attacks on Canadian border areas.

The North won the Civil War. It still had a huge, well trained army. Some Canadians feared that this army might be sent north. This way, the Americans could get even with Britain. They also could expand their borders. But Canada would be destroyed.

Confederation

The United States helped cause Canadian Confederation in 1867. The end of reciprocity forced us to find other ways to increase trade. Perhaps this could be done within a *united* Canada. Such unity also would help us defend ourselves against a possible American attack. As well, unity might help us develop our West more quickly. This would stop the American spread into that area.

Treaty of Washington

In 1871, our Prime Minister, John Macdonald, joined in some important **negotiations** in Washington. These talks involved Britain, Canada and the United States. Several issues needed to be settled. Among these were:
1. the right of Americans to fish in Canadian waters
2. the Canada-U.S. boundary between Vancouver Island and the mainland
3. American claims for damages caused by the British-built raider, the *Alabama*
Macdonald's main aim was to persuade the Americans to renew the reciprocity agreement. For this, he was ready to grant them generous fishing rights in our coastal waters. The Americans were not prepared to meet his price. They preferred to pay cash for the fishing rights. They were not interested in a large trade agreement. Britain's main goal was to improve its relations with the United States. To do so, they were prepared to be generous. In part, this meant sacrificing some of Canada's interests. The Americans knew this was the situation. Therefore, they put heavy pressure on the British. When Macdonald realized what was happening, he became frustrated and angry. He commented:

> "I must say that I am greatly disappointed at the course taken by the British Commissioners. They seem to have only one thing on their minds — that is, to go home to England with a treaty in their pockets, settling everything no matter at what cost to Canada."

1. What charge was Macdonald making? Do some extra research on the Washington negotiations. Was this charge true?
2. Try to find other examples in our history where the British might have "sold us out" to the Americans. For example, look at the peace treaties after the American Revolution and the War of 1812. Also consider the Alaska Boundary Dispute. (See the following insert.)
3. On the other hand, try to recall examples where Britain defended us against American pressures.
4. Britain controlled Canadian foreign policy both before and after Confederation. Indeed, they did so until the 1920s. Why would this be? What advantages and disadvantages could this offer to Canada? Is it likely that

Canada could have obtained better terms from the United States on its own? Explain your answer.

By the terms of the Treaty of Washington, the United States bought the right to fish in Canadian waters. Britain and the U.S. settled the Alabama claims peacefully. The Americans refused to pay for any damages caused by the Fenians. Instead, Britain made a cash payment to Canada.

The west coast boundary dispute was more complicated. The Portland channel separates Vancouver Island from the mainland. There are several islands in this channel, including San Juan. Both Britain and the United States claimed ownership of that island. Each side proposed a boundary line, giving San Juan to itself. Finally, the dispute was turned over to the Emperor of Germany. He acted as an **arbitrator** or referee. The boundary he chose gave San Juan Island to the United States (see accompanying map).

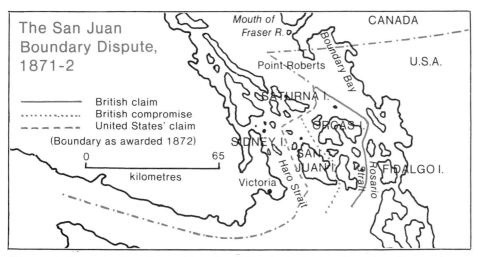

This map indicates the Canadian and American claims in the San Juan boundary dispute, plus the line of settlement.

The Alaska Boundary Dispute (1898-1903)

The United States bought Alaska from Russia in 1867. At that time, the boundary between the Alaskan "Panhandle" (see map) and Canada was not clear. Uneven coastline and rugged mountains made it hard to draw any clear cut line. For many years, this situation was not a real problem.

But, in 1898 gold was discovered in the Klondike. This was part of Canada's Yukon Territory. Miners and supplies came and went through Skagway, on the Pacific coast. Both Canada and the United States claimed the coastal land in that area. Look at the map to see the boundary lines each country wanted.

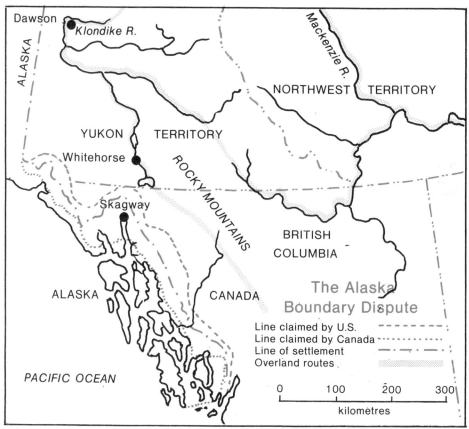

This map indicates the Canadian and American boundary claims in the Alaska boundary dispute, plus the line of settlement. Although more of the disputed territory was awarded to Canada, the U.S. won the basic argument. How can you *prove* this from the map?

Both sides agreed to turn over their dispute to a special commission. This body had six members. Three were American, two Canadian and one British. It chose a boundary line mid-way between those suggested by Canada and the United States. But this line gave Skagway to the United States. In fact, the Americans won this dispute. Canadians felt that they had been "sold out" by the British. Lord Alverstone, the British member of the commission, had sided with American interests.

The meeting of the Alaska Boundary Tribunal, London, England, October, 1903

Annexationism

Would you like to join, or be taken over by, the United States? If Canada were to be annexed to the United States, this would mean that we became part of that country. Annexationists are people who would like to see this happen. Such feelings have been expressed in Canada from time to time.

1849	1959
The editor of *The Saint John Morning News*:	*Farley Mowat,* Canadian novelist:

1849

The editor of *The Saint John Morning News*:
"Geographically speaking, we belong to the United States. We are connected by an imaginary line. We have sprung from the same stock, we speak the same language, profess the same literature, are not lacking the enterprise of our neighbours."
1. This article is saying that Canada is an "artificial" political unit. What is the "imaginary line" to which it refers? Look at a political and physical map of North America. Does the political boundary fit with, or clash with, natural geographic regions? Does this mean that we will one day become part of the U.S.?
2. According to this article, what things do Canadians have in common with

1959

Farley Mowat, Canadian novelist:
"In short, I now conclude that the only solution to our trouble with the Americans is to jine 'em; from which it follows that I no longer believe we can lick 'em ... in almost every important social, intellectual and economic aspect we have already become pseudo-Americans.

1. What are "pseudo-Americans"? Do you agree with Mowat that this is what we have become?
2. In what important ways are Canadians *different* from Americans? Are these differences enough to keep us apart from Americans? Explain your answer.

Americans? What *else* can you add to this list?

3. Which American state is *closest* to you? What Canadian province is *farthest* from you? Do you have more in common with the people of that American state or that Canadian province?

4. Do you feel that you have more in common with Americans or with French-Canadians? Why?

This is a Canadian political cartoon published during a federal election campaign of the late 19th century. Try to discover which election this was. To which issue in that election does the cartoon refer? Who are the people portrayed? What is the point of the cartoon? Which Canadian political party does it seem to support?

4.   THE TWENTIETH CENTURY

Canadian-American relations improved steadily between 1900 and 1945. Canada and Britain were allies against Germany in World War I (1914-1918). The United States came into the war on their side in 1917. This was the first time that Canada and the United States had been military allies. Thus, World War I helped to create a strong new bond between us.

This war produced another important result. Before it began, Britain was our major trading partner. It also was our main source of foreign investment. The war gave Canada's economy a chance to grow tremendously. To do so, it needed a lot of new **investment.** Britain was pouring its money into its own war effort. Therefore, we relied more than ever on American investment. By the end of the war, the United States had replaced Britain as our leading trade partner and supplier of foreign investment.

During the 1920s and 1930s, Canadians and Americans shared many common experiences. (Many of these are described in Unit 3, Chapter 2.) First came the prosperous, exciting "Roaring Twenties." These were followed by the "hard times" of the Depression in the "Dirty Thirties." At the end of this came World War II (1939-1945). In this war, Canada was an ally of Britain from the beginning. The United States joined the allies late in 1941.

During this war, Canadian-American relations became closer than ever before. There was great trust and good will between the two countries. We co-operated closely in military matters. Together we planned war production for our industries. The United States promised to defend us against any enemy invasion. Actually, the Americans did this mainly in their own interest. Still, Canadians were grateful for the promise of help from such a powerful friend. Together, the two countries made plans for the defence of North America. This close relationship lasted long after the war ended. It is still in effect today.

We also have kept our close economic ties with the United States. We have enjoyed great benefits from this relationship. Americans buy large quantities of raw materials from us. They provide investment funds to help us develop our economy. American **technology** is available to us. In most fields it is the best and most advanced in the world. The American economy produces many goods and services which Canadians enjoy. These also are available to us.

In the late 1940s, world tension began to increase again. This was mainly due to **competition** between the United States and the Soviet Union. This conflict became known as the "Cold War" (see Unit 6, Chapter 3). In this situation, Canada clearly sided with the United States. The Cold War grew even more serious during the 1950s. Understandably, our military and economic ties with the United States grew stronger than ever.

President Franklin Roosevelt
watches Prime Minister
Mackenzie King sign the
U.S.-Canada Trade
Agreement in Washington,
D.C., 17 November, 1938.

In the past few years, this trend has begun to change. World tension has eased somewhat. American relations with Communist countries like China and the Soviet Union have slowly improved. The danger of a major war has grown less. As we feel more secure, we place less value on American protection. Furthermore, Canadians have begun to see some bad aspects to our close ties with the U.S. Perhaps we have become too dependent on the Americans. Maybe they have too much influence over our government, culture and economy. These ideas have been emphasized in our media. This has helped to produce a certain amount of **anti-Americanism.** Canadian politicians have become quite sensitive about this issue. Thus, Canadian-American relations are of great interest in our society today. There are some sharp differences among our people on this question. No doubt, these differences will produce some lively debates among us in the next few years. The rest of this unit will help you learn more about this vital issue.

Canadians demonstrate in Washington for an all-Canadian St. Lawrence Seaway, 1954. Why would they have such a goal? For what reasons did our government reject this idea?

THINGS TO THINK ABOUT AND DO

Reviewing Key Words and Ideas

1. The following terms appeared in this chapter. Try to recall their meaning and how they were used.

annexation	competition	negotiations
anti-Americanism	Fenians	reciprocity
arbitrator	investment	technology
blockade	loyalty	United Empire
border dispute	Manifest Destiny	Loyalists

Remembering the Facts

1. Why do Canadians have a love-hate relationship with the United States?
2. For what reasons were Canadian-American relations poor between 1750 and 1850?
3. How did the United States help to bring about Canadian Confederation?

4. How did World Wars I and II affect Canadian-American relations? Why?

5. The United States replaced Britain as Canada's main trading partner and source of foreign investment. When did this happen?

6. In what ways is Canada heavily dependent on the U.S. today?

Analyzing Ideas

1. The Americans decided to fight for their independence from Britain; Canada decided to remain a loyal British colony. Does this suggest basic differences between the two peoples? How did these different decisions affect future Canadian-American relations?

2. "The real father of Confederation was neither Brown, Cartier nor Macdonald, but the United States Navy." Explain this quotation. Try to discover if this view was accurate.

3: In the 20th century, Canada gradually drew closer to the Americans and farther away from the British. Why did this happen? Has this change been good or bad for Canada? Explain your answer.

4. In 1961, President John F. Kennedy spoke in Ottawa. He said: "Geography has made us neighbours. History has made us friends." In what ways was he correct?

Applying Your Knowledge

1. Divide the class into three teams. Each must prepare a paper on the question: "Who won the War of 1812?" One team should write from the American viewpoint. The second should write a Canadian opinion. The third should be neutral, and take an unbiased approach. Present each paper in class. Who do you think *really* won the war? Why?

2. Do you think that having the United States as a neighbour helps keep Canada united? Why or why not?

3. Have some classmates imagine that they are Canadians who have moved to the United States. Have others play the part of Americans who have moved to Canada. Interview members of both groups. Ask them

(a) why they moved and

(b) how they find life in their new adopted country.

Use a tape recorder if possible. Replay the taped interviews several times. List the similarities and differences between Canadians and Americans, and their ways of life. Have you found new answers to earlier exercises in this chapter?

3

ECONOMIC LINKS

INTRODUCTION

"No nation, no people, have helped more than the U.S. to make Canada what it is today — one of the most desirable places to live in the world . . ."

"You are a serf, no more than that . . . and Massa lives away down south."

These statements conflict. They express different views on Canada's economic ties with the United States.

1. What is the opinion in the comment at left, above? Give some examples to support that view.

2. What is the opinion in the comment at right, above? Look up "serf" and

What point is this drawing trying to make?

"Massa" if you are not sure of their meaning. Do you think there is *any* truth in that remark? If so, how much?

Both statements have some truth. It is true that Canada has very close economic ties with the United States. These are much closer than with any other country. As a result, Canada enjoys many benefits. We have one of the highest **standards of living** in the world.

Our close economic links with the United States, the world's richest nation, help explain this. Without these links, the quality of our life would go down. Naturally we do not want this to happen. Therefore we depend on the United States a great deal. This dependence creates some problems for us.

We will explore our economic ties with the United States in this chapter. We will look at the good and the bad features of this "American Connection."

Before reading on, study the chart of Key Words and Ideas which follows.

KEY WORDS AND IDEAS IN THIS CHAPTER

Term	Meaning	Sample Use
capital investment	the placing of money into a business	Many foreigners invest money in Canadian businesses. Capital investment has both good and bad effects on our economy.
continentalism	the feeling that Canada and the U.S. are part of one North American unit	Some Americans would like Canadians to support continentalism. (Does it work the other way?) Then the U.S. could claim a share of our natural resources. (How does this relate to annexation and Manifest Destiny?)
entrepreneur	someone who organizes, manages and takes the risks of a business venture	Americans are among the world's best entrepreneurs. Canada also has some, but needs more.
foreign investment	money invested in Canada by non-Canadians	There is over $60 billion worth of foreign investment in Canada today.

foreign trade	trade between Canada and other countries	Foreign trade is a vital part of Canada's economy. Our main trading partner is the United States.
standard of living	the quality of life a person can have; this is determined by his/her income, and the cost of goods and services that are available	Canada has one of the highest standards of living in the world. This is partly due to our ties with the U.S., which is the richest country in the world.
trade deficit	an unfavourable balance of trade (where imports cost more than our exports are worth)	Canada has a trade deficit in automobiles and parts with the United States.

1. OUR TRADE WITH THE UNITED STATES

What Trade Is

Most of us know what the word trade means. Children often make several "deals" in one day. "I'll trade you my cap pistol for your rabbit." "You give me three sticks of gum plus two pennies, and I'll give you half of my popsicle." Sport fans know what it means if two teams make a trade. "Toronto Maple Leafs trade Darryl Sittler to Montreal Canadiens for Ken Dryden, a draft choice plus cash." Trade involves an exchange between two or more parties. Each wants something from the other. Each is willing to pay for what is wanted.

Foreign Trade

Trade goes on within each country. It also takes place between countries. This second type of trade is called foreign trade. Canada depends very heavily on foreign trade. We have a surplus (extra amount) of certain goods and natural resources. We try to trade these to other countries. In return, we take the money, goods or natural resources we may need. Items which we sell to other countries are called exports. Imports are those items which we buy.

Trade With the United States

Canada is one of the world's leading trading nations. We have dozens of trading partners around the world. But our most important trading partner is the United States. These charts give you information about Canada's foreign trade:

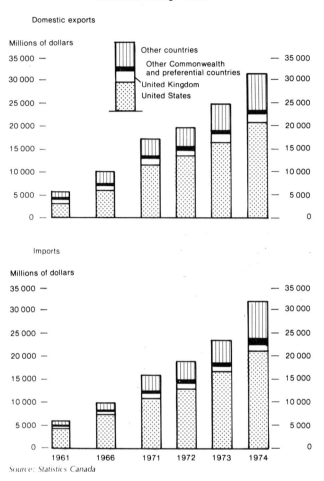

Canadian Foreign Trade

Source: Statistics Canada

Canada's Foreign Trade — Alternate Years 1966-1976 (in Millions of Dollars)

Year	Value of Exports	Value of Imports	Total Value of Trade	Balance of Trade
1966	10 325	9 866	20 191	+ 459
1968	13 624	12 358	25 982	+ 1 266
1970	16 820	13 952	30 772	+ 2 868
1972	19 977	18 655	38 632	+ 1 322
1974	32 441	31 692	64 133	+ 749
1976	38 053	36 582	74 635	+ 1 471

Source: Statistics Canada

Canada's Import Trade

	Value of Imports (Millions of Dollars)		
	1967	1971	1976
United States	8 016.3	10 944.0	25 650.2
United Kingdom	673.1	837.3	1 152.0
Japan	304.8	801.9	1 524.1
Venezuela	276.3	387.7	1 290.7
West Germany	256.9	429.4	817.6
France	130.8	213.1	438.8
Italy	110.3	157.5	365.3
Sweden	76.2	113.3	262.4
Switzerland	66.0	86.2	163.4
Netherlands	64.8	76.4	181.1
Belgium & Luxembourg	64.6	59.0	124.7
Australia	64.5	125.7	339.1
Hong Kong	51.0	80.2	284.6
Iran	33.2	66.6	695.6

Source: Statistics Canada

Canada's Export Trade

Country	Value of Exports (Millions of Dollars)		
	1967	**1971**	**1976**
United States	7 079.4	11 665.1	25 784.0
United Kingdom	1 169.1	1 345.9	1 852.6
Japan	572.2	789.3	2 389.1
West Germany	178.0	314.3	706.0
Netherlands	176.4	232.3	447.8
Australia	156.2	180.0	362.2
Italy	141.4	207.6	550.5
India	140.6	142.4	154.5
U.S.S.R.	128.7	125.8	535.7
Belgium & Luxembourg	100.9	178.6	481.7
People's Republic of China	91.3	204.1	195.0
Norway	87.4	185.8	152.3
Venezuela	82.0	119.9	341.1
France	80.6	153.1	402.4

Source: Statistics Canada

As you can see the United States is a huge **market** (buyer) for Canadian products. This is because they are a wealthy country with a large population. They need our products in large amounts. They can afford to pay for them. We need American goods and services. Many of these are very appealing.

Some are very complicated. These items might not be available from other countries. If they are, they might be more expensive or not as well made.

A Japanese ship unloads cargo at Vancouver docks. Canada's trade with Japan has increased rapidly since 1965.

Look at the chart on Canada's Export Trade. It lists the fourteen leading buyers of Canadian products in 1967. The countries are listed in order, one through fourteen, as of 1967.

1. Make your own version of this chart. Use the same headings. List the countries as they appear in the text. Then, instead of writing in the dollar figures, simply give each country a rank number, one through fourteen. Do this for each of the three years indicated.
2. In 1967, which country was the leading buyer of Canadian exports? Did it keep that position in 1971 and 1976?
3. What important changes in ranking occurred between 1967 and 1976? Which countries have become much more important customers for Canada? Which countries have become less important?
4. In percentage terms, which country increased its buying *most* between 1967 and 1976?
5. In 1976, Mexico bought $214.6 million worth of Canadian exports. Relate this figure to your chart. Where would this rank Mexico? Try to discover more recent developments in Canadian trade. The *Canada Yearbook* could be a useful source of information. Also, you might write to Statistics Canada or the Department of Industry, Trade and Commerce in Ottawa. With your teacher's help, try to relate your findings to Canadian foreign policy and general world developments. For example, why has Canada's trade with Japan been increasing so rapidly? What is important about the increase in our trade with the Soviet Union? India and China are large countries; together, they have about half the world's population. Why does our trade with them remain low?

A Not-So-Hot Deal for Canada?

Most industrialized nations make at least some of their own kinds of automobiles. For example, Sweden makes the Volvo, France the Renault, Germany the Mercedes, and so on. Is there a "Canadian" car? The answer, of course, is "no". There have been such cars in the past, but not today. We make "North American" cars of United States design.

The *Canada-United States Auto Trade Pact* was signed in 1965. It created a single automobile industry for both countries. Canada was to benefit from this pact. It was to mean more jobs and cheaper cars for Canadians. Cars and parts could move across the border without **tariffs** (customs duties). We would produce only certain car models. These would be sold in both Canada and the United States. The Americans would specialize in *other* models. We could import these models from them.

The huge General Motors of Canada Ltd. car and truck assembly plant at Oshawa, Ontario. This company is a subsidiary of the parent American corporation.

Canada has gained some benefits from this deal. However, recently we are buying more cars and parts from the U.S. than we are selling to them. This means we have a deficit in trade. Here are some figures:

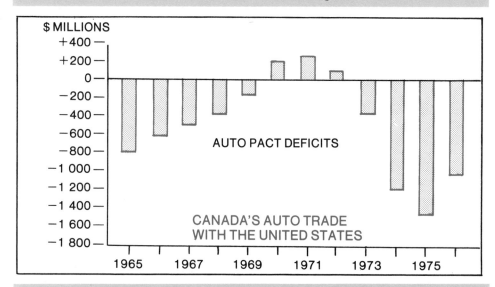

1. Canadian professor James Laxer claims that these deficits cost Canada up to 30 000 jobs. How could this be?
2. In 1977, a special government study made some serious criticisms of the Auto Trade Pact. It said that Canada had been given a secondary role to play in the car industry. We only assembled parts, and manufactured parts of medium to low technology. Not enough money was being put into research and development in Canada. Thus, the Americans kept control over key aspects of the industry. Once again, we were stuck with being "hewers of wood and drawers of water" in a key manufacturing industry.
What could Canada do about this situation? Consider other ideas and information provided by this chapter in your answer.

The following questions deal with the importance of Canada's trade with the United States:
1. Imagine that the United States stopped buying from Canada. Suggest reasons why this might happen. Use the charts in this chapter to help answer these questions. Where else might Canada look for customers? Which countries might want our products, and be able to afford them? Why is it unlikely that they could replace the U.S. as our main customer?
2. What if Canada could not replace the U.S. as a customer? How would you be affected? Why? (Make your answers as full as possible.)
3. Imagine that the United States stopped selling its goods and services to

Canada. Could we get the same things from other countries? If so, from whom? If not, why not?

4. What if we could not buy similar things from other countries? How would you be affected? Why? (Again, make a full answer.)

5. Discuss or debate this point: "THERE ARE MORE ADVANTAGES THAN DISADVANTAGES IN CANADA'S CLOSE TRADE TIES WITH THE UNITED STATES."

Let's look at some fairly recent examples of these issues.

In the early 1970s, the American economy faced some serious problems. Unemployment was high. So was inflation. Imports were growing faster than exports. In other words, the **balance of trade** was unfavourable. To help correct this, President Nixon placed a ten per cent **surcharge** (extra tax) on all imported goods. Many of these goods came from Canada. They now cost more to buy there. As a result, their sales fell. This action probably cost 90 000 Canadians their jobs over the next six months.

In 1971, President Nixon "froze" prices and wages for 90 days. His aim was to fight inflation in the United States. Our government said that this policy was not to apply in Canada. But two American-owned car companies did not agree. Ford of Canada announced a freeze on the price of its new 1972 models. Chrysler Canada held back a planned raise for its workers. These Canadian workers did not get their raise until the freeze ended in the United States.

Canadian Commodity Exports, 1969 and 1973
(in millions of dollars)

COMMODITY	1969	1973
Wheat	473	1 220
Animals & Other Edible Products	992	1 933
Metal Ores & Concentrates	1 139	1 997
Crude Petroleum	526	1 482
Natural Gas	176	351
Other Crude Inedible Materials	622	1 189
Lumber	696	1 598
Pulp	753	1 059
Newsprint	1 126	1 287
Fabricated Metals	1 499	2 082
Other Fabricated, Inedible Materials	1 089	2 168
Motor Vehicles and Parts	3 514	5 338
Other Machinery and Equipment	1 459	2 454
Other Domestic Exports	383	561
Re-exports	428	582
*TOTAL EXPORTS	14 875	25 301

*Figures might not add exactly, due to rounding.
SOURCE: Statistics Canada

Canadian Commodity Imports 1969 and 1973
(in millions of dollars)

COMMODITY	1969	1973
Food	933	1 625
Animals & Other Edible Products	130	356
Metal Ores & Concentrates	193	330
Crude Petroleum	393	941
Other Crude Inedible Materials	499	745
Fabricated Textiles	403	659
Chemical Products	662	1 023
Fabricated Metals	731	1 026
Other Fabricated Inedible Materials	1 109	1 573
Motor Vehicles & Parts	3 546	6 063
Other Machinery & Equipment	4 031	6 474
Other Imports	1 500	2 486
*TOTAL IMPORTS	14 130	23 303

Figures might not add exactly, due to rounding.
SOURCE: *Statistics Canada*

2.   AMERICAN INVESTMENT IN CANADA

The Nature of Investment

It is a hot summer day. The temperature is climbing above 30°C. Three young children get a smart idea. They will set up a cold drink stand in their neighbourhood. They will charge 10 cents a glass. First they need $2.00 to buy tins of frozen lemonade. They only have $1.00. They ask their mother for the other dollar. She says "no." They offer to give her half of any **profits** (gains) from their business. She changes her mind and gives them $1.00. She has just made an investment. She is now part owner of a new lemonade business.

When money is used this way it is called **capital.** Most businesses and industries need large amounts of capital to get started, and to keep going. People **invest** (put their money) in businesses to make **profits.** If the business in which they invest succeeds they will share in the rewards.

Canada is a highly industrialized country. Hundreds of large businesses employ thousands of workers. There are thousands of smaller operations too. Billions of dollars have been invested in these companies, large and small. Much of this capital has been invested by Canadians. Some, though, comes from other countries. This money is called foreign investment.

Kinds of Foreign Investment

Foreigners invest in Canada in several ways. They may loan money to Canadian businesses. They may also loan money to a government in Canada, national, provincial or local. This is done by buying the bonds put out by these governments.

Foreigners sometimes buy **stocks** (shares) in Canadian companies. As stockholders they are part-owners of the company. Sometimes foreigners buy an entire Canadian company. Or they buy a big enough share to take over control of the company. Such an action is called a **takeover.** Foreigners also can buy buildings, land or other kinds of property in Canada. Sometimes, foreign companies set up **branch plants** in Canada. Such plants are called branches because they are part of the main tree (the foreign company).

The end of a busy trading day on a Canadian stock exchange

The accompanying charts will help you see the nature and amount of foreign investment in Canada. More than 60 billion foreign dollars are invested in Canada. About 80 per cent of this amount is American.

1. Divide your class into small groups. Discuss the following questions:
a) What are some advantages of foreign investment in Canada?
b) What are some of the disadvantages?
c) Is it a good idea to get 80 per cent of our foreign investment from one country? Explain your answer.
2. Share your answers with another group. Try to provide examples for your main points.
3. Discuss these questions as a whole class. Is there much disagreement? What are the views of the majority on the main questions?

FOREIGN INVESTMENT IN CANADA
(Selected Major Industries)

Industry	Year	Ownership				Where the Money Came From (in percentage)			Control		
		Amount Invested (in billions of dollars)							Percentage of Financial Control of Industry		
		Canada	U.S.	Other	Total	Canada	U.S.	Other	Canada	U.S.	Other
Manufacturing	1968	10.3	9.7	1.7	21.7	48	44	8	42	46	12
	1973	14.5	13.7	2.8	31.1	47	44	9	41	44	15
	*1976	*	*	*	*	*	*	*	43	43	14
Petroleum and Natural Gas	1968	4.0	5.3	1.2	10.6	38	51	11	25	61	14
	1973	6.9	7.6	1.9	16.4	42	46	12	24	59	17
	*1976	*	*	*	*	*	*	*	27	57	16
Other Mining and Smelting	1968	2.3	3.0	0.6	5.9	39	51	10	32	58	10
	1973	3.8	3.8	0.9	8.5	44	45	11	43	45	12
	*1976	*	*	*	*	*	*	*	43	44	13
Railways	1968	4.6	0.4	0.6	5.6	82	8	10	98	2	—
	1973	5.2	0.4	0.5	6.1	85	7	8	98	2	—
	*1976	*	*	*	*	*	*	*	99	1	—

*Figures Not Available

Note: Figures might not add exactly, due to rounding.

Foreign Investment
(Specific Industries)

Industry	Year	Ownership Amount of $ Invested (in millions)			Where $ Came From (%)		Control Percentage of Financial Control of Industry	
		Total	Canada	Foreign (U.S. in brackets)	Canada	Foreign (U.S. in brackets)	Canada	Foreign (U.S. in brackets)
Aluminum	1968	871	225	646 (533)	26	74 (61)	—	100
	1973	944	302	642 (553)	32	68 (58)	100	—
Automobiles & Parts	1968	1 231	184	1,047 (1 044)	15	85	3	97
	1973	2 092	307	1,785 (1 774)	15	85	4	96
Chemicals	1968	2 405	849	1,556 (1 284)	35	65 (53)	19	81 (60)
	1973	2 888	815	2,073 (1 694)	28	72 (59)	14	86 (64)
Electrical Equipment	1968	1 160	404	756 (680)	35	65 (59)	22	78 (68)
	1973	1 784	640	1,144 (1 010)	36	64 (56)	27	73 (61)
Iron & Steel Mills	1968	1 332	1 151	181 (113)	86	14 (9)	99	1 (1)
	1973	1 893	1 709	184 (148)	90	10 (8)	97	3 (3)
Pulp & Paper	1968	3 462	1 415	2,047 (1 744)	41	59 (50)	50	50 (39)
	1973	4 714	2 003	2,711 (2 029)	43	57 (43)	50	50 (34)
Rubber	1968	362	127	235	35	65	1	99
	1973	564	162	402	29	71	1	99
Textiles	1968	908	698	210 (155)	77	23 (17)	76	24 (17)
	1973	1 317	961	336 (258)	74	26 (20)	70	30 (21)

Distribution of Foreign Ownership in Canada

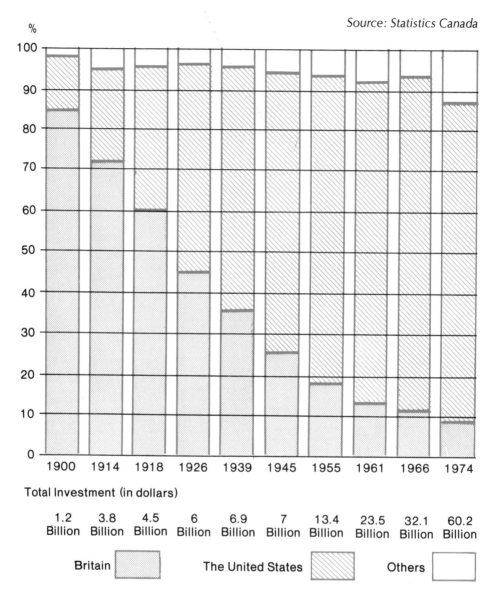

Source: Statistics Canada

Total Investment (in dollars)

| 1.2 Billion | 3.8 Billion | 4.5 Billion | 6 Billion | 6.9 Billion | 7 Billion | 13.4 Billion | 23.5 Billion | 32.1 Billion | 60.2 Billion |

Britain   The United States   Others

Analyzing The Charts:

1. Which industry seems to be growing fastest in Canada? Which employs the most people?
2. What do the charts tell you about the importance of *trade* to the Canadian economy?
3. Why are so few people employed in "primary industries"? How could we increase the number of jobs created by our own natural resources?
4. How does this chart relate to our list of advantages and disadvantages in foreign investment.

Employment by industrial group, 1965 and 1974

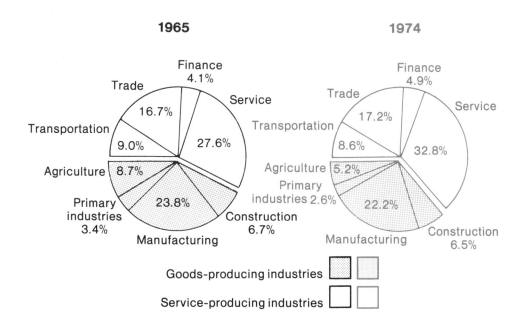

Some "Pros" and "Cons" of Foreign Investment

Advantages	Disadvantages
—Foreign investment has created hundreds of thousands of jobs in Canada.	—Foreign investors influence the Canadian economy. They are threatening to take away their money. This pressure can cause a Canadian government to act in a way they want.
—Businesses supported by foreign money pay salaries to Canadians. They also provide pensions and other benefits.	
—Canadians buy goods and services with this money. This helps other businesses in Canada.	—Foreign branch plants have to follow the orders to their parent companies. These orders can conflict with the laws or interests of Canada. Serious problems could result.
—Businesses supported by foreign money pay taxes on their profits to Canadian governments.	
—Foreign capital helps Canada develop resources. Without it, they might have to be left in the ground.	—An American branch plant in Canada must obey American law. For example, the United States government could ban trade with country "X". Its Canadian subsidiary then cannot trade with that country.
—Foreign companies in Canada often give business to Canadian-owned firms.	
—Some branch plants bring in advanced skills and machinery. They also "import" good businessmen from other countries.	—Sometimes foreign companies try to employ as few Canadians as possible. They ship Canadian raw or semi-finished products to the U.S. Americans are hired to finish these products. Often, these products are sold back to Canada. We can get lazy. Instead of developing our own skills and research, we rely on theirs.
—Canadians can buy shares in many foreign-owned businesses. They can profit from good investments.	

The American Eagle: Are We "Under its Wings" or "In its Claws"?

You will read some examples of the power of the eagle. After you have finished, answer the question in the title. Are we under its wings — enjoying its benefits and protection? OR are we in its claws — powerless to control our fate?

a) The United States has a *Trading with the Enemy Act*. This act forbids American companies to trade with an enemy of the United States. American branch plants in Canada are bound by this law too. Many Canadians work for these companies. These branch plants have had to turn down good business deals with countries like Cuba and China. Perhaps, some jobs were lost as a result.

b) Canada imports many of its manufactured goods. These include computers, instruments, machine tools and so on. For example, our **trade deficit** in manufactured goods was $10 billion! (The value of such goods imported was $10 billion more than the value of such goods exported.) We must pay this

difference, either in money or other exports. Meanwhile, our own manufacturing industry does not grow quickly enough. This means fewer jobs. Many of our imported manufactured goods come from the United States. Thus we remain heavily dependent on that country.

c) In 1977 a Canadian company, UNITOURS LTD., set up tours to Cuba. They advertised these trips in American magazines. About one thousand customers showed interest. At the time, Cuba was an American "enemy". The United States government stepped in. It probably suggested that UNITOURS would lose other American business if they proceeded. UNITOURS changed its mind about offering trips to Cuba to Americans. (More recently, Americans have been permitted to travel to Communist countries such as Cuba and Vietnam.)

d) Millions of dollars are made in the tourist business. Canada is anxious to attract American tourists. Governments can choose to discourage foreign travel by their citizens. In 1977, an American law cut back the travel and convention expenses which could be deducted from taxes. Many Canadian cities host conventions and conferences. Such gatherings often involve Americans. Many of these people were discouraged from travelling to Canada by the new law. The American president also urged his people to stay at home and spend their money in their own country. No doubt, such policies have helped the United States. However, they have been very costly to Canada. Toronto alone expected to lose $60 million per year.

1. List the types of businesses which would be hardest hit by a decline in tourism.

2. Who in your family work outside your home? Ask them if their jobs or businesses depend directly on ties with the United States. If they say "no", see if their positions depend *indirectly* on such ties.

3. General Motors is the main industry in Oshawa, Ontario. This city has a population of over 120 000. GM is an American-controlled automobile manufacturer. If, for some reason, the company decided to leave, Oshawa would be ruined. Is there a town or city near you in a similar situation? Is there a solution to this condition?

4. Search for statistics which will tell you the names of the ten largest companies in Canada. (Check the *Canada Yearbook* or the *Financial Post* as possible sources. You might write to Statistics Canada or the Department of Industry, Trade & Commerce in Ottawa.) Try to find out which of these companies are American-owned or controlled. Prepare a chart or graph with your data. If you are unsuccessful here, at least examine the charts in this chapter. They will show you the extent of foreign (including American) investment in Canada in certain key industries.

An automatic welder on the Ford Motor Company assembly line at St. Thomas, Ontario. The Ford Company employs thousands of Canadian workers. However, critics of the Auto Trade Pact suggest that Canada should obtain many *more* jobs from that agreement.

A Canadian research technologist at work. Our dependence on foreign investment and technology limits such job opportunities in Canada.

What is Being Done About Foreign Investment

We are becoming more aware of the problems of too much foreign investment. Television and newspapers comment frequently on this issue. Well-known Canadians have expressed their fears openly. The federal and provincial governments are paying more attention to the matter. Here are some things that have been done:

— No more than 25 per cent of Canadian banks can be owned by non-Canadians.
— Only Canadian citizens, or companies with 80 per cent Canadian ownership, can be granted broadcasting licenses for radio or TV.
— It has been made more difficult for foreigners to get oil and gas leases in the Yukon and Northwest Territories.
— Some provinces prevent foreigners from buying land. For example, Prince Edward Island has restrictions on foreign (and non-resident) ownership of ocean-front land.
— The federal government passed the *Foreign Investment Review Act.* This lets the government examine foreign bids to take over Canadian businesses. These bids can be rejected by the government.
— Some governments give special loans or tax advantages to Canadian-owned companies. For example, a few years ago the government of Ontario made a large loan to a Canadian publishing company. As a result, the company remained in Canadian hands.

What Could Be Done

Some Canadians feel that our politicians are not doing enough about limiting foreign investment. Examples of their thinking follow.

Some Canadians Speak Out On Foreign Investment

Walter Gordon

Walter Gordon was a member of the Pearson cabinet of the early 1960s. He upset the government by recommending steps to reduce foreign influence in Canada's economy. In the 1970s he was active in the *Committee for an Independent Canada* (CIC). This organization would like to see certain large American owned companies, such as IMPERIAL OIL (EXXON), **nationalized** (taken over by the Canadian government). It also wants some other foreign firms bought out by Canadian investors. The CIC feels that some basic industries should be owned, or at least controlled by Canadians. Mr. Gordon has warned that Canada will lose its political independence unless it reduces the amount of foreign control of its economy.

Walter Gordon, one of the first prominent Canadians to call for major limits on foreign investment spending

Mel Hurtig

Mr. Hurtig is a very outspoken Canadian publisher from Edmonton. He claims that over 90 per cent of the "new" foreign investment in Canada each year is actually Canadian money. It comes from profits on Canadian business, plus loans or grants from Canadian banks and governments. Americans and other foreigners are buying up *our* economy with *our* money. Also, he claims that over $600 000 leaves Canada every hour of every day. This is money earned by foreign investment in our country. Mr. Hurtig wants strict limits placed on future foreign investment here. He also wants Canada to buy back some of the existing investment.

James Laxer

Mr. Laxer is a Canadian professor of economics. He has been associated with the New Democratic Party. He has criticized Canadian governments for "selling out" to foreign investors, particularly Americans. One of his most bitter attacks was on the Alberta Tar Sands Project. These tar sands contain billions of barrels of oil. In the early 1970s, seven mainly American-owned companies were given the right to develop this potential. Much of the money will be supplied by Canadian banks and governments. Much of the profits will go to foreign owners.

1. Try to find an address for the Committee for an Independent Canada. Write to them for information on foreign investment in Canada.

2. Look for items in newspapers and on news broadcasts which show foreign investment as a "good thing".

3. Many other countries have tougher laws against foreign investment than we do. These include Britain, France, Italy, West Germany, Mexico and Japan. Why do you think Canada does not follow their example?

4. An American financial magazine once said: "The only U.S. business which wouldn't be cordially welcomed to Canada is *Murder Incorporated.*" What does this mean?

5. How could Canada "buy back" control of certain key industries from foreign investors? Where would the money come from?

6. If this were done, which industries should be bought out first. Why?

7. What *political* concerns might be involved in such a policy? Did you think of these when answering No. 3 above.

8. Try to discover what our major political parties have to say about American investment in Canada. Which answers do you prefer?

Professor Melville Watkins, a severe critic of foreign investment in Canada

Present Trend

Statistics presented earlier in this chapter showed that foreign investment in Canada is growing. Yet there is little pressure on our governments or politicians to resist this trend. This is despite the fact that the media frequently point out the facts. The following Gallup Poll was published in the summer of 1977:

QUESTION NO. 1: Do you think there is enough U.S. capital invested in Canada now, or would you like to see more?

ANSWERS	Enough Now	Like to See More	Don't Know
1964	46%	33%	21%
1967	60	24	16
1970	62	25	13
1972	67	22	11
1975	71	16	13
1977	69	20	12

QUESTION NO. 2: Some experts want Canada to buy back control — say 51% — of U.S. companies in Canada. This might mean a big reduction in our standard of living. Would you approve of this or not?

ANSWERS	YES	NO	PERHAPS	DON'T KNOW
NATIONAL - 1970	46%	32%	2%	19%
- 1975	58	26	2	14
- 1977	41	42	2	15
REGIONAL - 1977				
Atlantic	30	50	—	20
Quebec	41	44	1	14
Ontario	40	40	2	18
Prairies	51	39	2	8
British Columbia	45	44	4	8

1. In the middle and late 1960s, Canada was very prosperous. In the mid-1970s, our economy slowed down considerably, and unemployment grew. Also, Atlantic Canada has almost always had more economic problems than the rest of Canada. How are these facts reflected in the Gallup Poll above? Explain your answers.

2. What do you conclude about how Canadians feel today about foreign investment? How do you personally feel about this issue? Why?

3. Try to find the music and *Canadian* lyrics (words) to the song "This Land Is Your Land, This Land Is My Land." Sing the song together with your class. Now,

consider this title: "This Land Is *Their* Land" (a reference to foreign ownership in Canada). As a class, try to make up *new* lyrics for the song. Make them reflect the extent of foreign control of our economy, and how you feel about it.

3. ENERGY RESOURCES

The Energy Crisis

Several years ago, the north-eastern United States faced a huge power failure. In many large cities, the lights literally went out. Machinery run by electricity stopped. Household appliances went off. Elevators stopped running, trapping thousands of people. In the summer of 1977, the city of New York faced a complete power failure. It lasted almost two days. Industries shut down. Hospitals and other essential services faced huge problems. At night, the darkness encouraged crime. Many stores were looted and several fires were set. When power was restored, the city was struck by a record heat wave. Restrictions were placed on the use of certain equipment, including air conditioners, to prevent another power failure.

The energy crisis does not involve electricity alone. North America was hit by an oil shortage in 1973-74. In certain other countries, oil had to be rationed. We were very surprised by such developments. For years we had been told that North America had vast reserves of oil and natural gas. Perhaps this is one reason why we had begun to use them so much. Often, energy was used thoughtlessly. Companies in the energy business ran advertisements encouraging increased consumption of their products.

Suddenly, by the mid-1970s, everything was changing. Costs for discovering and processing resources rose quickly. Foreign suppliers began withholding oil, or increasing its price. Experts began to say that Canada and the United States could run out of oil and natural gas fairly soon. Such predictions were shocking. Energy is vital to our way of life. It is needed in industry, transportation, defence, home heating and many important activities. The items we use every day — radios, televisions, lawnmowers, air conditioners, outboard motors, hair dryers, electric blankets and so on are useless without power to run them.

A Canadian oil refinery working around the clock to maintain supplies of vital petroleum products. Most such refineries are controlled by foreign oil companies.

The Denison Mines Affair

Uranium is a key natural resource. Nuclear energy cannot be made without it. As we need more energy, uranium will become even more important. Canada is lucky to have large amounts of uranium.

In 1970, much of Canada's known reserves of uranium were controlled by a company called *Denison Mines.* The president of this company was Mr. Stephen Roman. He announced plans to sell his company's shares to a foreign firm. If this sale took place, less than 10 per cent of our uranium resources would have remained in Canadian hands. Therefore, the Canadian government blocked this sale.

Mr. Roman was very upset. He took the government to court. He felt that it

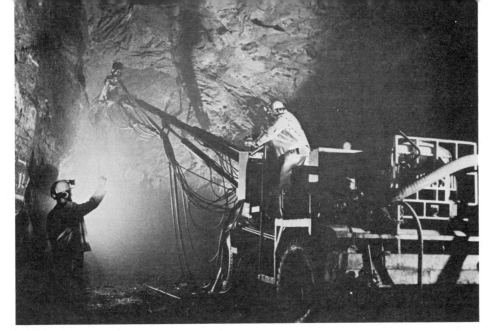
Operations inside a uranium mine in Canada

was interfering in his business. He had broken no law, he said. He felt he had the right to sell his business interests for the best possible price. In some ways, the government agreed with him. But it believed that uranium was too important a resource to be controlled by foreigners. It provided $30 million to Denison Mines. This let the company continue production of uranium at Elliot Lake, Ontario. In return, the company promised to keep this mine running until at least 1984.

Our government took further steps to keep the uranium industry in Canadian hands. Foreign ownership in this industry would be limited to 33 per cent or less. The courts helped too. They rejected Mr. Roman's legal action against the government.

The "Denison Affair" showed what the government *could* do about foreign ownership. But it has not continued this policy of strong action. Foreigners continue to buy up large chunks of Canadian land, industry and resources.

Who Owns Canada's Energy Resources?

Look at the charts earlier in this chapter. You can see that many of Canada's energy resources are owned or controlled by foreigners. This is particularly true of oil and natural gas. The largest companies in this field are American-owned. These companies have been selling large quantities of Canadian oil and natural gas to the United States for many years. Both Canadian and American governments co-operated in this. We made money from this arrangement. Some money went to our federal government. Some went to the governments of oil-producing provinces. Some money also went to Canadians who owned shares in, or worked for, those foreign companies.

Canadian Quotas

We are more careful now in these dealings. The demand for energy keeps growing. We realize that we must keep large reserves for our own future use. The United States would prefer to buy Canadian oil and natural gas (at reasonable rates). They too want to save their own shrinking supplies. Our government has begun to limit exports of Canadian oil and gas. Americans have claimed that we are backing out of deals. They say they are counting on our energy resources, and that we are letting them down.

Canadians reply that we must look after our own interests first. We do help out the Americans in emergencies. For example, the winter of 1976-77 was one of the coldest on record. Northern American states developed serious fuel shortages. We agreed to ship large amounts of oil and gas to them on a short term basis.

The Canadian government is planning to slowly cut our oil and gas exports over the next few years. This issue could cause serious trouble between our two countries. Hopefully, it will be settled peacefully.

The Sharing of Continental Resources: "What's Ours Is Ours, and What's Yours Is Ours."

Each year, the United States uses vast amounts of natural resources. It has a large population. They demand many goods and services. Many countries, including Canada, want the products of American industry. As a result, the United States is by far the world's biggest industrial producer. Many of the energy resources which they consume come from Canada. The American factories have huge appetites. Every year they grow hungrier.

American businessmen know how important Canada's natural resources are to their industries. This is one reason why they have bought up so many of those resources. They would like a guaranteed supply of our raw materials. The American government has tried to "sell" Canada a **continental resources sharing plan.** Here is the main idea: our natural resources should not be regarded as "Canadian" or "American." They should be held "in common." There would be no border between our two countries when it came to resources. We have seen examples of how "co-operative" Canada has been with the United States about our resources. But we still say "NO" to the idea of a continental resources sharing plan.

1. List the advantages to Canada of such a plan.
2. How do you feel about such a plan? Why?
3. The Americans can be tough bargainers in economic matters. In 1970,

POWER RESERVOIR

CANADA

macPherson *TORONTO STAR*

President Nixon cut in half the daily amount of Canadian oil allowed into the United States. This cost us millions of dollars per day. One reason for this action was to make us agree to a North American energy-sharing plan. We refused.

(a) Why did this action cost us money?

(b) Why would the United States not likely take a similar action today?

Canada did agree to sell an additional 189 billion cubic metres of natural gas to the Americans over the next several years. Why would we do this? (Afterwards, President Nixon removed the limits on imported Canadian oil.)

New Sources of Electricity

There could be a similar problem with electricity. The demand for it is also growing. For many years Ontario and Quebec have co-operated with American border states. They have set up a complex grid system. It is run by

Ontario Hydro's nuclear generating plant at Pickering, Ontario

Syncrude Canada Ltd.'s "Li'l Beaver" dragline was used in a test to see if the Athabaska Tar Sands could be mined profitably. Huge projects are now underway there.

computers. If any area runs short of power, extra energy can be fed in from other regions. We helped out the Americans during the great power failure of a few years ago. New York State has sent extra electrical power to Ontario on several occasions.

Ontario's hydro-electric potential is almost fully developed. It is beginning to rely more on nuclear-powered generators to produce electricity. There is concern on both sides of the border over nuclear power. Some of its dangers include possible nuclear leaks and pollution.

Will Canada and the United States be able to share electricity in the years to come? The answer is "maybe."

4.   THE DEBATE OVER A MACKENZIE VALLEY PIPELINE

As we have seen, both Canada and the United States need more oil and natural gas. Huge reserves have been discovered in Alaska. Smaller deposits have been found in the valley of the Mackenzie River. There is no question that these reserves have to be developed. However, problems have come up over how to bring them south to the waiting markets.

The United States has been anxious to start using Alaskan oil and gas as soon as possible. This could be brought south in one of two ways. One is by pipeline through Canada. The other is via a shorter pipeline to Alaska's south shore and then the rest of the way by ship. The Americans also hoped that Canada would continue to make its oil and gas available to them.

These questions produced several concerns in Canada. We were worried about damage to the northern environment. This could be caused, on land, by pipeline construction. It also could result at sea, because of spills fron huge oil tankers. Pipelines would create problems for our Native peoples. Their lifestyles would be greatly upset. Moreover, some of their land claims still had not been settled by our government. There might be court battles over who owned the land through which the pipelines would be built.

The Canadian government faced still more difficulties. They did not want to offend the Americans. It would be cheaper to co-operate with them. Otherwise, we would soon have to build our own pipelines, and without help. Still, we wanted to keep Canadian oil and gas mainly for our own use. Our gas and oil fields would be hooked up to pipelines running into the United States. In future, it could be hard to deny these supplies to our neighbours.

The decisions about oil were made first. The Americans built a pipeline across Alaska. The first oil through the line began arriving at the tanks on the south shore in the summer of 1977. From here, tankers would carry it south to waiting refineries on the American west coast. Almost immediately, problems arose with the pipeline. There were leaks, plus a serious explosion. These events seemed to justify earlier worries about the **environment.** They also influenced a key decision about natural gas pipelines.

Scenes from the opening of the Trans-Alaska Pipeline in 1977. Such projects present a real
danger of massive pollution of both the Canadian and American Arctic environment.

You Decide

In July 1977 the Canadian government made a major decision. It concerned the building of a natural gas pipeline in the Canadian North. You will be provided with some essential information. Also keep in mind what you have just read. Try to make the best possible decision. Then see if it is the same as the real one made by the government.

Here is the situation:

1. In 1972, several American and Canadian companies formed Canadian Arctic Gas Pipeline Limited (CAGPL). This new corporation would try to win a contract to build the main gas pipeline through the Far North. Among the contributing companies were Exxon, Shell and Gulf Oil.

Proposed Routes — Natural Gas Pipeline

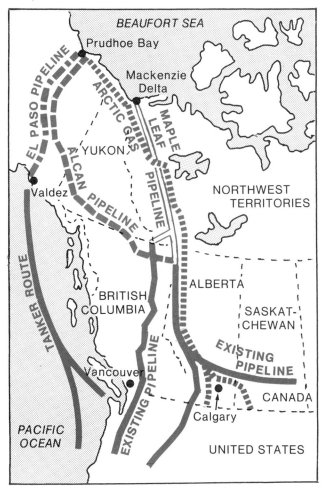

2. Over the next five years, CAGPL spent $140 million on studies and plans for their pipeline. The route they chose began at Prudhoe Bay, Alaska (see map). It ran east to the Mackenzie Delta and then south along the Mackenzie Valley into Alberta. It would carry both American and Canadian gas.

3. In 1974, the President of Alberta Gas Trunk Lines, Robert Blair, pulled his company out of CAGPL. He proposed a new plan. He would build a pipeline from Alaska through the Yukon to Vancouver and the United States (see map). He would follow the Alaska Highway rather than the Mackenzie Valley. His line would carry only American gas.

4. Also in 1974, the Canadian government created a commission to investigate the matter. It was headed by Justice Berger of the British Columbia Supreme Court. He conducted hearings across Canada. He took special care to consult the Native peoples. Their lands and lifestyles were at stake in this issue. In the spring of 1977 Justice Berger made his report. He said that a Mackenzie Valley pipeline would destroy the wildlife of that region. He also stated that time was needed to settle the land claims of Native peoples. In short, he wanted no northern pipeline for ten years. Also, he recommended against a Mackenzie Valley line at any time.

5. The Berger Report won both friends and enemies. **Environmentalists** praised it. So did the Native peoples. The New Democratic Party urged the Liberal government to adopt the report. However, leaders of business and industry said otherwise. The economy could not afford any delay. The natural gas would be needed by the early 1980s. The United States government also applied pressure. They wanted a decision by September 1, 1977. Otherwise, they might agree to a third plan.

6. The third plan was the El Paso project. An all-American company would build a gas pipeline across Alaska to Valdez (see map). From here, Alaskan gas would be carried by ship to U.S. markets. Canada would be excluded.

7. Stop at this point. Imagine that *you* are the Canadian government. What will you do? CAGPL has powerful companies behind it. They have spent millions. They are strongly financed. This is important, because the pipeline would be Canada's largest (3200 km long and 1.22 m in diameter). By 1977, its cost was estimated at about $10 billion. Over 3000 people, mostly Canadians, would be directly employed by the project.

8. Robert Blair's company argues back. His plan is cheaper than CAGPL's. Canadian gas reserves will be protected. He points out that he asks no government guarantees of financial support. On the other hand, CAGPL wants a promise that if its project runs over estimated costs, the government (taxpayers) will pay the difference.

9. CAGPL counters this argument. Blair's group is poorly financed. It could go bankrupt. It has done far less research on its plans. Its cost estimates could be

A tanker takes on oil off the coast of Alaska.

very inaccurate. Also, what will happen to Mackenzie Delta gas? How can it get to *any* markets — Canadian or American?

10. Blair replies that he will build a connecting line, the "Dempster Link", to tie in the Mackenzie Delta with the main line. He also reminds the government of the heavy American involvement in CAGPL. The latter's route will damage the environment just as the Berger Report fears. There will be trouble with the Native peoples. The public will be upset by these developments. The voters seem to feel that his plans leave more control in Canadian hands.

11. CAGPL again reminds the government of Blair's shaky financing and poor research. What if his company folds? Environmental damage can be limited, or repaired. Native land claims can be settled peacefully while construction goes on. Go with the stronger, more experienced company.

12. Washington is pressing you for a decision.

13. DECIDE!

In July of 1977 the Trudeau government rejected the CAGPL plan for a Mackenzie Valley gas pipeline. Instead, they decided to permit Robert Blair's company to build the pipeline. The pipeline would follow the Alaska highway route. The government insisted on one condition: that the "Dempster Link" must be built to connect Mackenzie Delta gas with the main line.

Note the location of the Dempster Link. The Canadian government insisted that it be built as a condition for awarding the contract. Why did it do so?

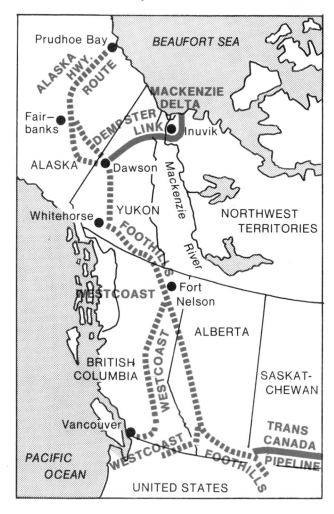

Northern Gas Pipeline — Route Chosen

Canadians as Entrepreneurs

Foreign control of Canada's economy can be offset in several ways. As we have seen, one way is government action. Another is the encouragement of Canadians to start more businesses of their own. We are sometimes criticized for being too cautious in business. For example, it is said that we save too much money. Our banks turn around and lend this money to foreigners. These people often seem more willing to take a chance on a new business venture.

However, this is not completely true. Canada has a growing number of **entrepreneurs** (builders of business). Here are three examples:

Gary Walker

In 1971, Mr. Walker was a young lawyer working for a development and construction company. Soon he had formed his own law firm. Next he turned to buying old houses, fixing them up and selling them for good profits. By 1973 he had built up a $500 000 fund. With this he was able to begin a large development firm, with himself as president. His company won multi-million dollar construction contracts. By 1977 he was a 33-year-old millionaire.

Edie Laquer

Edie Laquer is a successful young businesswoman in a large Canadian city. When she was nineteen years old, she went into partnership in a cosmetic company. Within two years the company had grown rapidly and was employing 250 people. At age twenty-one, Edie sold her half of the business. With this money, she invested in land. By 1977, she owned several valuable pieces of real estate. Her income had risen to over $100 000 per year. Such wealth enabled her to pursue an exciting lifestyle featuring travel, plus expensive cars and clothes.

Pedro Cabezuelo

Pedro, a native of Spain, was a waiter in 1974. By 1977, he was a partner in a company which owned several restaurants and pubs. To get his start, Pedro worked and saved very hard. When his chance came, he put all his life savings into the company. He also went into debt for several thousand dollars. His gamble paid off. Pedro is now a millionaire. He and his partners have plans for even more business expansion.

5. CONCLUSION

We have seen that the economic ties between Canada and the United States are very close. In many ways, this is a happy and pleasant relationship. But Canadians are becoming more aware that we pay a big price for this. We must count on American trade, investment and goodwill. We seem to be growing more dependent on these things. A few people are telling us that this threatens our *political* independence. This item will be discussed more fully in a later chapter. We should note that these warning voices seem to be in the minority. They have not really captured public attention. Both federal and provincial governments let us slip closer into the American embrace. Do you agree with this viewpoint? Why or why not?

A computer installation. The computer industry, largely American-controlled, will play a vital role in Canada's future.

THINGS TO THINK ABOUT AND DO

Reviewing Key Words and Ideas

The following terms appeared in this chapter. Try to recall their meaning and how they were used.

balance of trade	export	royalty
bonds	foreign investment	standard of living
branch plant	foreign trade	stocks
capital investment	import	subsidiary
CIC	market	surcharge
continental resource sharing	nationalize	surplus
deficit	pipeline	takeover
entrepreneur	quota	trade
environmentalist	rationing	

Remembering the Facts

1. What evidence is there that Canada has very close economic ties with the United States?
2. Summarize the good and bad aspects of this close relationship.
3. Why is energy a touchy issue in Canadian-American relations?
4. How could Canada gain more control over its own economy? Why are these steps difficult to take?

Analyzing Ideas

1. American foreign investment is spread all over the world. More than 25 per cent of it is in Canada. This amounts to many *billions* of dollars. Would it be fair for us to change the rules of investment in Canada after the American money has come in here? Is it reasonable to have controls that are at least as tough as those imposed by other countries (such as Britain and Japan) where Americans invest? Why would it be more difficult for us to apply similar rules?
2. Try to find more up-to-date statistics about foreign investment than the ones offered in this book. Compare the two sets of figures. What *trends* can you see? Do you like them?

Applying Your Knowledge

1. In 1971, the Canadian government published the *Gray Report*. This had been produced by a special committee led by Herb Gray. Mr. Gray was a cabinet minister in the Trudeau government. This report made a number of important recommendations about foreign investment in Canada. Shortly after, Mr. Gray lost his cabinet position. Students who are interested in economics could discover the details of the Gray Report. They should tell them to the class. Consider these questions. What, if anything, was done about the recommendations of the Gray Report? Why might Mr. Gray have been removed from the Cabinet? How does this incident compare with the experience of Walter Gordon?

2. Do you think it is right that any private people, Canadian or foreign, should own natural resources in Canada? Why do you feel this way? (This could be a good topic for a class discussion or debate.)

3. Try to involve *other* people in a discussion of United States influence in the Canadian economy. Parents, or other relatives, plus friends, would be ideal. See if they are aware of the nature and extent of this American influence. What do they think about it? If many of you feel concerned, what could you *do* about it? (Consider letters to politicians, radio and television stations, and so on.)

4

MILITARY AND POLITICAL ASPECTS

INTRODUCTION

Most of us have heard about "the longest undefended border in the world." Of course, this refers to the Canada-United States border. The fact that it *is* undefended shows the trust and good feelings which exist between us. For almost one hundred years, there has been no serious danger of war between Canada and the U.S. Indeed, since World War I, the two countries have been strong military allies.

1. What does it mean to be a "military ally" of another country?

2. What advantages could there be in having such an ally? Why might this also be a disadvantage or a danger?

3. Why are Canada and the United States military allies?

    Think about economic, geographical and historical reasons. You should also consider values or beliefs shared by the two countries.

Canada's military ties with the United States became very strong during and after World War II. These ties were slightly strained in the early 1960s. This happened again in the early 1970s. However, today Canada and the United States seem to be entering a new period of co-operation. In this chapter, we will study some of the reasons for these developments.

Before reading on, study the chart of Key Words and Ideas which follows.

KEY WORDS AND IDEAS IN THIS CHAPTER

Term	Meaning	Sample Use
Cold War	a war of words, and ideas. It is not "hot" because the two sides do not actually shoot at each other.	After World War II, a "Cold War" developed between the United States and the Soviet Union. Each country had several allies (friends) on its side.
deterrence	the act of persuading another person or group *not* to do something (usually done by threatening to take counter action)	Both the U.S. and the U.S.S.R. have huge weapons systems. Each has enough power to destroy the other. The principle of deterrence is at work for both nations.
espionage	various spying activities	Espionage is a key part of the Cold War. Most countries spy on suspected enemies (and even friends). They do this to discover new weapons, secret plans and so on. This reduces the chance of being surprised by future developments.
military ally	a friendly country with which you have a defence agreement. Allies promise to defend each other, and sometimes to co-operate in an attack on an enemy.	Canada and the United States have been military allies for many years.
obsolescence	a stage of being out of date or old-fashioned	Countries develop new weapons very quickly. Because of this their existing weapons reach a stage of obsolescence. Out of date weapons are of limited use, even though they might be very expensive.

1.   THE "COLD WAR"

As we have seen in Unit 3, Canadians and Americans fought side by side in two world wars. In World War II (1939-1945), the very safety and survival of North America were at stake. This experience made strong bonds between our two peoples. When the war had ended, many dangers to world peace remained. Therefore, Canada and the United States chose to remain allies.

Soviet Threat

The new danger to North America seemed to come from the Soviet Union. This country had been our **ally** in the war. This did not prevent problems from developing. The reasons for this are explained in more detail in Unit VI, Chapter 3. Still, it is necessary here to give at least a brief summary of them. Since 1918, the Soviet Union had been under a Communist government. Its leaders did not share our beliefs in democracy and human rights. This was a difference in basic values. It created tension and mistrust on both sides.

At the end of World War II, the Soviet Union was the strongest power in Europe. It used this power to take over several countries in central and Eastern Europe. The Communists believed in spreading their system as far as possible. Some democratic countries feared that the Soviet Union might attack them next. This was not really very likely. Still, it was possible. Their concern was real. Canada and the United States had to be prepared, just in case.

The Nature of the Cold War

This tense situation came to be called the "Cold War." It was "cold" because there was no actual shooting between the two sides. Instead, the conflict was more like a war of words, and nerves. Nonetheless, both sides built up their armed forces. They spent huge sums of money on planes, tanks, guns and other weapons. They also engaged in **espionage** on each other. This way, they hoped to learn about each other's latest military equipment, and their plans for using it.

2.   THE FORMATION OF NATO

These actions caused the Cold War to become more tense and dangerous. Canada and the United States became even more concerned about their safety. Several countries in western Europe had similar feelings. Therefore, in 1949 they joined together in a new and larger alliance. This was called NATO — or, the *North Atlantic Treaty Organization*. Details about NATO are offered in Unit VI, Chapter 3.

In 1945 Igor Gouzenko was a clerk in the Soviet embassy in Ottawa. He gave the Canadian government evidence of a large Soviet spy ring operating in Canada and the United States. This news increased suspicion of the Soviet Union. In this rare photograph taken in 1954, Gouzenko's identity is protected by a hood. Why was this necessary? Today he lives in an unknown location in Canada under constant R.C.M.P. protection.

The main goal of NATO was, and is, to provide security for its members. NATO officials worked out plans for their common defence. Basically, the idea was to present a united front against any enemy. Such unity would **deter** (discourage) an enemy attack.

In fact, the main enemy was expected to be the Soviet Union. NATO was geared to protect western Europe against a Soviet attack. Canada and the United States did not want that area to be taken over by the Russians. Thus, by protecting western Europe, we protected ourselves.

3.   CANADA AND THE UNITED STATES FORM NORAD

NATO did not do enough to protect North America from a *direct* Russian attack. This fact became clear in the 1950s. During this period, many new weapons were developed. The first two atomic bombs had been dropped on Japan in 1945. They destroyed the cities of Hiroshima and Nagasaki. They killed or wounded over 100 000 people. By the early 1950s, both the Soviet Union and the United States had developed **hydrogen bombs.** These were *much* more powerful than the bombs dropped on Japan! Moreover, aircraft

This is the type of atomic bomb dropped on Hiroshima, Japan, in 1945.

An atomic explosion

The ruins of Nagasaki after the dropping of an atomic bomb on that city

were becoming larger and more powerful. They could fly farther and faster. New jet bombers could carry hydrogen weapons from the Soviet Union to the United States and vice versa.

To meet these dangers, it was essential to improve the air defence of North America. Radar had been developed during World War II. It could warn of approaching aircraft. In the early 1950s, Canada agreed to help build and run new radar stations on our soil. If radar spotted attacking planes, jet fighters could be sent up to **intercept** (meet) them. Several lines of radar stations were built across Canada. The line farthest north was the DEW (Distant Early Warning) Line. It was completed in the early 1950s.

A radar installation on the Pinetree Line

Most of these bases were kept after 1945. Canada also agreed to use weapons and training methods similar to those of the Americans. In this way, the forces of both countries could work together more easily. Canadian and American soldiers took part in military exercises together. Canada also agreed to co-operate with the United States in other ways. We agreed to produce certain weapons, equipment and war supplies.

Still, these measures were not enough to deal with a modern nuclear attack. Even the radar lines were **obsolete** (out of date) almost as soon as they were built. This was because of the development of long range missiles. This took place in the late 1950s and early 1960s. The largest of these missiles were called **ICBM's** — Intercontinental Ballistic Missiles. These were huge rockets, with hydrogen warheads attached to them. An ICBM launched from certain places in the Soviet Union could hit Toronto or New York City within thirty minutes! Radar stations were of little use against such weapons.

These developments created major problems for NATO and for North America. Now, Canada and the United States were just as vulnerable to sudden attack as Europe was. If you had been responsible for North American air defence at this time what would you have done?

United States Offensive Missiles

These are the basic offensive missiles of the United States, drawn to scale. The Polaris and Poseidon missiles are fired from submarines. They are being replaced with more advanced Poseidon missiles with multiple warheads. Even the old ones had a **range** of (could travel up to) 4 800 km. The Minuteman missiles are land-based, and fired from underground silos. Some models could travel 16 000 km. They too are being fitted for multiple warheads. The Titan is a much larger missile. It can deliver a huge warhead up to 16 000 km. It is still in service.

Note: The ranges of several of these basic missiles have been or are being improved.

United States Offensive Missiles

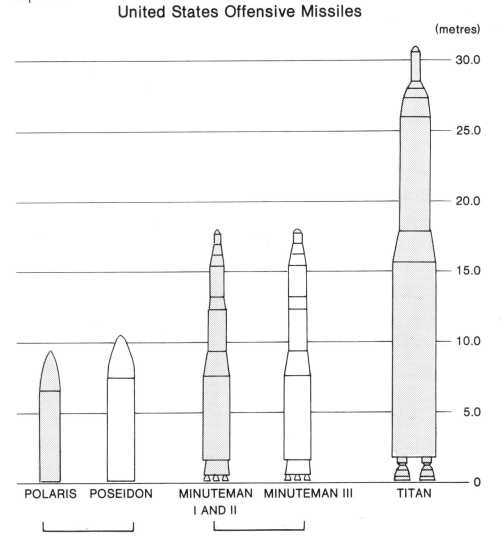

You Be The Military Expert

1. Here is an opportunity for you and your classmates to play the role of defence experts. Your responsibility is to plan the defence of North America against enemy air attacks. In the first stage, we will assume that the attackers have bombers only — no missiles. Let us say that they have about 800 bombers. Each of these aircraft can carry a hydrogen bomb powerful enough to wipe out a large city, or to destroy a large military unit. For this exercise, you will need paper and pencils, globe, and access to a good Learning Resources Centre.

2. First, what extra information do you need about the enemy?

3. Next, what important facts must you keep in mind about North America (the area you must defend).

4. Here are a few ideas to help you with No. 2 above: who would the enemy likely be? what would be the speed of enemy planes? where would enemy bases be located? how far are these bases from their targets? what is the estimated flying time to targets? what is the quality of enemy planes and pilots? what are the numbers and speed of enemy fighters to escort bombers? (assume twice as many fighters as bombers) and so on. Try to find such information about aircraft of the 1950s. Estimate realistically where necessary.

5. To help you with No. 3 above consider: the types and locations of most likely targets, the size of North America, the probable routes to targets which enemy planes would take, and so on.

6. Next, think about ways in which you could get warning of an enemy attack. Such warning could mean the difference between destruction and survival.

7. With regard to No. 6 above, a friendly telephone call is most unlikely. Most probably, you would rely on radar signals. These could spot the direction and approximate number of enemy planes from distances up to one thousand kilometres. It would be a good idea to have built lines of radar stations across northern Canada. (Why *northern* Canada?) This actually was done. Try to find

The Soviet TU-16 ("Badger") long-range bomber

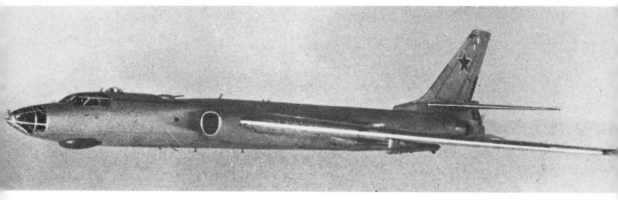

out details of these systems. Beyond this, you would have to rely on lucky sightings by friendly aircraft, or the pickup of stray signals by ships. Both of these are most unlikely to happen.

8. Once you had received warning of advancing enemy planes, how could you destroy them? Why would it be desirable to destroy them as far north, and as high in the air, as possible?

9. The enemy planes could be shot down by your planes, or in some cases by ground fire. By the end of the 1950s, there were also some ground-to-air missiles that could shoot down aircraft.

10. You also should have a good *offence*. This means you should have the ability to strike back at the enemy and destroy him no matter what. Why could this be an important part of your *defence?* (Remember the idea of **deterrence.**)

11. By now, you might be feeling confident that you have this problem under control. NOT SO! We are going to throw your plans into total confusion. Keep your paper and pencils handy!

12. By the early 1960s, the enemy is no longer relying mainly on its bomber force. It still has bombers, but it also has something better. This is the *ICBM* or Intercontinental Ballistic Missile. Such a missile can carry a gigantic hydrogen warhead over 8 000 km. They travel at several thousand kilometres per hour, many times faster than any aircraft. They also fly very high, beyond the reach of any known defence missile. An ICBM launched from Moscow could hit Toronto in less than 30 minutes.

A U.S. "Minuteman" missile, perched in its underground silo

Giant Soviet ICBMs on parade in Moscow's Red Square

13. What effect does the development of ICBM's have on your defence system? How useful will your radar be? What kinds of devices must you invent to deal with this new situation? Why must you also develop ICBM's of your own (if you don't already have them)?

14. Obviously, your radar is next to useless. You must develop new warning systems. Try to find out how space satellites could help in this regard. You must also try to develop weapons that will destroy incoming missiles. (This has proven to be very complex and extremely expensive.) Missiles are very difficult targets because of their speed, and the **altitude** (height) at which they fly. The super powers have found it somewhat less difficult to improve their own **offensive** (attacking) weapons. This way, they emphasize deterring the attack rather than trying to deal with it once it happens.

15. This is the end of our "game." Unfortunately, this nuclear arms race continues in real life. After the ICBM came the missile-firing submarine. Both the United States and the Soviet union have dozens of such submarines. These could fire up to sixteen missiles at targets 2 500 km away. And they

The Poseidon missile carrying a dummy multiple warhead assembly rises from the Atlantic off the coast of Florida to begin its second successful flight. The stubby 10 m long defence weapon was launched from the submerged nuclear submarine James Madison, whose extra tall antenna, used for tests, sticks out of the water at right.

could do so while submerged! Next came MIRV's (multiple-independently-targeted-reentry-vehicles). These were a new version of the ICBM. Instead of carrying just one warhead, a missile could now carry several. The missile would be launched. Then, while high above the earth, it would receive a signal and shoot the warheads off in different directions. Each warhead had a guidance system to take it to target with deadly accuracy.

By the late 1950s it was clear that North America needed a better system of air defence. This system was created in 1958. It is called NORAD (the North American Air Defence system). It provided for the complete **co-ordination** (linking) of Canadian and American air defence plans. It organized radar warning systems. These were connected with air bases, from which jet interceptors could rush up to meet enemy bombers. Huge new research projects were begun. These worked on new communications systems (such as satellites) to provide quick warning against missile attacks.

The headquarters of NORAD are situated near Colorado Springs. Here, a large mountain has been hollowed out at the centre. Inside are located the vital computers and communications equipment. They are in constant contact with all NORAD bases and forces — on land, at sea and in the air. If they received warning of an attack on North America, they would control the response of all NORAD defensive and offensive weapons.

By the terms of the NORAD agreement, an American is in overall command. He is assisted by a Canadian deputy. In a war situation, the

A space satellite

President of the United States has the *final* decision as to the use of NORAD forces. He could commit Canadian forces to battle. He also could order American forces to enter Canadian territory. Most likely, enemy missiles or bombers would be intercepted in our airspace. Naturally, this could have disastrous results on life in this country.

Canada has contributed to NORAD in other ways. We keep several squadrons of jet interceptors. Most of these planes are based in Quebec and New Brunswick. They could meet an enemy bomber attack. Until 1972, we kept BOMARC missile bases at North Bay, Ontario and Macaza, Quebec. These had nuclear warheads. They too were designed to destroy bombers. However, the BOMARC's have become **obsolete.** The bases have been removed.

Shopping List for a Modern Day Warrior

(or, "What every well-equipped nation is wearing these days")

In this chapter, we have been describing some of the weapons of modern warfare. On every day of every year, millions of dollars are spent developing, testing or buying various kinds of weaponry. It has been estimated that up to 50 per cent of the scientific work done by the United States and the Soviet Union is connected somehow to war. Here is a list of only a *few* of their latest projects:

● Each of the two super powers could "deliver" several thousand nuclear warheads against the other. (One American expert estimates that 400 such warheads would destroy 75 per cent of the industry of the Soviet Union and 33 per cent of its population.)

The main entrance to NORAD's underground headquarters near Colorado Springs. Inside there are eleven steel buildings, some of them three stories deep. They are under more than 400 m of granite.

This road, over 400 m long, leads into the NORAD command centre inside Cheyenne Mountain.

● Sensor devices are being tested. They would make the ocean "transparent" and reveal the hiding places of submarines. Then, special torpedoes moored to the ocean floor could be released. These would "listen" to the sound of the enemy vessels and use that sound to aim themselves and destroy those vessels.

● Hunter-killer satellites, using laser weapons, can destroy unarmed satellites now in space.

● "Smart" bombs and missiles are being developed. These have very accurate, built-in aiming devices to score direct hits on almost any target. Their guidance systems include radar, laser beams and television cameras.

● The United States has developed a nuclear-tipped "Cruise" missile. It is launched from a bomber. It is 4.3 m long and flies at 885 km/h. However, it can fly at treetop level, automatically adjusting for terrain. This means it is almost impossible to detect or effectively destroy. A Cruise missile can fly 2 400 km and strike within 30 m of its target.

● The United States has developed a small "Lance" missile with a warhead which can release millions of **neutrons.** These would bring slow, agonizing death to many people.

● Several countries have various kinds of nuclear missiles or bombs. These include China, France, and Britain. Many other countries could make such weapons if they wanted to do so.

● Many countries have chemical and bacteriological weapons. These can release gases that paralyze or kill, poison drinking water, ruin food supplies and spread various kinds of incurable diseases.

The arms race is increasing in speed and cost. Meanwhile, millions of human beings go without adequate food, clothing, shelter, education or medical attention. As one concerned person said at the United Nations: "Time is not on our side."

The deadly "Cruise" missile developed in the late 1970s by the United States

The controversial B-1 bomber. In 1977, President Carter decided not to proceed with the production of this new long-range aircraft. This decision could be reversed in the future.

4. CANADIAN SUPPORT FOR AMERICAN ACTIONS

Since World War II, Canada has supported most American military actions. We joined American forces fighting in Korea (see Unit VI, Chapter 2). We agreed with the first moves by U.S. soldiers in Vietnam in the early 1960s. We later became somewhat critical of American actions in Vietnam.

The United States has not been completely happy with Canada as an ally. For example, they feel that we should spend more money on defence. The Americans spend a much bigger *share* of their budget on defence than we do. Thus, they feel that we are not paying enough toward the costs of NATO and NORAD. For example, today there are about 170 000 servicemen in NORAD. They man about 400 separate bases. Almost 95 per cent of them are Americans. The United States also gives seventeen times more money than Canada does to NORAD. The figures are $2 billion to $115 million. Many Americans claim that we have not always supported them totally in time of trouble.

Let's look at the "Cuban Missile Crisis" of 1962 as an example. In that year, the United States learned that the Soviet Union was placing missiles in Cuba. These weapons could hit American targets in seconds. They also could reach parts of Canada. The Americans ordered the Soviets to remove the missiles. If they did not obey, they would face nuclear war. In time, the Russians *did* remove their weapons. Meanwhile, NORAD forces had been put on full alert. President Kennedy asked that all Canadian forces be put in a similar condition. For various reasons, Prime Minister Diefenbaker hesitated to do this. He and President Kennedy did not get along well together. Their personalities clashed. Also, the Americans were pressing Canada to adopt nuclear weapons. Mr.

A Soviet ship en route to Cuba, 1962. Crates of missiles can be seen lashed to the foreward deck.

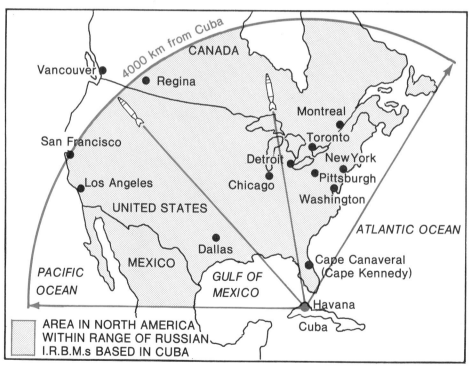

This map shows the potential range of the Soviet missiles being set up in Cuba in 1962. These missiles were removed because of American pressure.

Diefenbaker did not want to do this. Perhaps by refusing to "jump" when the Americans said to, he hoped to show that Canada had some independence.

The Americans resented this for a long time. They showed this by their actions towards Canadian forces. Canadians with NORAD were given less important duties. They also received less information about military developments. In 1973, American forces were again put on full alert. This time the trouble was in the Middle East. Canada's Defence Minister was informed eight hours later of President Nixon's decision!

Other military matters have strained Canadian-American relations at times. In the mid-1960s, Canada became critical of American actions in Vietnam. Prime Minister Pearson once spoke out in public against American bombing there. Lyndon Johnson, the President of the United States, was furious! In private, he attacked Mr. Pearson's "interference" in American affairs. Witnesses said that, the two men almost came to blows.

Canada has traded with some countries which the United States did not officially approve of. These included Cuba and China. Both have Communist governments. This fact largely explains American dislike. Moreover, Canada decided to "officially recognize" Communist China at a time when the United States did not.

Canada makes these decisions for several reasons. We are an independent country. We cannot be expected to always do what the United States wants. This is especially true when we do not agree with American policy. Also, Canadian politicians must please Canadian voters. Sometimes they can do this

Prime Minister Pearson (left) and President Johnson appeared to be happy in this meeting in 1966.

by "tweaking the noses" of the Americans — or appearing to do so. Still, our government must be very careful in this regard. They are constantly walking a tightrope — and it can be tricky! We cannot afford to push the United States too far. As one analyst has said:

> "It is not in the Canadian interest that the U.S. should be weakened and humiliated — even when it follows policies Canadians think foolish . . . The price Canadians pay for the national independence they have is that they do not push it too far . . . Canadians know that they would not survive if the United States ceased behaving towards them like a civilized country."

Concern Over the Northwest Passage

In 1969, the American supertanker *Manhattan* made an historic trip through the Northwest Passage (see map). Its purpose was to see if Alaskan oil could be shipped by this route to ports on the American east coast. Canada is concerned about these plans. There is great danger of oil spills from the tankers. This would seriously harm the Arctic environment. Also, Canada claims to control the waters involved. The United States argues that these are international waterways. If this is true, they can be used by anyone.

The United States is thinking about building an oil refinery at Eastport, Maine. This is where tankers coming from the Northwest Passage might dock. Canada is opposed to the shipping of oil through Canadian waters to Eastport. Again, pollution from oil spills is the main concern. Valuable fishing grounds could be badly hurt by such accidents.

THE NORTHWEST PASSAGE

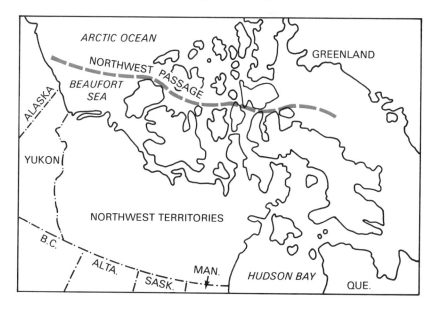

5.   AMERICAN POLITICAL INFLUENCE IN CANADA

The United States can put great pressure on Canadian politicians. Usually, our neighbours are very friendly. But they know what they want. They can be very persuasive. As the saying goes: "They can make us offers we *cannot* refuse."

To get their way they could harm our economy. They could put hundreds of thousands of Canadians out of work. Our living standards could be sharply lowered. They could literally ruin certain businesses, industries or whole communities. Just the threat of using such powers would probably be enough to make a Canadian politician cave in. We can see that Canada pays a steep price for having a *branch plant economy*.

Interference in Elections

American political leaders have, in the past, interfered in Canadian elections. They have helped candidates who favour American interests. Sometimes, they have wanted to see an "undesirable" Canadian politician beaten. This happened in 1963. American interests gave large funds to the campaign of the Liberal party. They hoped to help defeat the Progressive Conservative government of John Diefenbaker. (Some reasons have been suggested earlier in this chapter.) The Diefenbaker government *was* defeated.

1. American business corporations and labour unions have given money to Canadian politicans and political parties. Why would they do this? Should it be allowed?
2. It has been suggested that the United States government sometimes pressures American companies to make political contributions in Canada. Why would it do this?
3. In the past, American presidents have offered their own expert political advisers to certain Canadian leaders. Why? Should this be allowed?

Conclusion

One Canadian professor has suggested that no Canadian government can survive without American approval and support. This claim might be exaggerated. Still, it makes us stop and think.

ALL THINGS CONSIDERED, CAN WE REALLY CALL OURSELVES A SOVEREIGN, INDEPENDENT COUNTRY?

Does the United States Have a Plan to Invade Canada?

A few years ago, some Canadians were shocked by a newspaper story. In it reporters claimed to have evidence of an American plan for the invasion of Canada. There was no follow up to the story. Public interest died down. However, the story was probably true.

Every major country is concerned about its own safety. It must be ready for even the most unlikely events. This is why the United States Department of Defence prepares different kinds of plans. Some are for self-defence. Others are plans for attacks on other countries, if the need arises. These plans are kept up-to-date. New weapons and conditions cause them to change. In an emergency, there would be time only for action. Plans for such action must be made in advance.

1. What developments in Canada might cause the United States to send armed forces into this country? Why? Are any such developments likely to occur?
2. Could Canada defend itself against all kinds of American attacks? Against any kind?
3. Think about what you have read so far. Is it likely that Canadian officials would believe that the United States has plans for the invasion of Canada? Explain your answer.
4. Is it likely that Canada has any plans for defending against an American attack? For a Canadian attack on the U.S.? Why or why not?
5. A former RCMP security officer told an interesting story to a newspaper reporter. It concerned American reaction to the Quebec crisis of 1970 (see Unit 4, Chapter 4). He claimed that the American CIA (Central Intelligence Agency) sent dozens of spies into Quebec. Also, he said that the United States moved troops, tanks and other heavy weapons up close to the Quebec border. Why might the Americans do such things? When the former RCMP officer saw the story in print, he denied it. Why would he do this?

Canada: Two-Faced Over American Bombing

In the 1960s, several Canadians spoke out against the war in Vietnam. They were especially upset by the American bombing of cities and villages. Many innocent lives were lost in such attacks. The television news showed terrible scenes of people being killed or wounded. Some were shot, others stabbed or blown apart by shells. Firebombs filled with **napalm** (jellied gasoline) gave hideous wounds. Often victims were children or even babies.

It was a fact that Canadian factories were supplying Americans with some of their ammunition. Hundreds of workers owed their jobs to such business.

American B52 bombers bombing over Haiphong Harbour (North Vietnam)

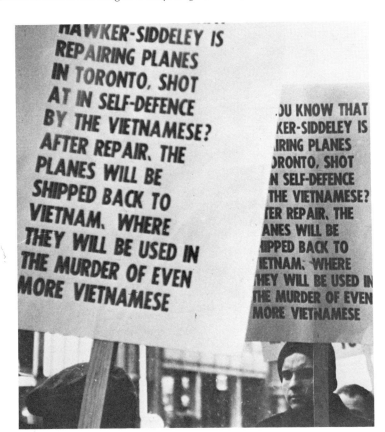

HAWKER-SIDDELEY IS REPAIRING PLANES IN TORONTO, SHOT AT IN SELF-DEFENCE BY THE VIETNAMESE? AFTER REPAIR, THE PLANES WILL BE SHIPPED BACK TO VIETNAM, WHERE THEY WILL BE USED IN THE MURDER OF EVEN MORE VIETNAMESE

Canadians protesting over our country's role in the Vietnam war. What charge are they making?

Some Canadians became wealthy from the profits. Even after condemning the bombing, we sold guns, bombs, ammunition and supplies to the United States.

1. Should Canadian factories sell weapons or ammunition to foreign countries at all? If so, under what conditions?
2. Could the Canadian government legally forbid Canadian companies to sell certain goods to other countries? Should it have such power?
3. What reasons could you suggest why such power was not used during the war in Vietnam?
4. Do you believe that Canadians were partly responsible for the effects of that war? Explain your answer.

THINGS TO THINK ABOUT AND DO

Reviewing Key Words and Ideas

The following terms appeared in this chapter. Try to recall their meaning and how they were used.

ABM system	espionage	NATO
atomic bomb	hydrogen bomb	NORAD
BOMARC	ICBM	obsolescence
branch plant economy	interceptor aircraft	radar
Cold War	military ally	"smart" bomb
deterrence	Minuteman	SPRINT
DEW Line	napalm	

Remembering the Facts

1. Why was NATO formed in 1949? Why was NORAD formed in 1958?
2. Why did the Cuban Missile Crisis strain Canadian-American relations?
3. How does the United States exert *political* influence on Canada?

Analyzing Ideas

1. In the early 1960s, John Diefenbaker's government came apart. Mr. Diefenbaker and some of his supporters argued that Canada should not adopt nuclear weapons. Why might they have felt this way? What arguments would there be for the opposite view? With which side do you agree? Why? Does Canada have nuclear weapons *today*?
2. Is it true that "the United States will defend us whether we want it or not"? If so, why don't we become **neutral?** — that is, try not to be anyone's ally or

enemy. What would we gain by becoming neutral?

3. If the United States invaded Canada (which is unlikely), the Soviet Union almost certainly would not help us. This is partly because the result would be a disastrous nuclear war. Also, they probably would not think a major change had occurred. They regard us as almost a colony of the United States. Are they right?

4. Think back on the main points made in this unit. Can our government consider itself fairly independent of the United States? Could it be more so? Explain your answers.

Applying Your Knowledge

1. The governments of Canada and the United States have some differences over certain issues today. These include:
   a) energy-sharing
   b) pollution control (air and water)
   c) control of Arctic waterways
   d) Canadian policy toward American investment
   e) Canadian defence spending

Try to find out about the specific problems in these areas. Your newspapers and news magazines will help. Check the files in libraries. What is Canada's position on each issue? Do you agree with these positions?

2. What other issues exist between our two countries? Which, in your opinion, is the most serious of all? Why?

5

AMERICAN CULTURAL INFLUENCE: CAN WE TELL "US" FROM "THEM"?

INTRODUCTION

"Canadian independence from the United States? — BIG DEAL! There isn't any important difference between the two countries anyway."

1. Have you ever heard that kind of statement before? Who would be *more* likely to say this — a Canadian, an American or someone from a third country? Why? Who would be least likely to say it? Why?
2. Can you state important differences between Canada and the United States? Between Canadians and Americans?
3. Set up a role play in your classroom. Create a team of four or five investigators. The rest of the students should represent people from several different countries. Obviously, these should include Canada and the United States. The job of the investigators is to pick out the Canadian and American members of the group. Set up your own details and rules. However, you cannot ask direct questions such as "What is your nationality?" Afterwards, the investigators will report to the class. Why did they choose the questions they used? What clues did they use?
4. Imagine that you could no longer live in Canada. In what other country would you choose to live? Why? Compare your answers with classmates, friends or family.
5. Use the ideas gained in No. 3 and No. 4 above to help you with your next task: make a list of important similarities and differences between Canadians and Americans. Include points about values, lifestyles, customs, culture, government and economics. Which seem to be greater — the similarities or the differences? Which are more important? Why?
6. How important do you think it is for Canada to be and feel different from the United States? Why? How could this question be connected to the idea of Canadian independence?

Holiday Inn® THE WORLD'S INNKEEPER®

M left nationalists frustrated

U.S. profit drive costs jobs here

TEXACO

McDonald's BILLIONS AND BILLIONS SERVED

HOWARD JOHNSON'S

Americans told they threaten Canada's culture

dge
RYSLER
Trucks

Kentucky Fried Chicken®

Arctic pipeline pact called sellout to U.S.

A&P

Before reading on, study the chart of Key Words and Ideas which follows.

KEY WORDS AND IDEAS IN THIS CHAPTER

Term	Meaning	Sample Use
Americanize	to make something American in nature or style	Canada is becoming Americanized in some ways. For example, we drive American cars, wear American-style clothes, use American chain hotels, motels and restaurants, and so on.
cultural identity	the feeling of a people that they know who and what they are	Canadians are developing a cultural identity. Sharing experiences, customs and arts helps this feeling to grow. The strong impact of the U.S. on Canadian life can make it hard to develop our own identity.
independence	the ability to get along without relying on anyone or anything else	Canada and the U.S. both gained independence from Britain. We are now trying to be independent of the U.S. The Americans have considerable influence in our affairs.
mass media	mass media are methods of communications which reach huge numbers of people; they include radio, television, newspapers and magazines	The mass media are important in shaping the ideas of the people. The media can help develop our culture, identity and unity. We are often exposed to American media and their influence.
nationalism	a feeling of pride in and loyalty to a particular country or nation	Most Americans feel strong nationalism. So do most Canadians, although we sometimes do not show it as clearly. This feeling must remain strong in Canada if our country is to survive.

| pop culture | This is "popular" culture. It appeals to the great majority of people. This includes television, most movies, popular music and so on. (It would not include opera, ballet or classical music) | Our pop culture is strongly influenced by the United States. Canadian identity is stronger in our "formal" arts such as painting and literature. |

1.   THE IMPORTANCE OF BEING DIFFERENT

We have been looking at the ties which exist between Canada and the United States. These ties are mainly economic, military and political. We have seen some of the benefits of these ties. Some of the problems have also been discussed. Perhaps the biggest danger in the American connection is that we lose our independence. Canada could lose its independence as a country in one of two ways.

First, we might be taken over by force. This seems unlikely. Still, we are very important to the United States. They need our natural resources. We also are a valuable market for their goods and services. In a way, we are their "Northern Shield". We stand between them and their major rival, the Soviet Union. The United States must have our military help. This is mainly needed to patrol our air space and coastal waters. It is unlikely that we would try to end our economic and military ties with the United States. (The reasons for this have been explained in previous chapters.) However, if we *did* try, we might force the Americans to act against us.

Canada could disappear as a nation in a second way. It is a sneaky, slow and fairly pleasant process. It is also the more likely and dangerous way. At the end of Chapter 3, we referred to the "American embrace". It is cozy, and very strong. As we settle into it, we feel more and more comfortable and safe. But if we do not take care we might "wake up" too late. We would discover that we had sold our riches. We had also lost control of our government and we had forgotten how to defend ourselves. Then that little scene in Ottawa where the Maple Leaf Flag is lowered, and replaced by the Stars and Stripes, might actually take place.

1. Think back to that imaginary scene which introduced this unit. How did it make you feel?

2. Try the same idea with your family and friends. How do *they* feel? Ask them to explain their reactions.

3. Look for opinion polls on the question of Canada becoming part of the United States. How do Canadians in general seem to feel about the idea?

4. Think about those Canadians who would not mind, or would actually prefer, joining the United States. What do you think are their reasons?

Irving Layton

Gabrielle Roy

Mordecai Richler

Margaret Atwood

Farley Mowat

Margaret Laurence

You may have studied the work of some of these Canadian writers

5. Now consider those Canadians who are against the idea. Why do they feel this way?

6. What seems to be the main difference between those in favour of joining the U.S. and those against?

You have probably discovered a key idea. Some Canadians have a much stronger sense than others of a true **Canadian identity.** They believe that Canada *is* different from other countries, including the United States. There are things about Canada that are special. These are worth preserving. If our country is to survive, a majority of Canadians must feel this way. Before they can feel this way, they must have reasons. The best reason would be that the differences are there, that we do have a Canadian identity.

At times, it is difficult to find this identity. American ideas, ways of doing things and goods seem to be everywhere in Canada. You can easily see this for yourself. Do a survey. Ask people to name favourite motel chains, fast food restaurants, types of cars, T.V. programmes and entertainment stars. Look carefully at the products in your home and school. How many of them are American? Do you see the problem?

It is true that the arts are flourishing in Canada. There are many fine Canadian writers, dancers, painters, poets, musicians and so on. However, in many cases very few Canadians know about their works.

On the other hand, there is another type of culture. We will call it "popular culture". Popular culture is known to, and enjoyed by, large masses of our people. We will now look at American influence on this level of our culture. We will also consider what we are doing about that influence.

The audience waits for the beginning of a performance in the Grand Theatre de Québec.

2. ENTERTAINMENT

A. Television

For most Canadian families, television is the main form of entertainment. A survey of Canadian television viewers was taken in February 1977. Look at the results.

— The top (the most popular) 8 shows were *all* American.

— Only 2 Canadian shows placed in the top 20. These were Saturday Night Hockey (9th) and Front Page Challenge (19th).

— Of the next 37 most-watched programs, only 17 Canadian-produced programs attracted one million or more viewers.

— During "prime time" (19:00-23:00) on the CBC network almost two thirds of the programs were Canadian. However, they captured only 42.5 per cent of Canadian viewers in those hours.

— During prime time on the CTV network, Canadian shows attracted only 21 per cent of that network's viewers. The other 79 per cent preferred its American programs.

— Almost half of the Canadian viewers on CBC and CTV were drawn to NHL Hockey. Without this, only about 10 per cent of viewers would be watching other Canadian programs.

— Re-runs of *Gilligan's Island* and *Bugs Bunny* cartoons (none of the cartoons were made after 1952) had larger audiences than well-made Canadian documentaries and educational programs.

Such statistics should make us worry. They show how hard it is to develop a Canadian culture. These percentages also make the problem worse. Making television programs in Canada costs a great deal. But American shows draw far larger audiences, both in the United States and Canada. Companies which advertise on U.S. television have vast audiences. They will pay high prices to sponsor popular American shows. In the U.S., an average of $175 000 is spent on a half-hour situation comedy. Compare this with a top price of $50 000 paid by CBC to produce the same type of show. It is easy to see why U.S. television can have more appeal. Many American shows have a high production quality and big name stars. So more people watch U.S. television. The advertisers are willing to buy time at high prices. And so the cycle goes on.

1. See if this viewing pattern is still true. Look at this week's TV Viewer Guide. Work with some friends or classmates. Choose the viewing hours you will survey. List the programs available. Make one for Canadian shows. Make another for American programs. If you are not sure, leave them out. How many Canadian shows are available? How many American programs? Compare the numbers. Does the pattern still hold?

2. Next, survey only Canadian television channels. List their Canadian programs. Then list the American shows they carry. What ratio do you find?

3. Now each person in the survey should choose the shows they would like to see this week. Be honest! Now, figure out the ratio of Canadian to American shows in your *own* viewing.

4. Rank your ten *favourites*. How many are American? Compare your findings with the other people in the survey. Average the results.

5. Try to find out the 20 top-rated television shows in Canada. How many are Canadian? How high do the Canadian shows place in the ranking?

A television cameraman holds a cue card during a live program.

"STAY WITH THE **LEAFS**, WE GOTTA GET OUR 60% CANADIAN"

Situation Comedies: A Slice Of Popular Culture

For many years, Americans have been able to see their own lifestyles shown on television. In the mid-1970s, many "average" or "typical" Americans could identify with such shows as:

— *All in the Family*
— *Rhoda*
— *The Jeffersons*

— *The Brady Bunch*
— *Mary Hartman, Mary Hartman*
— *Sanford and Son*

Many viewers also enjoyed, and some could identify with, such shows as *Chico and the Man*, the *Bob Newhart Show* and the *Mary Tyler Moore Show*.

Most of these shows are, or were, **situation comedies.** They work from the same basic setting each week. This is usually a family or job situation. The main characters remain the same. Both the characters and situations are typical — they are part of everyday life. This fact, plus their humour, makes them attractive to mass audiences. Thus they are part of **pop** (popular) **culture.** Such shows are about as popular in Canada as in the United States. This is despite their being American programs. Actually, there are very few Canadian shows of this type.

1. What reasons could you suggest for this situation?

2. Does this shortage say anything important about Canadian culture or identity? (If so, what?)

3. Can you name three Canadian shows of the type described above?

4. Do you identify with any of the characters on the shows listed above? If so, make a list of the reasons why. Your class might choose to discuss this question in small groups.

In the mid-1970s, a Canadian situation comedy *did* become very successful. The show was called *The King of Kensington*. It was about a Jewish family living in a highly ethnic neighbourhood in downtown Toronto. By 1977, the show had been bought by American television for showing in the U.S.

1. Is *The King of Kensington* still shown on TV? If so, try to watch it. What is there about the show that is appealing? Is there anything distinctively Canadian about it? How do you account for its appeal in the American market? (Is it because it portrays an attractive Canadian lifestyle? Is it the quality of the humour? The ability of the actors? Is it successful because it has *no* clear Canadian identity?)

2. Are there any *other* Canadian-made shows of this type on TV these days? If so, how successful are they? Do you watch them regularly? Are they shown on American networks as well?

3. Review the factors you have identified above. Create your own ideas for successful Canadian situation comedies. Perhaps there could be a class competition to judge the best ideas. An English, Theatre Arts or Drama teacher might be helpful here.

The star of *The King of Kensington*, Al Waxman

B.   Films

Movies are another popular form of entertainment. Look up movie advertisements in your local newspapers. How many Canadian-made films can you find? Are there other non-American films playing? If so, do they outnumber the Canadian movies? How many of the non-American films have you seen? How many would you like to see?

   It seems that Canadians prefer American movie stars too.

1. Choose your top ten favourite movies stars. How many are Canadian?

2. Again, compare your choices with friends, relatives or classmates. What is the trend?

3. Can you name five Canadian movie stars?

4. Why *do* Canadians seem to prefer American films and American stars? Which seems to be a more important factor — the film itself or the people playing in it. Why? Give some personal examples.

5. How might our heavy exposure to American shows and stars in television and movies affect us?

6. A recent study done in the United States showed that violence was increasing rapidly in American television. This was true even on children's shows and during family viewing time. Did you consider this effect in No. 5 above?

Canada's Feature Film Industry

How can we build a *Canadian* identity in films? Recently, our government has poured millions of dollars into the building of a feature film industry. This has helped Canadians to create such fine films as *Goin' Down the Road, Wedding in White, Kamouraska, Mon Oncle Antoine, The Rowdyman* and *Why Shoot the Teacher.*

   Most of these films were Canadian in every sense. They were written, produced, directed and performed by Canadians. They also dealt with Canadian places, events and themes. *Kamouraska* won some international recognition. This was probably because it dealt with "universal" themes such as loneliness, jealousy, infidelity and greed. However, it had a distinctive French-Canadian setting. Even more profitable was *The Apprenticeship of Duddy Kravitz.* This was based on the novel by Montreal writer, Mordecai Richler. An American actor was brought in to play the title role. Perhaps this had something to do with the film's box-office success. More likely, this was due to the quality of the story. The fact that the story took place in Canada was downplayed in American promotion. Thus, its themes and humour could be more easily shared by the large American audience.

   Feature films are commercial (business) ventures. Therefore, they must

A scene from *The Apprenticeship of Duddy Kravitz*. Although this film was based on a Canadian novel, and had a Canadian setting, its producers decided to bring in an American actor to play the title role.

A scene from *Mon Oncle Antoine*. This film won international recognition in several film festivals.

make profits for their investors. To succeed, they need large audiences. Not many Canadian films have markets outside Canada. This is especially true if they deal with Canadian themes and star Canadian performers. Even *within* the country, they must compete with American and other foreign films. Thus, Canadian film-makers face several difficult choices. They can make low-class movies which feature sex, violence, the supernatural and other "cheap" thrills. They can use American stars to "hype" (stimulate) the gate. Or, they can seek help from the Canadian government. The latter now offers tax advantages for films made in Canada. Unfortunately, this has attracted more foreign than Canadian producers to make films here. Also, the government has considered putting a special tax on tickets to non-Canadian movies.

1. How many of the above-mentioned Canadian films have you seen? Have you heard of any of them before? Ask your parents the same questions.
2. Name some other Canadian feature films. How many have you seen? Do you know whether they made profits?
3. Some of the Canadian films listed above were described as having "Canadian" themes. What are these? Make a list of examples. Why are they "Canadian"? Which of them could be of interest to foreigners? Which would not? Would the one type be commercially successful (make profits) and the other not? Are the Canadian themes worth developing in films? Why or why not? If so, should such films receive financial help from government?
4. Is it important to have a Canadian feature film industry? Explain your answer. If you say "yes", how could we encourage its growth? Should Canadians produce "garbage" movies with mass appeal? (Would you feel differently if you were an investor in Canadian films?) Should we import foreign directors and stars? Should we penalize foreign films and performers in Canada?

The Mass Media

The *mass media* are methods of communication which reach large numbers of people. Thus, they include such things as radio, television, newspapers, and magazines. The mass media affect our thoughts, and values, and so our culture. In Canada, the media are strongly influenced by the United States. We have seen how many Canadians prefer the American television and films to our own.

This is a serious situation. There are two reasons. First, the media *are* mass. They reach huge numbers of people. The most gifted Canadian high school teacher might reach 5000 to 6000 students in his or her career. A popular half-hour show on television will draw several million viewers. Secondly, we are exposed to the media for long periods of time.

Press coverage of a political party rally in a Canadian city

1. Survey your friends and classmates. How many hours of television do they watch in a day? What would be their total for a week? What would yours be? Take an average.

2. Extend your survey. Find out the amount of time spent doing these things in one day:

(a) listening to radio

(b) reading newspapers

(c) reading magazines (of all kinds)

What would be their total for a week? What would yours be? Take an average. Add it to the results of your first survey. How big a role do the mass media play in your life? In that of your classmates?

3. Separate males and females for a magazine survey. What are the three most popular magazines for each group? How many of these are Canadian? American? How do the reading habits of your parents or other adults compare?

4. A recent survey of Canadian teenagers, in a city high school showed the following:

— Students watched an average of 20 hours of television per week.

— Girls preferred "women's magazines" featuring fashions, dating etiquette

and "advice" regarding shopping, marriage, and so on. Most of these magazines were American.
— Boys preferred magazines on sports, sex and cars. All of the magazines mentioned were American.

How do your results compare with these?

Canadians rely heavily on American mass media. This must affect our culture. It seems to make us more 'American' in outlook and style. It becomes harder and harder to develop a *distinctive* culture.

But the problem will not be easy to solve. Here is an example to show you why. Imagine you owned a radio or television station in Canada. Of course you would want to attract the biggest possible audience. Then you can ask higher rates from advertisers. What would you do to gain a large audience? Would you tend to use Canadian or American material and performers? Now pretend you are a Canadian advertiser. You would naturally want to reach the most people. You would advertise in magazines, radio or television programs with large numbers of readers, listeners or viewers. Will these be mainly Canadian or American?

C.   Popular Music

Who are your favourite popular music performers and groups? Many of the top song-writers, record companies, studios, back-up musicians and tour organizers are Americans too. Make a class list. Are most of your favourites, Americans or Canadians. Do you know which they are? The biggest market for pop music is the United States. It is natural that it must appeal to American tastes. "American style" in popular music is copied by foreign performers and writers.

However Canadians have made a very strong impact in popular music. Here are some famous examples.

Anne Murray	Bachman-Turner Overdrive
Gordon Lightfoot	Tom Connors
The Band	Lighthouse
Murray McLauchlan	Gilles Vigneault
Ian and Sylvia Tyson	Joni Mitchell
Robert Charlebois	Burton Cummings
The Guess Who	René Simard

1. What names can you add to the list?
2. Do you think that popular music plays an important part in a country's culture? If so, can you explain why?

Gordon Lightfoot

Anne Murray

Stompin' Tom Connors

Robert Charlebois

3. Pick a Canadian "pop" musician, group, or song that you consider to have a Canadian identity. What makes the musician, group or song Canadian? Is it their style? Lyrics?

4. Which do you consider most important for developing Canadian culture — television, films or pop music? Explain your answer.

The "Talent Drain" or "Go South Young Woman/Man"

Many talented Canadians have had to go south to win success. This has been true of people in many fields. Business people, actors, musicians, comedians, film directors, athletes and writers are some examples.

1. Rich Little, Paul Anka, Jack Kent Cooke, Norman Jewison, Anne Murray, Donald Sutherland and others have found fame in the U.S. How many names can you add to this list?

2. Why do you think this happens? Does it make Canadian culture stronger or weaker? Does it affect American influence over us? Explain your answer.

3. What (if anything) could be done about this situation?

Sometimes talented Canadians have simply been ignored in their own country. More often, though, the chances for success are simply greater south of the border. The American market is ten times larger than ours. Salaries too are bigger. More money can be spent on production. Often Americans are more willing to risk money on new ventures than we are.

Something else limits chances for talented Canadian performers. Canadians often import American talent for big jobs in Canada. The Canadian National Exhibition is held each summer in Toronto. Its managers bring in many Americans to star in the big Grandstand Shows.

Some Canadian cities have cultural centres. These are used to stage plays, shows or other forms of entertainment. Often, the Canadian performances lose money. How do these centres survive? Some receive government grants. But most bring in American headliners to attract bigger crowds and thus earn more money. A performer is paid mainly on the basis of audience appeal. Thus, foreign stars are usually paid more than Canadians even while performing in Canada.

However, top-name Canadian performers can equal, or even out-draw, foreign competition. Recently, Anne Murray and Gordon Lightfoot starred in their own separate shows in Las Vegas. Both of them did well against such American "names" as Frank Sinatra and Liberace. However, Canadian-made films often star American or other foreign actors. Even in business, large companies sometimes bring in American executives to fill key positions. Why do you think this is done?

You can see why talented Canadians often seek their fame and fortune elsewhere, and mainly in the United States. Perhaps nothing can change these facts. We could look at it from another angle. Are you proud when you hear about a Canadian who has "made it" in the United States? Perhaps their success can boost Canada's image and make its culture stronger. It still seems sad, though, to see them leave for "greener fields".

1. On the other hand, some Canadians do *not* make it in the American "big time". Try to think of some examples. Are these "failures" victories for Canadian culture? Or are they just failures? Why?

2. Occasionally, specially talented Americans choose to live and work in Canada. Can you give some examples? Does their work retain an American character, or does it become "Canadian" in nature? Or, does it have a more universal appeal? Why might some American artists prefer to live here?

3. SPORTS

North Americans have been going wild over sports. This is especially true of professional sports. Vast numbers of people are involved in, or affected by sports. Sports has become "big business." Sports is an important part of our culture and way of life.

Can you find the differences between what is Canadian and what is American in 'pro' sports?

1. Name your five favourite sports. Can any of these be considered as native to Canada? What sports, if any, *are* natively Canadian? How popular are they in this country?

2. Which are your three favourite teams in your top five sports? Is the *first* choice in each your own hometown team? How many of your total favourites are based in the U.S.?

3. Look at the Sports Pages of a major newspaper. If it is the baseball season, find out how many teams are Canadian? Explain your findings. Hockey is more a *Canadian* game. If it is the hockey season, find out how many professional hockey teams are Canadian? American? Why is this?

4. Name your five favourite stars in each of your five top sports. How many are Canadian? American? Did you choose them because of their *nationality?* If not, why did you pick them? When you are watching a contest between Canadian and American teams, do you think about *this* aspect? (Do you think it is part of the competition? Why or why not?)

In 1977, Canada's Prime Minister Trudeau made a speech in Washington, D.C. He used professional sport as an example of Canadian-American

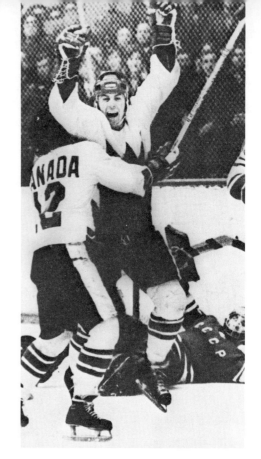

Paul Henderson scores the winning goal against the Soviet Union in the final game of the first ever Canada-U.S.S.R. hockey tournament, 1972. Did you see this game? If so, how did you feel at that moment?

harmony. He noted that Washington hockey fans support their NHL team without thinking that most of the players are Canadians. Similarly, Montreal and Toronto baseball fans cheer their almost entirely American teams.

However, not long ago, the Trudeau government had interfered with professional football in Canada. It stopped the new World Football League from setting up teams in Canada. This league was mainly American. But the backers of a proposed Toronto team were Canadians. Mr. Trudeau claimed that the Canadian Football League (CFL) had to be protected. Its championship game, for the Grey Cup, was a major Canadian custom. It was a part of our culture. It had to be preserved. Politics can be funny! Football is essentially an American game. Even in Canada, most of the top players, coaches and managers are Americans. Yet a football game is thought of as a part of our culture.

1. Are you a fan of Canadian football? (If not, pose these questions to someone who *is*.) How do you choose favourite players? By their ability? nationality? or for some other reason?

2. Do you believe that a certain number of players on each Canadian team *must* be Canadians, regardless of ability? Or, would you rather see your team go after the best possible players and ignore their nationality? Explain your

answer. If you prefer the second choice, how would you give Canadians the chance to play professional football? Look at another angle in this issue. What would happen to American hockey teams if U.S. fans insisted that their teams be mainly American?

3. Do you think that Canadian athletes playing in the U.S., represent a "threat" to American culture? Do American teams or athletes threaten *our* culture? Is it fair to compare the two situations? Explain your answers.

4. Should the Canadian Football League try to expand into the United States? Do you think that it would succeed? Why or why not?

5. Was the Canadian government right to stop the World Football League from establishing teams in Canada? How important are sports to the growth of a Canadian identity?

4. EDUCATION

Education helps shape our thoughts, ideas and values. There has been concern about American influence in this field. Many of the textbooks used in Canadian schools are written by Americans. More of them are published by American companies, or Canadian branches of such companies. American ways have affected Canadian education. The "credit system" used in many high schools is an American idea. Many of the teaching machines and lecture methods we use also began in the United States.

The large number of American professors in Canadian colleges worries some people. Most of our colleges and universities have Americans on their staffs. Sometimes they hold key positions. Often, Americans make up high percentages of the staff. There are two sides to this issue. Some people say that Canadian students must have the best professors. Why limit your choice to Canadians? Better professors will make our educational system stronger. This will enrich our culture. There is another side to the issue. Perhaps these foreign teachers present biased views. Shouldn't we offer jobs to Canadians first?

Many people want tighter controls on education. Politicians know this. Some provinces have limited the use of foreign textbooks. For example, Ontario publishes a booklet entitled *Circular 14*. It lists the textbooks approved by the government for use in Ontario schools. With a few rare exceptions these texts must be Canadian. This means that the books must be written by Canadian citizens. They must also be manufactured in Canada. Teachers are encouraged to use Canadian learning materials wherever possible. Special permission is needed to use a textbook not listed on Circular 14. It is usually more difficult to gain such permission for foreign texts.

Other measures have been taken to strengthen the "Canadian content" in our educational system. Some universities have placed limits on the hiring of foreign (mainly American) professors. Several years ago, the Canadian Studies

Citizenship of Teachers in Canadian Universities — by Region, 1974 - 75.

Region	Canada		United States		United Kingdom		Other Commonwealth		Other Countries	
	Number	Per-centage	Number	Per-centage	Number	Per-centage	Number	Per-centage	Number	Per-centage
Atlantic Provinces	2 046	64.6	481	15.1	323	10.2	120	3.7	195	6.1
Quebec	4 880	76.1	423	6.5	188	2.9	110	1.7	810	12.4
Ontario	7 948	67.0	1 807	15.2	1 061	8.9	352	2.9	680	5.6
Western Provinces	3 667	60.8	1 252	20.7	596	9.8	197	3.2	317	5.1
Total Numbers and Average Percentages	18 541	67.5	3 963	14.4	2 168	7.8	779	2.8	2 002	7.1

Note: Percentages might not add exactly due to rounding.
Source: *STATISTICS CANADA.*

Foundation (CSF) was created. Its members came from across Canada. They were experts in the field of education. The CSF tried to encourage more study of Canada in our schools. This was particularly true in History and Geography. The CSF also helped to develop new units and courses of study featuring things Canadian. Many provinces have responded. Now there is a much greater emphasis on the study of Canada. Another CSF goal was a core curriculum for all Canadian students. This would mean that all students would study the same basic things in certain required courses. So far, this goal has not been achieved.

1. Look through your own textbooks. Examine the pages at the beginning. They contain the name of the publisher. Often, they show where the book was published and printed. The names of the authors are found here too. Sometimes, their job title is included.

How many are published and printed in the United States? How many are written by Americans?

2. *This* textbook has been written by Canadians but published by an American subsidiary. Does this make it "dangerous" in any way by affecting content?

3. The authors wish to state that there has been no pressure whatsoever to present a pro-American viewpoint in this book. On the contrary, Canadian values and ideas have been stressed. Which do you think is more important — that your books be written by Canadians or published by Canadian-owned companies? Explain your answer.

4. Do you feel that you study *too much* about Canada in school? How much history, geography, literature and so on of other countries do you study? Do you feel it is enough? Why or why not?

5.   WHAT CAN BE DONE?

Obviously, American culture has a powerful influence on Canada. What can we do about this?

There are several choices. One would be to change the tastes of Canadians. This would be very difficult. We could do nothing about American cultural influence in Canada. This would be dangerous. Instead, governments in Canada have taken steps to *compromise* between these extremes.

Governments have given money to promote Canadian culture. Theatres and art schools have been built with these grants. The money has been used to hire teachers and to support struggling artists. Considerable money is being given to people in the feature film industry. "Canadian content" rules have been passed for television and radio broadcasting. These require stations to include specific amounts of Canadian material in their programming. There also are strict limits on the amount of foreign ownership in Canadian broadcasting.

In the early 1960s, the Canadian government began to help Canadian

magazines. It ended certain tax privileges for American publications.
Advertisers in these magazines had been allowed to deduct their advertising
costs from their income taxes. This was stopped. The American publications
protested. They were supported by the United States government. Therefore,
two powerful magazines, *Time* and *Reader's Digest,* were **exempted** from (not
included in) these new rules. However, in 1975, the Canadian government put
new demands on these magazines. Sixty per cent of their content would have
to be Canadian. Seventy-five per cent of the business would have to be
Canadian-owned. *Reader's Digest* met these terms. *Time* did not. It closed
down its Canadian offices. The American version of *Time* is still available, and
selling well.

Conclusion

The effort to develop a distinctive Canadian identity goes on. There are
two parts to the struggle. One involves building our own positive Canadian
culture. The other means resisting powerful foreign influences, especially that

CANADIAN INDENTITY?

THURSDAY, NOV. 10, 1977

of the U.S. Recently, a well known Canadian writer and editor spoke to an American audience in Washington. His remarks summed up the theme of this chapter. He said that, on the subject of Canadian culture, there are two groups in Canada. These are the nationalists and the "I don't cares." He expressed the fear that the latter group was winning. But, as he pointed out, we *must* be nationalistic. Otherwise, someone else's nationalism will roll right over us.

THINGS TO THINK ABOUT AND DO

Reviewing Key Words and Ideas

The following terms were used in this chapter. Try to recall their meaning and how they were used.

Circular 14	cultural identity	national identity
compromise	feature film	popular culture
CSF	international competition	prime time
culture	mass media	situation comedy

Remembering the Facts

1. In what two ways might Canada be "taken over" by the United States?
2. Why do Canadians watch so much American television? How is this related to our efforts to have our own identity?
3. Why is it difficult to develop a feature film industry in Canada?
4. How can sports help a country to develop an identity?
5. How does American influence reach us through the field of education? What are we doing about this?

Analyzing Ideas

1. "What the U.S. wants it will get. And if we don't give them what they want, they'll take it anyway. And what they want — is most of what we've got." What is the main *feeling* in this comment? Do you agree with it? Why might Canadians be more hopeful than this?
2. A recent comment in an American newspaper said that Canadians "worry too much" about the strength of their culture. It pointed out that Canada has produced *many* fine artists and writers. **Per capita** (per person in our population) we might have more such people than the United States. What do you think of this argument?
3. Do you think there is too much anti-Americanism in Canada? Why does some of this feeling exist? Is it good for Canada? Why or why not?

4. It has been suggested that one way to keep Canadian culture distinctive is to keep Quebec in Confederation. What is meant by this? Do you agree with the idea?

5. ". . . even the most intelligent Americans . . . neither know nor care that they share this continent with a Canadian culture distinct from their own." What is the point of this remark? Do you agree with it? How does it relate to anti-Americanism in Canada? Would it make any difference if Americans were more aware of Canadian culture, and our desire to be "different"?

6. Which do you think is more important to Canadian independence: economic freedom or cultural freedom? Explain your answer.

Applying Your Knowledge

1. "We like the Americans we know; we just don't like the United States." What does this mean? Use the material in this unit (Canadian-American Relations) to explain this quote.

2. The following ideas might be suitable for a class discussion: Consider the everyday life of "average" Canadians and Americans. What similarities and differences are there? Which are greater? Is the everyday life of most Canadians distinctively different? What are the implications of your ideas for Canadian culture and identity?

3. Debate this: RESOLVED: That international competition in sports helps to build Canadian unity (think of such examples as recent Olympics competitions and World Cup Hockey).

4. It has been suggested that Canadians have three main **options** (choices) regarding future relations with the U.S.: keep the same ties as we now have; move toward closer union; try to become more independent.

What would be the advantages and disadvantages of each choice? Which do you prefer. Conduct a poll to see how many people agree with you. Which path do you think our government is following at present? What makes you think so? Does Canada really have a *choice* about the strength of its ties with the U.S.? Explain your answer.

VI

Canadian Foreign Policy

1

UNDERSTANDING WHAT FOREIGN POLICY IS

INTRODUCTION

The term "foreign policy" means the interactions and ties that one nation has with other nations. Every country in the world has a foreign policy. Canada is no exception to this rule. Our main task in this unit is to try to discover what Canada's foreign policy is all about.

In this chapter, we will begin by exploring the meaning of the term "foreign policy." Next, we will consider the goals and methods of foreign policy. Then, we will look at some factors which influence such policy. This is followed by a section on how to judge a country's foreign policy. Finally, there is a brief discussion of the importance of foreign policy.

Here is a way to help you understand foreign policy. Think of a country as a person. Have you ever heard the saying: "No man is an island"? This suggests that no person can live a full or normal life if he or she is completely alone. Now, some quick wits among you are probably saying: "There are several countries that are islands, and I can name some." This is true, but only in a geographic sense. Countries, like people, cannot act as though no one else exists in the world. Such **isolation** cannot be, especially in our modern world.

1. What word do we use for a person who tries to live completely alone? Why might someone try to live in this way?
2. Try to imagine yourself in such a position. Why would it be practically impossible to live strictly alone? (Among other things, your answer should include references to modern methods of communication and transportation.)
3. Why would it be impossible for a country to be completely isolated from other countries?
4. Despite what we have said above, some people can live in more isolation than others. Suggest some reasons for this.
5. Now apply this thinking to countries. Why do certain countries need a lot of

contact with other countries? Why do others need fewer outside ties? Which of these reasons apply to Canada? Why?

Before reading on, study the chart of Key Words and Ideas which follows.

KEY WORDS AND IDEAS IN THIS CHAPTER

Term	Meaning	Sample Use
blockade	to cut off all travel to and from a country, usually by surrounding it with land, sea and air forces	A blockade can be used to weaken or punish a country, or to defeat it in war. It cuts off a country's foreign trade.
diplomacy	the art of conducting relations with foreign countries; involves the negotiation of treaties, alliances and other agreements; requires wisdom, skill and patience	Diplomacy is used to carry out a country's foreign policy. A diplomat is a nation's representative to other nations.
disarmament	the act of getting rid of armed forces and weapons of war	Disarmament can be a step toward reducing tension between countries. It tends to increase the chances for peace.
effectiveness	how well something works or succeeds	Foreign policy must show effectiveness. This is judged by seeing if its results match its aims.
foreign policy	the relations a country has with other countries; includes aims and actions	Foreign policy is the theme of this unit. We want to know what Canada's foreign policy is and how effective it is.
idealism	a belief in ideals or perfect values, and a tendency to base actions on such belief	Sometimes the actions of a country are the results of idealism. A country might try to make ideals such as truth, justice or equality come true in the world through its foreign policy.

ideology	a collection or set of ideals which have been worked into a system	Democracy, Communism and Christianity are examples of ideology. A country's ideology influences its foreign policy.
isolation	being alone	In the past, some countries have tried to act in isolation from the rest of the world. This has become almost impossible in modern times.
national self-interest	whatever is best for one particular country	Just like people, countries usually put their own (national) self interests first. This is a form of selfishness.
prosperity	"good times", particularly in the economic or financial sense	Countries try to increase their own prosperity through foreign policy. They can do this by trade agreements, investing money wisely, and so on.
security	safety	The main goal of a country's foreign policy is security. It wishes to survive, and to be safe from conquest or destruction.

Unit Preview/Review Questions

As you study this unit, keep these questions in mind. You may want to return to them when you have finished the unit.

1. What does Canada stand for in the world?
2. What do we want out of our ties with other countries?
3. How do we try to achieve these aims?
4. What do other countries think of Canada?
5. How important is Canada in world affairs?
6. Should we be making changes in our dealings with other countries?

1.   GOALS AND METHODS IN FOREIGN POLICY

Let us now return to our main idea. There are almost two hundred separate countries in our world. Each of them has to have at least some dealings with other countries. These dealings are called foreign policy. Naturally, every country wants its foreign policy to work well and succeed. This takes careful planning (not to mention some good luck). For example, a country must decide what its goals are. Then, it must consider what methods to use in order to achieve these goals. In making these decisions, several other things must be kept in mind. How weak or strong is this country compared to others? How rich or poor is it? How might other countries react to its plans? Which goals are most important? And so on. From this, you can see how complicated foreign policy can be.

Again, to help our understanding, let us think of a country as a person. Its foreign policy can be compared to a person's **social life** (relations with other people). Imagine that there is a fifteen-year-old boy who is interested in a certain fourteen-year-old girl. He would like to get her attention, become friends with her and, hopefully, get a date with her. These are his goals. Now he must decide upon the method or methods, by which he will achieve those goals. Here are a few possibilities:

- — impress her by showing off in front of her
- — offer to buy her a Big Mac
- — give her the impression that he has a lot of money
- — try to get an introduction through a friend
- — introduce himself and ask for a date
- — hit her to get her attention

1. What other suggestions could you make?
2. Rate all of the possible methods. Put them in order from most down to least effective. Have a reason for each decision.
3. Would some of these methods be good under certain conditions but poor under others? Which ones? Why?
4. Try to find methods whose effectiveness depends on the personalities of the people involved.

Applying Your Ideas

As with the social life of the boy above, a country's foreign policy has goals and methods. The following is a list of terms which relate to foreign policy. Be sure you know their meaning before proceeding with the activities below. (Get help from your classmates, your teacher or a dictionary if necessary.)

alliance	financial aid	security
blockade	foreign trade	spying
buildup of arms	immigration	threat of force
diplomacy	peace	tourism
disarmament	prosperity	war

Are you sure that you know the meaning of each term? Prove it by setting up a chart in your notebook like the one which follows. Do the terms in any order. They were listed alphabetically above.

Understanding Foreign Policy

Term	Meaning	Goal of Foreign Policy?	Method of Foreign Policy?	Both Method And Goal?	Example of Use
Example: foreign trade	an exchange of goods between two or more countries			✔	*As a goal:* Country "A" wishes to increase its foreign trade. It uses diplomacy to try to negotiate trade arrangements with other countries. *As a method:* Country "A" wishes to improve its relations with another nation. It tries to do this by offering attractive trade proposals.

How to Fill in the Chart ("Understanding Foreign Policy")

1. List the terms, in any order, down the left hand column.
2. Write in (briefly) the meaning of each term.
3. Pretend that you are the foreign minister of a country. This could be Canada or some other nation, real or imaginary. With each term, try to think of how it could be used as part of your foreign policy (refer to the example provided). Would this term be a *goal* or a *method* of policy? Put a check mark in the appropriate column. If you think it could be *both,* check the "Both" column instead.
4. How many items have you classified as "Both"? Would this tend to suggest that foreign policy is simple or complicated? Explain your answer.
5. Now *defend* your decisions. In the right hand column, give an *example* of the item being used in the way you have suggested.

6. Of all the items you have checked as "Methods", which is the most dangerous? Why? Could it also be the method of carrying out foreign policy which works best? How?

7. Review the items you have checked as "Goals". Which do you think is the most important? Why? What methods would help achieve this goal?

8. With regard to the goal you selected in No. 7, does it seem to you that most countries today have chosen this as their main goal? If not, why not?

Probably, most of us would choose *peace* as the most important goal. Certainly, it seems to be the most desirable. War is costly, and terribly destructive. In a major war using today's weapons every living thing on the face of the earth could be wiped out. In spite of this, most countries do not have peace as their main goal. Instead, they choose what they call security. This might seem strange, but is quite natural. A country, just like a living person, has an instinct for survival. It wants to live, and not be destroyed. Therefore, it will do almost anything to live, including fight. Like people, most countries prefer not to fight. However, they will do so to protect themselves. True, they might lose, and be destroyed. However, victory permits survival. Sometimes, it even brings great rewards. By winning a war, a country might gain land, riches, people, glory and so on. For these reasons, there are times when certain countries *do* attack others. Thus, it is sometimes possible to *judge* other countries. Like people, their actions are "good" or "bad", depending on the intentions and results of their actions.

Perhaps this is the most important point to remember about foreign policy: *the main goal of every country is to survive.* This causes it to seek security. In the end, all other factors give way — peace, war, good, bad, right, wrong. Obviously, this creates a kind of "jungle" in world affairs. The rule of "survival of the fittest" still applies. Until this changes, all of us must live with the possibility of world destruction through war. This is why the conduct of foreign policy is so important today.

2. FACTORS WHICH INFLUENCE FOREIGN POLICY

No two countries have exactly the same foreign policy. This is because the situation of each country is **unique** (special). There are several factors which can influence the foreign policy of a country.

One of the factors is **ideology.** This means the ideas or values for which a country stands. Some nations, like Canada and the United States, believe in democratic government. This means that they want people to have rights and freedoms. Thus, they tend to have friendly relations with other democratic countries. However, they are sometimes in conflict with countries that do not share these beliefs. Some of these countries believe in government by dictatorship.

Another factor in foreign policy is history. Your nation might have a long record of peace and friendship with another country. This is bound to affect your relations with each other. So would a long record of war or bad feelings.

Foreign policy is not a "one-way street". Therefore, how other nations feel and act toward your country affects its foreign policy. For example, you might wish to have friendly relations with the neighbouring country. You set this as a goal of your foreign policy. You try to encourage trade, tourism and military co-operation. These are methods of gaining your goal. However, the neighbouring country has been persuaded by a third country to help conquer you! Clearly, your policy is going to have to change when this fact becomes known.

1. How could you discover that your nation is in danger of attack?
2. What if you fail to discover this?
3. Can you see now why countries spy on each other? Why might even friendly countries, which seem to have good relations, spy on each other?
4. Is there any way the nations of the world could do away with spying on each other? Why or why not?

There are many other factors which influence a country's foreign policy. Some of these are:
 (i) geography,
 (ii) public opinion (the views of the people),
 (iii) military power,
 (iv) personal views of leaders,
 (v) the type of economy in the country.

Set up a chart in your notebook, something like this:

How Certain Factors Influence Foreign Policy

Factor	How It Influences Foreign Policy	Example of an Application to Canada

1. Take each of the five factors mentioned above, and list them down the left-hand column of your chart. (Leave plenty of space between each one.)
2. Try to explain how each factor could influence a country's foreign policy.
3. Next, try to create an example of how each factor has, or could have, an influence on Canadian foreign policy.
4. Compare your answers with those of classmates. Add their best ideas to your chart.

In a democracy, public opinion can influence foreign policy, sometimes strongly. Here, demonstrators gather outside the Parliament Buildings in Ottawa.

5. Below are listed several facts about Canada. Read each one carefully and then

    a) try to decide which of the five factors is being illustrated by the statement

    b) state how this fact could influence Canadian foreign policy

    c) if you have not thought of the idea, add it to the third column of your chart beside the appropriate factor

● A majority of Canadians trace their ancestry to Western Europe, particularly to Britain and France.

● Canada relies heavily on foreign trade; we need markets for raw materials and other products.

● Canada is "next door" to the richest and most powerful country in the world.

● Canada restricted its defence budget in the early 1970s, so that its armed forces now need new weapons and recruits.

● The Prime Minister, assisted by his Cabinet, is responsible for planning, and carrying out, Canadian foreign policy.

● Canada is a democracy, so that the government must answer to the people every few years in an election.

Factors Influencing Canadian Foreign Policy Decisions

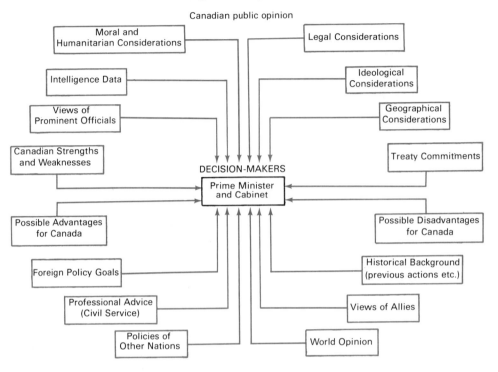

3. MAKING JUDGEMENTS ABOUT FOREIGN POLICY

We make judgements about the actions of people every day. We judge our parents, friends, teachers, bosses, business associates and so on. Usually, we judge them in terms of ability, intelligence, attractiveness, personality, moral qualities (honesty, loyalty, etc.) and the degree of success we think they achieve.

We can judge a country's foreign policy in a similar way. Basically, there are two standards of judgement. One of these is **effectiveness** (whether or not it works). This can be assessed by comparing a country's *goals* with the degree to which these goals are met. If most, or all, of its goals are won, then its foreign policy has been very effective. In short, it has been successful. The less progress made toward the goals, the lower the judgement of the policy.

Earlier, we had the example of a boy seeking ways of getting a date with a girl. You were asked to judge the value of several methods available to him.

Today's world is full of tension and conflict. Therefore, it is more important than ever before that our leaders carry out foreign policy with great care and wisdom.

How would we decide whether or not his policy was effective? (CORRECT! Did he get the date, or not?) Still, he might have finished somewhere between complete victory and defeat. Maybe he just missed getting the date, or was told he might get one in a week or two. These same ideas of victory, defeat, or something in between apply to foreign policy. Remember the main goal of every country is to survive. Beyond this, it wants to prosper and to give its people the best possible life. In the end its success or failure must be measured by the extent to which it does those things.

In a sense, these are selfish goals. The boy wants a date for himself. A country wants security or prosperity for itself — ahead of other countries if necessary. Thus, many of a country's actions are said to be based on its **self-interest.** To be exact, this is national self-interest.

There is a second standard for judging a country's foreign policy. This is called **idealism** (the opposite of self-interest). It means overall goodness or benefit for the world as a whole. Countries, like people, have different **motives** (reasons) for doing things. Sometimes they act selfishly. However, at times they do things that are of great help to others. Often, there is a mixture of motives behind their actions.

For example, let us imagine that a young girl notices an elderly blind man struggling along the street with an armful of groceries. She helps him carry his parcels home. Why did she do this? To help the old man? To have a chance at a reward of some kind? To make herself feel good? To relieve her guilt feelings for having ignored his problem once before? Will she ever really know why she did this? Does it really matter, so long as she, and the old man, both benefit?

The same issues come up when judging a country's foreign policy. Let us say that country "A" is rather poor and backward. Country "B" volunteers to send assistance. Part of this "help" consists of teachers and other experts who will train and educate the people of country "A". Why has country "B" done this? Is it an honest attempt to help? Will the teachers be agents and spies for their government? Will they fill the children's heads with foreign ideas? Does country "B" want to make a friend, or dependent, out of country "A"? How should we judge this policy? In terms of its results? In terms of the "good" or "bad" intentions behind it? Probably, each of us will judge on the basis of our own personal attitudes and values. This is why there can be much difference of opinion over the quality of a country's foreign policy. How good are you at judging motives behind foreign policy? Reproduce the following chart in your notebook. Make it large, and leave plenty of space between lines.

Action	Canadian Motives				Soviet Motives			
	Self-Interest	Idealism	Attacking	De-fending	Self-Interest	Idealism	Attacking	De-fending
1) build up of armed forces at home								
2) set up of military bases in other countries								
3) sending financial aid to poorer countries								
4) sending spies into other countries								
5) trying to increase trade with other countries								
6) investing money in the economies of other countries								
7) making a military alliance with one or more other countries								
8) ?								
9) ?								

1. Various foreign policy actions are listed down the left hand column. First you must *judge* the reasons behind such actions on the assumption that they are *Canadian* actions. Put check marks in any of the four appropriate columns under "Canadian Motives."
2. Next, judge the motives of such actions assuming they were performed by the Soviet Union. Check off the appropriate columns.
3. Do you find *different* reasons for the actions, depending on whether they are done by Canadians or Russians? If so, *why?*
4. Look at your assessment of Canadian motives. Do you think a Russian would agree? Why or why not?
5. What does this exercise tell you about *trust* in foreign policy? What does it tell you about judging foreign policy?
6. If possible, choose two other actions, add them to your list of seven, and complete the chart.
7. Canada actually does perform several of the above actions in its foreign policy. More of this will be described in later chapters.

To sum up this section, foreign policy can be judged in two *main* ways: how well it achieves its goals, and the amount of good it does for the world as a whole. Throughout history, nations have asked, "Did it [an action] work?" more often than "Did it help people?" Or, to put it another way, winning is more important than playing the game. Try to remember these ideas as you study the following chapters on Canadian foreign policy.

4.   THE IMPORTANCE OF FOREIGN POLICY

As we all know, the world today is full of problems and dangers. Among these are ignorance, disease, starvation, illiteracy, pollution, overpopulation and the threat of nuclear war. We in Canada are fortunate. Most of these problems are far less serious here than in other lands. Still, we are not just Canadians. We are members of a single human race. We are, whether we realize it or not, citizens of the entire world. Thus, the problems of the world are partly our problems. They will not disappear. We cannot pretend that they do not exist.

In some ways, the planet Earth is getting smaller. New means of transportation and communication are causing this to happen. Today, we can fly across Canada more quickly than most people could travel two hundred kilometers just eighty years ago. In 1976, Montreal hosted the Olympic Games. The events were telecast live, by satellite, to viewers as far away as Tokyo and Moscow.

However, these same wonders can bring up the bad side of life as well as the good. While we sit in front of our TV sets eating cake and ice cream, the news camera zooms in on the face of a starving child in Africa. At other times, we can see "in living colour" the effects of floods, earthquakes, wars or other

These photos depict important aspects of Canadian foreign policy.

Canadian officers discuss their part in the United Nations peacekeeping force on Cyprus.

A Canadian instructor advises Libyan farmers.

Canada supports disarmament. A Canadian sentry watches a German soldier check piles of weapons surrendered in World War II.

For self-protection, Canada still keeps armed forces at the ready.

human disasters in the comfort of our air-conditioned family rooms. The missile, another marvel of science, can drop destruction upon us from the other side of the world. This can happen in less time than it takes some of us to get to work or school.

We hope that these problems can be solved or at least made less dangerous. This can happen only if the nations of the world agree to co-operate in fighting them. To do so, *they must improve their relations with each other*. In this simple fact we find the real importance of foreign policy.

THINGS TO THINK ABOUT AND DO

Reviewing Key Words and Ideas

The following terms appeared in this chapter. Try to recall their meaning and how they were used.

alliance	idealism	peace
blockade	ideology	prosperity
diplomacy	isolation	security
disarmament	motive	spying
effectiveness	national self-interest	war

Remembering the Facts

1. What is the difference between goals and methods in foreign policy?
2. What are the main factors which influence foreign policy?
3. What are the two main standards by which a foreign policy can be judged?

Analyzing Ideas

1. Why is foreign policy so important in human life today?
2. How could a nation both defend itself and work for world peace at the same time?
3. Some people who talk about the shrinking earth say we are now living in a "global village".
a) What does this term mean?
b) What does it suggest about human life today?
c) How is this connected to the idea of the importance of foreign policy?
4. Some people believe that, in relations among countries, "might is right".
a) What do they mean by this?
b) How would such people judge a foreign policy — by effectiveness or idealism? Explain your answer.

c) Why is this view dangerous?

5. Some issues in a country's life are foreign, while others are "domestic" (internal). Here is a list of developments. Decide the nature of each, foreign or domestic, and say why this is so. Could any be *both*? If so, explain how.

alliance	industry	riot
crime	labour strike	trade
fishing	peace	treaty
immigration	revolution	war

Applying Your Knowledge

1. Organize a class debate on this idea: "Resolved — that in foreign policy, might *is* right."

2. Imagine that you are the leader of a country called "OZ." You are responsible for creating and carrying out the foreign policy of the Land of OZ. Invent names for three or four other countries to make up a "world". Give each country, including OZ, certain characteristics. Include size, population, wealth, economy, military power, history, geography, etc. (If necessary, review the section on "factors influencing foreign policy".) *Canada: Towards Tomorrow,* A.S. Evans, L.A. Diachun (McGraw-Hill Ryerson, 1976) has some ideas on pages 197-198 which might be helpful. Now, create a set of goals for the foreign policy of OZ. Then, suggest the most effective methods of securing these goals. Explain your decisions. Finally, compare your ideas with classmates, friends, or members of your family at home.

3. There are several *simulation games* which deal with some of the ideas presented in this chapter. Among these are DIPLOMACY, DANGEROUS PARALLEL and CRISIS. Perhaps your teacher or librarian could help you locate, and organize, one of these simulations.

2

CANADA'S SEARCH FOR PEACE AND SECURITY

INTRODUCTION

As we have seen, all nations want to be secure, or safe. This is the only way to be sure of survival. Each nation must decide for itself the best way to achieve this security. This is one of the main jobs of the government of a country.

So far, the government of Canada has done a good job of keeping our country secure. Since Canada was formed in 1867, no foreign enemy has set foot on our soil. The task of protecting Canada has not always been easy. Since 1900, we have been involved in two terrible world wars (see Unit 3, chapters 1 and 2). Fortunately, we were on the winning side in both of those conflicts.

When World War II ended in 1945, many Canadians believed that our security was now guaranteed. There would be no more troubles, or major wars, in the world. That hope has proven to be false. The world is still a very dangerous place. Canada, though reasonably secure, would be foolish to think itself completely safe.

This chapter will begin by describing Canada's position on world affairs by 1945. Next, it will show how we tried to arrange for our security in the years right after World War II. Then, it will explain how and why these plans were upset. Finally, we will consider why changes were made in Canada's security arrangements in the 1950s. These are basically the same plans on which our security rests today.

Before reading on, study the chart of Key Words and Ideas which follows.

KEY WORDS AND IDEAS IN THIS CHAPTER

Term	Meaning	Sample Use
aggression	an act of attacking — as in hurting someone, taking property or invading a country	The United Nations tries to stop aggression, because such activity can lead to war.
demobilization	reducing the size of armed forces	Demobilization took place quickly in Canada after World War II ended.
economic sanction	stopping trade or other business with a particular country	The United Nations sometimes asks its members to apply economic sanctions against an aggressor. These sanctions are meant to discourage its bad behaviour.
impartiality	fair-mindedness; freedom from prejudice or rigid views	Canada has a fairly high reputation for impartiality. This is partly because of its support for certain United Nations policies.
international law	law that applies throughout the world, not just in one country	The United Nations would be more effective if countries would agree to, and obey, international law.
middle power	a country that is neither a super power nor a weak nation but something in between	For a few years after 1945, Canada played the role of a middle power.
peacekeeping	getting between two fighting groups and acting firmly but fairly toward both to prevent more violence	Canada is a world leader in peacekeeping. This is mainly through support of United Nations work in world trouble spots.
refugee	a person who is fleeing from his or her homeland	Canada has admitted thousands of refugees since 1945. It provides a new and safe home for these people.

super power	a nation with great power and wealth	The United States and the Soviet Union are super powers today. Some other countries, such as China, could become super powers in the future.
veto	the power to block action by simply saying "no"	Several countries have veto power in the United Nations. This makes it very difficult for the U.N. to work effectively.
world government	just as it reads — a government for the whole world; it would have ruling power over all countries	Some people think world government is needed to prevent war. It could save the world from destruction.

1.   CANADA'S WORLD POSITION BY 1945

It has been said that Canada "came of age" in World War II (1939-1945) and became a truly independent country. Also, the war gave a boost to our economy. By the end of the war, Canada was one of the leading industrial nations of the world. It was a major producer of arms and ammunition.

The Honourable C. D. Howe, Minister of Munitions and Supply, inspects a shell offered by a munitions worker. During World War II, Canada became a leading manufacturer of munitions. Thousands of women such as the one shown here made a major contribution to Canada's war effort.

We came of age in yet another sense. Several great military powers had been crushed, at least temporarily. Among these were Germany and Japan. On the other hand, the Canadian Armed Forces had been built up to record size. Over 1 000 000 Canadian men and women were in uniform by the end of the war. This combination of factors lifted Canada to high rank. For a while, at least, we were the fourth or fifth strongest military power in the world!

This was a source of great pride to Canadians. So was the fine record of service built up by our forces during the war. Over 40 000 Canadian soldiers had lost their lives in the defence of their country. The Canadian people, and their government, felt that this sacrifice gave us the right to have a strong voice in world affairs. The Prime Minister, Mackenzie King, was determined that Canada should play an important part in the postwar world.

Obviously, we could not have as much influence as the "Great Powers." Among these, the United States and the Soviet Union were in a class by themselves. Next came Britain, France and China. However, on the next level down were medium-sized nations such as Canada. They were not "super-powers", but neither were they weak or unimportant. Thus, a key part of Canada's foreign policy after 1945 was to play the role of a "**middle power**." In the following sections, we will see how this was done.

2.   CANADA'S ARMED FORCES

Canada has never maintained large armed forces in peacetime. When World War I began in 1914, there were fewer than 5000 battle-ready troops in the entire country. Also, there was very little modern equipment or weapons. Almost the same situation existed in 1939, at the start of World War II. When that war ended, a decision had to be made about our forces. Should they be kept at their current high level? Should they be reduced a bit? Should they be severely cut back to our "normal" peacetime level? (The name for this last action is **demobilization**.)

The government of Mackenzie King decided to demobilize the Canadian Armed Forces. This does not mean that they were completely disbanded. However, by 1947 their numbers had been reduced to around 100 000 (from a wartime high of one million plus). This was done partly because the greatest danger seemed to end with the war. Also, it was very expensive to keep large armed forces. The people were sick of war, and tired of paying for it. Therefore, there was very little criticism of demobilization.

Since the late 1940s, Canada's security needs have changed from time to time. They seemed to be greatest through the 1950s and early 1960s (for reasons we will soon discover). In this period, our armed forces were kept around the 90 000 level. The defence budgets were high enough to pay for new weapons and equipment. However, world tension began to decrease in

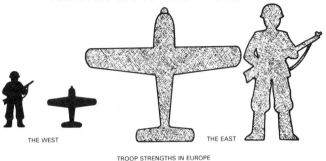

Comparison of Soviet Bloc and Western Forces After World War II

THE WEST   THE EAST

TROOP STRENGTHS IN EUROPE

	1945	1946
U.S.	3 100 000	391 000
U.K.	1 321 000	488 000
Canada	299 000	—
U.S.S.R.	4 000 000	4 000 000

the late 1960s and early 1970s. So too did our armed forces. The numbers fell below 80 000 for the first time since before World War II. Budgets were cut back. Weapons and equipment slowly became scarce and outdated. Beginning in 1976, the Canadian government moved to improve the situation. Budgets were once again increased, if only slightly. Plans were made to buy new aircraft, tanks and naval cruisers.

If you have read the chapter carefully so far, you should have noticed a problem. How could Canada expect to play a key role, as a "Middle Power", and yet reduce its military strength to a low level? How, indeed, could it even expect to remain secure?

The fact is that Canada was *not* able to play a "middle power" role for very long. We grew weaker. At the same time, other nations recovered or developed for the first time. It seems that we Canadians were a little too idealistic about the world. First, we forgot that the idea of "might is right" still counts for something. In the "crunch", the countries with the most "muscle" get the biggest say. These countries also have more influence on less powerful nations. For example, a developing nation might choose as its ally a country which can provide it with military arms for self defence. Secondly, we pinned too many hopes on a new world organization, the United Nations. The U.N. is the main theme of the next section in this chapter.

3.   THE FORMATION OF THE UNITED NATIONS

Most of us have heard the expression: "You can't take the law into your own hands."
1. What does this mean?
2. Give an example of someone trying to do this.
3. Why would someone want to do this?
4. Why is it not legal to do this? *Should* it be?

The idea we are getting at is that, in Canada, we have a set of laws (described in Unit II). These laws are designed to protect all of us. For them to work, we must all basically agree to obey them. Those who break the law must be punished. Otherwise the laws will become meaningless. The law controls our actions and punishes wrongdoers. The same does not occur in world affairs. There are a few rules which many nations have agreed to obey. These are called **international law.** They deal with such things as navigation on the oceans, and conduct in war. However, any country can ignore these ideas if it wishes. There is no effective way of enforcing them as yet.

Each nation is "a law unto itself." Its actions are based on what it wants to do. There is no law to limit its actions. It is limited only by its own power, and the wishes of other nations. This is why "might is right" is often true in foreign policy. This is also why so many wars occur.

As World War II was ending, several countries decided to try to do something to prevent future wars. Their idea was to create a world organization. All nations would some day belong to it. This was the start of the United Nations. The hope was to create a body that would try to enforce certain rules upon *all* members (just like a government does within a country). In this way, war could be prevented. Problems among nations could be solved peacefully.

In 1945, the San Francisco Conference created a Charter (or constitution) for the United Nations. This Charter was approved by fifty-one nations. It came into effect on 24 October, 1945. The Charter begins as follows:

> WE THE PEOPLES OF THE UNITED NATIONS DETERMINED to save succeeding generations from the scourge of war, which twice in our lifetime has brought untold sorrow to mankind, and to reaffirm faith in fundamental (basic) human rights, in the dignity and worth of the human person, in the equal rights of men and women of nations large and small, and to establish conditions under which justice and respect for the obligations arising from treaties and other sources of international law can be maintained, and to promote social progress and better standards of life in larger freedom ... HAVE RESOLVED TO COMBINE OUR EFFORTS TO ACCOMPLISH THESE AIMS.

Interpreting the Document

1. What does the word "scourge" mean? How would war have this effect?
2. To what events does the "twice in our lifetime" phrase refer?
3. Make a list of the *ideals* for which the United Nations stands.
4. What is meant by "international" law? What does any law need to be effective? Can the U.N. provide this key requirement?
5. What goals, other than preventing war, does the U.N. have, according to its Charter?
6. Why is the prevention of war its main goal?

As we have learned, the main goal of the United Nations is to prevent war. It can work toward this goal in a number of ways. The United Nations is a complex organization. The more important facts about the U.N. are summarized in the accompanying chart.

Organization of the United Nations

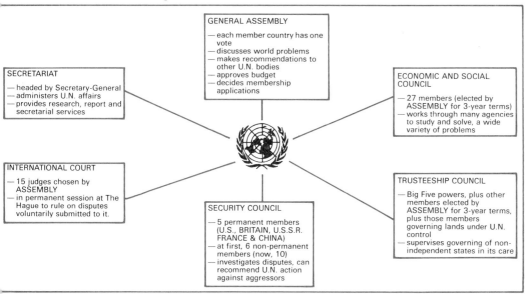

GENERAL ASSEMBLY
— each member country has one vote
— discusses world problems
— makes recommendations to other U.N. bodies
— approves budget
— decides membership applications

SECRETARIAT
— headed by Secretary-General
— administers U.N. affairs
— provides research, report and secretarial services

ECONOMIC AND SOCIAL COUNCIL
— 27 members (elected by ASSEMBLY for 3-year terms)
— works through many agencies to study and solve, a wide variety of problems

INTERNATIONAL COURT
— 15 judges chosen by ASSEMBLY
— in permanent session at The Hague to rule on disputes voluntarily submitted to it.

SECURITY COUNCIL
— 5 permanent members (U.S., BRITAIN, U.S.S.R. FRANCE & CHINA)
— at first, 6 non-permanent members (now, 10)
— investigates disputes, can recommend U.N. action against aggressors

TRUSTEESHIP COUNCIL
— Big Five powers, plus other members elected by ASSEMBLY for 3-year terms, plus those members governing lands under U.N. control
— supervises governing of non-independent states in its care

How The U.N. Works For Peace

Here are the main methods which the United Nations can use to keep peace and prevent war.

1. The United Nations tries to persuade countries to reduce their armed forces.

2. The U.N. sets up many agencies to fight world problems such as poverty, disease and illiteracy.

3. Serious disputes between countries can be discussed by the General Assembly *and* by the Security Council. Perhaps one of these bodies can arrange a peaceful solution.

4. The disputing countries could take their problem to the International Court.

5. If one or more countries misbehave, the United Nations can call for **economic sanctions** against them. This means that other countries would not trade with the misbehavers. This could hurt their economies. Therefore, they might correct their actions.

6. If one or more countries attacks another, the U.N. can threaten to use force against the attackers.

7. If necessary, the U.N. could ask member countries to contribute soldiers and weapons to a U.N. armed force. This force would be used against **aggressor** (attacking) nations.

The United Nations Building, New York City

The Office of Secretary - General

The Secretary-General is the official head of the United Nations. He or she supervises its office staff of several thousand employees. The Secretary-General must see that U.N. policies are carried out. Often, differences between member states must be smoothed out. Also, the Secretary-General is the spokesman for the U.N., explaining its actions to the press, and to the world as a whole.

To become Secretary-General, a person must first be **nominated** (proposed) by the Security Council. Then, the nominee must be elected by the General Assembly. The job calls for patience, courage and intelligence. It also demands **impartiality** (fairness, or freedom from prejudice). Member countries could not accept a U.N. leader who sided all the time with certain people or certain nations.

Since the U.N. began, there have been four Secretaries-General. Their photographs follow.

Secretaries-General of the United Nations

Trygve Lie (1946-1953)

Dag Hammarskjold (1953-1961)

U Thant (1961-1971)

Kurt Waldheim (1971-)

4. CANADA'S SUPPORT OF THE UNITED NATIONS

Canada has always been one of the strongest supporters of the United Nations. We are one of its fifty-one **charter** (original) members. Each year, we make a large contribution of money to the U.N. budget. We have supported U.N. efforts to achieve disarmament.

Canada also has worked through the United Nations to help poor countries. Most of you probably remember "Trick or Treating" on Halloween. Perhaps a few of you would confess to still doing this. The key phrase you shouted was "shell out" and this is what your neighbours did. Do you remember the "UNICEF" boxes that some of you carried around? You asked people to put money in them. This, whether your knew it or not, was to support a U.N. project — the *United Nations International Children's Emergency Fund.* It has helped children in countries ravaged by war. It also helps children in countries that have been struck by epidemics, floods, earthquakes and other disasters.

The accompanying chart lists the various help agencies of the United Nations.

United Nations Agencies

Year of Founding	Title and Abbreviation	Details of Operation
1865	International Tele-Communication Union (ITU)	This is the oldest international organization in the world. It supervises all forms of communication in the world.
1875	Universal Postal Union (UPU)	This body tries to speed the flow of mail throughout the world.
1919	International Labour Organization (ILO)	This agency tries to improve working conditions throughout the world. It encourages employers to pay fair wages and provide safe, healthy places to work.
1944	International Bank for Reconstruction and Development (IBRD)	Together, these agencies are called the "World Bank Group". They can make loans to any U.N. member. They try to help poorer countries. They do so by providing money for worthwhile projects — such as roads, hospitals and schools.
1956	International Finance Corporation (IFC)	
1960	International Development Association (IDA)	
1945	Food and Agricultural Organization (FAO)	This body tries to increase world food production. It provides fertilizers, farm equipment and training, especially to poor countries.
1945	International Monetary Fund (IMF)	Each country has a different money system. This can create problems for business and trade. The IMF helps to solve such problems.
1946	U.N. Educational, Scientific and Cultural Organization (UNESCO)	This is a very large agency. It tries to help poorer countries. This is done by financing schools, research, cultural centres and so on. It also tries to encourage world co-operation on common social problems.

1948	General Agreement on Tariffs and Trade (GATT)	This agreement tries to encourage world trade. It persuades countries to reduce, or remove, all **tariffs** (customs duties). It helps countries consult on problems of world trade.
1950	World Meteorological Organization (WMO)	WMO encourages countries to share information on weather. This can be very useful to the captains of ships and aircraft.
1957	International Atomic Energy Agency (IAEA)	This body tries to supervise the use of atomic energy throughout the world. It tries to discourage non-peaceful (as for weapons) atomic power use.
1958	Inter-Governmental Maritime Consultative Organization	This is a small agency. It encourages nations to co-operate in all matters affecting shipping.

Note: Canada is a member of each of the above agencies. To date, Canada has contributed over $85 million to them.

Canadian money has gone for the relief of drought, sickness, starvation and other human problems. We have helped to build dams, bridges, roads, schools, hospitals and other items in poor countries throughout the world. In addition, we have welcomed thousands of **refugees** to Canada.

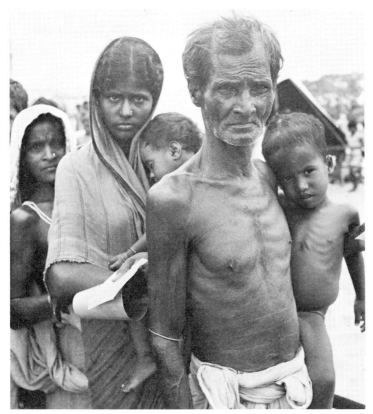

Refugees from East Pakistan. Canada has helped to meet the needs of such people for shelter, food, water, and health care.

Canada also has made important military contributions to the United Nations. In 1945, we argued for the creation of a special United Nations Force. We suggested that every member should contribute. They might provide — money, soldiers, ships, aircraft, guns or whatever they could afford. This force would be kept at the ready. It could be sent into action anywhere, at any time, to keep world peace. Unfortunately, this idea was not accepted.

However, in 1950 the United Nations decided to create a similar kind of force. This was needed to meet a special problem in Korea. This country is a peninsula in Asia (see map). After World War II, it was divided into North and South Korea. The dividing line was the 38th parallel of latitude. The North was

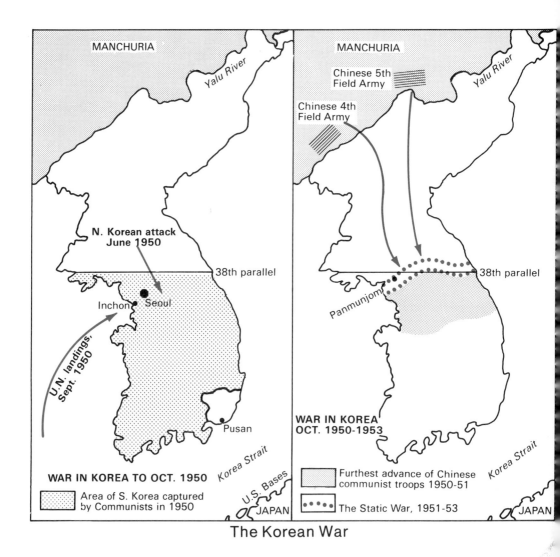

The Korean War

Communist and was supported by the Soviet Union. South Korea was protected by the United States.

In June of 1950 North Korea attacked South Korea. It seems that they were encouraged to do this by the Soviet Union. The United States asked the United Nations to take action against this **aggression** (attack). The Security Council met in special session. Eventually, it reached a decision. A United Nations armed force would be sent to Korea to turn back the invaders.

Over 300 000 troops served in the United Nations forces in Korea. About 85 per cent of these were American. Over thirty other members of the U.N. contributed in the same way to this force. Canada sent an army brigade of about 8 000 soldiers. It also provided three naval destroyers and an air transport squadron. Only the United States and Britain made larger contributions to the U.N. force. Over 1500 Canadian soldiers became casualties in the Korean War. Of these, 406 were killed.

The Korean fighting was finally ended by a **truce** (agreement to stop shooting) in July, 1953. The United Nations action saved South Korea. Perhaps even more important was the fact that the U.N. had shown it could be effective. In time, most of the U.N. forces went home. Canada's idea of a permanent U.N. force was still not accepted. However, our support of the U.N. in its hour of need was very valuable.

Canada has helped the United Nations in yet another important way. This is in the difficult job known as **peacekeeping.** Since World War II, several "trouble spots" have developed in the world. On many occasions, this has led to fighting. Sometimes the United Nations can persuade the two sides to stop fighting. This involves arranging a truce. However, this agreement to stop shooting does not always last. Therefore, the United Nations offers to provide a force to stand between the two sides. This U.N. force supervises the truce. It reports any violations made by either side. It also helps to solve misunderstandings. In this way, the U.N. force can usually prevent the conflict from breaking out again. Thus, this work is called "truce supervision" and "peacekeeping."

Canada is an ideal country for this type of role. We have a reputation for being quite **impartial** (fair-minded). We are not a large power; therefore we are not feared. Our government is keenly interested in peace. Our people want Canada to play a helpful role. They also seem willing to pay the cost. As a result, Canada has been very active in truce supervision and peace-keeping for the United Nations. We now are known throughout the world for this role. You could say it has become part of Canada's "identity."

The accompanying chart outlines Canada's peacekeeping role. It is not possible here to describe each one in detail. Therefore, we have chosen one for closer study: The Suez Crisis of 1956. (Your class might select one or two other trouble spots for deeper study.)

Aid by Canada in United Nations Peacekeeping Operations

Date	Area	Operation
1949-	KASHMIR	U.N. Military Observer Group, India/Pakistan
1950-54	KOREA	U.N. Command, Korea
1954-	PALESTINE	U.N. Truce Supervisory Organization
1954-	VIETNAM, LAOS, CAMBODIA	International Commissions established by 1954 Geneva Agreement
1956-67	EGYPT	U.N. Emergency Force
1958-59	LEBANON	U.N. Observer Group in Lebanon
1960-64	CONGO	U.N. Operation in the Congo
1962-63	WEST NEW GUINEA	U.N. Temporary Executive Administration
1963-64	YEMEN	U.N. Observer Mission Yemen
1964-	CYPRUS	U.N. Force in Cyprus
1965-66	INDIA/PAKISTAN	U.N. India/Pakistan Observer Mission

The Suez Crisis

The Middle East has been a major threat to world peace for many years. Basically, the problem revolves around the state of Israel. This is the national homeland of the Jewish people. Centuries ago, the Jews lived in this part of the world, near the eastern shore of the Mediterranean Sea. Then, in the first century A.D. they were expelled by the Romans. The Jews were scattered in all directions. However, they kept their belief that Israel was their "Promised Land". In the early 20th century, they began to return to this area in significant numbers.

This development was upsetting to the Arabs who lived in the region. They too had strong claims to the land going back for hundreds of years. They feared that the Jews might try to take away some of this land for their own state. After years of struggle, this finally did happen. The new state of Israel was created in 1948. It was recognized by the United Nations, but not by the Arabs. War broke out. The Arabs tried to destroy Israel, but were defeated instead. As a result of their victory, the Israelis gained considerable land. This only increased the anger and bitterness of the Arabs, who swore to take revenge.

Other factors helped to increase tension in the Middle East. This area has a very **strategic** (important) location. The Suez Canal is situated here. Many big powers, including Britain, France, the United States and the Soviet Union had vital interests in the region. To further these interests, they often took sides in the quarrel between Arabs and Jews. To make things even worse, they also sold large quantities of arms and ammunition to both sides.

The United Nations tried to help by sending truce observers to the area. It also tried to arrange a permanent settlement. This proved to be impossible.

Canadian soldiers on U. N. patrol in Egypt. Their jeeps contrast sharply with the more traditional form of desert transportation.

The Jews were determined to keep their newly won country plus the additional areas conquered in war. The Arabs, on the other hand, refused to recognize Israel. They were determined to destroy it. The uneasy truce lasted until 1956.

In that year, war began again. This time, Britain and France were directly involved. These countries relied heavily on the Suez Canal. It was important for both economic and military reasons. It had been controlled by Britain for many years. However, the Canal zone was inside Egyptian territory. Egypt was a major Arab nation. Its leader, General Nasser, decided to **nationalize** (take over for the state) the Canal zone. Britain and France decided to oppose the move.

Fighting broke out in October 1956. Israeli forces attacked Egypt and rushed toward the Suez Canal. To support Israel, British and French paratroops were dropped near the Canal zone. This attack was strongly criticized by most members of the United Nations. The Soviet Union threatened to **intervene** (come in) on the side of Egypt. The United States was deeply embarrassed. They were a supporter of Israel, and an ally of Britain and France. Still, they agreed with the Russians that the attack was wrong.

Finally, a way out was found. It was presented by Canada at a dramatic, all-night meeting of the General Assembly. The spokesman was Lester Pearson, our Secretary of State for External Affairs.

Pearson suggested the calling of an immediate end to the shooting. Next, he asked for a United Nations Emergency Force (U.N.E.F.) to preserve the truce. It would also supervise the withdrawal of all invading forces from Egypt. Next, the U.N.E.F. would patrol tense border areas. This plan was adopted and its terms were carried out. The U.N.E.F. grew to about 6000 troops. They were supplied by several countries, including Canada. Ours was the largest single contribution (about 800 men). The first Commander of the U.N.E.F. was a Canadian, General E.L.M. Burns.

Lester Pearson won the Nobel Prize for Peace in 1957. This was a great honour — for him, and for Canada. The Nobel Prize is an award that is widely recognized around the world. The U.N.E.F. remained in operation until June 1967, when President Nasser forced it to leave. There have been two further wars in the Middle East, in 1967 and 1973. After both of these, Canada agreed to contribute to new peacekeeping efforts there.

5. CANADA'S DISAPPOINTMENT WITH THE UNITED NATIONS

Thus far, the record of the United Nations might appear to you to be very good. In some respects, the record *has* been good. However, we must remember two key facts. First, the main goal of the United Nations is to prevent war. It has not achieved this aim. Secondly, Canada was counting on the U.N. for a measure of security. This could work only if the U.N. was able to prevent wars. In time, the weaknesses of the U.N. began to show. When that happened, Canada had to make other arrangements for its security.

What Went Wrong?

The United Nations has proved to be a disappointment for several reasons. To begin with, it does not have enough power. It cannot force any nation to do something it does not wish to do. It can only ask, advise or suggest. The U.N. has no permanent armed force of its own. In the General Assembly, each country has one vote, regardless of size, wealth or power. It has become, in some ways, a debating society where smaller, weaker or poorer nations can have their say. Therefore, it is often ignored by the big powers.

The big powers pay somewhat more attention to the Security Council. However, this body also has a serious weakness. Each of the five permanent members has the power of **veto.** This is the power to block any action with which it disagrees. In other words, all five permanent members must agree to any action before it can be taken. Look back at the earlier chart on the organization of the United Nations. Name the 5 members of the Security Council. As you might imagine, they often disagree. Unanimous (united) agreement is almost always impossible. It is true that there has been no World War since 1945. This might be partly due to the existence of the United Nations. More likely it is due to the wish of the big powers to survive. With modern weapons, a world war might destroy the whole world.

The basic problem of the U.N. is that it is not a **world government.** None of its members gives up any of its independence when joining. Each member is free to leave the U.N. It can support or reject U.N. policies as it sees fit. Earlier in this chapter, we saw that things cannot run this way in an individual country. All members of a society must agree to obey its laws. These laws must be enforced upon everyone. It seems that the countries and people of the world will not see the world as one society. They will not obey one set of laws. For these reasons, the U.N. has not become what its founders, including Canada, hoped it would be.

THINGS TO THINK ABOUT AND DO

Reviewing Key Words and Ideas

The following terms appeared in this chapter. Try to recall their meaning and how they were used.

aggression	intervention	refugee
demobilization	middle power	super power
economic sanction	nationalize	truce
impartiality	pacifist	veto
international law	peacekeeping	world government

Remembering the Facts

1. Why was World War II an important experience for Canada?
2. Why was Canada so anxious for the United Nations to succeed?
3. Summarize the main ways in which Canada has supported the United Nations.
4. How did Canada win world recognition in 1956?

Analyzing Ideas

1. What is the main reason for the weakness of the United Nations?
2. In the Suez Crisis of 1956, the United States was on one side and Britain on the other. Why would this be embarrassing and difficult for Canada?
3. The following is a list of several countries in the world today:

Britain	France	Poland
Canada	India	West Germany
Chile	Japan	U.S.A.
China	Kenya	U.S.S.R.

Which of these would be called "super powers"? Which others are major powers? Which are "middle powers"? In each case, explain your choices. Which countries are left? Why is Canada not a middle power today? Do you wish we were? If so, why?

4. Why do you think each permanent member of the Security Council insisted on having veto power? Canada opposed this idea. Suggest a reason for our attitude.

5. Many people criticize the United Nations. An American once said that such people reminded him "of the poor Roman who felt sorry for himself because he didn't have a shoe, until he saw a man who didn't have a foot". What was he saying about people who criticize the U.N.? Do you agree?

Applying Your Knowledge

1. What is meant by a *world government?* Why is the U.N. *not* one of these? With the help of classmates, try to plan the structure of a world government. You will have to think about rules, various bodies, budget, law enforcement, voting arrangements and so on. If you succeed in creating a model, try it out. Set up an imaginary world crisis, and take it to your world government for solution.

2. Based on your experience in No. 2 above, what is the most difficult part of making a world government work? Could this problem ever be solved?

3. Would you be in favour of Canada scrapping its armed forces as an example to the world? Explain your answer.

4. Debate the resolution that: "The United Nations is now little more than a glorified and costly debating society which should be dissolved."

5. Earlier in this chapter, there is a chart showing the main agencies of the United Nations. Together, they have brought great social and economic help to millions of needy people. You could write to the United Nations to obtain information about the work of these agencies. The address is:

Information Division,
United Nations,
New York 10017, N.Y.

3

CANADA AND THE "COLD WAR"

INTRODUCTION

- In Winnipeg, a member of the RCMP sits quietly in an unmarked car. He is in plain clothes. He is watching two men exchange parcels on a street corner. One man is a suspected Russian secret agent. The other is a former member of the Canadian Armed Forces. He is believed to be handing over military secrets to the Russian, in return for large amounts of cash.
- In Hamilton, Ontario, a middle-aged woman is finishing her shift in an ammunition factory. She is making shell cases. They will later be packed with explosives and sold to the United States. From there they will be shipped to American artillery units stationed in West Germany.
- Near Colorado Springs, Colorado, an officer of the Canadian Armed Forces is sitting in front of a huge map of the world. It is electrically lit, and is connected to several computers. This is NORAD command headquarters. The officer at this moment is in charge of the whole North American air defence system.
- Somewhere in Alberta, a Canadian scientist is busy in a secret laboratory. He is part of a team working on the development of a new chemical. This might be used in the production of a special nerve gas. The gas could paralyze a city of one million people.
- In Leningrad, U.S.S.R., a Canadian businessman is touring a Russian electronics firm. He has agreed to spy on Russian industry for the Canadian and American governments. He will bring home as much information as he can which might have military value.
- In Halifax, an 18-year-old Canadian seaman is walking down a gangplank. He is part of the crew of a sleek new destroyer. He has just finished a tour of duty in the North Atlantic. His ship joined vessels from several allied nations in a series of naval exercises.

All of these Canadians are involved in some aspect of the **"Cold War."**

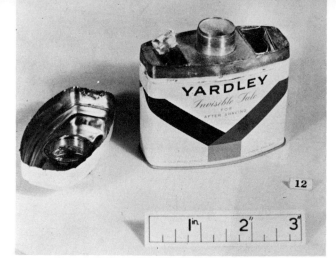

Evidence at a spy trial in Britain during the Cold War. A tiny radio transmitter was hidden in this can of after-shave powder.

Does this phrase strike you as unusual? Wars are normally described as "hot" — because of the fighting and violence involved. The term "Cold War" refers to a situation that developed in the world after 1945. It centred around the two great "super powers", the United States and the Soviet Union. These two countries did not actually go to war with each other. However, they became bitter enemies. Their conflict took the form of arguing, spying and competing with one another. Thus, their war was one of words and threats. Relations between them became very hostile — or frigid, you might say. Hence, the term "Cold War" was born.

This chapter begins by trying to explain the basic causes of the Cold War. Then, it will show how this threatened Canadian security. Next, we will study how Canada reacted to this threat. Finally, we will see how and why the Cold War began to "thaw." We will then see how the thaw affected Canadian foreign policy.

Before reading on, study the chart of Key Words and Ideas which follows.

KEY WORDS AND IDEAS IN THIS CHAPTER

Term	Meaning	Sample Use
arms race	a competition among countries to develop new weapons and build large quantities of them	Many countries are involved in the arms race today. Chief among these are the United States and the Soviet Union.
buffer state	a country located between two other countries which might come into conflict	Today, Poland acts as a buffer state between the Soviet Union and Western Europe.

collective security	the safety provided by numbers; several countries band together and promise to defend each other against attack	Canada tried to gain collective security through the United Nations. When this failed, we turned to military alliances such as NATO and NORAD.
conventional force	regular or normal weaponry (non-nuclear)	Canada's armed forces are a conventional force.
deterrent	the power to persuade someone *not* to do something	By keeping strong defences, plus the attacking power to destroy any enemy, the United States maintains a deterrent against attack.
flexible response	the ability to meet a situation in a variety of ways	NATO wants flexible response. It does not want to be forced to use only one kind of weapon to deal with an attacker.
Intercontinental Ballistic Missile (ICBM)	a missile which can carry a nuclear warhead thousands of kilometers (from one continent to another)	The U.S., the U.S.S.R. and China have ICBMs today.
NATO	North Atlantic Treaty Organization	NATO is a military alliance formed in 1948. Canada joined then, and has been a member ever since.
neutrality	not taking sides	Some people think that Canada should take a position of neutrality in world affairs. At the moment, we are not neutral. Some think this would be impossible and unwise for us.
NORAD	North American Air Defence (system)	NORAD was created in 1958 to improve North America's defence against attack from the air. Canada and the United States are members.
strategy	planning	NATO and NORAD both have strategy for carrying out their role of defending their members.

| **tactical nuclear weapons** | weapons of limited nuclear power, such as artillery shells or small bombs | NATO has tactical nuclear weapons, as part of its *strategy of flexible response.* |
| **Warsaw Pact** | a military alliance formed in 1955; it includes the Soviet Union and several countries of central and eastern Europe | The Warsaw Pact was the Russian answer to NATO. Its members promise to defend each other against "enemy attack". |

1.   HOW THE "COLD WAR" DEVELOPED

During World War II, Canada, the United States and the Soviet Union were allies. That is, they fought on the same side. Their common enemy was Germany. Once Germany was defeated, it was hoped that we could remain on friendly terms with the Soviets.

Unfortunately, this did not happen. One reason was that there were great **ideological** differences between the two sides. The Soviet Union is a Communist country. The **"West"** (Canada, U.S.A., Britain, etc) believe in democracy. Because of this difference, there was bound to be some mistrust and suspicion.

There was another important problem. Both the U.S.A. and the U.S.S.R. had become Super Powers. They were the two most powerful nations in the world. Each wanted to be "number one." Each wanted to expand its power and influence as much as possible. Naturally, this meant there would be **rivalry** (competition) between them.

The two sides also disagreed about the peace terms in Europe. The Soviet Union had borne the brunt of the land war against Hitler's forces. Millions of Soviet citizens had been killed. Cities were torn apart. Toward the end of the war, the Russian forces swept toward victory. They rolled over much of Eastern Europe. They wanted to keep their influence in this region. This would protect their western borders against a new German attack. It also would give security against a possible attack by Western Europe or the United States. The Russians wished to place very harsh terms on Germany. They insisted that Germany should remain weak and divided. This way, Germany could never again be a threat to peace, or to the Soviet Union.

The Western Allies did not completely agree with this approach. The United States was supported in this by Canada, Britain and France. They felt that the Soviet forces should withdraw from Eastern Europe, now that the war was over. Furthermore, they began to realize how Germany could be useful to them. They did not want Germany to threaten world peace again. However, if allowed to keep some military strength, Germany could act as a **buffer state**

The Communist Countries of Europe in 1978

Russia

Other Communist Countries

(shield). This way, it would help protect the West from Russian influence or expansion.

For these reasons, the Cold War began. Problems arose in different areas. The wartime allies were unable to agree on a final peace settlement in Europe. The West kept large forces in France, Holland, Belgium and western Germany. Russian forces remained in such countries as Poland, Hungary, Czechoslovakia and eastern Germany. In addition, the Soviet Union gave support to local Communist parties in those countries. With Soviet help, these parties gradually took over the governments of most East European nations. Russian agents also tried to arrange Communist takeovers of Greece and Turkey. (The latter country controls the Bosporus and the Dardanelles — the vital straits between the Black and Mediterranean Seas.)

In the late 1940s, Communist parties did well in elections in France and Italy. They also tried to stir up strikes and other troubles in several Western countries. From the Russian viewpoint, such actions were necessary and proper. They helped to spread Communism — a system in which the Soviet government believed strongly. Further, they helped to strengthen Soviet security. However, the West did not share this view. Canada, the United States and their allies saw great danger in these developments. Some people came to believe that there was a **"Communist conspiracy"** (plot) to take over the whole world. Also, Communist rule brought dictatorship. This would destroy freedom and democracy wherever it went. These were ideals which the West was determined to defend.

2.   THE FORMATION OF NATO

The proper name for NATO is the *North Atlantic Treaty Organization*. It was formed in 1948. Its aim was to meet the threat of Russian expansion. Canada was one of the first countries to join NATO. We did this with some regret. This is because we seemed to be admitting that the United Nations could not give us proper security. Forming this military alliance seemed to be a step backward. However, the danger from the Soviet Union appeared to be increasing. Our first responsibility was the protection of our country. The following countries belong to NATO:

Belgium	Luxembourg
Canada	Netherlands
Denmark	Norway
*France	Portugal
Federal Republic of Germany	Turkey
(West Germany)	United Kingdom
*Greece	United States

*Both France and Greece later withdrew from the NATO military command. Each country took back complete control over its own armed forces. However, both countries are committed to the common defence of all NATO members.

1. Locate each of these countries on a world map. In terms of position, what do most of them have in common? How does this help explain the title of their organization?
2. Who are the four most powerful members of NATO? Of these, which is strongest? Why?
3. How powerful is Canada in relation to its NATO allies?
4. Why would Canada and the United States be concerned about what happens in Europe? Why would it not be better for North America to simply defend itself, and let Western Europe do the same?

3. HOW NATO WORKS

The main idea behind NATO was **collective security.** In a sense, this means "One for all, and all for one." Each member of NATO promises to help all the other members. This includes financial and economic aid. It also means military help if necessary. Thus, if Canada is attacked by a hostile country, every other NATO member is bound to help us. In return, we must go to the aid of any other NATO member that is attacked. In this way, NATO provides group protection, or "collective security." No enemy country can attack one NATO member without having to take on *all* members.

Remember, the main purpose of NATO was (and is) to protect its members against the Soviet Union. You will better understand NATO's **strategy** (plans) if you look at a map of Europe. The Soviet Union has very powerful armed forces. Its troops and weapons are stationed throughout most of Eastern Europe. If they attacked westward, there would be heavy fighting in such countries as France and West Germany. These countries are our friends and allies. They would be heavily damaged by such fighting. Therefore, NATO adopted what it called a **"Forward Strategy."**

The main point of this plan was to meet a possible Russian attack as far to the east as possible. Therefore, NATO keeps large forces stationed in Western Europe. They are under a combined command. NATO headquarters are at Castean Mons in Belgium. Canada contributes to these forces in several ways. At the beginning, we agreed to keep a full army brigade (8000-10 000 soldiers) in Western Europe. Later, we added several squadrons of jet fighter aircraft. Portions of the Canadian navy also were assigned to NATO duty. These ships patrolled the seas, keeping track of Soviet fleets and submarines. All of this cost Canada several millions of dollars per year. It seemed to be a good investment for Canada's security.

Another part of NATO strategy is **flexible response.** This means that NATO planners want to be able to answer possible attackers in a variety of ways. Their first response would be with **conventional force.** This involves normal weapons of war. Then, if necessary, NATO could use **tactical nuclear weapons.** These include small atomic bombs and artillery shells; they have limited explosive power. As a last resort, NATO could turn to total nuclear war. This would be waged mainly by American forces. All kinds of nuclear weapons would be used, including huge bombs and missiles.

Naturally, such a war would bring destruction to all countries involved. As U Thant (former Secretary General of the United Nations) once said: "In modern war, there is only one victor, and his name is Death." Therefore, NATO hopes that its strength will act as a **deterrent** (discouragement) to potential enemies. Knowing that an attack would mean certain destruction, such an enemy would not dare begin a war.

The Soviet Response to NATO

The Soviet Union was very upset by the creation of NATO. It argued that no such alliance was needed. This was because the Soviet Union was *not* an aggressor. It posed no threat to Western Europe. On the contrary, the Russians argued that the creation of NATO was itself an aggressive act! They saw NATO as a threat to the security of Eastern Europe. Therefore, the Soviet Union persuaded many countries of that region to form their own alliance. This finally was done in 1955. The organization was called the **Warsaw Pact.** Its members are: Albania, Bulgaria, Czechoslovakia, East Germany, Hungary, Poland, Rumania and the Soviet Union.

All of this happened within ten years of the end of World War II. In that terrible conflict, over 100 million human beings had died. Nonetheless, the world by 1955 was once again divided into two hostile armed camps. The Cold War was on!

What Should Be Done With Canada's NATO Forces?

Membership in NATO has cost Canada hundreds of millions of dollars. In the past, most Canadians believed that this money was well spent. Much of it supported the armed forces which we kept in Europe. These included air and land units stationed in West Germany. Units of the Canadian Navy helped to patrol North Atlantic waters. Canadian money also helped some of the poorer NATO countries develop their economies and defence forces.

However, in recent years some Canadians have begun to question the value of NATO. The danger of a Soviet attack on Western Europe seems to have declined. Perhaps the large costs of keeping our troops in Europe could be better spent on problems here at home. Such people suggest that our money and troops are being wasted. Bring the forces home, where they could be of more use.

Soviet troops taking physical training. Soviet forces in Europe are more numerous and better prepared than the conventional NATO forces which they face.

Others claim that we must keep troops in Europe. This will show our allies that we still support them. They can trust us. Also, if we pull out, some countries might cut off their trade with us. The United States keeps large armed forces in Europe. They want us to help share the load. If we refuse, we will probably lose our voice in large NATO decisions. If trouble comes, we could find ourselves with no allies and few friends.

All of these factors place pressure on the Canadian government. But one thing is certain. If Canadian forces *stay* in Europe, they must be strengthened. Much of their equipment is out of date. Their weapons have little firepower. Improvements would be very expensive.

1. Look up current statistics which show the value of Canada's trade with NATO countries. The *Canada Yearbook* should be useful for this purpose. If time permits, write to Statistics Canada or to the Department of Industry,

Trade and Commerce. How valuable *is* this trade? Could we afford to risk losing it?

2. With the class, fully discuss the arguments for and against Canada removing its troops from Europe. Also consider the possibility of Canada leaving NATO altogether. What do you think our government should do about these questions. Why?

3. Try to find out what Canada *is* doing about these matters.

4. Some Americans and Europeans have accused Canada of trying to get a "free ride." What does this mean? *Do* we want the benefits of NATO membership, but not the responsibilities? Is the charge a fair one?

A Canadian CF 104 jet fighter. After 1971, these planes no longer carried nuclear bombs.

4.   CANADA AND THE UNITED STATES FORM NORAD

The Cold War went on throughout the 1950s. The Korean War (discussed in the previous chapter) was one aspect of this. So, too, was the Communist takeover in China in 1949. For a while, China and the Soviet Union appeared to become allies. This created a powerful combination against the West. Communist influence seemed to be spreading in Europe and Asia.

New developments in weaponry made the tension and danger even worse. Both the Soviet Union and the United States enlarged their armed forces. They became locked in an **arms race.** They were competing to see who could build the most and biggest weapons. These included very powerful hydrogen bombs. One such bomb was capable of wiping out a large city.

Normally, such bombs or "warheads" were carried to their targets by jet bombers. However, during the 1950s, **guided missiles** (rockets) became more important. Missiles fired from 10 000 km away could hit North America in about half an hour! Canada and the United States had plans for the defence of North America. However, these plans were several years old. These new weapons made the plans instantly out of date. To meet this danger, Canada and the United States formed the North American Air Defence System (NORAD) in 1958. The details of this system are described in Unit V, Chapter 4. Since 1958, Canada has reviewed its position every few years. On each occasion, we have decided to remain in NORAD. It is still one of the key links in our system of security and defence.

"O Canada — We Stand on Guard For Thee"

We all know these stirring lines. We sing them many times a year. Sometimes we have a quiver of emotion in our voices. They are the main theme of our national anthem. But are the words true? Do they have any meaning? Some defence experts say "NO." These people claim that they should be sung instead by the American Armed Forces.

The strength of Canada's defences has been debated for several years. The United States, and other allies, have been critical of Canadian defence policy. They point out that we are spending too little on weapons and equipment. Many of these items are now badly out of date. Some are useless. In addition, our armed forces are very small. They are "top-heavy." That is, there is too high a ratio of officers to ordinary soldiers. In other words "too many Chiefs and not enough Indians."

Several experienced members of Canada's Armed Forces have made similar points. For example, in 1976 the President of the Royal Canadian Armoured Corps Association charged publicly that:
— the Canadian Armed Forces had no thorough plans to handle a national emergency
— the Canadian Armed Forces did not have enough arms or ammunition even to train properly, let alone fight a war
— the Canadian Armed Forces had no tanks for training outside of New Brunswick; even there the tanks were few, old and slow
— the Canadian Armed Forces were keeping their old basic rifle (the Belgian FN) instead of replacing it with a modern, faster-firing weapon
— the Canadian militia (reserve) was in a terrible state; it had no real plans or ability to call up men

Army cadets receive their wings.

HMCS "Algonquin" on manoeuvres

A female mechanic learns a trade in the Canadian Armed Forces.

A Canadian paratrooper begins an exercise on winter survival.

— the Canadian Armed Forces could not even carry out peacetime duties properly because they lacked money, manpower and equipment
— Canadian defence policy had a "Band-Aid" approach
— in 1952, Canada spent 8 cents on welfare for every 44 cents spent on defence; today the reverse was true
— the Canadian Armed Forces, with a proud record and tradition, was becoming the "laughing stock" of the world

Do these charges seem extreme? False? They were labelled as "unfair" by the government. However, they were not denied. This is because they couldn't be. Most of those charges were basically true!

How could this be? There are several answers. First, defence is very costly. Taxes are already at record high levels in Canada. So is government spending. So is the national debt. Politicians have to see the whole picture. Increasing defence spending would cause other problems.

Also, today the danger of an enemy attack seems to be declining. We could be spending the money for nothing. Finally, it is argued that we could not *afford* to spend the money to really defend this huge land. We have too few people. And we are not rich enough. Better to count on the Americans to save us if necessary.

Recently the government has made some improvements. Almost $5 billion will be spent between 1977 and 1982 for new weapons and equipment. Most of this money will go for new tanks, jet fighters and long-range submarine tracker aircraft. The manpower of the forces will be slightly increased. These changes will help, and perhaps make us feel better. But they won't change one basic fact: CANADA CANNOT ADEQUATELY DEFEND ITSELF.

5. A NEW WORLD TAKES SHAPE

Fortunately, the tension of the Cold War began to ease somewhat in the 1960s. There were several reasons for this. Both the United States and the Soviet Union had come to accept each other as super powers. Each could destroy the other, but would be destroyed in return. It was clear that they simply had to get along somehow. Also, each got to know the other a little better. Perhaps this reduced their fear and suspicion somewhat. New leaders came forward in many countries. They did not have the same prejudices. They seemed more willing to work with one another, and to accept change.

There were many signs that the "Cold War" was beginning to thaw, at least a little. There was increased trade and travel between East and West. Cultural exchanges became more common. Government leaders held more conferences and made more agreements. For example, several countries signed a treaty which banned the use of nuclear weapons in outer space or on the ocean floor. They also agreed to try to stop the spread of nuclear weapons to other countries. The United States and the Soviet Union even began meetings to discuss limiting the numbers and types of their nuclear weapons.

The world was changing in other ways as well. Many new nations emerged. This was especially true in Asia and Africa. Nations of Western Europe, such as Germany, had recovered from World War II. They wanted to regain an important voice in world affairs. So did Asian nations, such as China and Japan.

Canada could not ignore these changes. Moreover, the Canadian public began to take a greater interest in world affairs. They could see that our foreign policy was becoming outdated. We still talked and acted like a middle power, yet had not been one for many years. The United Nations was becoming more ineffective as world tension declined, as did the need for concern about our security. Perhaps NATO and NORAD were outdated, or at least less important. On the other hand, Canadians became more aware of the poorer countries of the world. Perhaps we should be spending money on *their* problems, not on guns and missiles.

For these and other reasons, the Canadian government decided to do a complete review of our foreign policy. It began under our brand new Prime Minister, Pierre Trudeau. This review, and its results, are the subject of the next chapter.

THINGS TO THINK ABOUT AND DO

Reviewing Key Words and Ideas

The following terms appeared in this chapter. Try to recall their meaning and how they were used.

arms race	ICBM	rivalry
buffer state	ideology	strategy
collective security	isolationism	tactical nuclear
conventional force	NATO	weapon
deterrent	neutrality	Warsaw Pact
flexible response	NORAD	

Remembering the Facts

1. What were the main reasons for the beginning of the Cold War?
2. How did the Cold War affect Canada's foreign policy?
3. What were the two key agreements made by Canada to protect its security during the Cold War?
4. Why did the Canadian government begin a review of its foreign policy in the late 1960s?

Analyzing Ideas

1. What is a "buffer state"? In what way does Germany play this role? Is Canada a buffer state? Why or why not?

2. In the 1950s, the United States operated a Strategic Air Command, which later became part of NORAD. It kept armed bombers in the air at all times. Why would it do this? One of its pilots said: "The moment we get the order to fly into Russia and drop our bombs, we will have failed in our main mission." What did he mean by this?

3. Why would NORAD put its command headquarters inside a mountain?

4. It has been suggested that Canada should leave NORAD, because we are becoming too dependent on the United States. What do you think of this idea? Would the United States defend us anyway, whether we wanted this or not?

5. Recently, a critic of Canada's defence policy compared this country's position with that of Sweden. He pointed out that Sweden is usually a neutral nation. Nonetheless, it keeps strong armed forces. Most of its weapons and equipment are produced in Sweden itself. (Many of Canada's weapons are made in foreign countries.) If a large war broke out, Sweden's entire defence system could go underground. So could much of its war industry. Here it would be protected and could continue to function. Canada is not even close to having similar abilities. The critic concluded: " ... for some reason we Canadians think we can completely opt out of all of this ... What are we playing at? Isn't it unbelievable?" How do you react to these comments? Why?

Applying Your Knowledge

1. Part of NATO's strategy is to have a "flexible response." The following is a list of possible actions it could take in the event of a Soviet attack. Put these in order of severity, from least to most severe.

- send troops, guns, tanks and other "conventional" weapons to meet the invaders
- release nerve gas that would paralyze the enemy troops
- warn the Soviets to withdraw their troops
- drop "conventional" bombs on Russian cities and industrial centres
- use chemical weapons on the Soviet troops
- give the Soviets a time limit to withdraw their forces
- launch ICBM and MIRV missiles with nuclear warheads against the Soviet Union
- fire small tactical nuclear warheads on the Soviet troops
- drop bombs on the Soviet Union that would release deadly gases and 'germs' on the people

2. Do research on the latest missiles and other weapons being developed by the United States and the Soviet Union. Next, divide your class into two groups: half will be Russians and half Americans. Each group will discuss *privately*. Imagine that you are preparing for a meeting with the other country to try to agree on limiting or abolishing certain weapons. Argue if you must, but agree on a *plan*. What will you agree to give up? What do you want the other country to give up in exchange? Now, hold your conference with the other country.

(a) What happened? Why did it happen? What does this tell you about the arms race and about the problem of disarmament?

(b) Compare your results with "real life." Similar talks go on between the U.S. and the U.S.S.R. These are called SALT (Strategic Arms Limitation Talks.) They are often reported in newspapers and magazines. See what you can find. (These talks have been going on since the early 1970s.)

3. Debate this: RESOLVED: That without the existence of nuclear weapons, World War III would already have happened.

Negotiators from several major powers arrange an agreement for banning nuclear weapons testing in the atmosphere. This agreement in the early 1960s helped to start a "thaw " in the Cold War.

4

FOREIGN POLICY FOR A CHANGING WORLD: CANADA'S SEARCH FOR NEW ROLES

INTRODUCTION

As we learned in the previous chapter, the world was changing rapidly in the 1960s. Despite this fact, there had been no major review of Canadian foreign policy. Our goals and methods had remained basically the same for over fifteen years. In 1968, the way was cleared for such a review to begin. In that year, Prime Minister Lester Pearson retired from politics. He had been the main **architect** (designer) of Canada's foreign policy since 1950. Pierre Trudeau was Canada's next Prime Minister.

Mr. Trudeau was an exciting new personality in politics. He was well educated, fairly young, and very intelligent. He had played no part in the formation of earlier Canadian foreign policy. Therefore, he could look at it in an open, unbiased way. He was quite prepared to make changes in it if necessary. This attitude seemed to have the support of the Canadian public. Therefore, in 1968 Mr. Trudeau made an important announcement. There would be a complete review of Canadian foreign policy.

In this chapter, we begin by looking at the "Trudeau Review" of foreign policy. Then, we will see the results of this review. Next, we will consider some issues which still face Canada in world affairs. Finally, we will briefly summarize what we have learned in this unit about Canadian foreign policy.

Before reading on, study the chart of Key Words and Ideas which follows.

KEY WORDS AND IDEAS IN THIS CHAPTER

Term	Meaning	Sample Use
ambassador	a person sent by one country to represent it in a foreign nation	Canada sends ambassadors to most other countries in the world.
British Commonwealth	an organization of former British colonies; they cooperate in trade and other matters	Canada plays an important role in the British Commonwealth.
Canadian International Development Agency (CIDA)	an organization set up by our government to help poorer countries in the world	Through CIDA, Canada sends over $1 billion in aid to other countries each year.
Colombo Plan	an organization created in 1950 to provide aid to Southeast Asia	Canada was a leading supporter of the Colombo Plan.
colony	an area that is not independent, but rather is controlled by a foreign state	Canada is a *former* colony of Britain.
Canadian University Service Overseas (CUSO)	this organization sends university students to countries needing various kinds of assistance	CUSO is one of many ways in which Canada helps less fortunate countries.
developed nation	one that is industrialized, and therefore has a reasonably high standard of living	Canada, the United States and most Western European nations are examples of developed nations.
diplomatic recognition	a sign of official acceptance of one country by another	In 1970, Canada gave diplomatic recognition to the government of Communist China.
foreign aid	help which one country gives to another	Such aid is an important part of Canadian foreign policy.

la Francophonie	French-speaking parts of the world; most of these are former colonies of France	Quebec is interested in la Francophonie. The Trudeau government increased foreign aid to member countries.
gross national product (GNP)	the value of all goods and services produced by a country's economy in one year	Canada's GNP is well over $100 billion per year. We give about half of one per cent of this in foreign aid.
non-alignment	the policy of not taking sides in world affairs	Many nations in the world *are* aligned — with the U.S., the U.S.S.R. or China. Others follow a policy of non-alignment. Many of these belong to the "Third World."
Third World	refers to nations that are non-aligned, and usually underdeveloped	Most Third World countries are found in Africa and Asia.
tied aid	foreign aid that has "strings attached"	Some of Canada's aid is tied aid — we lend money to countries and then insist they buy Canadian products with some or all of the money.
under developed nations	these countries have had little industrial or urban growth; most are quite poor and need foreign aid	Underdeveloped nations are found mostly in the Third World. Many are bitter. They think the developed countries take advantage of them. They want a bigger share of the world's riches.

1. Setting Up The "Trudeau Review"

Prime Minister Trudeau invited the whole country to take part in this review. He encouraged the press and the public to say what they thought. He personally took part in debates on the subject in many parts of Canada. People were invited to talk to government committees. Many people took advantage of this chance. They included professors, businessmen, teachers, soldiers and diplomats.

To help guide the review, Mr. Trudeau set down a few guidelines. Any decisions made should meet certain conditions. His guidelines are listed below.
I Canada needed to *broaden* its ties with other countries. (We should not be too dependent on any one other nation.)
II Canadian foreign policy should not be controlled by our armed forces.
III Our foreign policy should reflect life in Canada. (It should be based on our ideals or values, on public opinion and on our needs.)
IV The goals of our foreign policy should be **realistic** (sensible).
V Any foreign policy decisions must serve these interests of Canada:
a) help our economy grow
b) keep us independent
c) maintain peace
d) protect our security
e)·be morally right (do *good* for people; be fair and honest)
f) help all peoples gain a better life
g) protect our environment (fight pollution, save resources, etc.)

Understanding The Guidelines

1. Why would Canadians be concerned about being too dependent on one country? How could the government help to *broaden* our ties?
2. Why would it be dangerous for any country to let its armed forces control foreign policy?
3. How do we set "realistic" goals in foreign policy? (Why should we consider our economic and military strength in doing this? Can we do whatever we want in foreign policy? Why or why not?)
4. In May 1968 Prime Minister Trudeau said this about Canadian foreign policy: "We shall do more good by doing well what we know to be within our resources to do, than to pretend, either to ourselves or to others, that we can do things clearly beyond our national capacity." In simple terms, what was he saying? To which one of his guidelines (above) does this comment refer? Why do you think so? Do you agree with his view?
5. Look at number V again. List these factors in order of importance as you see them. Be sure you have reasons for your decisions. Compare your ideas with classmates.

2.   FINDINGS AND SUGGESTIONS OF THE TRUDEAU REVIEW

The results of the review of foreign policy were published in 1970. The publication was called *Foreign Policy for Canadians* (available in most libraries). It took the form of six separate booklets. The first provided a general plan for Canadian foreign policy. The other five booklets were called "sector papers."

They dealt with Europe, the Pacific, Latin America, the United Nations and foreign aid to poorer countries. The accompanying chart presents some of the key ideas from *Foreign Policy for Canadians*.

Europe

● Canadians have strong ties with Europe. About 96 per cent of all Canadians are of European ancestry. About 14 per cent of all Canadians were born in Europe.
● Canada has diplomatic and trade ties with every European country.
● Canada's future relations with Europe are very important.
● Europe can help Canada reduce its dependence on the United States.
● We should trade more with Europe.
● We should encourage more Europeans to invest in Canada.
● We should take advantage of the "thaw" in the Cold War. This would involve seeking closer ties with central and eastern Europe, not just the western portion.

The Pacific

● Canada is not just an Atlantic coast nation. We also are a country on the rim of the Pacific.
● Tremendous changes are taking place in Asia.
● Canada's relations with Pacific nations are important. This is especially true of such countries as China, Japan, Australia, Indonesia, Malaysia and the Philippines.
● Canada should increase its exports to, and investments in, the Pacific region.
● Canada should encourage an exchange of people, culture and ideas with Pacific nations.
● Canada should increase its aid to poor Pacific nations.
● Canada should avoid large military commitments in this region.

Latin America

● We live in the same hemisphere as the Latin American peoples. Nonetheless, we have not felt particularly close to them in the past.
● Canada has few historical or cultural ties with Latin America.
● Canada should seek stronger ties with countries of Latin America. This is especially true in terms of trade. Latin America has a large, rapidly growing population. It could become an important market for Canadian goods. Also, Latin America has many valuable resources, such as oil, which Canada needs.
● Canada and Latin America share a common concern regarding heavy American influence. This could be a base on which to build closer ties, and thus to reduce our dependence on the U.S.

United Nations

● Canada has been one of the strongest supporters of the U.N.
● The U.N. has been a disappointment to Canada, particularly on the topic of preserving peace.
● Canada should not count on the U.N. as much as it has in the past.
● Canada should continue to support the U.N. However, less emphasis should be placed on peacekeeping. More stress should go on helping poor nations, working for disarmament, and winning more respect for human rights and international law.

Foreign Aid

● Canada has had a fairly good record in this regard. However, it still does not meet the amount of aid suggested by the U.N.
● Canada can and should increase its foreign aid to poorer countries.
● Canadians *think* that their foreign aid is more generous than is really the case.
● Canada's foreign aid should stress **development assistance.** (This means that it should aim to help countries become more self-sufficient.) Previously, much of our aid was to help immediate problems such as starvation or disease.
● Our foreign aid should become broader in scope. It should not all be given out through the U.N. and the British Commonwealth.

This kind of slum area is all too common in underdeveloped countries. Canada has increased its aid to such countries in recent years.

Canada and the British Commonwealth

Another important part of Canada's foreign policy is our membership in the British Commonwealth. At one time, Great Britain controlled a huge world empire. The statement "The sun never sets on the British Empire" was literally true. The empire stretched right around the world. When the sun was setting on one part, it was rising on another.

However, after World War II the sun *did* set on the British Empire. Almost all of the areas which Britain held as **colonies** (dependent lands) are now independent. Still, many of them have decided to remain associated with Britain and to each other. They do this through membership in the British Commonwealth. This organization contains one quarter of the world's population. It occupies one fifth of the world's land area. All major continents and racial groups are represented. Usually, relations among its members are friendly and harmonious. The Commonwealth acts as an example to the world of how peoples of different language, race and culture *can* co-operate. In this sense, it is similar to the United Nations.

Canada has been a member of the Commonwealth from the very beginning. We developed some important trade ties within it, especially with Britain and South Africa. Our association with the Commonwealth nations reduces our dependence on the United States, if only slightly. Membership in the Commonwealth also could help Canadian security. Other members might be willing to help Canada in time of trouble. In addition, Canada gave a great deal of foreign aid to certain Commonwealth countries. This was given mainly to poorer nations in Africa and Asia.

For example, the **Colombo Plan** was created in 1950. Its goal was to ensure economic progress throughout Southeast Asia. Canada has been a major supporter of this plan. We have given tens of millions of dollars for such projects as a cement plant in Pakistan, a nuclear reactor in India, plus power, irrigation and transportation systems in several countries.

By the late 1960s, Canada had become one of the leading members of the British Commonwealth. Despite this, our role in that organization came under review in 1968-1970. In *Foreign Policy for Canadians*, there was no sector booklet on the Commonwealth. Instead, individual member countries were considered as part of the region in which they were located. Canada still plays an active part in the British Commonwealth. Many Canadians feel that membership in the Commonwealth is part of Canada's identity in the world community. However, this is not regarded as a vital part of our foreign policy. As of 1977, there were 36 countries in the British Commonwealth. They are named on the accompanying chart.

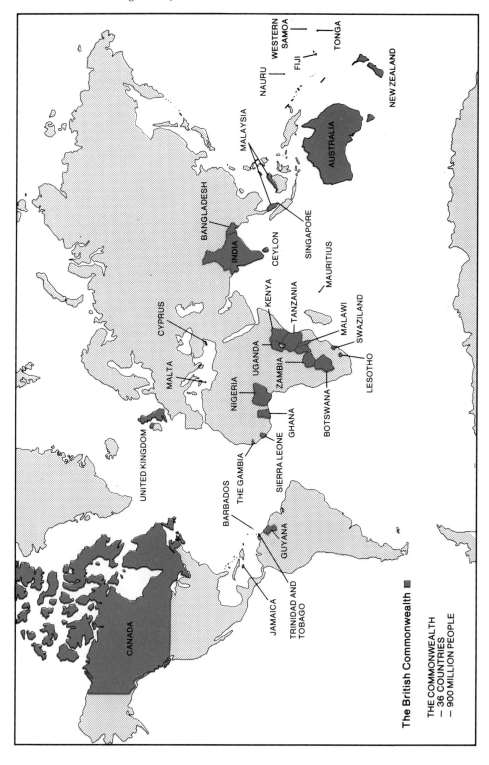

The British Commonwealth ■

THE COMMONWEALTH
– 36 COUNTRIES
– 900 MILLION PEOPLE

Members of the British Commonwealth

	Capital	Population	Date of Membership
Australia	Canberra	13 338 300	1 January 1901*
The Bahamas	Nassau	200 000	10 July 1973
Bangladesh	Dacca	71 479 071	18 April 1972
Barbados	Bridgetown	247 500	30 November 1966
Botswana	Gaborone	675 000	30 September 1966
Britain	London	55 968 300	
Canada	Ottawa	22 446 300	1 July 1867*
Cyprus	Nicosia	660 000	13 March 1961
Fiji	Suva	559 813	10 October 1970
The Gambia	Banjul	495 000	18 February 1965
Ghana	Accra	9 200 000	6 March 1957
Grenada	St. George's	110 000	7 February 1974
Guyana	Georgetown	830 000	26 May 1966
India	New Delhi	604 000 000	15 August 1947
Jamaica	Kingston	1 982 700	6 August 1962
Kenya	Nairobi	12 000 000	12 December 1963
LeSotho	Maseru	1 181 330	4 October 1966
Malawi	Lilongwe	4 916 000	6 July 1964
Malaysia	Kuala Lumpur	11 930 000	31 August 1957
Malta	Valletta	297 600	21 September 1964
Mauritius	Port Louis	881 944	12 March 1968
Nauru	Nauru	7 000	31 January 1968
New Zealand	Wellington	3 100 000	26 September 1907*
Nigeria	Lagos	79 759 000†	1 October 1960
Papua-New Guinea	Port Moresby	2 570 780	16 September 1975
Seychelles	Victoria	58 000	28 June 1976
Sierra Leone	Freetown	3 000 000	27 April 1961
Singapore	Singapore	2 219 100	15 October 1965
Sri Lanka	Colombo	13 180 000	4 February 1948
Swaziland	Mbabane	494 396	6 September 1968
Tanzania	Dar es Salaam	14 500 000	9 December 1961
Tonga	Nuku'alofa	90 000	4 June 1970
Trinidad and Tobago	Port of Spain	1 033 000	31 August 1962
Uganda	Kampala	10 500 000	9 October 1962
Western Samoa	Apia	151 251	28 August 1970
Zambia	Lusaka	4 500 000	24 October 1964

Date on which Dominion status was acquired.
†Provisional

Note: Four countries have left the Commonwealth since its creation: Burma (1948), Ireland (1949), South Africa (1961), Pakistan (1972).

Canada had something to do with South Africa's withdrawal from the Commonwealth. There was a dispute over South Africa's policy of discrimination known as **apartheid.** Most Asian and African members condemned this policy. So did Canada. As a result of this criticism, South Africa withdrew.

1. Where are Commonwealth members concentrated?
2. Which ones are not named on this map?
3. Find out where these countries are located.
4. What do you notice about the time at which these countries joined the Commonwealth? Does this give you a clue as to when this map was originally drawn?

3.   Results of the Trudeau Review of Foreign Policy

Even before the results of the review were published, the Trudeau government had begun to take action. One of the most important steps concerned defence policy. In April 1969, Prime Minister Trudeau announced changes in Canada's NATO role. Over the next few years, we would abandon our nuclear role. That is, Canadian forces working with NATO would no longer have nuclear weapons. Also, the number of Canadian ground troops in Europe would be reduced by almost 50 per cent. Further, Canada's defence budget was frozen at 1.82 billion dollars per year until 1972. This made Canada one of the lowest spenders on defence of any NATO country.

Mr. Trudeau meets the late Mao Tse-tung, the revolutionary leader who turned China into a Communist state, during his 1973 visit to China.

In 1970, the Trudeau government made another very important move. It gave official **diplomatic recognition** to China. (This means that we accepted the Communist government of China as the legal government. We also exchanged ambassadors with China.) This was important for several reasons. First, we showed our independence from American policy. (The United States did not yet recognize Communist China.) Secondly, we showed that we accepted the fact that some countries preferred to live under Communism. (This is an example of the *realism* which Mr. Trudeau called for.) Thirdly, we showed that we regarded Asia as a vital area of the world. China is a key power in that area, and will become even more important in the future.

As we said earlier, *Foreign Policy for Canadians* was published in 1970. After this, our government responded to it in several ways. Many of these are summarized in the accompanying chart.

Government Responses to the Trudeau Review

Canada and Europe

— Trudeau government carried on with reduction of Canadian forces in Europe. Army brigade reduced to about 5000 men. Nuclear weapons abandoned.

— Canada dropped opposition to Britain's entry into European Economic Community. Instead, the government appointed a special ambassador to the E.E.C. Canada has also tried to arrange new trade terms. Canada seeks certain favours as well as investment capital from European nations. (French and Swedish auto manufacturers already have established branch plants in Quebec and Nova Scotia. French, German and Swiss money is being invested in Canadian industries).

— Canada now attends the meetings of the important Council of Europe.

— Canada has signed agreements to share scientific and technological information with various European countries. It also belongs to the Committee on the Challenges of Modern Society.

— The Trudeau government signed trade, scientific and cultural agreements with the Soviet Union. We want to sell products to the U.S.S.R. and its Eastern European allies.

— Prime Minister Trudeau visited the Soviet Union. His goal was to strengthen good will and to see how the Soviets have developed their far northern areas. Canada hopes to borrow Soviet know-how in this field.

— Canada's relations with France became somewhat strained. France seemed to show sympathy for the separatist movement in Quebec. Canada regarded this as unwanted interference in its internal affairs.

Canada and the Pacific

— P.M. Trudeau has travelled more widely there than any previous Canadian Prime Minister. This action underlines the importance of this region.

— Canada has kept close ties with Commonwealth members of Pacific region.

A Canadian businessman shows a truck to interested Chinese at a trade exhibition in Peking.

— Japan is becoming our second most important trading partner and source of foreign investment.

— The federal government has greatly enlarged port facilities on the coast of British Columbia.

— Trade with Australia and New Zealand is growing rapidly.

— Canada has established diplomatic relations with Communist China. Trade and cultural exchanges with China are increasing.

— Canada has altered its immigration policy to admit more Asians.

— The federal government sponsors Asian studies programs in Canadian universities. It also has set up a Pacific Economic Advisory Committee.

— In 1973, Canada agreed to serve on the International Commission of Control and Supervision (I.C.C.S.) created to observe the Vietnam peace settlement. (Canada soon found it necessary to withdraw from that body.)

— Canada has increased its foreign aid to Pacific nations.

— In the autumn of 1973, Ottawa announced a three-year wheat deal with China having a potential value of $1 billion. This coincided with an official visit to China by P.M. Trudeau.

— By the late 1970s, Taiwan and Hong Kong had become major sources of imported goods to Canada. These imports were low-priced. Some of them threatened the jobs of Canadian workers in similar industries, such as clothing. The government put limits on the amount of textiles (mostly clothing) which could be imported. Their aim was to protect Canadian businesses and workers. The government also considered limiting textile imports from certain Asian countries. This too was designed to help Canadian companies and workers.

Canada and Latin America

— Canada has been very cautious in dealing with the nations of this region. This is because we have commitments elsewhere. Also, the United States has a special interest in Latin America.

— Canada has investments in, and trade ties with, many Latin American countries. These ties are growing. However, they are still on quite a small scale.

— Canada has continued to reject membership in the Organization of American States (O.A.S.).

— Canada has increased its development aid to Latin America.

— Canadian ties with Mexico have grown. Mexico is now our second largest market in Latin America. We consult each other on common problems. These include pollution, drug traffic and laws of the sea.

— Canada admitted hundreds of political refugees from Chile after a revolution took place in that country.

— Canadian trade and tourism with Cuba have increased recently.

Canada and the United Nations

— Canada no longer counts heavily on the U.N. to handle threats to world peace.

— Canada has maintained, and even increased, its support for U.N. aid programs.

— Canada continues to assist, when asked, in peacekeeping operations. One example was the force sent to the Middle East in 1973.

— In 1977, Canada agreed to serve on a possible U.N. assignment in Rhodesia. The whites might agree to turn over power to the black majority. A "neutral" U.N. force might be needed to keep the peace while the changeover takes place.

— Canada's overall feeling about the U.N. was expressed by Mitchell Sharp in September 1969: "Canada believes that the United Nations must fail to reach its goals if it cannot come to grips with its own problems . . . The U.N. . . . is drowning in a sea of words . . . This has led governments to attach less importance to the United Nations' activities. . ."

Canada and International Development

— The government body responsible for running Canada's assistance program is the Canadian International Development Agency (C.I.D.A.)

— The Trudeau government made foreign aid a major feature of its foreign policy. The goal of the 1975-76 federal budget was to set aside 3/4 of 1% of Canada's gross national product to such assistance.

— The countries receiving development aid from Canada are located in Asia, Africa, Latin America and the Caribbean.

— A greater share of Canadian aid is now going to French-speaking countries, especially in Africa.

— In Asia, the state of Malaysia has been a special object of Canadian aid in recent years.

— Peru, Brazil and Colombia are examples of Latin American nations with which Canada has developed new aid programs.

— In the Caribbean, Canada has increased assistance to fellow Commonwealth countries.

As we all know, Canada is one of the richest countries in the world. Canadians live a better, fuller life than do most of the people of the world. Most of us have more luxuries and comforts than we could ever need or use. If you don't agree that life in Canada is very good, ask yourself the following questions:
1. Have I ever had to worry about where my next meal was coming from?
2. If I become injured or sick, would it be impossible to get medicine, or decent medical attention?
3. Have I ever seen a child suffering from serious malnutrition?
4. Have I ever seen a person actually dying of starvation or thirst?
5. Is it impossible for me to get a decent education even if I want it badly?
6. Is it fairly normal to see dead bodies in the streets of my neighbourhood?

For most of us, the answer to each of those questions is "no." However, to millions of human beings the answers would all be "yes." In comparison with us, many countries in the world are poor and are often referred to as the **underdeveloped nations.** More recently, they have been referred to as countries of **The Third World.**

These countries want, but do not have, the standard of living enjoyed by the industrialized nations of the world. They are called the *Third* World because most of them are **non-aligned.** This means that they have no firm commitments either to the East or the West. In the "Cold War", they do not support either side. Most of these countries are found in Africa and Asia. There also are many under-developed countries in Latin America. However, most of these are aligned with the United States — at least, up to a point.

Here are some statistics which show how badly the underdeveloped nations need help:
● 900 million people in the world receive only half as much money as an average Canadian family gets from Family Allowance payments alone.
● Almost half of all children alive today suffer from some form of malnutrition.
● About 30 per cent of all adults alive today cannot read or write.
● The average income for a person living in Haiti is about 1/35 of the average income in Canada.
● Nigeria has one doctor for every 35 000 people; Canada has one for every 750 people.
● A Canadian consumes about 2.3 kg of food per day; the average person in India consumes about 560 g, of which 2/3 is rice.
● In Canada, about one child in forty dies before it is one year old, in South America and Asia the figure is one in ten.
● On a **per capita** (per person) basis, the developed countries consume twenty-five times the resources that underdeveloped countries use.
● About 20 percent of the world's population enjoy about 80 percent of its income.

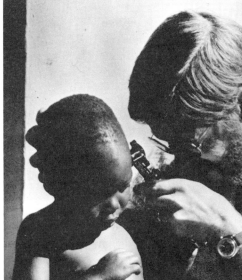

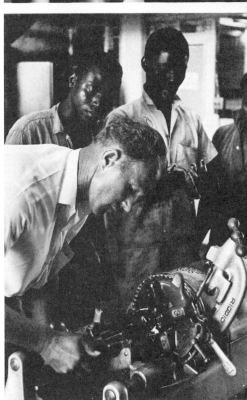

These photos show aspects of Canada's foreign aid program. What *kinds* of aids are shown? Why would they be especially valuable? What continents seem to be on the receiving end of this aid?

- In 1977, the world spent about $300 billion on military (war) items; this is twenty-six times as much aid as was sent to underdeveloped countries.
- CANADA has 0.6 per cent of the world's population. However, we claim:
  — 7.3 per cent of the world's land surface
  — 15 per cent of the world's known fresh water
  — 10 per cent of the world's productive forest
  — 10 per cent of the world's nickel supply
  — 21 per cent of the world's recoverable uranium
  — 8 per cent of the world's coal
  — the riches of the world's longest coastline (29 766 km)

1. What seem to be the main problems of the Third World?
2. Experts tell us that the **gap** (difference) between rich and poor nations is growing *larger,* not smaller. Why would this be?
3. It appears that we Canadians have far more than our share of the world's key resources. Why is this?
4. As you stuffed yourself with your third hamburger or second milkshake, did you ever think about the possibility that a young person somewhere in the world was starving to death? Do you think Canadians feel guilty about the richness of their life compared to that of most other peoples? Should they? Explain your answers.

Most of the developed nations of the world try to help underdeveloped countries. They do so for two main kinds of reasons: self-interest and idealism. These motives were discussed in chapter 1. If necessary, review their meaning.
1. Give an example of foreign aid based on the motive of self-interest.
2. Now give an example of aid based on idealism.
3. Which motive do you suspect is most common? Why?
4. Which motive do you think is uppermost with Canada's aid?
Which motive *should* be? Explain your answers.

Since World War II, Canada has spent tens of millions of dollars on foreign aid. Before the Trudeau Review, most of this went to poor Commonwealth countries, or was distributed through the United Nations. We still provide help through both of these channels. However, since 1970 some important changes have occurred in our aid programme.

First, as recommended in the Trudeau Review, we have increased the *amount* of aid. Years ago, the United Nations suggested "giving a guideline" for wealthy nations. This was 0.7 of one per cent of **gross national product** (G.N.P.) per year. (GNP is the value of all goods and services produced by an economy in a year.) Thus, if country A had a G.N.P. of $100.00 (unlikely!), it should give 70¢ in foreign aid.

1. Go to a library and look at the latest figures on Canada's gross national product. (You will find that it is well above one hundred billion dollars per year.)

2. Write the figure down. Calculate: what is 0.7 of one per cent of that amount? This is how much the United Nations says Canada should contribute to foreign aid. Check out your sources. Have we actually achieved this target? If not, how far short are we?

3. Do you think that the U.N. guideline of 0.7 of one per cent of GNP to foreign aid is reasonable? Why or why not?

4. In 1961, Canada was contributing only 0.2 of one per cent of our GNP to foreign aid. By 1974 this had grown to 0.5 of one per cent. Still, about one half of this aid was *tied*. In other words, there were "strings attached". For example, we might lend $10 million to country X, but insist that half of that money be spent buying Canadian-made farm machinery. In this way, we could make a lot of money. We collected interest on the loan. Also, we helped our own industry and trade. We increased our exports, created jobs in Canada and made profits on manufacture of the machinery. In recent years, much less of Canada's foreign aid is "tied". Also, many of our loans are either interest free, or are "forgiven" — that is, we do not ask to be paid back.

In addition to increasing the amount of our foreign aid, we have begun to distribute it more evenly. Between 1945 and 1965, the bulk of our assistance went to two Commonwealth countries: India and Pakistan. In Africa, we tended to favour Nigeria and Ghana. One goal of the Trudeau government has been to increase aid to former French colonies. French-Canadians often felt that we favoured former British colonies and ignored the French-speaking world *(la Francophonie)*.

Much of Canada's foreign aid is now disbursed (distributed) through the *Canadian International Development Agency* (CIDA). By 1977, its yearly budget was around one billion dollars. We also operate the *Canadian University Service Overseas* (CUSO). This organization has sent thousands of volunteers to foreign countries. They are university trained. They work in underdeveloped countries as teachers, doctors, technicians or as advisers on various problems.

5. ISSUES FACING CANADIAN FOREIGN POLICY TODAY

Canada still has to make some very difficult decisions in its foreign policy. Here are a few of the issues facing us. They will be discussed briefly in this section.
- Defence policy
- Attitude to racist governments
- Resource sharing
- Foreign aid
- Relations with the United States.

Canada's Foreign Aid (including food) by Region

(Fiscal Year)	1970/71	1971/72	1972/73	1973/74	1974/75
			($ millions rounded)		
Asia	180	148	175	204	244
	(68.4%)	(55.6%)	(55.4%)	(56.0%)	(49.5%)
Commonwealth Africa	25	50	54	64	109
	(9.5%)	(18.8%)	(17.1%)	(17.6%)	(22.1%)
Francophone Africa	30	45	59	67	99
	(11.4%)	(16.9%)	(18.7%)	(18.4%)	(20.1%)
Caribbean	19	14	16	16	20
	(7.2%)	(5.3%)	(5.1%)	(4.4%)	(4.1%)
Latin America	9	9	12	13	21
	(3.4%)	(3.4%)	(3.8%)	(3.6%)	(4.3%)
TOTAL	263	266	316	363	493
	(100%)	(100%)	(100%)	(100%)	(100%)

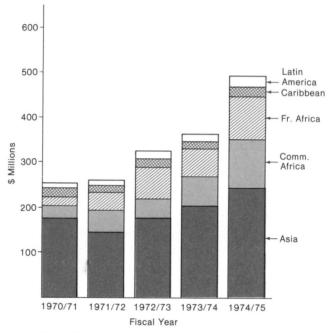

Source: Historical Statistics, Policy Branch, CIDA

Analyzing The Chart

1. Over the years shown, which African region has received the most aid from Canada?

2. Try to discover if Canadian aid to former French Africa increased as Mr. Trudeau intended.

3. Which region received the greatest *increase* in aid over the five years shown?

4. What was the total amount of aid given to all countries shown in 1970-71? What was the total for 1974-75? What is the *percentage increase?*

5. Uganda was a Commonwealth country during the period shown. However, it received little aid from Canada. A unique political situation there helps to account for this. Try to discover what that situation was.

In the late 1970s, Canadian defence planners had to choose a new jet fighter for our use in the 1980s. One of the aircraft considered was the American F-15A "Eagle." Two "Eagles" are shown here at Canadian Forces Base, Trenton, Ontario.

To strengthen its ground forces, Canada purchased new "Leopard" tanks in the late 1970s. These were made in West Germany. They are faster and more powerful than the old Centurion tank. Some of the Leopards are on duty with NATO forces in Europe.

With regard to defence policy, Canada remains a member of NATO and NORAD. However, we have little control over whether another major war occurs. As we have seen, such decisions are mainly in the hands of the great powers. The United States probably would "defend" us, whether we wished this or not. The U.S. could not allow another foreign power to gain control of us. Moreover, the world is troubled by the arms race. This grows more costly and dangerous with each passing day. However, our defence budget has been fairly limited. Many of our weapons are outdated or inadequate. The questions are:

SHOULD WE SPEND A LOT OF MONEY TO ACQUIRE NEW WEAPONS?

SHOULD WE "STAND PAT" WITH WHAT WE HAVE?

SHOULD WE DECLARE NEUTRALITY?

SHOULD WE COMPLETELY DISARM, AND HOPE THAT OTHER COUNTRIES WILL FOLLOW OUR EXAMPLE?

Canada also faces some difficult decisions concerning racism. Two countries pose the biggest problem. These are Rhodesia and South Africa. In both countries, the majority of people are black. However, in each case the white minority rules. The blacks are denied basic human rights, including an equal voice in their government. Canada has many ties with both countries. Most of these are economic, involving trade and investment.

SHOULD WE CONTINUE TO DO BUSINESS WITH GOVERNMENTS WHOSE POLICIES ARE OPPOSITE TO OUR IDEALS?

SHOULD WE INTERFERE IN THE INTERNAL AFFAIRS OF THOSE COUNTRIES?

IF WE ENDED OUR ECONOMIC TIES WITH THOSE COUNTRIES, WE WOULD LOSE MONEY, BUT WOULD WE CHANGE THE SITUATIONS THERE?

IF WE CUT OFF AID TO THOSE COUNTRIES, WOULD THIS HELP OR HURT THE BLACK MAJORITIES THERE?

Canada is blessed with natural resources. Most of the world's people are not so fortunate. In some ways, our lifestyle is bloated (swollen) with luxuries we really do not need. The United States, our major ally, is using up resources at a tremendous rate. They want access to ours as well. Many underdeveloped nations are ever more desperate for us to share our natural wealth.

SHOULD WE HOARD (KEEP) OUR RESOURCES FOR OUR OWN USE?

IS THERE ANY POINT IN SENDING AID TO POOR COUNTRIES IF THEY CANNOT BRING THEIR POPULATION GROWTH UNDER CONTROL?

SHOULD WE REGARD OURSELVES FIRST AS CANADIANS OR AS CITIZENS OF THE WORLD?

Canada has very close ties with the United States. These provide both benefits and disadvantages to us. The Americans will probably want to draw closer to us in future. This is particularly true in the economic and military sense. On the other hand, we sense a danger to our independence.

HOW CAN WE ASSERT OUR INDEPENDENCE FROM THE AMERICANS AND YET KEEP GOOD RELATIONS WITH THEM?

IS CANADA REALLY CAPABLE OF PLAYING AN IMPORTANT ROLE IN WORLD AFFAIRS AS A SEPARATE COUNTRY?

SHOULD WE AGREE TO BECOME A SATELLITE OR COLONY OF THE U.S.?

These photos show how non-whites suffer racial discrimination in South Africa. What *information* can you gather about South Africa's racial policies from the photos?

6.   CONCLUSION

In the four chapters of this unit, we have seen Canada's foreign policy go through several stages. By the end of World War II (1945), Canada was quite important in world affairs. Militarily, we ranked fourth or fifth in the entire world. Although we faced certain security problems through the Cold War, we were quite confident. This mood continued through the 1950s. Although our military declined, our economy grew rapidly. We had a fairly clear idea of our role in the world — namely, that of a middle power.

However, the world was beginning to change rapidly. As we moved into the 1960s, the old bases of our foreign policy came into question. Our power and influence in the world declined noticeably. Meanwhile, our doubts and questions about our role began to grow. The Trudeau Review helped to reorganize the goals and methods of our foreign policy. However, many issues remain to be solved. No doubt, they will remain with us for many years to come.

THINGS TO THINK ABOUT AND DO

Reviewing Key Words and Ideas

The following terms appeared in this chapter. Try to remember their meaning and how they were used.

ambassador	CUSO	GNP
apartheid	developed nation	non-alignment
British Commonwealth	development assistance	Third World
CIDA	diplomatic recognition	tied aid
Colombo Plan	foreign aid	underdeveloped
colony	la Francophonie	nation

Remembering the Facts

1. Why did it become necessary to review Canadian foreign policy in the late 1960s?
2. What actions did the Trudeau Review suggest to reduce Canada's dependence on the United States?
3. What other important changes resulted from the Trudeau Review?
4. What is meant by "the Third World"? What regions are part of it?
5. What are the main issues facing Canadian foreign policy today?

Analyzing Ideas

1. Some Third World countries accuse Canada of following a "White is Right" policy. What is implied in this? Is it an accurate charge?

2. Joseph Stalin was the former ruler of the Soviet Union. While once contemplating a certain action in foreign policy, he was advised against it. The reason: this action would be opposed by the Pope. Supposedly, Stalin replied: "And how many *divisions* does the Pope have?" What is a division? What point was Stalin making? Give an example from the world today that would support his point.

Applying Your Knowledge

1. Refer back to Mr. Trudeau's goals in foreign policy. Design a chart in your notebook. List the goals, in order and widely spaced, down the left hand margin of your page. Next, review this chapter on foreign policy. Beside each goal, list actions which Canada has taken to try to achieve these goals. By doing extra research, you can add to, and update, this chart. In a third column, give the policy a rating of "excellent", "good", "fair", or "poor." In the fourth column, briefly defend your thinking. Compare your views with classmates.

2. Together with the whole class, give Canadian foreign policy an assessment. Suggest ways in which it could be improved.

3. In 1969 a crew of American astronauts blasted off from earth. They would soon become the first humans to set foot on the moon. As their spaceship moved farther and farther from earth, they began to describe their thoughts. Naturally, the earth appeared as a distant sphere, getting gradually smaller. They marvelled at its beauty. They also said how silly human conflicts suddenly seemed. The earth was a mere speck in the universe, yet its people were divided by differences of race, language and basic beliefs. What were they trying to tell us? How does the "global village" idea fit in here? What signs do you see that the world is moving in this direction? Are you encouraged or discouraged? Is time on our side?

VII

Who are We? (Epilogue)

THE CANADIAN IDENTITY

What is a Canadian? The question has been asked often. The answers have often been vague and not always satisfactory. Perhaps many Canadians are not very concerned with this issue. Are you? Could you put into words what sets you as a Canadian apart from anyone else in the world? Today, with the future of Canada threatened as never before, the issue of the "Canadian identity" is again important.

Do countries have "national characteristics" in the same way that individuals have "personalities"? Mention the word "Canada" to foreigners and what image do they form?
— a nation of hockey players
— miles of open prairie land
— an endless wasteland of tundra
— a country of ice, snow, and igloos
— a land of vast resources and great potential

Can others know us as well as we know ourselves? What is our image of Canada and Canadians? If Canada disappeared tomorrow, what unique qualities would disappear with her?

> "Canada is a land of freedom and toleration. People of different backgrounds are welcomed. They are encouraged to retain their own unique cultural values. They may call themselves English-Canadian, French-Canadian, German-Canadian or Italian-Canadian."

Is this truth or myth? As Canadians we have long prided ourselves over our tolerance toward minority groups. We may begin to form doubts, however, when we read about vicious attacks on minority groups in our large cities; or when we hear loud complaints about immigrants; or when we learn that Quebec's Bill 101 denies children the right to be educated in the language of their choice.

> "Canada's history is different from that of any other country. Our nation is founded on loyalty to the Crown."

As history this is true. But can a national character really depend on its head

of state? Is the United States identified with Jimmy Carter? Russia with Leonid
Brezhnev? Uganda with Idi Amin? Canada with a monarch who is head of state
in name only? It may be a mistake to try.

> "Canada has developed a unique culture. We have distinctive Canadian
> singers, authors, painters, athletes, and stage, movie, and television
> performers."

Of course most of us could name a number of individuals under each
category. Go ahead. The list will be quite impressive. But reflect for a moment.
How distinctly Canadian is the culture they produce? Hockey may be a
"Canadian game", yet only three of the eighteen teams in the NHL are
Canadian. As for our singers and actors, in what respects do their performances
reflect Canadian culture? With the exception of a handful of successful singers
such as Gordon Lightfoot and Stompin' Tom Connors, Canadian music is little
different from American. It is this very fact which makes it popular. In most
cases our performers must go to the United States to make a name for
themselves before they are accepted as "Canadian stars".

Is there then no such thing as a Canadian identity? If you were to poll your
classmates, the majority would probably answer that indeed they are
Canadians and want to continue to be. They may not be able to tell you
specific reasons why. The answer may well be that the Canadian identity is an
idea. It exists if its citizens want to believe that Canada is different from any
other country in the world. It will continue to exist if Canadians across the
country are willing to make the effort and sacrifices necessary to preserve it.

As you read the poem by Native Canadian Duke Redbird, reflect on what
being Canadian means to him. Then, study the collage of photos which follows
and try to pick out various aspects of the Canadian identity. Examine the
statistics as well. What does being a Canadian mean to you?

I am a Canadian

I'm a lobster fisherman from Newfoundland
I'm a clambake in P.E.I.
I'm a picnic, I'm a banquet,
I'm a mother's homemade pie
I'm a few drafts
   in a legion hall in Fredericton
I'm a kite-flyer in a field in Moncton
I'm a nap on the porch,
   after a hard day's work is done.
I'm a snowball fight in Truro Nova Scotia
I'm small kids playing jacks
   and skipping rope
I'm a mother,
   who lost a son in the last great war
And I'm a bride, with a brand new ring
And a chest of hope
I'm an Easterner,
I'm a Westerner
I'm from the North
And I'm from the South
I've swam in two big oceans
And I've loved them both
I'm a clown, in Quebec during carnival
I'm a mass in the Cathedral of St. Paul
I'm a hockey game in the Forum
I'm Rocket Richard and Jean Beliveau

I'm a coach for little league Expos
I'm a baby sitter for sleep-defying rascals
I'm a canoe trip down the Ottawa
I'm a holiday on the Trent
I'm a mortgage, I'm a loan
   I'm last week's unpaid rent

I'm Yorkville after dark
I'm a walk in the park
I'm Winnipeg gold-eye
I'm a hand-made trout fly
I'm a wheat-field and a sunset
Under a prairie Sky.

I'm Sir John A. MacDonald
I'm Alexander Graham Bell
I'm a pow-wow dancer
And I'm Louis Riel

I'm the Calgary Stampede
I'm a feathered Sarcee
I'm Edmonton at night
I'm a bar-room fight
I'm a rigger, I'm a cat
I'm a ten-gallon hat
And an unnamed mountain
   in the interior of B.C.
I'm a maple tree and a Totem pole
I'm sunshine showers
And fresh-cut flowers
I'm a ferry-boat ride to the Island.

I'm the Yukon
I'm the North-West Territories
I'm the Arctic Ocean and the Beaufort Sea
I'm the prairies, I'm the Great Lakes
I'm the Rockies, I'm the Laurentians
I am French
I am English
I am Métis
But more than this
Above all this
I am a Canadian
   And proud to be free.

Population by ethnic group, 1971

Ethnic group	1971	
	No.	**%**
British Isles		
English		
Irish	9 624 115	44.6
Scottish		
Welsh and other		
French	6 180 120	28.7
Other European	4 959 680	23.0
Austrian	42 120	0.2
Belgian	51 135	0.2
Czech and Slovak	81 870	0.4
Danish	75 725	0.4
Finnish	59 215	0.3
German	1 317 200	6.1
Greek	124 475	0.6
Hungarian	131 890	0.6
Icelandic	27 905	0.1
Italian	730 820	3.4
Jewish	296 945	1.4
Lithuanian	24 535	0.1
Netherlands	425 945	2.0
Norwegian	179 290	0.8
Polish	316 425	1.5
Portuguese	96 875	0.4
Romanian	27 375	0.1
Russian	64 475	0.3
Spanish	27 515	0.1
Swedish	101 870	0.5
Ukrainian	580 660	2.7
Yugoslavic	104 950	0.5
Other	70 460	0.3
Asiatic	285 540	1.3
Chinese	118 815	0.6
Japanese	37 260	0.2
Other	129 460	0.6
Other	518 850	2.4
Eskimo	17 550	0.1
Native Indian	295 215	1.4
Negro	34 445	0.2
West Indian	28 025	0.1
Other and not stated	143 620	0.7
Total	21 568 310	100.0

Source: Statistics Canada

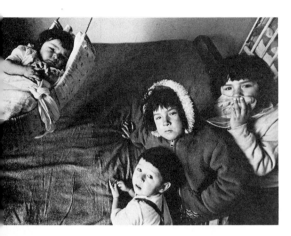

Photo Credits

Public Archives Canada

Art Gallery of Ontario — p. 59; Courtesy Boots Records Ltd. — p. 379 (lower left); British Columbia Government Photograph — p. 308; City of Montreal, Public Relations Department — p. 467 (lower centre); Courtesy The Canadian Armed Forces — pp. 419, 432, 434, 457; Courtesy The Canadian International Development Agency — p. 453 (upper right, lower left and right); Canadian Forces Photo — pp. 346, 353, 402 (middle right); Canadian Press, Courtesy Government of Canada — p. 262; Courtesy Capitol Records — E.M.I. of Canada Ltd. (photo by Raoul Vegg) — p. 379 (upper right); Courtesy Denison Mines Ltd. — p. 327; Courtesy The Department of External Affairs — p. 24, 357, 448; Courtesy Documentation photographique, directions generale de l'edition, Ministere des Communications, gouvernement du Quebec — p. 379 (lower right); Courtesy Early Morning Productions — p. 379 (upper left); Eatons of Canada Ltd. — p. 167; Fisheries and Environment Canada — p. 467, (upper right); Courtesy of Ford Motor Co. of Canada — p. 166; Courtesy Ford of Canada News Services — p. 320; Glenbow — Alberta Institute — p. 175; Courtesy Government of Quebec — pp. 235, 262, 370; F.T. Guthrie — p. 457 (upper); Hockey Hall of Fame Toronto — p. 467 (lower left); Courtesy I.B.M. Canada Ltd. — p. 338; Courtesy Imperial Oil Ltd. — p. 287, 326; Courtesy International Cinemedia Centre Ltd. and Minotaur Film Productions Inc., Montreal — p. 375 (upper); Metropolitan Toronto Police — p. 82 (lower left, lower right); Miller Services Toronto — pp. 39, 263, 345, 348, 350, 356, 397, 424, 431; National Film Board — p. 467 (centre right); Courtesy of The National Film Board of Canada & The Canadian Press — p. 262 (upper); Courtesy The National Research Council of Canada — p. 321; Courtesy The New Democratic Party (photo by Ronald Stephenson) — p. 323; Courtesy Nova Scotia Communication & Information Service — pp. 60, 62; N.F.B. Phototheque — pp. 252 (photo by Duncan Cameron), 326, 371, 375 (lower), 377, 450 (photo by Frank Mayrs); Courtesy Ontario Hydro — p. 330 (upper); Courtesy of the Ontario Ministry of Correctional Services — pp. 109, 110; Courtesy of the Ontario Ministry of Education Experience, 177 Project: *People at Work in Toronto, 1977* directed by the Women's Studies Dept., Toronto Board of Education, Photographer: Tom Quinn — p. 92; Courtesy the Ontario Ministry of Industry & Tourism — pp. 49, 57, 369; Courtesy of the Public Archives of Nova Scotia — p. 160; Saskatchewan Archives — p. 173; Courtesy Syncrude Canada Ltd. — p. 330 (lower); Courtesy Ting and the London Free Press — p. 372; Toronto Star Syndicate — pp. 192, 236, 245, 251 (upper), 256, 266, 268, 329, 382, 386, 467 (upper left); Courtesy the Toronto Stock Exchange — p. 313; Tourisme Québec — p. 467 (centre left); Courtesy Tourist Branch, Government of Quebec — p. 233; Transport Canada Photo — p. 241; Courtesy the United Nations — pp. 402 (upper & middle left), 412, 413, 415, 444, 453 (upper left), 459; Courtesy the United Nations/J.P. Laffunt — p. 399; Courtesy the United States Air Force — p. 355; Courtesy United States Information Service — pp. 286, 322, 335, 345 (upper & middle), 349, 351, 352, 354, 438; Courtesy Walter Gordon — p. 322; Courtesy Wide World Photos & the Canadian Press — p. 344.

ACKNOWLEDGEMENTS

page 27 From *Memoirs of a Bird in a Gilded Cage* by Judy LaMarsh reprinted by permission of the Canadian Publishers, McClelland & Stewart Ltd., Toronto.

p. 48-51 From the *Constitutional Conference Proceedings,* Second Meeting, February 10-12, 1969.

p. 72, 98 Courtesy of Metropolitan Toronto Police Department.

p. 99 Edmund Vaz, "Delinquent Behaviour Among Middle Class Boys" in Canadian Journal of Sociology and Anthropology.

p. 101 Harris Poll, 1965.

p. 174 From *The Winter Years* by James Gray; reprinted by permission of the Macmillan Company of Canada.

p. 251 From *Federalism and the French Canadians* by Pierre Trudeau, 1968, p. 170. Reprinted by permission of The Macmillan Company of Canada Limited, Toronto.

p. 258 From an article by Marcel Chaput in *The Canadian Commentator,* July-August 1961, Baxter Publishing, Toronto.

p. 297 From an article entitled "Let's Apply for Admission as the 51st State" by Farley Mowat in *Maclean's Magazine,* June 6, 1959. Reprinted by permission of Maclean-Hunter Limited, Toronto.

p. 358 From *The Better Part of Valour: Essays on Canadian Diplomacy,* by John W. Holmes, pp. 140, 178; reprinted by permission of The Canadian Publishers, McClelland and Stewart Limited, Toronto.

p. 465 "I am a Canadian" by Duke Redbird by permission of Duke Redbird.

INDEX